Visions of Grace

VISIONS *of* GRACE

An Anthology of Reflections

Compiled by William Sykes

 The Bible Reading Fellowship

Compilation and introductions
copyright © William Sykes 1997

The author asserts the moral right
to be identified as the author of this work

Published by
The Bible Reading Fellowship
Peter's Way
Sandy Lane West
Oxford OX4 5HG
ISBN 0 7459 3503 6
Albatross Books Pty Ltd
PO Box 320, Sutherland
NSW 2232, Australia
ISBN 0 7324 1566 7

First edition 1997
10 9 8 7 6 5 4 3 2 1 0

Acknowledgments

Unless otherwise stated, Scripture is taken from
The Revised Standard Version of the Bible,
copyright © 1946, 1952, 1971 by the Division of
Christian Education of the National Council of the
Churches of Christ in the USA.

Extracts are reproduced by permission of the
publishers, or, in some cases, by permission of
the holders of the rights of reproduction.

Extracts from the Authorized Bible (The King
James Bible) the rights in which are invested in
the Crown, are reproduced by permission of the
Crown's patentee, Cambridge University Press.

New English Bible © 1970 by permission of
Oxford and Cambridge University Presses.

Every effort has been made to trace and contact
copyright owners. If there are any inadvertent
omissions in the acknowledgments we apologize
to those concerned.

A catalogue record for this book is available
from the British Library

Printed and bound in Great Britain
by Redwood Books Limited, Trowbridge

Contents

Adoration	15	Greatness	108	Opportunity	207
Age	17	Growing	111	Pacifism	210
Ambition	20	Happiness	115	Patience	212
Art	22	Heart	118	Peace	214
Aspiration	25	Holiness	121	Perfection	217
Awareness	27	Hope	123	Personality	219
Baptism	31	Humility	126	Poetry	223
Beauty	33	Ideals	130	Poverty	226
Blessedness	37	Imagination	133	Praise	229
Character	41	Immortality	136	Presence	231
Cheerfulness	44	Influence	139	Progress	234
Christian	46	Inspiration	142	Psychology	237
Compassion	49	Intellect	144	Purity	240
Conscience	52	Joy	147	Quietness	243
Contemplation	55	Kindness	151	Relationships	246
Contentment	58	Leadership	154	Renewal	248
Courage	60	Life	156	Sacraments	252
Darkness	64	Light	159	Sacrifice	254
Divinity	67	Listening	162	Seeking	257
Education	70	Literature	165	Self	259
Eucharist	73	Loneliness	168	Serenity	262
Evolution	76	Longing	171	Sex	264
Experience	80	Love	173	Sorrow	266
Fellowship	83	Marriage	178	Thinking	269
Freedom	85	Materialism	182	Understanding	272
Friendship	88	Mercy	184	Union	274
Fulfilment	91	Mind	187	Vision	278
Genius	94	Money	190	War	281
Glory	96	Music	193	Wisdom	283
God Within	99	Nature	197	Wonder	287
Good	102	Neighbour	200	Word of God	290
Grace	105	Obedience	204	Youth	293

Preface
A READER'S VIEW

Steve Sheppard teaches law in Michigan in the United States. He was at University College, Oxford, pursuing his D. Phil. from 1989 to 1992. He has written prefaces for *Visions of Hope, Visions of Love Visions of Glory* and *Visions of Faith*. This is what he has now written about *Visions of Grace*...

This book is an immunization against the excesses of our times. For many of us, the barrage of information is too intense to concentrate, and in the clutter we are unlikely to learn enough about any one idea to make it our own. The age is too cynical to allow us seriously to think about our souls. What we might see of the glorious is usually cloaked in garb too twee or pretentious to apply to ourselves.

Into this morass whisks an unlikely hero in the form of Bill Sykes, the chaplain. Seeing Bill at the rugby touch line in a surreptitious conker-throwing duel with the college head porter, one might not believe one sees the architect of books that change the lives of their readers. But it is exactly that humour (and the concentration that makes it so hard to catch him at it) that has led, over the last two decades, to the scope and usefulness in these covers. *Visions of Grace* collects quotations and essays culled from thousands of years of the writings of the world's finest minds and greatest souls. From them, the reader will inevitably be captivated by a single question and find a platform for constructing an answer from within.

When I first met Bill, *Visions of Grace* was still bound in massive note books, heaped around Bill's rooms in college. My accomplices and I would meet once weekly during the term, having been gathered by one another more with an eye to mutual insult than grand insight. We would haul out these notebooks to consider their themes. Someone would eventually pick a topic from the index , and we would each nurse cups of Bill's tea whilst silently digesting the material from these pages for twenty minutes. With Bill's gentle prodding the discussion would begin, the student on the hot seat inventing a quick lie to explain why the topic was chosen. The conversations that followed could be predictable, but at times they were a furnace of inspiration, driven by these readings and catalysed by Bill's insightful questions. These meetings were now some years ago, and they remain with me as memories much stronger than meetings last week.

Thankfully, Bill has completed his project of publishing the notebooks. Now, there is no need to be in Oxford to explore these ideas, because *Visions of Grace* and its companion volumes are at hand anywhere. While each is independent and complete, there is little overlap among them. I find that friends I have given copies of the earlier volumes among *Visions of Faith, Hope, Love* and *Glory* are particularly happy to receive later volumes. From time to time I will hear from someone, long after I have forgotten of the gift, that they have found one of these books to be a source of comfort and inspiration.

This long-lived usefulness is unsurprising. The care and economy with which Bill has chosen his readings and wrapped them into the topics, and the straightforward way in which he has written of his own experiences and ministry in each, pay the reader a rich reward of thoughtful insight for a small investment of time and thought. This, indeed, is a manual for overcoming the modern struggle.

Steve Sheppard

HOW A SCHOOLMASTER USES AN ANTHOLOGY
OF REFLECTIONS

Robert Aldred is a former housemaster at St Edward's School, a boys' boarding school in Oxford. A few years ago his wife, Alison, was the nurse at University College, and working closely in that capacity with the chaplain of the college, Bill Sykes. Through that contact Robert discovered Bill Sykes' first anthology, the original *Visions of Faith* (now out of print, but superseded by a new edition), and from the moment he read it he realized what an invaluable resource it was. He has been using it for various groups in the school ever since and I asked him how.

'I use it in just one way,' he told me. 'We have copies of the book for the boys. We had a set of about forty at one stage, but over the years they have diminished. It is a very stimulating book, and sometimes a boy will say, "Can I borrow it?" And he will take it away for a while and then bring it back—but not always!

'What I do is to give them just one section of quotations to look at in one period, which usually lasts for forty minutes. They stay in the classroom and I ask them just to go through the quotations, to think about them, and to make notes. Then the following week they come back and we discuss them. I use the book two or three times a year, and I try to choose subjects which the boys themselves are interested in pursuing.

'Basically, I use the same method that Bill uses himself, in order to get people to think about whatever subject it is, and to meditate upon it. I actually use the word meditate, and I say to them, "To meditate means to chew it over and to thrash it through, to ask yourself whether you agree with it, and to ask yourself: *What is it actually saying? What does it mean by this phrase, and that phrase?*" I find that it raises the intellectual level of discussion to a much more serious one.

'Quite often a group will tend to treat things at the level where they are, which can be rather shallow. But I have found that this book forces them to go to a level which is more mature and more demanding, and there is a greater level of seriousness in the discussion. This year I have got four groups. Three of them are fine, but one is rather hard work, because of the level of input (or the lack of it) from the various members. There is a group within the group who are somewhat immature, and they tend to be flippant and a bit silly. But using Bill's book has forced them to be more thoughtful.

'It is enormously stimulating, and it provides a broad spectrum of types of writing. To give you an example, I wanted to do something with the sixth form on marriage and sexuality, and when I was looking through those sections I found this marvellous quotation from *The Prophet* by Kahlil Gibran:

> But let there be spaces in your togetherness,
> and let the winds of heaven dance between you.

'Brilliant! First of all I found it strange to see that juxtaposed against the Christian view of marriage. But then I thought, "Well, there's nothing much wrong with that!" And it made me realize how good it was to read people who were writing from all backgrounds, and from all walks of life and all the Church traditions. It's an enlarging experience.

'It is interesting how the pupils invariably pick out that passage from *The Prophet*. And when we are looking at the theme of suffering they almost always pick out the passage by Margaret Fishback Powers (and often known as 'Footprints'):

> One night a man had a dream. He dreamt he was walking along the beach with his Lord. Across the sky flashed scenes from his life. For each scene he noticed two sets of footprints in the sand, one belonging to him, the other to the Lord. When the last scene in his life flashed before him he looked back at the footprints on the sand. He noticed that many times along the path of his life there was only one set of footprints. He also noticed that it happened at the very lowest and saddest times of his life. This really bothered him, and he questioned the Lord about it. 'Lord, you said that, once I decided to follow you, you would walk with me all the way. But I've noticed that during the most difficult times in my life there is only one set of footprints. I don't understand why, in times when I needed you most, you would leave me.' The Lord replied, 'My precious child, I love you and would never leave you during your trials and sufferings; when you see only one set of footprints, it was then that I carried you.'

The Reverend Shelagh Brown
Bible Reading Fellowship

The story behind *Visions of Grace*
HOW IT CAME INTO BEING AND HOW TO USE IT

A priest who lost his faith
What happens when a priest thinks he has lost his faith? I was thirty years old, and faced with this situation saw three options: leave the Church; stay put in the Church and go through the motions; or stand my ground and fight. I had one thing on my side in making the choice—fresh memories from being a Gurkha officer. I had to fight.

Where he started the fight to find it
I started anew in the book of Genesis. In the story of the creation of man, God is depicted as fashioning and shaping man in his own image. He breathed into man and man became a living being. I was fascinated by this simple story. I took it to mean that God breathed something of his own nature into man, giving a divine potential to life.

Then I turned to the Gospels and found this 'something of God in man' worked out in the man—Jesus Christ. He found the Father in the depths of himself. He tried to explain this to the disciples: 'Do you not believe that I am in the Father and the Father in me? . . . the Father who dwells in me does his works' (John 14:10). As I struggled with what these words meant, I began to understand Jesus as the image of the invisible God.

Starting to see the way of grace
This understanding brought me a new insight Jesus discovered not only the presence of 'the Father' in himself, but also discovered this presence is *grace*, not just as an abstraction, but for people individually: 'And the Word became flesh and dwelt among us, full of grace and truth' (John 1:14). The writer of St John's Gospel spelt out the implications of this verse for us in a crucial sentence: 'And from his fulness have we all received, grace upon grace.' (John 1:16). The vision of grace was beginning to take shape.

I went back to the Epistles. Paul discovered that what Christ had experienced in his life, we can all experience in some measure. Some time after his conversion on the Damascus road, Paul wrote: 'It is no longer I who live, but Christ who lives in me . . .' (Galatians 2:20). 'In him the whole fullness of deity dwells bodily and you have come to fullness of life in him' (Colossians 2:9–10). I knew this meant much to me, that the whole power of the Trinity could be found in each of us: life, light, truth, joy, glory—and grace! Paul outlines this insight in an important passage: 'But by the grace of God I am what I am, and his grace toward me was not in vain. On the contrary, I worked harder than any of them, though it was not I, but the grace of God which is with me.'

(1 Corinthians 15:10). I held fast to this vision and thought of Christ's words: 'I came that they may have life, and have it abundantly' (John 10:10). But I still felt that I was missing some part of his vision for me.

Dust and divinity

Then something clicked into place: *that which was fashioned and shaped in the image and likeness of God was taken from the dust of the earth.* I saw then that in addition to being born with a 'divine' potential, we are still earthy and creaturely. This was no news to me, but now I saw that if either side was repressed or allowed too much sway the consequences would be negative and destructive.

But how could I make such a balance? I went back again to the Gospels. What do we find in the life of Christ? An integration of the divine and the earthy, the godly and the creaturely—'very God and very man'—a perfect combination of the divine and the human. I now began to understand why he was called 'the second Adam'. By his death and resurrection he had pioneered a way of integrating both sides of his nature, and so became the prototype of a new humanity. The vision of grace underlying this anthology finally made sense.

In many people over many years

Granted this vision of grace, I thought I might find evidence of it in the experience of men and women in the last 2,000 years. I started searching for signs of this vision in the thoughts and words of others. First, I sought it in the recorded experience of saints and theologians; secondly, from poets, novelists, playwrights, musicians and artists; thirdly, from philosophers, scientists, states-men, historians, politicians, economists and psychologists.

The material I found has been set out in ninety-six topics. These contain many aspects of grace, and their opposites—with some related topics.

How to grow in the vision

The aim of the anthology is to provide a means to grow in this vision of grace. This is done primarily through the practice of reflection, hence the subtitle, *An Anthology of Reflections.*

The *Concise Oxford Dictionary* defines 'reflection' as to 'go back in thought, meditate, or consult with oneself, remind oneself, or consider'. Reflection indicates a way of thinking with the mind, the imagination, intuition and feelings. It includes 'lateral thinking' and 'vertical thinking' thinking which takes into account the spiritual dimension. A good description comes from the Collect for the Second Sunday in Advent (a prayer for the study of the Scriptures): 'Grant that we may in such wise hear them, read, mark, learn and inwardly digest them.' Reflection can have such a devotional aspect, and merge into meditation and contemplation. I hope *Visions of Grace* can be used in many ways—as a book to dip into from time to time—as a bedside book—as a guide in time of need—as an aid to keeping a journal—as a personal book of devotion.

How to run a reflection group

As Chaplain and Fellow of an Oxford college, I have used the material for 'reflection groups'. These have been very popular, and in term-time at least thirty groups of up to five students meet each week.

I have been asked to describe in detail how these groups function. We meet for an hour a week at a mutually convenient time. We begin with a cup of tea, coffee or hot chocolate and briefly catch up on news. A list of topics is circulated and after two or three minutes a topic is chosen by consensus. Each topic consists of an introduction and some twenty quotations, two from the Old Testament, two from the New Testament, and the remaining sixteen from a wide variety of sources. Each person in the group is then given a copy of this material and the reflection group gets under way.

We then have about half an hour of silence. We look through the quotations, thinking them through, and working out what they mean to us individually. Some of our participants are not used to being quiet and find silence difficult at first, so I make available a clipboard, pen and paper. We have found that writing down thoughts and insights have eased this period of silence and been a useful way of developing ideas.

As convenor of the group, I use this half-hour period to go through the quotations in the same way as the others, but in addition to formulate some questions. These can be useful for stimulating discussion in the second half of the reflection group.

At the half-way stage, I ask if everyone has completed the material. I then ask, 'Was there any particular reason for choosing this topic?' Someone usually comes forward with a reason. My next question is: 'Did you find anything helpful?' The person who has chosen the topic responds, and then the other members of the group join in. Having reflected on the same material, conversation comes fairly easily. As convenor, my role is mainly to listen and make sure everyone has an opportunity to contribute. Sometimes the questions formulated by me earlier are a help, often they are not needed. The group ends promptly on the hour. (Time is precious in an eight-week term).

How a reflection group begins

I usually start a new group with one person. Before long he or she usually suggests a person to join. Sometimes the addition is actually uninterested in religion but a good thinker. Sometimes it is someone committed to a particular creed, often not that of the first in the group. The two of them then invite a third member and so on. So the groups are based on trust and friendship, not orthodoxy. In the groups we have Roman Catholics, Methodists, members of the Church of England, the United Reformed Church, and the Christian Union, and the occasional Jew, Hindu, Muslim, Buddhist, atheist and agnostic.

Sometimes a group doesn't grow. Some people are shy, and are not ready for the group experience. Others want to go forward slowly. A few need individual attention. Some function quite happily in twos and threes. I reckon four or five is the best working number. Trust can still be maintained, and everyone can fully participate. Above this number, communication tends to break down.

I see *Visions of Grace* as a skeleton (or framework) of grace—and I leave it to the individual to put upon it (to clothe it with) his or her own flesh and blood.

Bill Sykes

ADORATION

'Adoration'—regarding with the utmost respect and affection:
worshipping as a deity; reverence.

We had a tragedy in college. One of our retired Fellows had a daughter with a tumour on the brain. She was married, with a two-year-old son. The surgeon had operated on her several times, but was unable to remove the roots of the tumour. He feared he might irretrievably damage her speech and eyesight, some considerable time before she died, which sadly now seemed inevitable.

I was visiting her in hospital after one of these operations. I had only been there a few minutes when there was a knock on the door and in came her son—along with other members of the family. What followed was one of the most beautiful sights I have ever seen.

He quickly made his way to her bedside and looked adoringly into her eyes. Contact was made and suddenly they gave each other a look of sheer delight and wonder—the look reserved for a person greatly loved and adored. This was a look of extreme joy, and ecstasy. For a few moments they gazed at each other with the utmost respect and affection, and there were other elements present, namely, something akin to the worship of a deity—and reverence.

Adoration forms an important part of our institutional worship. This is true also of our vocal prayer. When I was originally taught to say my prayers 'adoration' was given a prominent position in the opening section of 'thanksgiving'. Nowadays I find in reflection a natural way and means of bringing adoration to the forefront.

Let the heavens be glad, and let the earth rejoice, and let them say among the nations, 'The Lord reigns!' Let the sea roar, and all that fills it, let the field exult, and everything in it! Then shall the trees of the wood sing for joy before the Lord, for he comes to judge the earth. O give thanks to the Lord, for he is good; for his steadfast love endures for ever!

1 Chronicles 16.31-34

And behold, the glory of the God of Israel came from the east; and the sound of his coming was like the sound of many waters; and the earth shone with his glory.

Ezekiel 43.2

And we all, with unveiled face, beholding the glory of the Lord, are being changed into his likeness from one degree of glory to another; for this comes from the Lord who is the Spirit.

2 Corinthians 3.18

Through him then let us continually offer up a sacrifice of praise to God, that is, the fruit of lips that acknowledge his name.

Hebrews 13.15

It is a beauteous evening, calm and free,
The holy time is quiet as a Nun
Breathless with adoration.

William Wordsworth, *The Poetical Works of William Wordsworth*, edited by E. de Selincourt and Helen Darbishire,
Oxford at the Clarendon Press, 1954, Volume III, page 17, *Miscellaneous Sonnets*, 'It is a Beauteous Evening,' l.1

Man is most truly himself, as the Eastern Church well knows, not when he toils but when he adores. And we are learning more and more that all innocent joy in life may be a form of adoration.

Vida D. Scudder, *The Privilege of Age*, J.M.Dent & Sons Ltd., 1939, page 30

Imagine an artist whose inspiration was ceaseless and continuously followed by realization—a Shakespeare or a Beethoven constantly at his best. All we can do to form an idea of God's personality should be in that direction, removing limitations all the time. That is prayer and that is adoration!

Ernest Dimnet, *What We Live By*, Jonathan Cape Ltd., 1932, page 67

To worship is to quicken the conscience by the holiness of God, to feed the mind with the truth of God, to purge the imagination by the beauty of God, to open the heart to the love of God, to devote the will to the purpose of God. All this is gathered up in that emotion which most cleanses us from selfishness because it is the most selfless of all emotions—adoration.

William Temple, *The Hope of a New World*, SCM Press Ltd., 1940, page 30

To adore . . . means to lose oneself in the unfathomable, to plunge into the inexhaustible, to find peace in the incorruptible, to be absorbed in defined immensity, to offer oneself to the fire and the transparency, to annihilate oneself in proportion as one becomes more deliberately conscious of oneself, and to give one's deepest to that whose depth has no end.

Pierre Teilhard de Chardin, *Le Milieu Divin*, William Collins Sons & Co. Ltd., 1960, page 188

Worship is essentially an act of adoration, adoration of the one true God in whom we live and move and have our being. Forgetting our little selves, our petty ambitions, our puny triumphs, our foolish cares and fretful anxieties, we reach out towards the beauty and majesty of God. The religious life is not a dull, grim drive towards moral virtues, but a response to a vision of greatness . . . The pattern prayer given by our Lord offers us the clue to right worship. It begins and ends with words of adoration.

Thomas F. Green, *Preparation For Worship* (Swarthmore Lecture), George Allen & Unwin Ltd., 1952, page 17

Adoration is the first and greatest of life's responses to its spiritual environment; the first and most fundamental of spirit's movements towards Spirit, the seed from which all other prayer must spring. It is among the most powerful of the educative forces which purify the understanding, form and develop the spiritual life. As we can never know the secret of great art or music until we have learned to look and listen with a self-oblivious reverence, acknowledging a beauty that is beyond our grasp—so the claim and loveliness remain unrealized, till we have learned to look, to listen, to adore. Then only do we go beyond ourselves and our small vision, pour ourselves out to that which we know not, and so escape from our own pettiness and limitations into the universal life.

Evelyn Underhill, *The Golden Sequence*, Methuen & Co. Ltd., 1932, page 162

We must be prepared to find that the last step of our relationship with God is an act of pure adoration, face to face with a mystery into which we cannot enter.

We grow into the knowledge of God gradually from year to year until the end of our life and we will continue to do so through all eternity, without coming to a point when we shall be able to say that now we know all that is knowable of God. This process of gradual discovery of God leads us at every moment to stand with our past experience behind us and the mystery of God knowable and still unknown before us.

The little we know of God makes it difficult for us to learn more, because the more cannot simply be added to the little, since every meeting brings such a change of perspective that what was known before becomes almost untrue in the light of what is known later.

Anthony Bloom, *Living Prayer*, Darton, Longman & Todd, 1966, page 106

For Christian experience, the life and person of Christ stand apart as the greatness of these self-revelations; the perfect self-expression of the Holy in human terms, and the supreme school and focus of man's adoring prayer. For here the Invisible God, by the most wonderful of His condescensions, discloses His beauty and attraction—the brightness of His glory and the express image of His person—in a way that is mercifully adapted to our limitations, and meets us on our own ground. Therefore the events of Christ's life—alike the most strange and the most homely—are truly 'mysteries.' They contain far more than they reveal. They are charged with Spirit, and convey the supernatural to those who are content to watch and adore. Because of this, Christian devotion moves ever to and fro between adoring and intimate prayer; passing through the incarnational veil to the Absolute Beauty, and returning to find the Absolute Beauty shining through the incarnational veil. 'Let thy thoughts be always upward to God and direct thy prayer to Christ continually,' says Thomas à Kempis. Thus the great horizon gives its meaning to the welcoming figure; and the welcoming figure makes the great horizon safe and fair.

Evelyn Underhill, *The Golden Sequence*, Methuen & Co. Ltd., 1932, page 165

The patience of Jesus was the expression of his humble, adoring love. So it must be with us.

Humility does not consist in feeling wretched, miserable and so forth; one can feel all these things and not be humble at all.

Humility means putting oneself aside, not considering self, thinking of others. It means seeing always the good and refusing to criticize.

Criticism of others always springs from wounded self-love, jealousy or some similar selfishness. Humility means making light of our own wounds and hurt feelings. This is true humility. In this way we offer God adoring love. It is a continual communion with the heart of Jesus.

In the light that falls on our souls from the eyes of the humbled Saviour we see ourselves: 'Human pride must be abased.'

More difficult to accept than humiliations from without are humiliations from within—the consciousness of our proneness to evil, forces we cannot control, inability to think of God and holy things . . . But prone in the mud we are one with Jesus. This is the supreme moment. Now our adoration must rise up pure, intense, sweet, one with the adoration of Christ.

Ruth Burrows, in *The Watchful Heart*, edited by Elizabeth Ruth Obbard, Darton, Longman & Todd, 1988, page 32

AGE

'Age'—length of time or of existence, duration of life required for a purpose, latter part of life.

I am a great admirer of one of my elderly cousins. When she left school, she went to college and then became a schoolteacher. Her early years were spent in developing teaching skills. She never married, and turned her attention to other things. As a gifted linguist she became fluent in six languages. Intent on making the most of life she developed a love of travel. In school holidays she visited many different parts of the world. She learnt to climb and succeeded in getting to the top of the Matterhorn. She was equally adept underground with potholing.

The years sped by. Eventually she became a headmistress. In this capacity she went on an exchange year in America and greatly enjoyed the experience, making many new friends. For several years she carried out her responsibilities with devotion and skill, and continued to spend most of her holidays abroad.

In retirement, she pursued her exploration of the world with greater enthusiasm and vigour. There are now few countries in the world unknown to her. She is a fascinating person to meet, and has many stories to tell of her adventures. Moreover she has a whole host of friends in many different parts of the world.

A few years ago she had hip trouble. She bravely faced up to two hip-replacement operations, and to the possibility of this being the end of her travels. However, she made a remarkable recovery, and at the first opportunity resumed her travels. Now well into her eighties, she continues to travel the globe. She is a role model for us all in her determination to live life to the full, and to the very end.

I said, 'Let days speak, and many years teach wisdom.' But it is the spirit in a man, the breath of the Almighty, that makes him understand. It is not the old that are wise, nor the aged that understand what is right.

Job 32.7-9

Do not cast me off in the time of old age; forsake me not when my strength is spent.

Psalm 71.9

Stay with us, for it is toward evening and the day is now far spent.

Luke 24.29

... grow in the grace and knowledge of our Lord and Saviour Jesus Christ.

2 Peter 3.18

The evening of life brings with it its lamps.

Joseph Joubert, *Pensées and Letters*, George Routledge & Sons Ltd., 1928, page 66

In seed time learn, in harvest teach, in winter enjoy.

William Blake, *The Complete Writings of William Blake*, edited by Geoffrey Keynes, Oxford University Press, 1974, page 150, *The Marriage of Heaven and Hell*, Plate 7, 'Proverbs of Hell,' l.1

I believe one has to be seventy before one is full of courage. The young are always half-hearted.

D.H. Lawrence, *The Selected Letters of D.H. Lawrence*, edited by Diana Trilling, Farrar, Straus & Cudahy, 1956, page 212

Old age has its pleasures, which, though different, are not less than the pleasures of youth.

W. Somerset Maugham, *The Summing Up*, Bernhard Tauchnitz, 1938, page 229

To know how to grow old is the master-work of wisdom, and one of the most difficult chapters in the great art of living.

Henri Frédéric Amiel, *Amiel's Journal*, translated by Mrs Humphry Ward, Macmillan & Co. Ltd., 1918, page 218

Youth, large, lusty, loving—youth full of grace, force, fascination. Do you know that Old Age may come after you with equal grace, force, fascination?

Walt Whitman, *The Complete Poems*, edited by Francis Murphy, Penguin Books Ltd., 1982, page 254, 'Youth, Day, Old Age and Night,' l.1

Old places and old persons in their turn, when spirit dwells in them, have an intrinsic vitality of which youth is incapable; precisely the balance and wisdom that comes from long perspectives and broad foundations.

George Santayana, *My Host The World*, The Cresset Press, 1953, page 169

Grow old along with me!
The best is yet to be,
The last of life, for which the first was made:
Our times are in His hand
Who saith, 'A whole I planned,
Youth shows but half; trust God: see all nor be afraid!'

Robert Browning, *The Poetical Works of Robert Browning*, Volume I, Smith, Elder & Co., 1899, page 580, *Dramatis Personae*, 'Rabbi Ben Ezra,' st.i, l.1

The soul's dark cottage, batter'd and decay'd,
Lets in new light, through chinks that time has made:
Stronger by weakness, wiser men become,
As they draw nearer to their eternal home;
Leaving the old, both worlds at once view,
That stand upon the threshold of the new.

Edmund Waller, *The Works of the English Poets, from Chaucer to Cowper*, Dr Samuel Johnson, 1910, Volume VIII, page 81, 'On The Foregoing Divine Poems'

For is it not possible that middle-age can be looked upon as a period of second flowering, second growth, even a kind of second adolescence?... Discontent, restlessness, doubt, despair, longing, are interpreted falsely as signs of decay. In youth one does not as often misinterpret the signs; one accepts them, quite rightly, as growing pains. One takes them seriously, listens to them, follows where they lead.

Anne Morrow Lindbergh, *Gift From The Sea*, Chatto & Windus Ltd., 1974, page 86

Many people as they grow older fear the coming of old age. They regret the failing of physical and mental powers, the withdrawal from active life, posts of leadership and the satisfaction of being used creatively. These increasing diminishments can be seen as a hollowing-out of the material and the temporal, in order to be ready to be filled with the spiritual and the eternal.

George Appleton, *Journey for a Soul*, William Collins Sons & Co. Ltd., 1976, page 47

The nearer we approach to the middle of life, and the better we have succeeded in entrenching ourselves in our personal standpoints and social positions, the more it appears as if we had discovered the right course and the right ideals and principles of behaviour... We wholly overlook the essential fact that the achievements which society rewards are won at the cost of diminution of personality. Many—far too many—aspects of life which should also have been experienced lie in the lumber-room among dusty memories. Sometimes, even, they are glowing coals under grey ashes.

C.G. Jung, *Psychological Reflections*, selected and edited by Jolande Jacobi, Routledge & Kegan Paul Ltd., 1953, page 110

When the signs of age begin to mark my body (and still more when they touch my mind); when the ill that is to diminish me or carry me off strikes from without or is born within me; when the painful moment comes in which I suddenly awaken to the fact that I am ill or growing old; and above all at that last moment when I feel I am losing hold of myself and am absolutely passive within the hands of the great unknown forces that have formed me; in all those dark moments, O God, grant that I may understand that it is You (provided only my faith is strong enough) who are painfully parting the fibres of my being in order to penetrate to the very marrow of my substance and bear me away within Yourself.

Pierre Teilhard de Chardin, *Le Milieu Divin*, William Collins Sons & Co. Ltd., 1960, page 69

My life is worth living if I can learn to transform everything that happens to me into love, in imitation of Jesus: because *love is for living*...
  When I have to live with people who do not see things the way I see them, who say they are enemies of my faith, I shall love them, and in loving them I shall sow the seeds of future dialogue in my heart and theirs; because *love is for living*...
  When I see time's destructive traces in my body and the approach of old age, I shall try to love even more in order to transform the coldest season of life into a total gift of myself in preparation for the imminent holocaust: because *love is for living*.
  When I see the evening of my life, or, on the tarmac in a car accident, in the agony of a fatal illness, in the ward of a geriatric hospital, feel the end coming, I shall reach out again for love, striving to accept in joy whatever fate God has had in store for me; because *love is for living*.

Carlo Carretto, *Love is for Living*, translated by Jeremy Moiser, Darton, Longman & Todd, 1976, page 135

In order to face suffering in peace:

Suffer without imposing on others a theory of suffering, without weaving a new philosophy of life from your own material pain, without proclaiming yourself a martyr, without counting out the price of your courage, without disdaining sympathy and without seeking too much of it.

We must be sincere in our sufferings as in anything else. We must recognize at once our weakness and our pain, but we do not need to advertise them ... We must face the fact that it is much harder to stand the long monotony of slight suffering than a passing onslaught of intense pain. In either case what is hard is our own poverty, and the spectacle of our own selves reduced more and more to nothing, wasting away in our own estimation and in that of our friends.

We must be willing to accept also the bitter truth that, in the end, we may have to become a burden to those who love us. But it is necessary that we face this also ... It takes heroic charity and humility to let others sustain us when we are absolutely incapable of sustaining ourselves.

Thomas Merton, *No Man is an Island*, Hollis & Carter, 1955, page 81

To a man of middle age, existence is no longer a dream, but a reality. He has not much more new to look forward to, for the character of his life is generally fixed by that time. His profession, his home, his occupations, will be for the most part what they are now. He will make few new acquaintances—no new friends. It is the solemn thought connected with middle age that life's last business is begun in earnest and it is then, midway between the cradle and the grave, that a man begins to look back and marvel with a kind of remorseful feeling that he let the days of youth go by so half enjoyed. It is the pensive autumn feeling,— it is the sensation of half sadness that we experience when the longest day of the year is past, and every day that follows is shorter, and the lights fainter, and the feebler shadows, tell that nature is hastening with gigantic footsteps to her winter grave. So does man look back upon his youth. When the first grey hairs become visible—when the unwelcome truth fastens itself upon the mind, that a man is no longer going up the hill, but down, and that the sun is already westering, he looks back on things behind. Now this is a natural feeling, but is it the high Christian tone of feeling? ... We may assuredly answer, No. We who have an inheritance incorruptible and undefiled, and that fadeth not away, what have we to do with things past? When we were children we thought as children. But now there lies before us manhood, with its earnest work: and then old age, and then the grave, and then home.

And so manhood in the Christian life is a better thing than boyhood, because it is a riper thing and old age ought to be brighter, and a calmer, and a more serene thing than manhood.

F.W. Robertson, *Sermons*, Kegan Paul, Trench, Trubner & Co. Ltd., 1893, First Series, page 63

AMBITION

'Ambition'—ardent desire for distinction; aspiration (to be, to do); object of such desire.

I received a letter from Australia. It was from one of our former postgraduates. He was letting me know he and his fiancée were getting married on 23 September in Sydney. 'If you happen to be in Australia at the time, would you please come and officiate at our wedding?' I showed the letter to the Head Porter. He fell for it at once. 'Let's go,' he said, 'Sue [his wife] would love to see Australia.' An immediate decision was made, and just before the wedding, we set off for Australia.

Rob Egerton had come to University College just over two years previously. He was a brilliant rugby player—a full-back—and a crowd-puller. When under pressure he was reluctant to kick the ball in to touch. He would either run the ball (for he was very fast) or do a monster kick ahead, sprint through the opposition, catch the ball, and score a try. He managed to do this in a Varsity match, much to the delight of the crowd.

When Rob left Oxford, he coached rugby in schools, and was selected to play for Australia in the World Cup. Australia and England ended up in the final. The night before the match, Rob rang me up. 'You have given me a problem Rob. Who do I support tomorrow?' Quick as a flash he came back with—'You can support fifteen Englishmen and one Australian.'

One of Rob's endearing qualities was his modesty. Ambition was not for him the all-important thing. The following year he accompanied his wife (Julia) to America. She had won a prestigious scholarship, and in their relationship, it was now her turn. A humble approach to ambition is invaluable.

Then they said, 'Come, let us build ourselves a city, and a tower with its top in the heavens, and let us make a name for ourselves, lest we be scattered abroad upon the face of the whole earth.
Genesis 11.4

This book of the law shall not depart out of your mouth, but you shall meditate on it day and night, that you may be careful to do according to all that is written in it; for then you shall make your way prosperous, and then you shall have good success.
Joshua 1.8

So the last will be first, and the first last.
Matthew 20.16

But if you have bitter jealousy and selfish ambition in your hearts, do not boast and be false to the truth.
James 3.14

Such joy Ambition finds.
John Milton, The Poetical Works of John Milton, edited by the Rev. H.C. Beeching, Oxford at the Clarendon Press, 1900, page 249, Paradise Lost, Book IV, l.92

Where ambition ends, happiness begins.
Hungarian proverb

No bird soars too high, if he soars with his own wings.
William Blake, The Complete Writings of William Blake, edited by Geoffrey Keynes, Oxford University Press, 1974, page 151, The Marriage of Heaven and Hell, Plate 7, 'Proverbs of Hell,' page 15

Put personal ambition away from you, and then you will find consolation in living, or in dying, whatever may happen to you.
Henri Frédéric Amiel, Amiel's Journal, translated by Mrs Humphry Ward, Macmillan & Co. Ltd., 1918, page 2

All ambitions are lawful except those which climb upward on the miseries or credulities of mankind.
Joseph Conrad, A Personal Record, 'A Familiar Preface,' J.M. Dent & Sons Ltd., 1923, page xx

Ambition, like a torrent, ne're looks back;
And is a swelling, and the last affection
A high mind can put off.
Ben Jonson, Ben Jonson, edited by C.H. Herford and Percy Simpson, Oxford at the Clarendon Press, 1965, Volume V, page 477, 'Catiline,' Act III, l.247

A proud ambition cares little for popularity. It will not seek it. It will hardly bend to receive it. A vain ambition courts it by every art, and spreads every sail to catch the least breath of popular applause.
Henry Edward Cardinal Manning, Pastime Papers, Burns & Oates Ltd., 1892, page 35

Ambition! We must be careful what we mean by it. If it means the desire to get ahead of other people—which is what I think it does mean—then it is bad. If it means simply wanting to do a thing well, then it is good. It isn't wrong for an actor to want to act his part as well as it can possibly be acted, but the wish to have his name in bigger type than the other actors is a bad one.

C.S. Lewis, *God in the Dock*, edited by Walter Hooper, William B. Eerdmans Publishing Company, 1970, page 55

Ambition raises a secret tumult in the soul, it inflames the mind, and puts it into a violent hurry of thought: it is still reaching after an empty, imaginary good, that has not in it the power to abate or satisfy it. Most other things we long for can allay the cravings of their proper sense, and for a while set the appetite at rest: but fame is a good so wholly foreign to our natures, that we have no faculty in the soul adapted to it, nor any organ in the body to relish it an object of desire placed out of the possibility of fruition. It may indeed fill the mind for a while with a giddy kind of pleasure, but it is such a pleasure as makes a man restless and uneasy under it and which does not so much satisfy the present thirst, as it excites fresh desires, and sets the soul on new enterprises. For how few ambitious men are there, who have got as much fame as they desired, and whose thirst after it has not been as eager in the very height of their reputation, as it was before they became known and eminent among men!

Joseph Addison, *The Works of Joseph Addison*, edited and published by Henry G. Bohn, 1856, Volume III, page 162

Aristotle (*Nicomachean Ethics* 4.3) described the virtue of *megalopsychia* ('greatness of soul or mind'), which was translated into Latin as *magnanimitas*, from which 'magnanimity' is derived. According to Thomas Aquinas (*ST* 11–11.129), magnanimity, 'the stretching forth of the mind to great things,' is a moral virtue that inclines people to excellence, especially but not only in virtues, and it moderates the pleasure that a person derives from external honors: 'Magnanimity is about honors in the sense that a man strives to do what is deserving of honor, yet not so as to think much of the honor accorded by man.' It is part of the virtue of fortitude or courage, because it is directed toward firmness or steadfastness in the face of what is difficult.

Its opposite vices by way of excess are presumption (striving for excellence beyond one's ability), ambition (inordinate desire for honors), and vainglory (inordinate desire for glory); its opposite vice by way of defect is pusillanimity ('small-mindedness'), which keeps a person from attempting what is commensurate with his or her ability. There are obvious problems in adapting magnanimity to Christian ethics, especially its temptation to pride or loss of humility. One possible corrective is to attribute abilities, excellencies, and success to God; for example, Thomas Aquinas noted that 'magnanimity makes a man deem himself worthy of great things because of the gifts he holds from God.'

James F. Childress, in *A New Dictionary of Christian Ethics*, edited by James F. Childress and John Macquarrie, SCM Press Ltd., 1986, page 364

ART

'Art'—skill applied to imitation and design, as in painting, etc., of artistic design, etc., thing in which skill may be exercised.

I wonder if art is yet another consequence of the divine inbreathing in the Genesis story of the creation of man. In that story God is depicted as fashioning and shaping man in his own image and likeness, and the last thing he does is breathe into man and man becomes a living being. I take that to mean something akin to an artistic spirit is to be found in the depths of our being. When catalysed or triggered off, artistic talent can grow and develop. This is certainly in line with scripture. The writer of Exodus records of Bezalel the son of Uri—'I have filled him with the Spirit of God, with ability and intelligence, with knowledge and all craftsmanship, to devise artistic designs, to work in gold, silver, and bronze, in cutting stones for setting, and in carving wood, for work in every craft.'

Some years ago we had a talented artist in college. I had been out to Mürren (a village in the Swiss Alps) to look after the English Church over the Christmas and New Year period. Whilst there I came across a teenage girl who was trying to get in to the Ruskin School of Drawing and Fine Art in Oxford. As her home town was close to Oxford I suggested she might like to meet our gifted artist and find out more about the Ruskin from her.

Three weeks later our meeting took place in my rooms in college. I was surprised to hear our gifted artist coming out with a vision of art entirely in line with this book. In fact, she was conscious of an 'artistic spirit' in the depths of her being, though she spoke of it entirely in artistic terms.

Blessed be the Lord, the God of our fathers, who put such a thing as this into the heart of the king, to beautify the house of the Lord which is in Jerusalem.

Ezra 7.27

A word fitly spoken is like apples of gold in a setting of silver. Like a gold ring or an ornament of gold is a wise reprover to a listening ear.

Proverbs 25.11-12

And there are varieties of working, but it is the same God who inspires them all in every one.

1 Corinthians 12.6

For we are his workmanship, created in Christ Jesus for good works, which God prepared beforehand, that we should walk in them.

Ephesians 2.10

Great art is an instant arrested in eternity.

James Huneker, *The Pathos of Distance*, T. Werner Laurie Ltd., 1913, page 120

Nature is a revelation of God; Art a revelation of man.

Henry Wadsworth Longfellow, *Hyperion*, George Routledge & Sons Ltd, 1887, page 196

Fine art is that in which the hand, the head, and the *heart* of man go together.

John Ruskin, *The Two Paths*, George Allen, 1905, page 57

Art, unless quickened from above and from within, has in it nothing beyond itself, which is visible beauty.

John Brown, *Horae Subsecivae*, T. Nelson & Sons, Ltd., 1928, page 176

True art, is the desire of a man to express himself, to record the reactions of his personality to the world he lives in.

Amy Lowell, *Tendencies in Modern American Poetry*, The Macmillan Company, 1917, page 7

The Fine Arts once divorcing themselves from *truth*, are quite certain to fall mad, if they do not die.

Thomas Carlyle, *Latter-Day Pamphlets*, Chapman & Hall Ltd., 1899, page 271

The art which is grand and yet simple is that which presupposes the greatest elevation both in artist and in public.

Henri Frédéric Amiel, *Amiel's Journal*, translated by Mrs Humphry Ward, Macmillan & Co. Ltd., 1918, page 249

Art is the gift of God, and must be used
Unto His glory. That in Art is highest
Which aims at this.

Henry Wadsworth Longfellow, *The Poetical Works of Longfellow*, Humphrey Milford, Oxford University Press, 1913, page 793, *Michel Angelo*, Part I, section 3

Painting is an art, and art is not vague production, transitory and isolated, but a power which must be directed to the improvement and refinement of the human soul.

Wassily Kandinsky, *Concerning the Spiritual in Art*, translated by M.T.H. Sadler, Dover Publications, 1977, page 54

To draw a moral, to preach a doctrine, is like shouting at the north star. Life is a vast and awful business. The great artist sets down his vision of it and is silent.

Ludwig Lewisohn, *The Modern Drama*, B.W. Huebsch, 1915, page 109

All great art is the work of the whole living creature, body and soul, and chiefly of the soul. But it is not only *the work* of the whole creature, it likewise *addresses* the whole creature.

John Ruskin, *The Stones of Venice*, edited by Jan Morris, Faber & Faber Ltd., 1981, page 233

The man who has honesty, integrity, the love of inquiry, the desire to see beyond, is ready to appreciate good art. He needs no one to give him an art education; he is already qualified.

Robert Henri, *The Art Spirit*, compiled by Margery A. Ryerson, J.B. Lippincott & Co., 1960, page 66

But the artist appeals to that part of our being which is not dependant on wisdom; to that in us which is a gift and not an acquisition—and, therefore, more permanently enduring. He speaks to our capacity for delight and wonder, to the sense of mystery surrounding our lives; to our sense of pity, and beauty, and pain.

Joseph Conrad, *The Nigger Of The 'Narcissus'*, J.M. Dent & Sons Ltd., 1929, page viii

So in Art's wide kingdoms ranges
One sole meaning still the same:
This is Truth, eternal Reason,
Which from Beauty takes its dress,
And serene through time and season
Stands for aye in loveliness.

Johann Wolfgang von Goethe, *The Works of Thomas Carlyle*, 'Wilhelm Meister's Apprenticeship and Travels,' Chapman & Hall Ltd., 1899, Volume II, page 329

When the artist is alive in any person, whatever his kind of work may be, he becomes an inventive, searching, daring, self-expressing creature. He becomes interesting to other people. He disturbs, upsets, enlightens, and he opens ways for a better understanding. Where those who are not artists are trying to close the book, he opens it, shows there are still more pages possible.

Robert Henri, *The Art Spirit*, compiled by Margery A. Ryerson, J.B. Lippincott & Co., 1960, page 15

Art is a kind of innate drive that seizes a human being and makes him its instrument. The artist is not a person endowed with free will who seeks his own ends, but one who allows art to realize its purposes through him. As a human being he may have moods and a will and personal aims, but as an artist he is 'man' in a higher sense—he is 'collective man,' a vehicle and moulder of the unconscious psychic life of mankind. That is his office, and it is sometimes so heavy a burden that he is fated to sacrifice happiness and everything that makes life worth living for the ordinary human being. As K.G. Carus says: 'Strange are the ways by which genius is announced, for what distinguishes so supremely endowed a being is that, for all the freedom of his life and the clarity of his thought, he is everywhere hemmed round and prevailed upon by the Unconscious, the mysterious god within him so that ideas flow to him—he knows not whence; he is driven to work and to create—he knows not to what end; and is mastered by an impulse for constant growth and development—he knows not whither.

C.G. Jung, *The Collected Works of C.G. Jung*, Volume XV, 'The Spirit in Man, Art,and Literature,' translated by R.F.C. Hull, Routledge & Kegan Paul Ltd., 1966, page 101

ASPIRATION

'Aspiration'—drawing of breath; desiring earnestly—for or after.

I think I have always been susceptible to aspiration. I remember the first few days away at School, and mulling over the words of the School motto: '*Semper ad coelestia*'— 'Always to the celestial things'. In retrospect I now wonder if this motto had more influence over me than I was aware of originally—an unconscious factor leading me to ordination.

Another special time of aspiration was a visit to Oxford at the age of fifteen. This was a Schools' Hockey Festival. We were accommodated in a college and got the feel of the life of an undergraduate. We spent three days playing against schools not normally in our ambit. In spare time I took a good look at the other colleges and the university buildings and it was then that aspiration hit me. I was suddenly fired with a burning desire to study in Oxford. From then onwards I worked hard at my studies, and was delighted some years later to get a place at Balliol.

A smaller aspiration, which bore fruit later, was watching the coronation on television, and seeing the Gurkhas for the first time. Later I saw them again, taking part in the Edinburgh Tattoo. When I came to do National Service, I soon became aware of a burning desire to serve with them. I was greatly privileged to be with them in Singapore and what is now Malaysia.

What is the difference between inspiration and aspiration? Inspiration is an inward influence, a divine inbreathing—as in the Genesis story of the creation of man. Aspiration is an outward influence, something which sparks off externally, yet a possible consequence of having first been inspired from within.

So now give me this hill country of which the Lord spoke on that day; for you heard on that day how the Anakim were there, with great fortified cities: it may be that the Lord will be with me, and I shall drive them out as the Lord said.

Joshua 14.12

How lovely is thy dwelling place, O Lord of hosts! My soul longs, yea, faints for the courts of the Lord; my heart and flesh sing for joy to the living God.

Psalm 84.1-2

And ... he breathed on them, and said to them, 'Receive the Holy Spirit.'

John 20.22

Set your minds on things that are above, not on things that are on earth.

Colossians 3.2

My ... aspirations are my only friends.

Henry Wadsworth Longfellow, *The Poetical Works of Longfellow*, Humphrey Milford, Oxford University Press, 1913, page 688, 'The Masque of Pandora,' III. 74

I have immortal longings in me.

William Shakespeare, *Anthony and Cleopatra*, Act V. sc.ii. l.279

A good man, through obscurest aspiration,
Has still an instinct of the one true way.

Johann Wolfgang von Goethe, *Faust*, translated by Bayard Taylor, Sphere Books Ltd., 1974, page 26, Part I, 'Prologue in Heaven,' l.328

By aspiring to a similitude of God in goodness or love, neither man nor angel ever transgressed, or shall transgress.

Francis Bacon, *The Advancement of Learning*, Cassell and Company Ltd., 1905, page 156

And thou my mind aspire to higher things:
Grow rich in that which never taketh rust.

Sir Philip Sidney, *The Poems of Sir Philip Sidney*, edited by William A. Ringler, Jr., Oxford at the Clarendon Press, 1962, page 161, 'Leave me, O Love'

Strong souls
Live like fire-hearted suns to spend their strength
In farthest striving action.

George Eliot, *The Spanish Gypsy. A Poem*, William Blackwood and Sons, 1868, page 303, Book IV

An aspiration is a joy for ever, a possession as solid as a landed estate, a fortune which we can never exhaust and which gives year by year a revenue of pleasurable activity.

Robert Louis Stevenson, *Familiar Studies of Men and Books, Virginibus Puerisque, Selected Poems*, William Collins Sons & Co. Ltd., 1956, page 293

Enflam'd with the study of learning, and the admiration of virtue; stirr'd up with high hopes of living to be brave men, and worthy patriots, dear to God, and famous to all ages.

John Milton, *Complete Works of John Milton*, Oxford University Press, 1959, Volume II, page 385, 'Of Education'

Yet some there be that by due steps aspire
To lay their just hands on that golden key
That opes the palace of eternity.

John Milton, *The Poems of John Milton*, edited by John Carey and Alastair Fowler, Longmans, Green & Co. Ltd., 1968, page 176, 'Comus,' l.12

O Lord, I, a beggar, ask of Thee
More than what a thousand kings may ask of Thee;
Each one has something he needs to ask of Thee,
I have come to ask Thee to give me Thyself.

Al-Ansari, *The Persian Mystics*, translated by Sardar Sir Jogendra Sing, John Murray Ltd., 1939, page 31, 'The Invocations of Sheikh Abdullah Ansari of Herat'

The sensual man is at home in worldliness because he has no higher aspiration. The spiritual man, however much attracted to worldliness, cannot be at home in the world of sense because he is groping towards the world of spirit.

Hubert van Zeller, *Considerations*, Sheed & Ward Ltd., 1974, page 84

For rigorous teachers seized my youth,
And purged its faith, and trimmed its fire,
Showed me the high, white star to Truth,
There bade me gaze, and there aspire.

Matthew Arnold, *The Poems of Matthew Arnold*, edited by Kenneth Allott, Longmans, Green & Co. Ltd., 1965, page 288, 'Stanzas from the Grande Chartreuse,' xii. 67

It was my duty to have loved the highest:
It surely was my profit had I known:
It would have been my pleasure had I seen.
We needs must love the highest when we see it.

Alfred, Lord Tennyson, *The Poems of Tennyson*, edited by Christopher Ricks, Longmans, Green & Co. Ltd., 1969, page 1741, *Idylls of the King*, No. 474, 'Guinevere,' l.652

A man who loves Jesus and the truth, who is delivered from undisciplined desires and really lives the inward life, can turn to God with nothing to hold him back. In spirit he can rise beyond himself and rest in peace and joy.

Thomas à Kempis, *The Imitation of Christ*, translated by Betty I. Knott, William Collins Sons & Co. Ltd., 1979, page 85

The religious spirit is in us. It preceded the religions, and their task as well as that of the prophets, of the initiated, consists in releasing, directing, and developing it. This mystical aspiration is an essentially human trait. It slumbers at the bottom of our souls awaiting the event, or the man capable, in the manner of an enzyme, of transforming it into true mysticism, into faith.

Lecomte du Noüy, *Human Destiny*, Longmans, Green & Co. Ltd., 1947, page 178

I should like to make every man, woman, and child whom I meet discontented with themselves, even as I am discontented with myself. I should like to awaken in them, about their physical, their intellectual, their moral condition, that divine discontent which is the parent, first of upward aspiration and then of self control, thought, effort to fulfil that aspiration even in part. For to be discontented with the divine discontent, and to be ashamed with the noble shame, is the very germ and first upgrowth of all virtue.

Charles Kingsley, *Health and Education*, W. Isbister & Co., 1874, page 20

No aspiring soul, . . . has not at some time bowed in worship before the wonder, mystery and beauty of this world. The glorious forms and colours of sunset and dawn; the ripple of moonlight on the surface of some quiet lake; the majesty of mountain peaks; and the quaintly flowing music of mountain streams, remind every lover of Nature that God is not apart from His world, but can be found hidden there as the very Spirit of it all—'Beauty Itself among beautiful things'. The beauty is there for all to see, but men dwell in the shadows of their own creation and their eyes are blind to it. We miss the joy of the beautiful so often, because we are wrapped up in ourselves.

Raynor C. Johnson, *A Pool of Reflections*, Hodder & Stoughton Ltd., 1975, page 143

The spiritual life is a gift. It is the gift of the Holy Spirit, who lifts us up into the kingdom of God's love. But to say that being lifted up into the kingdom of love is a divine gift does not mean that we wait passively until the gift is offered to us. Jesus tells us to set our hearts on the kingdom. Setting our hearts on something involves not only serious aspiration but also strong determination. A spiritual life requires human effort. The forces that keep pulling us back into a worry-filled life are far from easy to overcome. Here we touch the question of discipline in the spiritual life. A spiritual life without discipline is impossible. Discipline is the other side of discipleship. The practice of a spiritual discipline makes us more sensitive to the small, gentle voice of God. The prophet Elijah did not encounter God in the mighty wind or in the earthquake or in the fire, but in the small voice . . .

Through a spiritual discipline we prevent the world from filling our lives to such an extent that there is no place left to listen. A spiritual discipline sets us free to pray or, to say it better, allows the Spirit of God to pray in us.

Henri J.M. Nouwen, in *Circles of Love*, edited by John Garvey, Darton, Longman & Todd, 1990, page 41

AWARENESS

'Awareness'—a condition of conscious knowing.

W hen I was young I used to go to concerts in Huddersfield Town Hall. At that time there was an arrangement whereby children could go and sit in spare places in the orchestra at a reduced rate. I remember a concert given by the Yorkshire Symphony Orchestra in which I was sitting close to the tuba player. I observed him carefully. There he was, in his evening dress and black tie. During the concert he played only a dozen notes, and I remember feeling extremely sorry for him. What a life—a two-hour concert, sitting with that monstrous instrument by his side, only twelve notes played, and this was his occupation, his career, his life. No wonder he downed a pint during the interval.

This particular concert was a turning point in my life and gave me a conscious awareness of other people. I felt a certain sympathy for many different people and somehow wanted to help them, though at the time did not know how this could be done.

Life moved on with school, National Service and university, following in rapid succession. Even so, in my early twenties I was still aware of these feelings of sympathy for other people.

About this time I became conscious of the Holy Spirit and the importance of the spiritual dimension. Tentatively I moved forward in the direction of ordination and there discerned a need for heightened awareness. The crucial breakthrough came with the discovery of a 'listening' form of prayer. Quotations collected over the years were gathered together in *Visions of Faith, Hope, Love* and *Glory*, and used to further this practice of 'listening'—mulling over the contents in Reflection. This has led to increased awareness, both within and without.

O Lord, thou hast searched me and known me! Thou knowest when I sit down and when I rise up; thou discernest my thoughts from afar.

Psalm 139.1

I, wisdom, dwell in prudence, and I find knowledge and discretion.

Proverbs 8.12

Watch and pray that you may not enter into temptation; the spirit indeed is willing, but the flesh is weak.

Matthew 26.41

Take heed what you hear.

Mark 4.24

Our most important task is to become aware of the fact that our new consciousness of space no longer admits the traditional religious imagery by which we represent to ourselves our encounter with God. At the same time, we must also recognize that this traditional imagery *was never essential to Christianity*. We must recover the New Testament awareness that our God does not need a temple (Acts 7.47-53) or even a cathedral. The New Testament teaches in fact that God has one indestructible temple: which is man himself (1 Cor. 3.17). To understand that God is present in the world *in man* is in fact no new or radical idea. It is, on the contrary, one of the most elementary teachings of the New Testament.

Thomas Merton, *Conjectures of a Guilty Bystander*, Burns & Oates Ltd., 1968, page 274

The Holy Spirit is that power which opens eyes that are closed, hearts that are unaware and minds that shrink from too much reality. If one is open towards God, one is open also to the beauty of the world, the truth of ideas, and the pain of disappointment and deformity. If one is closed up against being hurt, or blind towards one's fellow-men, one is inevitably shut off from God also. One cannot choose to be open in one direction and closed in another. Vision and vulnerability go together. Insensitivity also is an all-rounder. If for one reason or another we refuse really to *see* another person, we become incapable of sensing the presence of God. The spirit of man is that facility which enables each of us to be truly present to another. The spirit of God is that power of communion which enables every other reality, and the God who is within and behind all realities, to be present to us.

John V. Taylor, *The Go-Between God*, SCM Press Ltd., 1972, page 19

Silence enables us to be aware of God, to let mind and imagination dwell upon his truth, to let prayer be listening before it is talking, and to discover our own selves in a way that is not always possible when we are making or listening to noise. There comes sometimes an interior silence in which the soul discovers itself in a new dimension of energy and peace, a dimension which the restless life can miss. If the possibilities of silence were often hard in biblical times they are infinitely harder in the world in which we live today. A world frightening in its speed and noise is a world where silence alone may enable man's true freedom to be found.

The ways in which meditation interpenetrates the praying of the Church and of the Christian are legion. A time of silence enables the Christian to share more deeply in the Church's sacramental worship... Into the Christian's use of silence there may flow the wonder of God the Creator, the recollection of the life and death and resurrection of Jesus, the recalling of scenes in his life, often a passage of the Bible, the glories of nature in which the finger of God is present, gratitude for personal blessings or the words of poets who tell of wonder and beauty. All these may stir meditation, and its course may be unpredictable.

Michael Ramsey, *Be Still and Know*, William Collins Sons & Co. Ltd., Fount Publications, 1982, page 83

Will we ever know whether we are living witnesses to the light or serving the prince of darkness? That is the question for the four priests who participated in the revolution in Nicaragua and are now members of the Sandinista cabinet. That, too, is the question for Christians active in agrarian reform, in the developement of cooperatives for the *campesinos*, and in programmes for better health and housing.

Christians are called to live in the world without being of it.

But how do we know whether we are just in it, or also of it? My feeling is that all Christians who are serious about their vocation have to face this question at some point.

Discernment remains our lifelong task. I can see no other way for discernment than a life in the Spirit, a life of unceasing prayer and contemplation, a life of deep communion with the Spirit of God. Such a life will slowly develop in us an inner sensitivity, enabling us to distinguish between the law of the flesh and the law of the spirit. We certainly will make constant errors and seldom have the purity of heart required to make the right decisions. We may never know whether we are giving to Caesar what belongs to God. But when we continuously try to live in the Spirit, we at least shall be willing to confess our weakness and ask for forgiveness every time we find ourselves again in the service of Baal.

Henri J.M. Nouwen, in *Circles of Love*, edited by John Garvey, Darton, Longman & Todd, 1990, page 48

Slowly on You, too, the meanings: the light-sparkles on water, tufts of weed in winter—the least thing—dandelion and groundsel.

Have you seen the wild bees' nest in the field, the cells, the grubs, the transparent white baby-bees, turning brown, hairy, the young bees beginning to fly, raking the moss down over the disturbed cells? the parasites?

Have you seen the face of your brother or sister? Have you seen the little robin hopping and peering under the bushes? Have you seen the sun rise, or set? I do not know—I do not think that I have.

When your unquiet brain has ceased to spin its cobwebs over the calm and miraculous beauty of the world;

When the Air and Sunlight shall have penetrated your body through and through; and the Earth and Sea have become part of it;

When at last, like a sheath long concealing the swelling green shoot, the love of learning and the regard for elaborate art, wit, manners, dress, or anything rare or costly whatever, shall drop clean off from you;

When your Body—for to this it must inevitably return—is become shining and transparent before you in every part (however deformed);

Then (O blessed One!) these things also transparent possibly shall surrender themselves—the least thing shall speak to you words of deliverance.

Edward Carpenter, *Towards Democracy*, George Allen & Unwin Ltd., 1931, page 90

Another lesson I learned was that the intensity of prayer is not measured by time, but by the reality and depth of one's awareness of unity with God. I learned to look on prayer not as a means of influencing the Creator in my favour, but as an awareness of the presence of God—everywhere.

I also learned a few helpful ideas about sin. Broadly speaking, I learned to recognize sin as the refusal to live up to the enlightenment we possess. To know the right order of values and deliberately to choose the lower ones. To know that, however much these values may differ with different people at different stages of spiritual growth, for one's self there must be no compromise with that which one *knows* to be the lower value.

I learned, too, that to condemn others is a grave mistake, since hatred, and even the wrong kind of criticism, is an evil which recoils upon its author and poisons every human relationship.

That does not mean we should be blind to the weaknesses or wickednesses of others, any more than to our own, but that we should learn to look at them as the limitations of birth and circumstance, limitations which it is our duty to help them to rise above. In this I have found that example and service are more helpful than advice or preaching. It has enabled me to get some little glimpse of the meaning behind that great truth—that all the living are as one, in the Great Life of the Universe.

And it carries with it a deep sense of rest. It gives a meaning to life, and a happiness which nothing else can give and no one but ourselves can take away. It is a road to be travelled with a shout of joy—a most exciting road!

Margaret Bondfield, *What Life Has Taught Me*, edited by Sir James Marchant, Odhams Press Ltd., 1948, page 27

BAPTISM

'Baptism'—religious rite of immersing (person) in, or sprinkling
with, water in sign of purification and (with Christians) of
admission to the Church, generally accompanied by name-giving.

T his definition fails to mention an important part of baptism—namely, spiritual rebirth. At the beginning of a baptism service I usually draw attention to the Genesis story of the creation of man and of the divine inbreathing. I point out the person to be baptized already has seeds of an enormous source of life in the depths of their being—something of the Father, the Son and the Holy Spirit, as well as divine attributes, such as life, light, truth, joy and love. In baptism, these 'seeds' or 'sparks of divine life' are triggered off or catalysed into life in a spiritual rebirth. In the cleansing of water, the priest sprinkles water on the forehead of the person being baptized and says—'*N*. I baptize you in the name of (nature of) the Father, in the name of (nature of) the Son, and in the name of (nature of) the Holy Spirit.' These are words not just of cleansing but of spiritual rebirth. This is followed with the signing of the cross, and the giving of a lighted candle to the godparents—symbolic of Christ the light of the world, now present in the life of the baptized person.

I usually end my brief introduction to the baptism service with a word about godparents. They are called 'godparents' because they have the task of nurturing and stimulating the 'godly' dimension catalysed and triggered off in baptism. Seen from this perspective what an important role godparents have and what an important sacrament baptism is.

And thus you shall do to them, to cleanse them: sprinkle the water of expiation upon them.
Numbers 8.7

Wash me thoroughly from my iniquity, and cleanse me from my sin!
Psalm 51.2

Truly, truly, I say to you, unless one is born of water and the Spirit, he cannot enter the kingdom of God. That which is born of the flesh is flesh, and that which is born of the Spirit is spirit. Do not marvel that I said to you, 'You must be born anew.' The wind blows where it wills, and you hear the sound of it, but you do not know whence it comes or whither it goes; so it is with every one who is born of the Spirit.
John 3.5-8

He has put his seal upon us and given us his Spirit in our hearts as a guarantee.
2 Corinthians 1.22

The true and availing baptism is a baptism into the life, death, and resurrection of Christ, and cleanses the soul of its sins and produces 'a good conscience toward God'—the old sinful man is buried and a new and Christlike man is raised.
Rufus M. Jones, *Spiritual Reformers in the 16th and 17th Centuries*, Macmillan & Co Ltd, 1914, page 110

This birth must be wrought within you. The heart, or Son of God must arise in the birth of your life, and then you are in Christ and He is in you, and all that He and the Father have is yours; and as the Son is one with the Father, so also the new man is one with the Father and with the Son, one virtue, one power, one light, one life, one eternal paradise, one enduring substance, one Father, Son, and Holy Ghost, and thou His child!

Rufus M. Jones, *Spiritual Reformers in the 16th and 17th Centuries*, Macmillan & Co. Ltd., 1914, page 197

Don't bother at all about that question of a person being 'made a Christian' by baptism. It is only the usual trouble about words being used in more than one sense. Thus we might say a man 'became a soldier' the moment he joined the army. But his instructors might say six months later 'I think we have made a soldier of him.' Both usages are quite definable, only one wants to know which is being used in a given sentence. The Bible itself gives us one short prayer which is suitable for all who are struggling with the beliefs and doctrines. It is: Lord I believe, help thou my unbelief.

C.S. Lewis, *Letters of C.S. Lewis*, edited by W.H. Lewis, Geoffrey Bles Ltd., 1966, page 239

The direct incoming of the Divine Spirit, producing a rebirth and a new creation in the man himself, is the only baptism which avails with God or which makes any difference in the actual condition of man. Baptism in its true significance is the reception of cleansing power, it is an inward process which purifies the heart, illuminates the conscience, and is not only necessary for salvation but in fact *is* salvation. Christian baptism is therefore not with water, but with Christ: it is the immersion of the soul in the life-giving streams of Christ's spiritual presence... the reception of *Christ's real baptism*, an inner baptism, a baptism of spirit and power, by which the believing soul, the inner man, is clarified, strengthened, and made pure.

Rufus M. Jones, *Spiritual Reformers in the 16th and 17th Centuries*, Macmillan & Co. Ltd., 1914, page 80

Imagine not infants but crowds of grown-up persons already changed in heart and feelings; their 'life hidden with Christ and God,' losing their personal consciousness in the laver of regeneration; rising again from the depths into the light of heaven, in communion with God and nature; met as they rose from the bath with the white raiment, which is 'the right-eousness of the saints,' and ever after looking back on that moment as the instant of their new birth, of the putting off of the old man, and the putting on of Christ. Baptism was to them the figure of death, burial, and resurrection all in one, the most apt expression of the greatest change that can pass upon man, like the sudden change into another life when we leave the body.

Benjamin Jowett, *Selected Passages from the Theological Writings of Benjamin Jowett*, edited by Lewis Campbell, John Murray Ltd, 1902, page 60

For thousands of years, rites of initiation have been teaching spiritual rebirth; yet, strangely enough, man forgets again and again the meaning of divine procreation. This is surely no evidence of a strong life of the spirit; and yet the penalty of misunderstanding is heavy, for it is nothing less than neurotic decay, embitterment, atrophy and sterility. It is easy enough to drive the spirit out of the door, but when we have done so the salt of life grows flat—it loses its savour. Fortunately, we have proof that the spirit always renews its strength in the fact that the central teaching of the ancient initiations is handed on from generation to generation. Ever and again human beings arise who understand what is meant by the fact that God is our Father. The equal balance of the flesh and the spirit is not lost to the world.

C.G. Jung, *Modern Man in Search of a Soul*, translated by W.S. Dell and Cary F. Baynes, Kegan Paul, Trench, Trubner & Co. Ltd., 1933, page 142

By the sacrament of Baptism, whenever it is properly conferred in the way the Lord determined and received with the proper dispositions of soul, man becomes truly incorporated into the crucified and glorified Christ and is reborn to a sharing of the divine life, as the Apostle says: 'For you were buried together with him in baptism, and in him also rose again through faith in the working of God who raised him from the dead.'

Baptism, therefore constitutes the sacramental bond of unity existing among all who through it are reborn. But baptism, of itself, is only a beginning, a point of departure, for it is wholly directed toward the acquiring of fullness of life in Christ. Baptism is thus ordained toward a complete profession of faith, a complete incorporation into the system of salvation such as Christ himself willed it to be, and finally, toward a complete integration into eucharistic communion.

Vatican Council II, *The Conciliar and Post-Conciliar Documents*, 1981 Edition, general editor, Austin Flannery, O.P., Fowler Wright Books Ltd., page 409

Baptism is not an offer made by man to God, but an offer made by Christ to man. It is grounded solely on the will of Jesus Christ, as expressed in His gracious call. Baptism is essentially passive—*being baptized, suffering* the call of Christ. In baptism man becomes Christ's own possession. When the name of Christ is spoken over the candidate, he becomes a partaker in this Name, and is baptized 'into Jesus Christ'. From that moment he belongs to Jesus Christ. He is wrested from the dominion of the world, and passes into the ownership of Christ.

Baptism therefore betokens a *breach*. Christ invades the realm of Satan, lays hands on His own, and creates for Himself His Church. By this act past and present are rent asunder. The old order is passed away, and all things have become new. This breach is not effected by man's tearing off his own chains through some unsatiable desire for a new life of freedom. The breach has been effected by Christ long since, and in baptism it is effected by our own lives, as in the lives of others before us … The baptized Christian has ceased to belong to the world and is no longer its slave. He belongs to Christ alone.

Dietrich Bonhoeffer, *The Cost of Discipleship*, translated by R.H. Fuller, SCM Press Ltd, 1948, page 174

BEAUTY

'Beauty'—combination of qualities, as shape, proportion, colour, in human face or form, or in other objects, that delight the sight; combined qualities, delighting the other senses, the moral sense, or the intellect.

I have been conscious of beauty as far back as I can remember. In childhood I quickly discovered the beauty of nature in our garden—in the flowers, the trees and the shrubs. After this I became aware of the beauty of the seasons—snow in winter, crocuses and daffodils in springtime, the sun, sea and sky in summer, and the rich hues of autumn.

My parents were quick to introduce me to the beauties of music and this continues to be a constant source of joy. I've always enjoyed orchestral music, but singing has become more important to me, especially taking part in our rich heritage of Church music.

Later in life travel opened up fresh vistas of beauty. I can still see in my mind's eye the flying fish accompanying our troopship, the *Empire Fowey*, as we sailed through the India Ocean. I saw brightly coloured birds and butterflies in the jungles of Malaysia. In recent years I have come to appreciate the beauty of mountains, the Himalayas, Mount Kenya and the Alps. Dawn and dusk are constant reminders of the beauty of the world.

In my thirties I became conscious of another source of beauty in the depths of myself. This I took to be a consequence of the divine inbreathing and led to an awareness of a seed or a spark of beauty deep inside myself. The Psalmist invites us to enter in to this beauty—'let the beauty of the Lord our God be upon us.' Happy are those who accept this invitation.

And let the beauty of the Lord our God be upon us.

Psalm 90.17 (AV)

Know how much better the Lord of them is: for the first author of beauty hath created them … for by the greatness and beauty of the creatures proportionably the maker of them is seen.

Wisdom of Solomon 13.3,5 (AV)

And how can men preach unless they are sent? As it is written, 'How beautiful are the feet of those who preach good news!'

Romans 10.15

Finally, brethren, whatever is true, whatever is honourable, whatever is just, whatever is pure, whatever is lovely, whatever is gracious, if there is any excellence, if there is anything worthy of praise, think about these things.

Philippians 4.8

He has a daily beauty in his life.

William Shakespeare, *Othello*, Act V. sc.i. l.19

Nothing in human life, least of all religion, is ever right until it is beautiful.

Harry Emerson Fosdick, *As I See Religion*, SCM Press Ltd., 1932, page 128

Though we travel the world over to find the beautiful, we must carry it with us, or we find it not.

Ralph Waldo Emerson, *The Works of Ralph Waldo Emerson*, edited by George Sampson, George Bell & Sons Ltd., 1906, Volume I, *Essays and Representative Men*, page 191

I want to help you to grow as beautiful as God meant you to be when he thought of you first.

George Macdonald, *The Marquis of Lossie*, Everett & Co. Ltd., 1912, page 68

For when with beauty we can virtue join,
We paint the semblance of a form divine.

Matthew Prior, *The Poetical Works of Matthew Prior*, edited by Charles Cowden Clarke, William P. Nimmo, 1868, page 401, 'Verses Spoken to Lady Henrietta Cavendish-Holles Harley, Countess of Oxford,' l.17

The hours when the mind is absorbed by beauty are the only hours when we really live.

Richard Jefferies, *The Pageant of Summer*, Chatto & Windus Ltd., 1911, page 39

Every bit of beauty in this world, the beauty of man, of nature, of a work of art, is a partial transfiguration of this world, a creative break-through to another.

Nicolas Berdyaev, *Christian Existentialism*, selected and translated by Donald A. Lowrie, George Allen & Unwin Ltd., 1965, page 323

For beauty being the best of all we know
Sums up the unsearchable and secret aims
Of nature

Robert Bridges, *Poetical Works of Robert Bridges*, Humphrey Milford, Oxford University Press, 1913, page 191, Sonnet: 'The Growth of Love,' st.viii, l.1

Physical beauty is the sign of an interior beauty, a spiritual and moral beauty which is the basis, the principle, and the unity of the beautiful.

Friedrich Schiller, *Essays, Aesthetical and Philosophical*, George Bell & Sons Ltd., 1875, page 4

(God) Himself has imparted of His own to all particular beings from that fountain of beauty—Himself. For the good and beautiful things in the world could never have been what they are, save that they were made in the image of the archetype, which is truly good and beautiful.

Philo, *Three Jewish Philosophers*, selections, edited by Hans Lewy, Harper & Row, Publishers, Inc., 1945, page 84

Spirit of Beauty, whose sweet impulses,
Flung like the rose of dawn across the sea,
Alone can flush the exalted consciousness
With shafts of sensible divinity—
Light of the World, essential loveliness.

Alan Seeger, *Poems*, Constable & Co. Ltd., 1917, 'An Ode to Natural Beauty,' page 4

A thing of beauty is a joy for ever:
Its loveliness increases; it will never
Pass into nothingness; but still will keep
A bower quiet for us, and a sleep
Full of sweet dreams, and health, and quiet breathing.

John Keats, *The Poems of John Keats*, edited by E. de Selincourt, Methuen & Co. Ltd., 1927, page 242

But a celestial brightness—a more ethereal beauty—
Shone on her face and encircled her form, when, after confession,
Homeward serenely she walked with God's benediction upon her.
When she had passed, it seemed like the ceasing of exquisite music.

Henry Wadsworth Longfellow, *The Poetical Works of Longfellow*, Humphrey Milford, Oxford University Press, 1913, page 144, *Evangeline*, 'Part the First,' l.59

It's only now I am beginning to see again and to recognise again the beauty of the world. Take the swallows to-day their flutter-flutter, their velvet-forked tails, their transparent wings that are like the fins of fishes. The little dark head and breast golden in the light. Then the beauty of the garden, and the beauty of raked paths … Then, the silence.

Katherine Mansfield, *Journal of Katherine Mansfield*, edited by J. Middleton-Murry, Constable & Co. Ltd., 1927, page 242

Man is so inclined to concern himself with the most ordinary things, while his mind and senses are so easily blunted against impressions of beauty and perfection, that we should use all means to preserve the capacity of feeling them … Each day we should at least hear one little song, read one good poem, see one first-rate picture, and if it can be arranged, utter some sensible remarks.

Johann Wolfgang von Goethe, *William Meister's Year of Apprenticeship*, translated by H.M. Waidson, John Calder (Publishers) Ltd., 1978, Volume II, page 74

Beauty is something wonderful and strange that the artist fashions out of the chaos of the world in the torment of his soul. And when he has made it, it is not given to all to know it. To recognise it you must repeat the adventure of the artist. It is a melody that he sings to you, and to hear it again in your own heart you want knowledge and sensitiveness and imagination.

W. Somerset Maugham, *The Moon and Sixpence*, William Heinemann Ltd., 1928, page 84

The wonder of Creation suggests another gateway to worship: the door of Beauty. Whatever kind of beauty stirs us to delight or to painful longing, we can use as a ladder to rise above ourselves. For this love of beauty is divinely implanted. The touch of beauty, when we feel it, is not to be merely a passing delight: it is the call of God, inviting us gently and sweetly to turn to Him. St. Augustine says: 'Thy whole creation praises Thee without ceasing … and to the end that, using Thy creatures as stepping stones, and passing on to Him who made them so wonderfully, our soul might shake off its despondence and soar up to Thee. There is refreshment and true courage.' To the man or woman who 'means only God' the beauty of Creation may become a transparent veil, half revealing and half concealing the presence of Love itself.

Olive Wyon, *The School of Prayer*, SCM Press Ltd., 1943, page 89

The Beautiful, says Hegel, is the spiritual making itself known sensuously. It represents, then, a direct message to us from the heart of Reality; ministers to us of more abundant life. Therefore the widening of our horizon which takes place when we turn in prayer to a greater world than that which the senses reveal to us, should bring with it a more poignant vision of loveliness, a more eager passion for Beauty as well as for Goodness and Truth. When St. Augustine strove to express the intensity of his regret for wasted years, it was to his neglect of the Beauty of God that he went to show the poignancy of his feelings, the immensity of his loss. 'Oh Beauty so old and so new! too late have I loved thee!'

It needs a special training, I think—a special and deliberate use of our faculties—if we are to avoid this deprivation; and learn, as an integral part of our communion with Reality, to lay hold of the loveliness of the First and only Fair.

Evelyn Underhill, *The Essentials of Mysticism*, J.M. Dent & Sons Ltd., 1920, page 113

You flowers and trees, you hills and streams, you fields, flocks and wild birds, you books, you poems, and you people, I am unutterably alone in the midst of you. The irrational hunger that sometimes gets into the depths of my will, tries to swing my deepest self away from God and direct it to your love. I try to touch you with the deep fire that is in the centre of your heart, but I cannot touch you without defiling both you and myself, and I am abashed, solitary, and helpless, surrounded by a beauty that can never belong to me.

But this sadness generates within me an unspeakable reverence for the holiness of created things, for they are pure and perfected and they belong to God and they are mirrors of His beauty. He is mirrored in all things like the sunlight in clean water: but if I try to drink the light that is in the water I only shatter the reflection.

And so I live alone and chaste in the midst of the holy beauty of all created things, knowing that nothing I can see or hear or touch will ever belong to me, ashamed of my absurd need to give myself away to any one of them or to all of them.

Thomas Merton, *The Sign of Jonas*, Hollis & Carter, 1953, page 232

The Beauty of the world, as many have felt, is the strongest evidence we have of the goodness and benevolence of the Creator. Not, of course, that the world was made beautiful for our sakes. It is beautiful because its Author is beautiful, and we should remember that when the old writers spoke of God as the Author of nature, they used the word in much the same sense as if we said that a man was the author of his own photograph. But we are allowed to see and enjoy beauty, although the gift cannot be proved to promote our own survival. It looks like a free gift of God. Beauty is a general quality of nature, and not only of organic nature; crystals are very beautiful; the perceiving mind must also be beautiful and healthy. The vile or vulgar mind not only cannot discern beauty; it is a great destroyer of beauty everywhere.

The love of beauty is super-personal and disinterested, like all spiritual values; it promotes common enjoyment and social sympathy. Unquestionably it is one of the three ultimate values, ranking with Goodness and Truth.

W.R. Inge, *Outspoken Essays*, Longmans, Green & Co. Ltd., 1922, Second Series, page 30

Suppose a curious and fair woman. Some have seen the beauties of Heaven in such a person. It is a vain thing to say they loved too much. I dare say there are ten thousand beauties in that creature which they have not seen. They loved it not too much but upon false causes. Nor so much upon false ones, as only upon some little ones. They love a creature for sparkling eyes and curled hair, lily breasts and ruddy cheeks: which they should love moreover for being God's Image, Queen of the Universe, beloved by Angels, redeemed by Jesus Christ, an heiress of Heaven, and the temple of the Holy Ghost: a mine and fountain of all virtues, a treasury of graces, and a child of God. But these excellencies are unknown. They love her perhaps, but do not love God more: nor men as much: nor Heaven and Earth at all. We should be all Life and Mettle and Vigour and Love to everything; and that would poise us ... But God being beloved infinitely more, will be infinitely more our joy, and our heart will be more with Him, so that no man can be in danger by loving others too much, that loveth God as he ought.

Thomas Traherne, *Centuries*, The Faith Press Ltd., 1969, page 87

BLESSEDNESS

'Blessedness'—happiness; enjoyment of divine favours.

I n the early 1970s I went and stayed with some friends in Kenya during a summer vacation. We visited some game parks and tried to climb an active volcano in the Rift Valley, called Ol Doinyo Lengai. On one occasion we were returning in our Land Rover from one of these mini safaris and came across a crowd of people in the road. A young girl, aged about fourteen, was lying face downwards by the side of the road in a pool of blood. She had either been run over or hit by a passing vehicle. All the indications were that she was dead. We gingerly made our way round the crowd, and somewhat distressed, continued our journey.

That night I began to take stock of this experience. Here was I, alive and well, with all my faculties intact. Back home in England I had food, a roof over my head, clothing, and an interesting job of work to do. How fortunate I was—compared with this poor young girl, whose life had been untimely ended today. My thoughts and feelings moved on. I was at a stage of life when I was discovering the life of the inner man. Gradually I was becoming conscious of an inner presence of the Father, and the Son, and the Holy Spirit. Soon this was to grow into a discovery of an inner presence of divine attributes, such as life, light, joy, truth, love, grace and glory; that these could be brought to the surface in reflection—and enjoyed.

Most people aim for happiness, but there is a longer, higher, deeper and wider state which includes happiness and yet is even more fulfilling. This is 'blessedness' and as in the definition above means 'enjoyment of divine favours'. This is a free gift of God, and it is ours for the asking.

The Lord bless you and keep you: The Lord make his face to shine upon you, and be gracious to you: The Lord lift up his countenance upon you, and give you peace
Numbers 6.24-26

For I will pour water on the thirsty land, and streams on the dry ground; I will pour my Spirit upon your descendants, and my blessing on your offspring.
Isaiah 44.3

But seek first his kingdom and his righteousness, and all these things shall be yours as well.
Matthew 6.33

And God is able to provide you with every blessing in abundance, so that you may always have enough of everything and may provide in abundance for every good work.
2 Corinthians 9.8

Blessed is he who has found his work; let him ask no other blessedness.
Thomas Carlyle, *Past and Present*, Ward, Lock & Co. Ltd., lxxx, page 136

There is in man a HIGHER than Love of Happiness: he can do without Happiness, and instead thereof find Blessedness.
Thomas Carlyle, *Sartor Resartus*, Ward, Lock & Co. Ltd., lxxx, page 128

He is blessed who is assured that the animal is dying out in him day by day, and the divine being established.
Henry David Thoreau, *Walden*, The New American Library of World Literature, Inc., 1960, page 149

Amid my list of blessings infinite,
Stand this the foremost, 'That my heart has bled.'
Edward Young, *Night Thoughts*, Thomas Nelson, 1841, page 210

Blesse mee in this life but with the peace of my conscience,
command of my affections, the love of thy selfe and my dearest
friend, and I shall be happy enough to pity *Caesar*.

Sir Thomas Browne, *The Works of Sir Thomas Browne*, edited by Geoffrey Keynes, Faber & Faber Ltd, 1964, Volume I, *Religio Medici*, page 93

Blessings, we enjoy daily. And for most of them, because they be so common, most men
forget to pay their praises: but let not us; because it is a sacrifice so pleasing to Him that
made that sun and us, and still protects us, and gives us flowers, and showers, and
stomachs, and meat, and content, and leisure.

Izaak Walton, *The Complete Angler*, Macmillan & Co. Ltd., 1906, page 174

Blessedness lieth not in much and many, but in One and oneness ... All the great works and
wonders that God has ever wrought or shall ever work in or through the creatures, or even
God Himself with all His goodness ... can never make me blessed, but only in so far as they
exist and are done and loved, known, tasted and felt within me.

Theologia Germanica, translated by Susanna Winkworth, Stuart Watkins Ltd., 1966, page 48

You never enjoy the world aright, till the Sea itself floweth in your veins, till you are clothed
with the heavens, and crowned with the stars and perceive yourself to be the sole heir of
the whole world, and more than so, because men are in it who are every one sole heirs as
well as you. Till you can sing and rejoice and delight in God, as misers do in gold, and Kings
in sceptres, you never enjoy the world ...

All things were made to be yours, and you were made to prize them according to their
value: which is your office and duty, the end for which you were created, and the means
whereby you enjoy. The end for which you were created, is that by prizing all that God hath
done, you may enjoy yourself and Him in Blessedness.

Thomas Traherne, *Centuries*, The Faith Press Ltd., 1969, pages 14, 6

That blessed mood
In which the burthen of the mystery,
In which the heavy and the weary weight
Of all this unintelligible world,
Is lightened:— that serene and blessed mood,
In which the affections gently lead us on,—
Until, the breath of this corporeal frame
And even the motion of our human blood
Almost suspended, we are laid asleep
In body, and become a living soul:
While with an eye made quiet by the power
Of harmony, and the deep power of joy,
We see into the life of things.

William Wordsworth, *The Poetical Works of William Wordsworth*, edited by E. de Selincourt, Oxford at the Clarendon Press, 1944, Volume II, page 260, 'Lines composed a few miles above Tintern Abbey,' l.37

Things worth remembering:
The value of time,
The success of perseverence,
The pleasure of working,
The dignity of simplicity,
The worth of character,
The improvement of talent,
The influence of example,
The obligation of duty,
The wisdom of economy,
The virtue of patience,

The joy of originating,
The power of kindness.

Anon.

Faith is not a thing of the mind, it is not an intellectual certainty or a felt conviction of the heart, it is a sustained decision to take God with utter seriousness as the God of our life; it is to live out the hours in a practical, concrete affirmation that he is Father and he is 'in heaven'. It is a decision to shift the centre of our life from ourselves to him, to forgo self-interest and make his interests, his will our sole concern. This is what it means to hallow his name as Father in heaven. Often it may seem that we only act 'as if', so unaffected are our hearts, perhaps even mocking us: 'where is your God?' It is this acting 'as if' which is true faith.

All that matters to faith is that God should have what he wants and we know that what he wants is always our own blessedness. His purposes are worked out, his will is mediated to us in the humblest form, as humble as our daily bread.

Ruth Burrows, *Living Love and Our Father*, Darton, Longman & Todd, 1990, page 113

Magnificent weather. The morning seems bathed in happy peace, and a heavenly fragrance rises from mountain and shore; it is as though a benediction were laid upon us... One might believe oneself in a church—a vast temple in which every being and every natural beauty has its place. I dare not breathe for fear of putting the dream to flight,—a dream traversed by angels... In these heavenly moments the cry of Pauline rises to one's lips. 'I feel! I believe! I see!' All the miseries, the cares, the vexations of life, are forgotten; the universal joy absorbs us; we enter into the divine order, and into the blessedness of the Lord. Labour and tears, sin, pain, and death have passed away. To exist is to bless; life is happiness. In this sublime pause of things all dissonances have disappeared. It is as though creation were but one vast symphony, glorifying the God of goodness with an inexhaustible wealth of praise and harmony. We question no longer whether it is so or not. We have ourselves become notes in the great concert and the soul breaks the silence of ecstasy only to vibrate in unison with the eternal joy.

Henri Frédéric Amiel, *Amiel's Journal*, translated by Mrs Humphry Ward, Macmillan & Co. Ltd., 1918, page 188

You are as prone to love, as the sun is to shine; it being the most delightful and natural employment of the Soul of Man: without which you are dark and miserable. Consider therefore the extent of Love, its vigour and excellency. For certainly he that delights not in Love makes vain the universe, and is of necessity to himself the greatest burden. The whole world ministers to you as the theatre of your Love. It sustains you and all objects that you may continue to love them. Without which it were better for you to have no being. Life without objects is sensible emptiness, and that is a greater misery than Death nor Nothing. Objects without Love are the delusion of life. The Objects of Love are its greatest treasures: and without Love it is impossible they should be treasures... To love all persons in all ages, all angels, all worlds, is divine and heavenly. To love all cities and all kingdoms, all kings and all peasants, and every person in all worlds with a natural intimate familiar love, as if him alone, is blessed. This makes a man effectually blessed in all worlds, a delightful lord of all things, a glorious friend to all persons, a concerned person in all transactions, and ever present with all affairs. So that he must ever be filled with company, ever in the midst of all nations, ever joyful, and ever blessed. The greatness of this man's love no man can measure; it is stable like the sun, it endureth for ever as the moon, it is a faithful witness in heaven. It is stronger and more great than all private affections. It representeth every person in the light of eternity, and loveth him with the love of all worlds, with a love conformable to God's, guided to the same ends, and founded upon the same causes. Which however lofty and divine it is, is ready to humble itself into the dust to serve the person beloved. And by how much the more sublime and glorious it is, is so much the more sweet and truly delightful, majesty and pleasure concurring together. Now you may see what it is to be a son of God more clearly. Love in all its glory is the friend of the most High. It was begotten of Him, and is to sit in His Throne, and to reign in communion with Him. It is to please Him and to be pleased by Him, in all His works, ways, and operations. It is ordained to hold an eternal correspondence with Him in the highest heavens. It is here in its infancy, there in its manhood and perfect stature.

Thomas Traherne, *Centuries*, The Faith Press Ltd., 1969, page 86

CHARACTER

*'Character'—moral strength, backbone; reputation, good
reputation; description of person's qualities.*

I was in my early twenties before I felt the full impact of Christ's character. Up to that point I got little glimpses here and there. Some of these came from the Gospels, others from the Church, and a few from religious education classes in school.

The main impact came later through a bishop who wisely guided me away from himself, to the character of Jesus Christ as portrayed in the Gospels. I began reading my newly acquired Bible and at last discovered a role model. Before long I began to get a new sense of identity and a value-system based on quality of life.

Dostoyevsky wrote a letter in which he expressed his belief that there is nothing lovelier, deeper, more sympathetic, more rational, more manly and more perfect than the Saviour. He went on to add there is in the world only one figure of absolute beauty: Christ—and he described him as an infinitely lovely figure.

His character obviously made an impact on those fortunate enough to meet him, but in the Resurrection appearances the disciples were aware of His presence in a new and wonderful way. With the coming of the Holy Spirit and the passage of two thousand years we know more of his character now than those early believers.

Visions of Grace brings together some of these character traits from the last two thousand years of lived Christian and religious experience. Reflecting on this material enables us, in the words of St Paul, 'to put on the Lord Jesus Christ'.

If I have walked with falsehood, and my foot has hastened to deceit; (Let me be weighed in a just balance, and let God know my integrity!) if my step has turned aside from the way, and my heart has gone after my eyes, and if any spot has cleaved to my hands; then let me sow, and another eat; and let what grows for me be rooted out.

Job 31.5-8

As he thinketh in his heart, so is he.

Proverbs 23.7 (AV)

You will know them by their fruits. Are grapes gathered from thorns, or figs from thistles?

Matthew 7.16

Show yourself in all respects a model of good deeds, and in your teaching show integrity.

Titus 2.7

He was his Maker's Image undefac'd!

Samuel Taylor Coleridge, *The Poetical Works of Samuel Taylor Coleridge*, edited by James Dykes Campbell, Macmillan & Co. Ltd, 1893, page 372, *Remorse*, Act II. sc.i

An honest man's the noblest work of God.

Alexander Pope, *An Essay on Man*, Cassell and Company Ltd., 1903, 'Epistle IV,' page 54

Happiness is not the end of life, character is.

Henry Ward Beecher, *Life Thoughts*, Alexander Strahan & Co., 1895, page 95

The foundation of every noble character is absolute sincerity.

Anon.

A talent is formed in stillness, a character in the world's torrent.

Johann Wolfgang von Goethe, *Torquato Tasso,* 1709, Act I. sc.ii. l.66

Character is higher than intellect... A great soul will be strong to live, as well as strong to think.

Ralph Waldo Emerson, *The Works of Ralph Waldo Emerson,* edited by George Sampson, George Bell & Sons Ltd., 1906, Volume III, *Society and Solitude: Letters and Social Aims: Addresses,* page 381

Let us be true: this is the highest maxim of art and of life, the secret of eloquence and of virtue, and of all moral authority.

Henri Frédéric Amiel, *Amiel's Journal,* translated by Mrs Humphry Ward, Macmillan & Co. Ltd., 1918, page 47

(Jesus)—the most innocent, the most benevolent, the most eloquent and sublime character that ever has been exhibited to man.

Thomas Jefferson, *The Writings of Thomas Jefferson,* Taylor and Maury, 1854, Volume IV, page 476

This above all: to thine own self be true,
And it must follow as the night the day
Thou canst not then be false to any man.

William Shakespeare, *Hamlet,* Act I. sc.iii. l.78

Friends, suffering, marriage, environment, study and recreation are influences which shape character. The strongest influence, if you are generous enough to yield to it, is the grace of God.

Hubert van Zeller, *Considerations,* Sheed & Ward Ltd., 1974, page 13

Character cannot be developed in ease and quiet. Only through experiences of trial and suffering can the soul be strengthened, vision cleared, ambition inspired and success achieved.

Helen Keller, *Helen Keller's Journal,* Michael Joseph Ltd., 1938, page 66

Our characters are shaped by our companions and by the objects to which we give most of our thoughts and with which we fill our imaginations. We cannot always be thinking even about Christ, but we can refuse to dwell on any thoughts which are out of tune with Him. We can, above all, quite deliberately turn our minds towards Him at any time when those thoughts come in.

William Temple, *Christian Faith and Life,* SCM Press Ltd., 1963, page 43

It is the character only of a good man to be able to deny and disown himself, and to make a full surrender of himself unto God; forgetting himself, and minding nothing but the will of his Creator; triumphing in nothing more than in his own nothingness, and in the allness of the Divinity. But indeed this, his being nothing, is the only way to be all things; this, his having nothing, the truest way of possessing all things.

John Smith the Platonist, *Select Discourses,* Cambridge at the University Press, 1859, page 401

What do we mean when we speak of a man of integrity? One who will be true to the highest he knows; who will never betray the truth or trifle with it; one who will never make a decision from self-regarding motives; one who will never yield to the persuasion of friends or the pressure of critics unless either conforms to his own standards of right and wrong; one who will face the consequences of his attitudes, decisions and actions, however costly they may be; one who will not be loud in self-justification, but quietly confident and humbly ready to explain.

George Appleton, *Journey for a Soul,* William Collins Sons & Co. Ltd., 1976, page 96

Now these mental and moral possessions are their own reward. They cannot, like earthly possessions, be taken away from us. For those who know what they are worth, the world is a much brighter place than for those who think that a man's life consisteth in the abundance of the things which he possesseth. The man whose 'mind to him a kingdom is' does not complain much of the injustices of life. Still less does the true Christian complain. He has found the joy that no man taketh from him. This world is not a bad place in his eyes, because he finds it full of love and beauty and wisdom. He knows that it is God's world, even though, in sad times like this, it seems to be 'full of darkness and cruel habitations.' Amid all the horrors of war and strife he sees the pure gold of love and heroism and devotion shining brightly.

W.R. Inge, *Personal Religion and the Life of Devotion*, Longmans, Green & Co. Ltd., 1924, page 59

The crown and glory of life is character. It is the noblest possession of a man, constituting a rank in itself, and an estate in the general good-will; dignifying every station, and exalting every position in society. It exercises a greater power than wealth, and secures all the honour without the jealousies of fame. It carries with it an influence which always tells; for it is the result of proved honour, rectitude, and consistency—qualities which, perhaps more than any other, command the general confidence and respect of mankind. Character is human nature in its best form. It is moral order embodied in the individual. Men of character are not only the conscience of society, but in every well-governed State they are its best motive power; for it is moral qualities in the main which rule the world.

Samuel Smiles, *Self Help*, S.W. Partridge & Co. Ltd., 1912, page 285

Where there is charity and wisdom
there is neither fear nor ignorance.
Where there is patience and humility,
there is neither anger nor disturbance.
Where there is poverty with joy,
there is neither covetousness nor avarice.
Where there is inner peace and meditation,
there is neither anxiousness nor dissipation.
Where there is fear of the Lord to guard the house (cf. Lk. 11.21),
there the enemy cannot gain entry.
Where there is mercy and discernment,
there is neither excess nor hardness of heart.

St Francis of Assisi, *Francis and Clare, The Complete Works*, translated by Regis J. Armstrong, OFM, Cap., Ignatius C. Brady, OFM, SPCK, 1982, page 35, *The Writings*, XXVII, 'How virtue drives out vice'

The fact that our being necessarily demands to be expressed in action should not lead us to believe that as soon as we stop acting we cease to exist. We do not live merely in order to 'do something'—no matter what... We do not live more fully merely by doing more, seeing more, tasting more, and experiencing more than we ever have before...

Everything depends on the *quality* of our acts and our experiences. A multitude of badly performed actions and of experiences only half-lived exhausts and depletes our being.

By doing things badly we make ourselves less real. This growing unreality cannot help but make us unhappy and fill us with a sense of guilt...

There are times, then, when in order to keep ourselves in existence at all we simply have to sit back for a while and do nothing. And for a man who has let himself be drawn completely out of himself by his activity, nothing is more difficult than to sit still and rest, doing nothing at all...

We must first recover the possession of our own being before we can act wisely or taste any experience in its human reality.

Thomas Merton, *No Man is an Island*, Hollis & Carter, 1955, page 107

The unity is one of character and its ideal. That character of the completed man, raised above what is poor and low, and governed by noble tempers and pure principles, has in Spenser two conspicuous elements. In the first place, it is based on manliness... It is not merely courage, it is not merely energy, it is not merely strength. It is the quality of soul which frankly accepts the conditions in human life, of labour, of obedience, of effort, of unequal success, which does not quarrel with them or evade them, but takes for granted with unquestioning alacrity that man is called—by his call to high aims and destiny—to a continual struggle with difficulty, with pain, with evil, and makes it the point of honour not to be dismayed or wearied out by them. It is a cheerful and serious willingness for hard work and endurance, as being inevitable and very bearable necessities, together with even a pleasure in encountering trials which put a man on his mettle, an enjoyment of the contest and the risk, even in play. It is the quality which seizes on the paramount idea of duty, as something which leaves a man no choice; which despises and breaks through the inferior considerations and motives—trouble, uncertainty, doubt, curiosity—which hang about and impede duty; which is impatient with the idleness and childishness of a life of mere amusement, or mere looking on, of continued and self-satisfied levity, of vacillation, of clever and ingenious trifling.

R.W. Church, *Spenser, English Men of Letters*, edited by John Morley, Macmillan & Co. Ltd., 1883, page 151

CHEERFULNESS

'Cheerfulness'—being contented, in good spirits, hopeful, animating, pleasant; being willing, not reluctant.

T he Gurkhas are noted for their cheerfulness. On jungle patrols my platoon sergeant, Sgt Nandaraj, would come and see me as soon as we had bivouacked for the night. With nostrils still twitching and eyes twinkling, he would give me his latest *sungur* (wild pig) report. He had just reconnoitred the area, and knew exactly where the wild pigs were. He was extremely keen to ambush them and supplement our basic army rations.

On one occasion we were positioned close to a rubber plantation, and the ground was more open than usual. On the return journey from our ambush position he decided to play a trick on me in the darkness. As a natural hunter he could move without making any noise at all. Before I was aware of what was afoot he quietly disappeared into the night. After a couple of minutes I realized I was on my own and hastily looked round for him. Just as I was beginning to feel utterly lost and panicky there was a hollow cough just behind my right ear, and I nearly jumped out of my skin. He enjoyed this and chuckled quietly to himself. He had been there all the time, though I didn't know it.

On another occasion we were by the sea, and manoeuvres were over by 4 pm. The Gurkhas went off crabbing, again to supplement their *bhat* (curry). That night Sgt Major Kabiram dug his fingers into the curry, and pulled out a huge crab's claw. In broken English he said, 'Ah, this afternoon, you ate me; now, I eat you.' With that he popped the claw into his mouth, crunched the contents and scoffed the lot. With the Gurkhas, cheerfulness, linked with loyalty, made them excellent soldiers and companions.

Behold, God will not reject a blameless man, nor take the hand of evildoers. He will yet fill your mouth with laughter, and your lips with shouting.

Job 8.20-21

A cheerful heart is a good medicine, but a downcast spirit dries up the bones.

Proverbs 17.22

Be of good cheer.

Matthew 14.27 (AV)

Rejoice always.

1 Thessalonians 5.16

That which befits us ... is cheerfulness and courage.

Ralph Waldo Emerson, *The Works of Ralph Waldo Emerson*, edited by George Sampson, George Bell & Sons Ltd., 1906, Volume I, *Essays and Representative Men*, page 353

Health and cheerfulness mutually beget each other.

Joseph Addison, *The Works of Joseph Addison*, edited and published by Henry G. Bohn, 1856, Volume III, page 363

A cheerful temper, joined with innocence, will make beauty attractive, knowledge delightful, and wit good-natured.

Joseph Addison, *The Works of Joseph Addison*, edited and published by Henry G. Bohn, 1856, Volume II, page 153

And so of cheerfulness, or a good temper—the more it is spent, the more of it remains.

Ralph Waldo Emerson, *The Conduct of Life, Nature, and Other Essays*, J.M. Dent & Sons Ltd., 1911, page 279

I have always preferred cheerfulness to mirth. The latter I consider as an act, the former as an habit of the mind. Mirth is short and transient, cheerfulness fixed and permanent.

Joseph Addison, *The Works of Joseph Addison*, edited and published by Henry G. Bohn, 1856, Volume III, page 356

Good nature is worth more than knowledge, more than money, more than honour, to the persons who possess it, and certainly to everybody who dwells with them, in so far as mere happiness is concerned.

Henry Ward Beecher, *Proverbs from Plymouth Pulpit*, Charles Burnet & Co., 1887, page 20

Mirth is like a flash of lightning, that breaks through a gloom of clouds and glitters for a moment; cheerfulness keeps up a kind of day-light in the mind, and fills it with a steady and perpetual serenity.

Joseph Addison, *The Works of Joseph Addison*, edited and published by Henry G. Bohn, 1856, Volume III, page 356

His harmonical and ingenious soul did lodge in a beautiful and well proportioned body ... Of a very cheerful humour. He would be cheerful even in his gout-fits, and sing ... Temperate man, rarely drank between meals. Extreme pleasant in his conversation, and at dinner, supper, etc: but satirical ...

Said of John Milton in *Brief Lives*, John Aubrey, *The English Spirit*, compiled by Paul Handley, Fiona MacMath, Pat Saunders and Robert Van de Weyer, Darton, Longman & Todd in association with Little Gidding Books, 1987, page 113

It is important to remind ourselves often that the cultivation of a right sense of humour can be one of the forms of piety. Cultivate a sense of humour in yourself about other people, and in other people about yourself: learn to laugh rather than be vexed by other people's foibles, but learn the ability also to let other people laugh at your own.

Gerald Vann, *The Divine Pity*, Sheed & Ward Ltd., 1945, page 52

Use your sense of humour. Laugh about things. Laugh at the absurdities of life. Laugh about yourself and about your own absurdity.

We are all of us infinitesimally small and ludicrous creatures within God's universe. You have to be serious, but never be solemn, because if you are solemn about anything there is a risk of you becoming solemn about yourself.

Michael Ramsey, in *Through the Year with Michael Ramsey*, edited by Margaret Duggan, Hodder & Stoughton Ltd, 1975, page 81

O we can wait no longer.
We too take ship O soul,
Joyous we too launch out on trackless seas,
Fearless for unknown shores on waves of ecstasy to sail,
Amid the waiting winds,
(thou pressing me to thee, I thee to me O Soul.)
Caroling free,—singing our song to God.
Chanting our chant of pleasant exploration ...
O daring joy, but safe!

are they not all the seas of God?
O farther, farther, farther sail!

Walt Whitman, *The Complete Poems*, edited by Francis Murphy, Penguin Books Ltd., 1982, *Passage to India*, ll.175, 254

O pure of heart! thou need'st not ask of me
What this strong music in the soul may be!
What, and wherein it doth exist,
This light, this glory, this fair luminous mist,
This beautiful and beauty-making power.
Joy, virtuous Lady! Joy that ne'er was given,
Save to the pure, and in their purest hour,
Life, and Life's effluence, cloud at once and shower,
Joy, Lady! is the spirit and the power,
Which wedding Nature to us gives in dower
A new Earth and new Heaven,
Undreamt of by the sensual and the proud—
Joy is the sweet voice, Joy is the luminous cloud—
We in ourselves rejoice!
And thence flows all that charms or ear or sight,
All colours a suffusion from that light.

Samuel Taylor Coleridge, *Coleridge's Poems*, edited by E.H. Coleridge, Oxford at the Clarendon Press, 1975, Volume I, *Poems*, Dejection: An Ode, l.59

CHRISTIAN

'Christian'—an adherent of Christianity.

Although I had been baptized as a child, and confirmed in my teens, I had very little idea of what a Christian is until I went to university. Edward Young's *Night Thoughts* influenced me to a certain extent with his verse—'A Christian is the highest style of man.' This initially attracted me to Christianity.

At university, I took a step of faith and made a commitment to the person of Jesus Christ. In the first instance, I believed I was committing myself to an historical person. In the second instance, because of the resurrection and the coming of the Holy Spirit, I believed I was committing myself to a presence—the spiritual presence of Jesus Christ.

This two-pronged commitment kept me going for several years. My understanding of being a Christian was someone who, in the words of the doggerel—'kept close to Christ all the way'.

The next stage came with a realization my faith was narrow and blinkered. I had concentrated so much on Christ, I had missed out on God the Father. In theology God the Father is seen as the Creator. Miss out the Creator, and you miss out on the creation.

The Genesis story of the creation of man introduced me to the concept of the 'God within', fully worked out in the person of Jesus Christ. St Paul discovered that what Christ had experienced we can all in some measure also experience.

For me, a Christian is someone who discovers something of the Father, the Son, the Holy Spirit, and a whole plethora of divine attributes in the depths of his/her being, and lives this out to the full. Happy the person who discovers their divine heritage and single-mindedly lives it.

You are the salt of the earth.
Matthew 5.13

You are the light of the world.
Matthew 5.14

Let your light so shine before men, that they may see your good works and give glory to your Father who is in heaven.

Matthew 5.16

For Christ also died for sins once for all, the righteous for the unrighteous, that he might bring us to God, being put to death in the flesh but made alive in the spirit.

1 Peter 3.18

A Christian is the highest style of man.

Edward Young, *Night Thoughts*, Thomas Nelson, 1841, page 64

O noble testimony of the soul by nature Christian!

Tertullian, *The Writings of Tertullian*, Hamilton & Co., 1869, Volume I, page 87, Apology No.17

If a man cannot be a Christian in the place where he is, he cannot be a Christian anywhere.

Henry Ward Beecher, *Life Thoughts*, Alexander Strahan & Co., 1859, page 135

The greatest of all blessings, as it is the most ennobling of all privileges, is to be indeed a Christian.

Samuel Taylor Coleridge, *Letters of Samuel Taylor Coleridge*, edited by Ernest Hartley Coleridge, William Heinemann, 1895, Volume II, page 775, Letter No. 209

Those who reject Christian beliefs, cannot count on keeping Christian morals.

Sir Richard Livingstone, *On Education*, Cambridge at the University Press, 1954, page 133

The Christian is the man who has ceased to do what he likes, and who has dedicated his life to do as Christ likes.

William Barclay, *The Gospel of Matthew*, The Saint Andrew Press, 1974, Volume I, page 21

The only absolute for the Christian is love, and on *that* you have got to be prepared to take *unconditional* stands and say, 'Here I stand, I can no other.'

John A.T. Robinson, *The Roots of a Radical*, SCM Press Ltd., 1980, page 55

He only is a Christian in fact in whom Christ dwelleth, liveth and hath His being, in whom Christ hath arisen as the eternal ground of the soul. He only is a Christian who has this high title in himself, and has entered with mind and soul into that Eternal Word which has manifested itself as the life of our humanity.

Rufus M. Jones, *Spiritual Reformers in the 16th and 17th Centuries*, Macmillan & Co. Ltd., 1914, page 170

To be a Christian does not mean to be religious in a particular way, to make something of oneself (a sinner, a penitent, or a saint) on the basis of some method or other, but to be a man—not a type of man, but the man that Christ creates in us. It is not the religious act that makes the Christian, but participation in the sufferings of God in the secular life.

Dietrich Bonhoeffer, *Letters and Papers from Prison*, edited by Eberhard Bethge, translated by R.H. Fuller, SCM Press Ltd., 1967, Second Revised Edition, page 198

It is not *Opinion*, or *Speculation*, or *Notions* of what is *true*; or *Assent* to, or the Subscription of Articles, or Propositions, tho' never so soundly worded, that ... makes a Man a *True* Believer, or a *True* Christian. But it is a *Conformity* of Mind and Practice to the *Will of God*, in all Holiness of Conversation, according to the Dictates of this Divine Principle of Light and Life in the Soul, which denotes a Person *truly* a Child of God.

William Penn, *A Collection of the Works of William Penn*, 1726, Volume II, page 781

He (Sebastian Franck) is especially interesting and important as an exponent and interpreter of a religion based on inward authority because he unites, in an unusual manner, the intellectual ideals of the Humanist with the experience and attitude of the

Mystic. In him we have a Christian thinker who is able to detach himself from the theological formulations of his own and of earlier times, and who could draw, with a breadth of mind and depth of insight, from the wells of the great original thinkers of all ages, and who, besides, in his own deep and serious soul could feel the inner flow of central realities.

Rufus M. Jones, *Spiritual Reformers in the 16th and 17th Centuries*, Macmillan & Co. Ltd., 1914, page 46

He is a Christian that wholly giveth himself up into Christ's incarnation, suffering, and death, and dieth to his hypocrisy in the death of Christ, and riseth from the death of Christ in a new will and obedience, and who, according to his inward ground, is and liveth in Christ, who himself becometh the temple of Christ, wherein Christ worketh with his power and virtue, and thereby killeth sin in the flesh. Such a one is a Christian in Christ, and may rightly enter into the resemblance of Christ, and exercise his Christianity therein.

Such a one will hear God's word, and keep and ponder it in his heart.

Jacob Boehme, *Mysterium Magnum*, translated by John Sparrow, John M. Watkins, 1924, Volume II, page 714

It is quite easy to be a genial libertine—friendly with everyone you meet, if you have for yourself and them no moral standard. And it is fairly easy for you to set up a moral standard for yourself and others—no doubt underlining the words '*for others*'—if you allow yourself in the process to become hypercritical, unsympathetic and censorious, which is to be a Pharisee. But to set up a standard for others and yourself—with the words '*for yourself*' underlined—and still show sympathy and love to those who fail to reach it, without letting the standard down, that is very hard. But that is to be a Christian.

William Temple, *The Church Looks Forward*, Macmillan & Co. Ltd., 1944, page 166

And each of us has to become Jesus. This is the Christian's sole aim which is nothing other than the destiny of all people; it is what human beings are for, what the world is for. This is the essence of all effective apostolate—to live the depth and breadth of the human vocation.

When we say 'Jesus' we are holding together two profound realities. We mean the living Lord in the glory of his victory, the surrendered One who is all God's. Our roots are in this victorious One. He is the ground on which we stand, the unshakeable rock, our perfect security.

But the risen Jesus is lost to our human gaze. He too is in light inaccessible which our poor earthly sight cannot cope with. And we are not meant to try. Standing on his victory, drawing our life from his inexhaustible well-spring, we are gently turned away from him in splendour to contemplate him in his mortal existence. This is what we are doing when we meditate on the Gospels. This is how we meet him, learn from him. We learn from him in the days of his flesh, when he too must contemplate the mystery of the Father, not face to face but in a mirror darkly as we do.

Ruth Burrows, *Living Love and Our Father*, Darton, Longman & Todd, 1990, page 135

Again we are called as Christians to a faith which both cares intensely about this world and is also set upon another world beyond it. The first is an immediate test of our Christianity. Our concern in action for the hungry and the homeless, for right dealing between different races, for the laws of conduct which God has given us, shows whether we love God whom we have not seen by the test of our love for the brother we have seen.

But as we serve this world and its needs we are all the while laying hold of something beyond this world, an eternal life which gives this world its true perspective. Let not that be forgotten. We are here not only to do things, we are here to be something, to become something—and that is the meaning of our being called to be saints. Christianity is about our doing things here, and about our being something whose goal is beyond here. The Christians are in the world as the soul is in the body by keeping alive for themselves and for others the hope of heaven ...

To this he has called us, and has made us one with all in every place who have the same call and dare not look back.

Michael Ramsey, *Canterbury Pilgrim*, SPCK, 1974, page 97

The indwelling Spirit of Christ radiates its benign influence as Life, as Light, and as Love. Christ is the eternal principle of life in all that lives. 'That which came into being, in Him was Life, and the Life was the Light of men.' He came 'that we might have Life, and have it more abundantly.' The call of Christ is the call to a more vivid, earnest, strenuous life. It has been said of a great man that he passed through the dream of life as one awake and that is what all Christians ought to do. 'Now it is high time to awake out of sleep.' Spiritual wakefulness means concentration of purpose. The world may be divided into those who have a purpose in life, and those who have none, or who fluctuate between several. Few things are more striking than the change which comes over even the outward appearance of a man or woman between youth and old age, according to whether he or she has or not a fixed purpose which is being carried out day by day. The face of the man who has found his work shows, in each decade of his life until the failure of his powers, increasing strength and dignity, and even beauty; while the man who lets himself drift shows in every line of his face that his will has been overpowered by disorderly impulses, or has simply abdicated. The portraits of good and great men at various ages, and the faces of those who are neither good nor great, are instructive in this way.

W.R. Inge, *Personal Religion and the Life of Devotion*, Longmans, Green & Co. Ltd., 1924, page 73

COMPASSION

'Compassion'—pity inclining one to spare or help.

L ooking back over life I have come to see the people who exercised the greatest influence over me were invariably compassionate and kindly people.

At primary school I can still remember a teacher who took a personal interest in me, and elicited a positive response in all aspects of learning. He was kindness personified and I was heartbroken when he left our school to take up another post.

In secondary school I can think of three masters who took a personal interest in me and were excellent teachers in their subjects. The memory of them still continues to influence me.

We tend to think of the Army as an institution devoid of compassion. I was fortunate enough to come across a National Service doctor whose kindly concern restored me to health, when there was a possibility of being invalided back to the UK.

As an undergraduate I had a brilliant tutor who took pains and trouble to see me through a difficult patch. I would not be here now but for his understanding and compassionate help.

At theological college we had a kindly Principal who was well aware of the dilemmas and difficulties most of us were going through. There was an instance when an ordinand was in danger of going off the rails. The Principal virtually wrote him a blank cheque, which did the trick and got him back on course.

I expect most of us can look back over our lives and recall compassionate and kindly people whose timely help has proved invaluable. Perhaps Dostoyevsky is right when he describes compassion as the chief, and perhaps the only law of all human existence.

The steadfast love of the Lord never ceases, his mercies never come to an end; they are new every morning; great is thy faithfulness. 'The Lord is my portion,' says my soul, 'therefore I will hope in him.'

Lamentations 3.22-24

The mercy of man is toward his neighbour; but the mercy of the Lord is upon all flesh: he reproveth, and nurtureth, and teacheth, and bringeth again, as a shepherd his flock.

Ecclesiasticus 18.13 (AV)

We who are strong ought to bear with the failings of the weak, and not to please ourselves; let each of us please his neighbour for his good, to edify him.

Romans 15.1-2

Have unity of spirit, sympathy, love of the brethren, a tender heart and a humble mind.

1 Peter 3.8

Compassion was the chief and, perhaps, the only law of all human existence.

Fyodor Dostoyevsky, *The Idiot*, translated by David Magarshack, Penguin Books Ltd., 1983, page 248

Jesus *found him.* The man did not find Jesus; Jesus found him. That is the deepest truth of Christian faith; Jesus found me. Our fellowship with Him is rooted in His compassion.

William Temple, *Readings in St. John's Gospel*, First and Second Series, Macmillan & Co. Ltd., 1947, page 160

Pity may represent little more than the impersonal concern which prompts the mailing of a cheque, but true sympathy is the personal concern which demands the giving of one's soul.

Martin Luther King, *Strength to Love*, William Collins Sons & Co. Ltd., 1980, page 32

If you think of your fellow-creatures, then you only want to cry, you could really cry the whole day long. The only thing to do is to pray that God will perform a miracle and save some of them. And I hope that I am doing that enough!

Anne Frank, *The Diary of Anne Frank*, Pan Books Ltd., 1954, page 111

Jesus' 'lack of moral principles.' He sat at meal with publicans and sinners, he consorted with harlots. Did he do this to obtain their votes? Or did he think that, perhaps he could convert them by such 'appeasement'? Or was his humanity rich and deep enough to make contact, even in them, with that in human nature which is common to all men, indestructible, and upon which the future has to be built?

Dag Hammarskjöld, *Markings*, translated by Leif Sjoberg and W.H. Auden, Faber & Faber Ltd, 1964, page 134

But to share with Christ his passion, his crucifixion, his death, means to accept unreservedly all these events, in the same spirit as he did, that is, to accept them in an act of free will, to suffer together with the man of sorrows, to be there in silence, the very silence of Christ, interrupted only by a few decisive words, the silence of real communion; not just the silence of pity, but of compassion, which allows us to grow into complete oneness with the other so that there is no longer one and the other, but only one life and one death.

Anthony Bloom, *Living Prayer*, Darton, Longman & Todd, 1966, page 16

The fact that human love or sympathy is the guide who conducts us to the heart of life, revealing to us God and Nature and ourselves, is proof that part of our life is bound up with the life of the world, and that if we live in these our true relations we shall not entirely die so long as human beings remain alive upon this earth. The progress of the race, the diminution of sin and misery, the advancing kingdom of Christ on earth,—these are matters in which we have a *personal* interest. The strong desire that we feel—and the best of us feel it most strongly—that the human race may be better, wiser, and happier in the future than they are now or have been in the past, is neither due to a false association of ideas, nor to pure unselfishness. There is a sense in which death would not be the end of everything for us, even though in this life only we had hope in Christ.

W.R. Inge, *Christian Mysticism*, Methuen & Co. Ltd., 1899, page 327

In his feeling I see him (Christ) supremely as a man of compassion. That is, he entered into every aspect and event of human life, knowing it in its truth and reality, sharing all that human beings experienced, not only perceiving what women and men felt, but feeling with them. With those who needed tenderness he was tender, but his love was not always gentle. He would not spare people the truth, even when it had to hurt. He could love the rich young man and yet say to him that he could not inherit eternal life if he did not give up his riches. He flayed the oppressors of the poor with the most biting invective that has ever been used. His love could be gentle, but it could also be stern and austere, intensely demanding.

I see him deeply involved in the conflict of his time, not standing aside offering advice or principles from on high, but deeply involved, right *in* the conflict, followed round by contentious groups, supported or attacked, applauded or derided, loved or feared. He was a man of passion, not only in his suffering, but throughout his life and ministry.

Kenneth C. Barnes, *The Creative Imagination* (Swarthmore Lecture Pamphlet), Friends Home Service Committee, 1967, page 33

Jesus' compassion is characterized by a downward pull. That is what disturbs us. We cannot even think about ourselves in terms other than those of an upward pull, an upward mobility in which we strive for better lives, higher salaries, and more prestigious positions. Thus, we are deeply disturbed by a God who embodies a downward movement... Here we see what compassion means. It is not a bending toward the underprivileged from a privileged position; it is not a reaching out from on high to those who are less fortunate below; it is not a gesture of sympathy or pity for those who fail to make it in the upward pull. On the contrary, compassion means going directly to those people and places where suffering is most acute and building a home there. God's compassion is total, absolute, unconditional, without reservation... It is the compassion of a God who does not merely act as a servant, but whose servanthood is a direct expression of his divinity.

The great mystery of God's compassion is that in his compassion, in his entering with us into the condition of a slave, he reveals himself to us as God... His self-emptying and humiliation are not a step away from his true nature... Rather, in the emptied and humbled Christ we encounter God, we see who God really is, we come to know his true divinity.

Henri J.M. Nouwen, Donald P. McNeill, Douglas A. Morrison, *Compassion*, Darton, Longman & Todd, 1982, page 27

Out of kindliness springs compassion, which is a fellow-feeling with all men; for none can share the griefs of all, save him who is kind. Compassion is an inward movement of the heart, stirred by pity for the bodily and ghostly griefs of all men. This compassion makes a man suffer with Christ in His passion; for he who is compassionate marks the wherefore of His pains and the way of his resignation; of His love, His wounds, His tenderness; of His grief and His nobleness; of the disgrace, the misery, and the shame He endured; of the way in which He was despised; of His crown; of the nails of His mercifulness; of His destruction and dying in patience. These manifold and unheard-of sorrows of Christ our Saviour and our Bridegroom, move all kindly men to pity and compassion with Christ.

Compassion makes a man look into himself and recognize his faults, his feebleness in virtues and in the worship of God, his lukewarmness, his laziness, his many failings, the time he has wasted and his present imperfection in moral and other virtues; all this makes a man feel true pity and compassion for himself. Further, compassion marks the errors and disorders of our fellow-creatures, how little they care for their God and their eternal blessedness, their ingratitude for all the good things which God has done for them, and the pains He suffered for their sake; how they are strangers to virtue, unskilled and unpractised in it, but skilful and cunning in every wickedness; how attentive they are to the loss and gain of earthly goods, how careless and reckless they are of God, of eternal things, and their eternal bliss. When he marks this, a good man is moved to compassion for the salvation of all men.

Such a man will also regard with pity the bodily needs of his neighbours, and the manifold suffering of human nature; seeing men hungry, thirsty, cold, naked, sick, poor, and abject; the manifold oppressions of the poor, the grief caused by loss of kinsmen, friends, goods, honour, peace; all the countless sorrows which befall the nature of man. These things move the just to compassion, so that they share the sorrows of all.

John of Ruysbroeck, *The Adornment of the Spiritual Marriage*, translated by C.A. Wynschenk Dom, edited by Evelyn Underhill, John M. Watkins, 1951, page 30

CONSCIENCE

'Conscience'—a moral sense of right and wrong.

T he 'still small voice' first came into prominence with Elijah in the wilderness. Elijah did not find the Lord in the wind, or the earthquake, or the fire, but after the fire there was a 'still small voice'. William Cowper in his poem *The Task* also wrote of the 'still small voice'.

I wonder if the 'still small voice' is yet another consequence of the divine inbreathing in the Genesis story of the creation of man. As I look back I can see a number of factors which played an important part in the development of my conscience. First there was home and parental upbringing. Secondly there was school which helped to educate my conscience in those early formative years. Thirdly there was the influence of the media— radio, television, films, books, newspapers and the like. Even a radio programme like Dick Barton, with its emphasis on right and wrong, might have exercised a certain influence on the development of my conscience. If you remember, the 'baddies' never actually won. Dick, Jock and Snowy always got them in the end. Even so, when I got to university and was thinking these things out for myself, I rediscovered the still small voice and came to rely on its dictates. This led to a listening form of prayer and keeping a journal (a spiritual diary) which has been an invaluable companion for over thirty years. The Bible, the Church, Christian tradition and theology have all been influential in developing my conscience, but ultimately the 'still small voice' now guides my conscience.

Look carefully at Nicolas Berdyaev's contribution. This comes close to verbalizing my understanding of conscience.

Be angry, but sin not; commune with your own hearts on your beds, and be silent.
Psalm 4.4

Who can say, 'I have made my heart clean; I am pure from my sin'?
Proverbs 20.9

When Gentiles who have not the law do by nature what the law requires, they are a law to themselves, even though they do not have the law. They show that what the law requires is written on their hearts, while their conscience also bears witness and their conflicting thoughts accuse or perhaps excuse them on that day when, according to my gospel, God judges the secrets of men by Christ Jesus.
Romans 2.14-16

We have renounced disgraceful, underhanded ways; we refuse to practice cunning or to tamper with God's word, but by the open statement of the truth we would commend ourselves to every man's conscience in the sight of God.
2 Corinthians 4.2

The still small voice.
William Cowper, *The Poetical Works of Cowper*, edited by H.S. Milford, Oxford University Press, 1950, page 214, *The Task*, V. l. 685

Conscience is the voice of the soul, the passions are the voice of the body.
Jean Jacques Rousseau, *Emile or Education*, translated by Barbara Foxley, J.M. Dent & Sons Ltd., 1911, page 249

Labour to keep alive in your breast that little spark of celestial fire, called conscience.
George Washington, in *The Life of George Washington*, Jared Sparks, Henry Colburn, Publisher, 1839, page 401

In early days the conscience has in most
A quickness, which in later life is lost.
William Cowper, *The Poetical Works of Cowper*, edited by H.S. Milford, Oxford University Press, 1950, page 244, 'Tirocinium,' l.109

The church must be reminded that it is not the master or the servant of the state, but rather the conscience of the state.

Martin Luther King, *Strength to Love*, William Collins Sons & Co. Ltd., 1980, page 62

Our secret thoughts are rarely heard except in secret. No man knows what conscience is until he understands what solitude can teach him concerning it.

Joseph Cook, *Conscience*, R.D. Dickinson, 1879, page 90

Yet still there whispers the small voice within,
Heard through Gain's silence, and o'er Glory's din:
Whatever creed be taught, or land be trod,
Man's conscience is the Oracle of God.

Lord Byron, *The Poetical Works of Lord Byron*, edited by Ernest Hartley Coleridge, John Murray, 1948, page 759, *The Island*, 'Canto the First,' st.vi., l.120

By 'conscience' I mean the individual's conviction concerning right and wrong. Sometimes it is a reflective judgement, sometimes an emotional reaction, sometimes an intuitive perception. At its best it combines all three.

William Temple, *Citizen and Churchman*, Eyre & Spottiswoode, 1941, page 29

Some good must come by clinging to the right. Conscience is a man's compass, and though the needle sometimes deviates, though one often perceives irregularities in directing one's course by it, still one must try to follow its direction.

Vincent van Gogh, *Dear Theo: An autobiography of Vincent van Gogh*, edited by Irving Stone, Constable & Co. Ltd., 1937, page 208

The more productively one lives, the stronger is one's conscience, and, in turn, the more it furthers one's productiveness. The less productively one lives, the weaker becomes one's conscience; the paradoxical— and tragic —situation of man is that his conscience is weakest when he needs it most.

Erich Fromm, *Man For Himself*, Routledge & Kegan Paul Ltd., 1975, page 160

The glory of a good man is the witness of a good conscience. Have a good conscience, and you will always have gladness; for a good conscience is able to endure a great deal, and be glad even in adversity, whereas a bad conscience is always fearful and restless. You will enjoy quiet rest if conscience does not condemn you.

Thomas à Kempis, *The Imitation of Christ*, translated by Betty I. Knott, William Collins Sons & Co. Ltd., 1979, page 91

Deep within his conscience man discovers a law which he has not laid upon himself but which he must obey. Its voice, ever calling him to love and to do what is good and to avoid evil, tells him inwardly at the right moment: do this, shun that. For man has in his heart a law inscribed by God. His dignity lies in observing this law, and by it he will be judged. His conscience is man's most secret core, and his sanctuary. There he is alone with God whose voice echoes in his depths. By conscience, in a wonderful way, that law is made known which is fulfilled in the love of God and of one's neighbour.

Vatican Council II, *The Conciliar and Post Conciliar Documents*, 1981 Edition, general editor, Austin Flannery, OP, Fowler Wright Books Ltd., page 916

Conscience is that depth of human nature at which it comes in touch with God, where it receives God's message and hears His voice... Conscience is the remembrance, in our sinful life, of God and of life Divine. When, in the most sinful and criminal man, conscience awakes, this means that he remembers about God, and how it is to live a godly life, although he may not express it in these words. Conscience is the organ of reception of religious revelation of truth, of good, of integral truth. It is not a separate side of human nature or a special function; it is the wholeness of man's spiritual nature, its very heart... Conscience is also the source of original primary judgements about the world, and about life. More than this, conscience judges God, or about God, because it is an organ of the perception of God. Conscience may judge about God only because it is an organ of the perception of God. God acts on man's conscience, awakens his conscience, awakens his memories of a higher world. Conscience is the remembrance of what man is, to what world he belongs by the idea of his creation, by whom he was created, how and why he was created. Conscience is a spiritual, supernatural element in man, and it is not at all of social origin. What is of social origin is rather an obstruction or deformation of conscience. Conscience is that depth of human nature where it has not fallen completely away from God, where it has maintained contact with the Divine world.

Nicolas Berdyaev, *Christian Existentialism*, selected and translated by Donald A. Lowrie, George Allen & Unwin Ltd., 1965, page 88

The ability to arrive at a view of what is morally right and wrong.

In the history of Christian tradition, discussions and disagreements about conscience have arisen on two related issues: in what this ability might consist; and what authority conscience enjoys.

Accounts of what conscience is fall broadly into two families. According to one version, conscience is nothing other than our normal powers of reasoning as applied to practical matters, and in particular moral decisions. It is therefore not a special faculty with unique powers, but rather enjoys the ordinary powers and limitations of human reasoning generally. This position is defended by Aristotle, and by Thomas Aquinas in his account of the function of right reason (*recta ratio*) in the discovery of natural law. Writers in this tradition would generally stress that our reasoning powers in practical matters cannot arrive at the clarity which is at least theoretically possible in matters of logic or even in the physical sciences. Aristotle counsels against seeking greater precision in moral questions than the subject-matter allows, and Aquinas remarks that there is progressively greater difficulty in arriving at correct moral judgements the more detailed and specific these judgements try to be. It would commonly be held, however, that any normal adult would be clearly aware of at least general moral truths.

The alternative account of conscience regards it as a kind of moral sense or sensibility, on the analogy of our physical senses. Conscience according to this account grasps the moral quality of actions, or the truth of moral principles, directly and non-discursively. Joseph Butler gives one of the most authoritative defences of this position. It would be characteristic of this view to stress the clarity and certainty of judgements of conscience, and to align it with an intuitionist rather than a rationalist approach to morality. In principle, both views can be integrated into the Christian tradition, and each is compatible with the view that conscience is in some sense authoritative. There are, however, notable differences in the ways in which this is typically done by each account.

On the first, rationalist, account, reason is seen as one of God's gifts to human kind. The moral truths discovered by our human reasoning can to that extent be regarded as discoveries about the will of God for us. However, it would be acknowledged that our reasoning powers in general are fallible, and that this is true also of our moral reasoning. Our claims to discover moral truths may turn out to be in fact mistaken claims. Nevertheless, in the last analysis a human being can do no more than commit himself or herself to the truth as it is perceived to be. For this reason, Aquinas among others defended the view that we are bound to follow our conscientious judgement, even in cases where (as it turns out) that judgement is mistaken. Conscience is authoritative not because it always judges correctly, but because as rational beings we have no alternative but to do what, in our best judgement, we believe we ought to do.

On the alternative account, it is easier to claim that conscience is somehow infallible (although it is not essential to this view to make such a claim), and that in a more direct sense it is the 'voice of God' within us. The authority of conscience is thus directly linked with the authority of God, and the duty to follow the dictates of conscience is immediately obvious. Especially those writers who, for theological reasons, believe that human reasoning is unreliable as a result of the Fall will stress that conscience is not a matter of human *reasoning* at all, but derives from the inspiration of the grace of God which makes our moral duty clear to us.

Gerard J. Hughes, in *A Dictionary of Pastoral Care*, edited by Alastair V. Campbell, SPCK, 1987, page 47

CONTEMPLATION

'Contemplation'—gazing upon; viewing mentally.

As far back as I can remember I have always had a contemplative side to my nature. When I was nearing the end of National Service I took some leave and spent a quiet day on the beach at Port Dixon, near Penang, northern Malaya (as it was then). I took very little with me—a swimming costume, a towel and some food—and finding a secluded spot, spent the whole day on the beach, doing absolutely nothing at all.

At first numerous thoughts and feelings came to the surface, mainly to do with the last twenty months—my time as a private soldier in Exeter, four months at Mons Officer Cadet School, Aldershot, and now almost a year in Singapore. My mind relaxed further and for a while went blank. I listened to the ebbing of the sea, and was able to absorb something of the sun into my being.

I began to muse over the early part of my life and then, almost like a drowning man, my past life flashed before me. Here, thousands of miles from home, I was able to view my life from a different perspective. Precious truths and insights came to the surface. New ideas took root, and I began to think of the future and what to do in life.

In the evening there was a gentle breeze and my mind went blank again. After a while I became aware of something stirring inside me which I was unable to identify and put into words. With the passage of time and in the light of recent experience I think this had something to do with a consciousness of the spiritual dimension, and my first real experience of contemplation. I now try to spend a day on the beach every year, and contemplate.

Be still, and know that I am God.
Psalm 46.10

I commune with my heart in the night.
Psalm 77.6

Continue steadfastly in prayer, being watchful in it with thanksgiving.
Colossians 4.2

Pray constantly.
1 Thessalonians 5.17

Contemplatives are not useful, they are only indispensable.
Ernest Dimnet, *What We Live By*, Jonathan Cape Ltd., 1932, page 195

What we plant in the soil of contemplation we shall reap in the harvest of action.
Meister Eckhart, *Meister Eckhart*, translated by Raymond B. Blakney, Harper & Row, Publishers, Inc., 1941, page 111

All civil mankind have agreed in leaving one day for contemplation against six for practice.
Ralph Waldo Emerson, *The Works of Ralph Waldo Emerson*, edited by George Sampson, George Bell & Sons Ltd., 1906, Volume IV, *Miscellaneous Pieces*, page 431

I think there is a place both inside and outside of religion for a sort of contemplation of the Good, not just by dedicated experts but by ordinary people: an attention which is not just the planning of particular good actions but an attempt to look right away from self towards a distant transcendent perfection, a source of uncontaminated energy, a source of *new* and quite undreamt-of virtue.
Iris Murdoch, *The Sovereignty Of Good Over Other Concepts*, Cambridge University Press, 1967, page 94

For not, surely, by deliberate effort of thought does a man grow wise. The truths of life are not discovered by us. At moments unforeseen, some gracious influence descends upon the soul, touching it to an emotion which, we know not how, the mind transmutes into thought. This can happen only in a calm of the senses, a surrender of the whole being to passionless contemplation. I understand, now, the intellectual mood of the quietist.

George Gissing, *The Private Papers of Henry Rycroft*, J.M. Dent & Sons Ltd., 1964, page 134

Contemplation is the state of union with the divine Ground of all being. The highest prayer is the most passive. Inevitably; for the less there is of self, the more there is of God. That is why the path to passive or infused contemplation is so hard and, for many, so painful—a passage through successive or simultaneous Dark Nights, in which the pilgrim must die to the life of sense as an end in itself, to the life of private and even of traditionally hallowed thinking and believing, and finally to the deep source of all ignorance and evil, the life of the separate, individualized will.

Aldous Huxley, *The Perennial Philosophy*, Chatto & Windus Ltd., 1974, page 259

Prayer is one of the means towards the end, as the mystic strives to attain the goal. There must be continued and unbroken perseverence in prayer, in order to secure unmoved tranquillity of mind and perpetual purity. Pure and sincere prayer is only obtained by laying aside all anxiety about material things, and all distractions. When purification and cleansing have done their part, there must be no self-satisfaction, but only a deep humility: then the soul must concentrate its thoughts and little by little it will begin to rise to the contemplation of God and to spiritual insight.

John Cassian, in *Studies in Early Mysticism in the Near and Middle East*, Margaret Smith, Sheldon Press, 1931, page 67

The contemplation of God—and contemplative prayer is, I believe, not necessarily an advanced state but something accessible to us very backward Christians—the waiting upon God in quietness can be our greatest service to the world if in our apartness the love for people is on our heart. As Aaron went into the holy of holies wearing a breastplate with jewels representing the twelve tribes upon it, so the Christian puts himself deliberately into the presence of God with the needs and sorrows of humanity upon his heart. And he does this best not by the vocal skill with which he informs the Deity about the world's needs but by the simplicity of his own exposure to God's greatness and the world's need. 'As the soul is in the body' wrote the unknown author of the Letter to Diognetus, 'so are the Christians in the world.'

Michael Ramsey, in *Spirituality For Today*, edited by Eric James, SCM Press Ltd., 1968, page 139

All too easily when we talk about the interior life of prayer or contemplation we have in mind some sort of refined human activity going on within; it can be cultivated and grow to wonderful proportions.

But let us substitute the words 'interior life' for 'depth life' and we come nearer to what it means to be a contemplative. A contemplative lives below the surface, is present to what really is and not in the ephemeral, often illusory world of impressions.

Contemplation is based on faith. Only faith takes us behind appearances; only faith roots us in naked reality and keeps us there steadfastly, refusing to allow us to escape into pleasant fantasy, to make excursions into 'if only', into what our ego wants for its satisfaction and comfort.

Faith says: You are for God. You must abandon all desire to cling to boundaries, to your own limits, your own idea of things. You have to allow yourself all the time to be drawn up and away, or down and beyond, to God Himself.

Ruth Burrows, in *The Watchful Heart*, edited by Elizabeth Ruth Obbard, Darton, Longman & Todd, 1988, page 15

Contemplation is to see and to hear from the heart. It takes us beyond sense perception. It is to relate to things as they are.

All so-called spiritual knowledge is useless if simply retained in the head. It is a waste of time and leads to self-delusion. It is to know about rather than to know.

The same is true of theological knowledge. This has to be diverted towards the contemplative experience through meditation, otherwise it remains apart from life and is of no ultimate value.

Contemplative seeing is not selective. It is not processed by the brain nor conditioned by previously held concepts and attitudes. It constitutes a whole way of life, a way to be followed by the true disciple of Jesus.

Traditionally, contemplation has been thought of as an Eastern approach to religion. Action in this world has been seen as its opposite and typical of the Western understanding. Today's world requires a marriage of the two, that is, contemplation in action.

Bede Griffiths OSB, in *The Universal Christ*, edited by Peter Spink, Darton, Longman & Todd, 1990, page 28

The nature of contemplation is passive.

Contemplation comes from beyond. When I contemplate I do not look inside myself, I look ahead of me.

What do my ideas matter? I know them, and they die one after the other.

What engages me in contemplation is an idea that cannot die, and this comes from God. That is why I believe in contemplation.

One ounce of transcendence is dearer to me than any amount of reasoning.

If reasoning is there at all, it comes beforehand. All my life I have been reasoning! Now I am trying to do without reasoning for a time, while I lay myself before God and let Him act upon me.

I prefer to do as Elijah and wait for His coming in the cave of Horeb.

Contemplation is passive; it is God's coming into us, into our consciousness. God lets us know *Him as He is*, not as He may appear to be from outside.

In contemplation I attain the fullness of my earthly life and I feed on eternal life, because eternal life is what I am destined for. All the rest can take care of itself, because it counts for little compared with eternal life.

Carlo Carretto, *The God Who Comes*, translated by Rose Mary Hancock, Darton, Longman and Todd, 1974, page 38

We like to look on the spiritual life as something very noble, very holy but also very peaceful and consoling. The word 'contemplation' easily tempts those who have not tried it to think that the mystical life consists in looking at the Everlasting Hills, and having nice feelings about God. But the world of contemplation is really continuous with the world of prayer, in the same way as the high Alps are continuous with the lower pastures. To enter it means exchanging the lovely view for the austere reality; penetrating the strange hill-country, slogging up stony tracks in heavy boots, bearing fatigue and risking fog and storm, helping fellow-climbers at one's own cost. It means renouncing the hotel-life level of religion with its comforts and conveniences, and setting our face towards the snows not for any personal ambition or enjoyment, but driven by the strange mountain love. 'Thou hast made us for Thyself and our hearts shall have no rest save in Thee.' Narrow rough paths, slippery shale, the glimpse of awful crevasses, terrible storms, cold, bewildering fog and darkness—all these wait for the genuine mountaineer. The great mystics experience all of them, and are well content so to do.

One of the best of all guides to these summits, St. John of the Cross, drew for his disciples a picturesque map of the route. It starts straight up a very narrow path. There are two much wider and better paths going left and right; one of them is marked 'the advantages of this world' and the other 'the advantages of the next world'. Both must be avoided for both end in the foothills, with no road further on. The real path goes very steeply up the mountain, to a place where St. John has written, 'After this there is no path at all' and the climber says with St. Paul, 'Having nothing I possess all things.'

Here we are already a long way from the valley and have reached the stage which is familiar to all climbers, where we feel exhilarated because we think we see the top, but are really about to begin the true climb. This is the Illuminative Life; and here, says St. John, on these levels, the majority of souls come to a halt. For the next thing he shows us is an immense precipice towering above us, and separating the lovely Alpine pastures of the spiritual life from the awful silence of the Godhead, the mysterious region of the everlasting snows. No one can tell the climber how to tackle the precipice. Here he must be led by the Spirit of God; and his success must depend on his self-abandonment and his courage—his willingness to risk, to trust, and to endure to the very end. Every one suffers on the precipice. Here all landmarks and all guides seem to fail, and the naked soul must cling as best it can to the naked rock of reality. This is the experience which St. John calls in another place the Dark Night of the Spirit. It is a rare experience, but the only way to the real summit; the supernatural life of perfect union with the self-giving and outpouring love of God. There His reality, His honour and His glory alone remain the very substance of the soul's perpetual joy. And that, and only that, is the mystic goal.

Evelyn Underhill, *Collected Papers of Evelyn Underhill*, Longmans, Green & Co. Ltd., 1946, page 118

CONTENTMENT

'Contentment'—being in a state of satisfaction, well pleased—
originally it meant a state of being bounded (in one's desires).

I n 1973 a group of four of us from University College, London, went on an expedition to the Asian part of Turkey. Our aim was to visit archaeological sites, such as Troy and Ephesus, and see some of the remoter parts of Turkey.

We acquired a Triumph 2000 estate car, giving us sufficient room for personnel and camping equipment, and carefully worked out an itinerary which would take us through several European countries and capital cities.

We arrived at a small campsite late one evening in Germany. An elderly couple ran this site. They seemed genuinely pleased to see us and gave us a warm welcome. They gently eased us through some basic rules and regulations and left us free to settle down.

We pitched our tent, cooked and ate our evening meal, and talked about the day's events over the washing-up. All of us were impressed with this elderly couple, so we decided to go and have a chat with them before settling down for the night.

We soon picked up their air of contentment. In our conversation with them they told us they enjoyed their outdoor life and being close to nature. Both spoke with pride of their work and the feeling of fulfilment it gave them. It was obvious they worked together well as a team and were devoted to each other. They also enjoyed meeting people, especially people like ourselves from different backgrounds, and related well with them. Here was a couple, happy with their lot, exuding contentment. They made a lasting impression on us.

The lines have fallen for me in pleasant places; yea, I have a goodly heritage.

Psalm 16.6

Happy is the man who finds wisdom, and the man who gets understanding... Her ways are ways of pleasantness, and all her paths are peace.

Proverbs 3.13,17

... I have learned, in whatever state I am, to be content.

Philippians 4.11

Keep your life free from love of money, and be content with what you have; for he has said, 'I will never fail you nor forsake you...'

Hebrews 13.5

The noblest mind the best contentment has.

Edmund Spenser, *Spenser's Faerie Queene*, edited by J.C. Smith, Oxford at the Clarendon Press, 1964, page 13, Book I, Canto I, st.xxxv, l.4

A contented mind is a continual feast.

English proverb

A mind content, both Crown and Kingdom is.

Robert Greene, *Farewell to Folly*, 1587, st.ii, l.12

Of unattainable longings sour is the fruit; griding madness.

C.S. Lewis, *Poems*, edited by Walter Hooper, Geoffrey Bles Ltd., 1964, 'Pindar Sang', page 17

To be content with little is difficult; to be content with much, impossible.

Old proverb

Content is Wealth, the Riches of the Mind;
And happy He who can that Treasure find.

John Dryden, *The Poems of John Dryden*, edited by James Kinsley, Oxford at the Clarendon Press, 1958, Volume IV, page 1715, 'The Wife of Bath Her Tale,' l.466

Better a handful of dry dates and content therewith than to own the Gate of Peacocks and be kicked by a broody camel.

Arab proverb

… nobody who gets enough food and clothing in a world where most are hungry and cold has any business to talk about 'misery' …

C.S. Lewis, *They Stand Together—The Letters of C.S. Lewis to Arthur Greeves (1914-1963)*, edited by Walter Hooper, William Collins Sons & Co. Ltd., 1979, page 161

Those who face that which is actually before them, unburdened by the past, undistracted by the future, these are they who live, who make the best use of their lives; these are those who have found the secret of contentment.

Alban Goodier, SJ, *The School of Love*, Burns & Oates & Washbourne Ltd., 1920, page 68

My crown is in my heart, not on my head;
Not deck'd with diamonds and Indian stones,
Nor to be seen: my crown is call'd content;
A crown it is that seldom kings enjoy.

William Shakespeare, *King Henry VI*, Part III, Act III. sc.i. l.62

For not that, which men covet most, is best,
Nor that thing worst, which men do most refuse;
But fittest is, that all contented rest
With that they hold: each hath his fortune in his brest.

Edmund Spenser, *Spenser's Faerie Queene*, edited by J.C. Smith, Oxford at the Clarendon Press, 1964, page 414, Book VI, Canto IX, st.xxix, l.6

How calm and quiet a delight
It is alone, To read, and meditate, and write,
By none offended, nor offending none;
To walk, ride, sit, or sleep at one's own ease,
And pleasing a man's self, none other to displease!

Charles Cotton, *Poems*, chosen and edited by J.R. Tutin, published by the editor, 1903, 'The Retirement,' page 16

Let us be contented with what has happened to us and thankful for all we have been spared. Let us accept the natural order in which we move. Let us reconcile ourselves to the mysterious rhythm of our destinies, such as they must be in this world of space and time. Let us treasure our joys but not bewail our sorrows. The glory of light cannot exist without its shadows. Life is a whole, and good and ill must be accepted together. The journey has been enjoyable and well worth making—once.

Winston S. Churchill, *Thoughts and Adventures*, Thornton Butterworth Ltd., 1932, page 19

To live content with small means; to seek elegance rather than luxury, and refinement rather than fashion; to be worthy, not respectable, and wealthy, not rich; to study hard, to think quietly, talk gently, act frankly; to listen to stars and birds, to babes and sages, with open heart; to bear all cheerfully, do all bravely, await occasions, hurry never. In a word, to let the spiritual, unbidden and unconscious, grow up through the common. This is to be my symphony.

William E. Channing, *A Series of Miscellaneous Illustrated Cards*, 1902, 'My Symphony,' page 37

Contentedness, in all accidents brings great peace of spirit... If I fall into the hands of thieves or of publicans and sequestrators; what now? They have left me the sun and moon, fire and water, a lovely wife, and friends to pity me, and some to relieve me, and I can still discourse; and unless I list, they have not taken away my merry countenance, and my cheerful spirit, and a good conscience: they still have left me the providence of God, and all the promises of the gospel, and my religion, and my hopes of heaven, and my charity to them too; and still I sleep and digest, I eat and drink, I read and meditate; I can walk in my neighbour's pleasant fields, and see the varieties of natural beauties, and delight in all that in which God delights—that is, in virtue and wisdom, in the whole creation, and in God himself.

Jeremy Taylor, *Holy Living*, abridged by Anne Lamb, The Langford Press, 1970, pages 62, 65

God is the master of the scenes; we must not choose which part we shall act; it concerns us only to be careful that we do it well, always saying, 'If this please God, let it be as it is': we, who pray that God's will may be done in earth as it is in heaven. For is not all the world God's family? Are not we His creatures? Do we not live upon His meat, and move by His strength, and do our work by His light? And shall there be a mutiny among the flocks and herds, because their lord or their shepherd chooses their pastures, and suffers them not to wander into deserts and unknown ways? If we choose, we do it so foolishly that we cannot like it long, and most commonly not at all; but God is wise, affectionate to our needs, and powerful. Here, therefore, is the wisdom of the contented man, to let God choose for him; for when we have given up our wills to Him, our spirits must needs rest, while our conditions have for their security the power, the wisdom, and the charity of God...

Let us prepare our minds against changes, always expecting them, that we be not surprised when they come; for nothing is so great an enemy to tranquillity and a contented spirit as our unreadiness when our fortunes are violently changed. Our spirits are unchanged if they always stood in the suburbs and expectation of sorrows.

Jeremy Taylor, *Holy Living*, abridged by Anne Lamb, The Langford Press, 1970, page 62

COURAGE

'Courage'—bravery, boldness, ability to nerve oneself to a venture.

I n recent years we have had several physically handicapped undergraduates in college. All of them have had something in common, namely, a quiet courageous approach to life. This has caused me to think about the nature of their courage.

I found some clues in the words of Cardinal Manning. He wrote in *Pastime Papers*— 'the Italians call it *Coraggio*, or greatness of heart; the Spaniards, *Corage*; the French, *Courage*, from whom we have borrowed it. And we understand it to mean manliness, bravery, boldness, fearlessness, springing not from a sense of physical power, or from insensibility to danger or pain, but from the moral habit of self-command, with deliberation, fully weighing present dangers, and clearly foreseeing future consequences, and yet in the path of duty advancing unmoved to its execution.'

This fits in roughly with my observations. Very rarely have they complained about their condition. Each has had a certain greatness of heart quietly bubbling away in them.

All of them have developed this moral habit of self-command, able to face the future, calmly, deliberately and courageously. Somehow they have found an inner strength which carries them through their various difficulties.

I wonder if this is yet another consequence of the divine inbreathing in the Genesis story of the creation of man. Some of us may be unaware of the precise nature of this inner strength, and yet be highly dependent on it. I often wonder where great-heartedness comes from. Heredity? Environment?—or both of these together in a combination of the human with the divine?

Be of good courage, and let us play the man for our people, and for the cities of our God.
1 Chronicles 19.13

Wait for the Lord; be strong, and let your heart take courage; yea, wait for the Lord!
Psalm 27.14

Be watchful, stand firm in your faith, be courageous, be strong. Let all that you do be done in love.
1 Corinthians 16.13-14

I can do all things in him who strengthens me.
Philippians 4.13

Great things are done more through courage than through wisdom.
German proverb

Where true Fortitude dwells, Loyalty, Bounty, Friendship and Fidelity may be found.
Sir Thomas Browne, *The Works of Sir Thomas Browne*, edited by Geoffrey Keynes, Faber & Faber Ltd., 1964, Volume I, Christian Morals, page 258

Courage is what it takes to stand up and speak; courage is also what it takes to sit down, and listen.
Anon.

The Courage we desire and prize is not the Courage to die decently, but to live manfully.
Thomas Carlyle, *The Works of Thomas Carlyle*, Chapman & Hall Ltd., 1899, *Critical and Miscellaneous Essays*, Volume III, 'Boswell's Life of Johnson,' page 123

Oh courage... oh yes! If only one had that... Then life might be liveable, in spite of everything.
Henrik Ibsen, *Hedda Gabler*, edited by James Walter McFarlane, translated by Jens Arup and James Walter McFarlane, Oxford University Press, 1966, Volume VII, page 225, Act II

Courage is the basic virtue for everyone so long as he continues to grow, to move ahead.
Rollo May, *Man's Search For Himself*, George Allen & Unwin Ltd., 1953, page 224

Courage is sustained, not only by prayer, but by calling up anew the vision of the goal.
A.D. Sertillanges, OP, *The Intellectual Life*, translated by Mary Ryan, The Mercier Press, 1948, page 157

The greatest virtue in life is real courage, that knows how to face facts and live beyond them.
D.H. Lawrence, *The Selected Letters of D.H. Lawrence*, edited by Diana Trilling, Farrar, Straus & Cudahy, 1958, page 243

It requires moral courage to grieve, it requires religious courage to rejoice.
Søren Kierkegaard, *The Journals of Søren Kierkegaard*, a selection edited and translated by Alexander Dru, Oxford University Press, 1938, page 87

Courage is not simply *one* of the virtues but the form of every virtue at the testing point, which means at the point of highest reality.

C.S. Lewis, in *The Unquiet Grave*, Cyril Connolly, Hamish Hamilton, 1945, page 75

The stout heart is also a warm and kind one: Affection dwells with Danger, all the holier and lovelier for such stern environment.

Thomas Carlyle, *The Works of Thomas Carlyle*, Chapman & Hall Ltd., 1899, Critical and Miscellaneous Essays, Volume III, *Corn-Law Rhymes*, page 147

Unbounded courage and compassion joined,
Tempering each other in the victor's mind,
Alternately proclaim him good and great,
And make the hero and the man complete.

Joseph Addison, *The Works of Joseph Addison*, edited and published by Henry G. Bohn, 1856, Volume I, 'The Campaign', page 48

Yet I argue not
Against heavens hand or will, nor bate a jot
Of heart or hope; but still bear up, and steer
Right onward.

John Milton, *The Poetical Works of Milton*, edited by the Rev. H.C. Beeching, Oxford at the University Press, 1900, page 89, 'To Mr. Cyriack Skinner upon his Blindness', l.6

Courage is required not only in a person's occasional crucial decision for his own freedom, but in the little hour-to-hour decisions which place the bricks in the structure of his building of himself into a person who acts with freedom and responsibility.

Rollo May, *Man's Search For Himself*, George Allen & Unwin Ltd., 1953, page 229

Heroism is the brilliant triumph of the soul over the flesh—that is to say, over fear; fear of poverty, of suffering, of calumny, of sickness, of isolation, and of death. There is no serious piety without heroism. Heroism is the dazzling and glorious concentration of courage.

Henri Frédéric Amiel, *Amiel's Journal*, translated by Mrs Humphry Ward, Macmillan & Co. Ltd., 1918, page 4

We must accept our existence as far as ever it is possible; everything, even the unheard of, must be possible there. That is fundamentally the only courage which is demanded of us: to be brave in the face of the strangest, most singular and most inexplicable things that can befall us.

Rainer Maria Rilke, *Letters to a Young Poet*, translation by Reginald Snell, Sidgwick & Jackson, 1945, page 38

Courage cannot be explained with reference solely to itself. A courageous man is one who has courage to do something, to be something. That is, he believes that there is more to be done with life than prolong it. It is said that a man must have the courage of his convictions, but he can have no courage unless he has convictions. The New Testament in general, and the Sermon on the Mount in particular, makes it clear that the courageous man's first victory is a conquest over anxiety. Anxiety can be described under these headings: (1) *Material*—Fear of increased prices, inflation, unemployment, changes in trade, nationally and internationally, illness, infirmity. These might be summarized as a general, though vague, feeling of political and economic insecurity. (2) *Spiritual*—Fear of loss of freedom and power to keep one's identity. Fear of being a hypocrite or incapable of significant action. Fear of being inadequate in personal relationships especially in the family. (3) *Religious*—Fear of the failure and disappearance of the church on account of the small number of practising members. Fear through a reluctance to think and live in the light of the fact that Christians walk by faith and not by sight and therefore cannot answer all the questions men may ask. Christians do not claim that only Christians can be courageous but that a man, or woman, requires courage to be a Christian in any century—whether in facing violence, torture and death or enduring the constant battle to be fought out against anxiety. It is brave to accept dangers oneself but it is even braver to allow and even exhort others to be courageous in their particular spheres of living—for example, a bishop ordaining clergy, parents encouraging their sons and daughters to leave home and take full responsibility for themselves, friend helping friend to make a decision where one should be made no matter at what cost.

Christians learn that courage is a necessity rather than a virtue through their frequent meditation on the passion and triumph of our Lord. In every generation orthodox doctrine and individual piety are most clearly expressed in the compassion and courage of church members. Where there is no courage, compassion dwindles and where compassion is absent courage tends to become arrogant self-display.

R.E.C. Browne, in *A Dictionary of Christian Ethics*, edited by John Macquarrie, SCM Press Ltd., 1967, 'Courage,' page 76

DARKNESS

'Darkness'—state of no or relatively little light, being unilluminated, gloomy, sombre; the evil, atrocious, cheerless side to things; sadness, sullenness.

O ur university expedition to Nepal in 1963 was an exciting adventure. We completed our scientific projects on time; we very nearly got into Tibet; and we made a film of village life on the slopes of Annapurna which was later shown on television.

Not all, however, was plain sailing. We had our fair share of darkness. As with Longfellow—metaphorically speaking:

Into each life some rain must fall,
Some days must be dark and dreary.

On the second day of our trek we had a long exhausting day. We planned to stay in a village by a river. We reached our destination late in semi-darkness, ate a hasty meal, pitched our tent, and were about to go to sleep when there was a pitter-patter, heralding torrential rain, which fell throughout the night. The rain was so heavy it came straight through the canvas of our tent. The sewn-in groundsheet made matters worse. There was no outlet. Much to our dismay, the level of the water rose during the night making it impossible for us to sleep in sodden sleeping bags—a night never to be forgotten.

Two days later there was a tremendous storm. This time we were camped on a ridge. We had to hold on to the tent poles, for fear of losing our tent—another sleepless night. Finally our return journey on foot to Pokhara took place in the context of three days of solid rain. The lesson learnt from these 'times of darkness' is that they are all a part of life as a whole, and have to be gone through as patiently and creatively as possible.

I will turn the darkness before them into light, the rough places into level ground. These are the things I will do, and I will not forsake them.

Isaiah 42.16

Arise, shine; for your light has come, and the glory of the Lord has risen upon you. For behold, darkness shall cover the earth, and thick darkness the peoples; but the Lord will arise upon you, and his glory will be seen upon you.

Isaiah 60.1-2

And even if our gospel is veiled, it is veiled only to those who are perishing. In their case the god of this world has blinded the minds of the unbelievers, to keep them from seeing the light of the gospel of the glory of Christ, who is the likeness of God . . . For it is the God who said, 'Let light shine out of darkness,' who has shone in our hearts to give the light of the knowledge of the glory of God in the face of Christ.

2 Corinthians 4.3-6

Now this I affirm and testify in the Lord, that you must no longer live as the Gentiles do, in the futility of their minds; they are darkened in their understanding, alienated from the life of God because of the ignorance that is in them, due to their hardness of heart.

Ephesians 4.17-18

The mass of men lead lives of quiet desperation.

Henry David Thoreau, *Walden*, The New American Library of World Literature, Inc., 1960, page 10

Darkness is more productive of sublime ideas than light.

Edmund Burke, *Burke's Works*, printed for J. Dodsley, Volume I, page 145, 'Light: On the Sublime and Beautiful,' I.17

Into each life some rain must fall,
Some days must be dark and dreary.

Henry Wadsworth Longfellow, *The Poetical Works of Longfellow*, Humphrey Milford, Oxford University Press, 1913, page 63, 'The Rainy Day,' st.iii, l.44

Resolve to be thyself; and know that he,
Who finds himself, loses his misery!

Matthew Arnold, *The Poems of Matthew Arnold*, edited by Kenneth Allott, Longmans, Green & Co. Ltd., 1965, page 144, 'Self-Dependence,' l.31

And out of darkness came the hands
That reach through nature, moulding men.

Alfred, Lord Tennyson, *The Poems of Tennyson*, edited by Christopher Ricks, Longmans, Green & Co. Ltd., 1969, page 974, No.296, 'In Memoriam A.H.H.,' st.cxxiv, l.23

That Jesus fought despair and triumphed we know from his prayers on the cross which began with 'My God, why have your forsaken me?' and ended with 'Into your hand, Lord, I commend my spirit.' However near we come to despair, we have this precedent to refer to.

Hubert van Zeller, *Considerations*, Sheed & Ward Ltd., 1974, page 76

If I stoop
Into a dark tremendous sea of cloud,
It is but for a time; I press God's lamp
Close to my breast; its splendour, soon or late,
Will pierce the gloom: I shall emerge one day.

Robert Browning, *The Poetical Works of Robert Browning*, Smith, Elder & Co., 1899, Volume I, *Paracelsus V*, page 72

And when he can no longer *feel* the truth, he shall not therefore die. He lives because God is true and he is able to know that he lives because he knows, having once understood the word, that God is truth. He believes in the God of former vision, lives by that word therefore, when all is dark and there is no vision.

George Macdonald, *Unspoken Sermons*, First Series, Alexander Strahan, Publisher, 1867, page 144

When the heart is hard and parched up, come upon me with a shower of mercy.
    When grace is lost from life, come with a burst of song.
    When tumultuous work raises its din on all sides shutting me out from beyond, come to me, my lord of silence, with thy peace and rest.
    When my beggarly heart sits crouched, shut up in a corner, break open the door, my king, and come with the ceremony of a king.
    When desire blinds the mind with delusion and dust, O thou holy one, thou wakeful, come with thy light and thy thunder.

Rabindranath Tagore, *Gitanjali*, Macmillan & Co Ltd., 1971, page 30

The man of to-day pursues his dark journey in a time of darkness, as one who has no freedom, no mental collectedness, no all-round development, as one who loses himself in an atmosphere of inhumanity, who surrenders his spiritual independence and his moral judgment to the organised society in which he lives, and who finds himself in every direction up against hindrances to the temper of true civilisation. Of the dangerous position in which he is placed philosophy has no understanding, and therefore makes no attempt to help him. She does not even urge him to reflection on what is happening to himself.

Albert Schweitzer, in *Albert Schweitzer: Christian Revolutionary*, by George Seaver, James Clarke & Co., 1944, page 94

It would be wrong to assume that what John of the Cross speaks of as 'Dark Night' has nothing in common with ordinary, non-religious human experience. The image is not alien.

How many pages of literature, how many paintings and songs, have as their theme a dark night when what once had meaning now has none—when life's light has been extinguished, the heart bruised, the mind bewildered.

Bereavement, disappointment, failure, old age and, on the wider scene, the threat of atomic destruction; these and countless other common experiences engulf us in night.

All of them confront us with our finitude, raise fundamental questions on human existence and contain a challenge to accept our human vocation, whether we know the shape of that vocation or not.

Every human being is for God and an openness for God. It is not only around us who know his name but around every single person that the sun is shining, seeking an entrance. He uses every occasion to illumine us and his illumination is most often perceived as darkness.

Ruth Burrows, *Ascent to Love*, edited by Elizabeth Ruth Obbard, Darton, Longman & Todd, 1988, page 48

Oh, how dare I mention the dark feeling of mysterious dread which comes over the mind, and which the lamp of reason, though burning bright the while, is unable to dispel! Art thou, as leeches say, the concomitant of disease—the result of shattered nerves? Nay, rather the principle of woe itself, the fountain head of all sorrow co-existent with man, whose influence he feels when yet unborn... for... woe doth he bring with him into the world, even thyself, dark one, terrible one, causeless, unbegotten, without a father...

Then is it not lawful for man to exclaim, 'Better that I had never been born!' Fool, for thyself wast not born, but to fulfil the inscrutable decrees of thy Creator and how dost thou know that this dark principle is not, after all, thy best friend; that it is not that which tempers the whole mass of thy corruption? It may be, for what thou knowest, the mother of wisdom, and of great works: it is the dread of the horror of the night that makes the pilgrim hasten on his way. When thou feelest it nigh, let thy safety word be 'Onward'; if thou tarry, thou art overwhelmed. Courage! build great works—'tis urging thee—it is ever nearest the favourites of God—the fool knows little of it. Thou wouldst be joyous, wouldst thou? then be a fool. What great work was ever the result of joy, the puny one? Who have been the wise ones, the mighty ones, the conquering ones of this earth? the joyous? I believe not.

George Borrow, *Lavengro*, Thomas Nelson & Sons Ltd., 1933, page 119

For an hour past I have been the prey of a vague anxiety; I recognise my old enemy... It is a sense of void and anguish; a sense of something lacking: what? Love, peace,—God perhaps. The feeling is one of pure want unmixed with hope, and there is anguish in it because I can clearly distinguish neither the evil nor its remedy... Of all the hours of the day, in fine weather, the afternoon, about 3 o'clock, is the time which to me is most difficult to bear. I never feel more strongly than I do then, *'le vide effrayant de la vie,'* the stress of mental anxiety, or the painful thirst for happiness. This torture born of the sunlight is a strange phenomenon. Is it that the sun, just as it brings out the stain upon a garment, the wrinkles in a face, or the discoloration of the hair, so also it illumines with inexorable distinctness the scars and rents of the heart? Does it rouse in us a sort of shame of existence? In any case the bright hours of the day are capable of flooding the whole soul with melancholy, of kindling in us the passion for death, or suicide, or annihilation, or of driving us to that which is next akin to death, the deadening of the senses by the pursuit of pleasure. They rouse in the lonely man a horror of himself; they make him long to escape from his own misery and solitude...

People talk of the temptations to crime connected with darkness, but the dumb sense of desolation which is often the product of the most brilliant moment of daylight must not be forgotten either. From the one, as from the other, God is absent but in the first case a man follows his senses and the cry of his passion; in the second, he feels himself lost and bewildered, a creature forsaken by all the world.

Henri Frédéric Amiel, *Amiel's Journal*, translated by Mrs Humphry Ward, Macmillan & Co. Ltd., 1918, page 200

DIVINITY

'Divinity'—theology; being divine, Godhood.

O ne of our undergraduates was helped in her understanding of the Christian faith by some words of Meister Eckhart in this section. These came from his second contribution, particularly the last paragraph—'The seed of God is in us. Given an intelligent farmer and a diligent fieldhand, it will thrive and grow up to God whose seed it is, and accordingly its fruit will be God-nature. Pear seeds grow into pear trees; nut seeds into nut trees, and God-seed into God!'

Through these words she was able to understand baptism (and confirmation) as a cleansing and *a spiritual rebirth*. She linked this up with the parable of the grain of wheat which falls into the ground and dies before bearing much fruit. She knew, of course, the seed did not entirely die merely the outer case—thus allowing the nutrients of the soil to catalyse growth from the centre of the seed. This simple parable enabled her to understand more fully the nature of her baptism and confirmation.

She moved on to consider the words of the confirmation service; that 'she may... daily increase in your Holy Spirit more and more, until she comes to your everlasting Kingdom.' She worked out spiritual rebirth, initiated in baptism and confirmation, needed to grow in prayer, as in reflection.

She then moved on to the service of Holy Communion and realized how apt these words were. At one level she received bread and wine, at another level the body and blood of Christ, the Father, the Holy Spirit, life, light, truth, joy, love and so on.

She now came to understand Divinity as a 'divine life', rather than a 'divine science', and she was changed by it.

He who is of God hears the words of God; the reason why you do not hear them is that you are not of God.
John 8.47

Little children, you are of God, and have overcome them; for he who is in you is greater than he who is in the world.
1 John 4.4

No man has ever seen God; if we love one another, God abides in us and his love is perfected in us.
1 John 4.12

We know that we are of God.
1 John 3.19

There's a divinity that shapes our ends,
Rough-hew them how we will.
William Shakespeare, *Hamlet*, Act V. sc.ii. l.10

There is surely a peece of Divinity in us,
something that was before the Elements, and owes no homage unto the Sun.
Sir Thomas Browne, *The Works of Sir Thomas Browne*, edited by Geoffrey Keynes, Faber & Faber Ltd., 1964, Volume I, *Religio Medici*, page 87

The mystery of a Person, indeed, is ever divine, to him that has a sense for the Godlike.
Thomas Carlyle, *Sartor Resartus*, Ward, Lock & Co. Ltd., page 92

Reason is our Soules left hand, Faith her right,
By these we reach divinity.
John Donne, *The Satires, Epigrams and Verse Letters*, Oxford at the Clarendon Press, 1967, page 90, Verse Letters: 'To the Countess of Bedford,' l.1 'Strong is the soul, and wise, and beautiful'

The seeds of godlike power are in us still;
Gods are we, bards, saints, heroes, if we will!

Matthew Arnold, *The Poems of Matthew Arnold*, edited by Kenneth Allott, Longmans, Green & Co. Ltd., 1965, page 53, 'Written in Emerson's Essays,' l.11

Were I indeed to define divinity, I should rather call it a *divine life*, than a *divine science*; it being something rather to be understood by a spiritual sensation, than by any verbal description...

John Smith the Platonist, *Select Discourses*, Cambridge at the University Press, 1859, page 1

There is a power in the soul untouched by time and flesh, flowing from the Spirit, remaining in the Spirit, altogether spiritual. In this power is God, ever verdant, flowering in all the joy and glory of his actual self.

Meister Eckhart, *Meister Eckhart*, Franz Pfeiffer, translated by C. de B. Evans, John M. Watkins, 1956, Volume I, page 36

That only which we have within, can we see without. If we meet no gods, it is because we harbour none. If there is grandeur in you, you will find grandeur in porters and sweeps. He only is rightly immortal, to whom all things are immortal.

Ralph Waldo Emerson, *The Conduct of Life, Nature and Other Essays*, J.M. Dent & Sons Ltd., 1911, page 262

O give thyself unto me, for without thee no gift at all can satisfy. And because thou thyself art the gift, O give me what thou art, that I may give thee what I am, and be made a partaker of the divine nature.

Thomas Traherne, in *Landscapes of Glory*, edited by A.M. Allchin, Darton, Longman & Todd, 1989, page 36

Divinity is essentially the first of the professions, because it is necessary for all at all times; law and physic are only necessary for some at some times. I speak of them, of course, not in their abstract existence, but in their applicability to man.

Samuel Taylor Coleridge, *Table Talk of Samuel Taylor Coleridge*, George Routledge & Sons Ltd., 1884, page 186

Since it is through the possession of happiness that people become happy, and since happiness is in fact divinity, it is clear that it is through the possession of divinity that they become happy. But by the same logic as men become just through the possession of justice, or wise through the possession of wisdom, so those who possess divinity necessarily become divine. Each individual is therefore divine. While only God is so by nature, as many as you like may become so by participation.

Boethius, *The Consolation of Philosophy*, translated by V.E. Watts, Penguin Books Ltd., 1969, page 102

In the life which wells up in me and in the matter which sustains me, I find much more than Your gifts. It is You Yourself whom I find, You who makes me participate in Your being, You who moulds me. Truly in the ruling and in the first disciplining of my living strength, in the continually beneficent play of secondary causes, I touch, as near as possible, the two faces of Your creative action, and I encounter, and kiss, Your two marvellous hands—the one which holds us so firmly that it is merged, in us, with the sources of life, and the other whose embrace is so wide that, at its slightest pressure, all the springs of the universe respond harmoniously together.

Pierre Teilhard de Chardin, *Le Milieu Divin*, William Collins Sons & Co. Ltd., 1960, page 56

The Scriptures say of human beings that there is an outward man and, along with him, an inner man.

To the outward man belong those things that depend on the soul but are connected with the flesh and blended with it, and the co-operative functions of the several members such as the eye, the ear, the tongue, the hand, and so on. The Scripture speaks of all this as the old man, the earthy man, the outward person, the enemy, the servant.

Within us all is the other person, the inner man, whom the Scripture calls the new man, the heavenly man, the young person, a friend, the aristocrat...

The seed of God is in us. Given an intelligent farmer and a diligent fieldhand, it will thrive and grow up to God whose seed it is, and accordingly its fruit will be God-nature. Pear seeds grow into pear trees; nut seeds into nut trees, and God-seed into God!

Meister Eckhart, *Meister Eckhart*, translated by Raymond B. Blakney, Harper & Row, Publishers, Inc., 1941, page 74

The centre of life is neither in thought nor in feeling, nor in will, nor even in consciousness, so far as it thinks, feels, or wishes. For moral truth may have been penetrated and possessed in all these ways, and escape us still. Deeper even than consciousness there is our being itself, our very substance, our nature. Only those truths which have entered into this last region, which have become ourselves, become spontaneous and involuntary, instinctive and unconscious, are really our life—that is to say, something more than our property. So long as we are able to distinguish any space whatever between truth and us we remain outside it. The thought, the feeling, the desire, the consciousness of life, are not yet quite life. But peace and repose can nowhere be found except in life and in eternal life, and the eternal life is the divine life, is God. To become divine is then the aim of life: then only can truth be said to be ours beyond the possibility of loss, because it is no longer outside of us, nor even in us, but we are it, and it is we; we ourselves are a truth, a will, a work of God. Liberty has become nature; the creature is one with its creator—one through love. It is what it ought to be; its education is finished, and its final happiness begins. The sun of time declines and the light of eternal blessedness arises.

Our fleshly hearts may call this mysticism. It is the mysticism of Jesus: 'I am one with my Father, ye shall be one with me. We will be one with you.'

Henri Frédéric Amiel, *Amiel's Journal*, translated by Mrs Humphry Ward, Macmillan & Co. Ltd., 1918, page 44

EDUCATION

'Education'—bringing up (young persons); giving intellectual and moral training; development of character or mental powers.

I n this section I like the quotation which suggests education is not learning; it is the exercise and development of the powers of the mind; and the two great methods by which this end may be accomplished are in the halls of learning or in the conflicts of life.

In University College, Oxford, the exercise and development of the powers of the mind are given a top priority. Each week in term-time an undergraduate is given an essay title, along with a reading list, and he/she then has to write the essay and read this out to the tutor in a tutorial. In the tutorial the tutor will often take the undergraduate to task, arguing this way and that, sometimes destroying the main thrust of the essay. In this process the tutor is not just checking how much of the reading list has been covered, but is attempting to sharpen and bring out the powers of the mind of the undergraduate.

In college life another great method of education is taking place, namely, the conflicts of life. School timetables are a thing of the past and undergraduates are left free to organize their own schedules. Some find this difficult. Sadly, an increasing number have to face the trauma of family breakdown. A few experience bereavement with the loss of a parent or a loved one. Newly found relationships in college also break down and some experience pains of rejection. Later they will face the full thrust of competition and the workaday world. Yes, education does not just reside in the halls of learning, but also in a creative response to the conflicts of life, which are manifold.

You shall therefore lay up these words of mine in your heart and in your soul; and you shall bind them as a sign upon your hand, and they shall be as frontlets between your eyes.
Deuteronomy 11.18

Apply your mind to instruction and your ear to words of knowledge.
Proverbs 23.12

Take my yoke upon you, and learn from me; for I am gentle and lowly in heart, and you shall find rest for your souls.
Matthew 11.29

Who is wise and understanding among you? By his good life let him show his works in the meekness of wisdom.
James 3.13

Deep verst in books and shallow in himself.
John Milton, *The Poetical Works of Milton*, edited by Rev. H.C. Beeching, Oxford at the Clarendon Press, 1900, page 495, *Paradise Regain'd*, Book IV, l.327

Education has for a chief object the formation of character.
Herbert Spencer, *Social Statics*, Williams and Norgate, 1892, page 81

The direction in which education starts a man will determine his future life.
Plato, *The Republic of Plato*, translation by B. Jowett, Oxford at the Clarendon Press, 1881, page 110, Book IV, 425B

To be what we are, and to become what we are capable of becoming, is the only end of life.

Robert Louis Stevenson, *Familiar Studies of Men and Books, Virginibus Puerisque, Selected Poems*, William Collins Sons & Co. Ltd., 1956, page 112

Finally, education, alone, can conduct us to that enjoyment which is, at once, best in quality and infinite in quantity.

Horace Mann, *Lectures and Reports on Education*, Cambridge: published for the editor, 1867, page 84

But warm, eager, living life—to be rooted in life—to learn, to desire, to know, to feel, to think, to act. That is what I want. And nothing less. That is what I must try for.

Katherine Mansfield, *Journal of Katherine Mansfield*, edited by J. Middleton Murry, Constable & Co. Ltd., 1927, page 251

Education is not learning; it is the exercise and development of the powers of the mind; and the two great methods by which this end may be accomplished are in the halls of learning or in the conflicts of life.

Anon.

One impulse from a vernal wood
May teach you more of man,
Of moral evil and of good,
Than all the sages can.

William Wordsworth, *The Poetical Works of William Wordsworth*, edited by E. de Selincourt and Helen Darbishire, Oxford at the Clarendon Press, 1958, Volume IV, page 57, 'The Tables Turned,' st.vi, l.21

Education... is the leading human souls to what is best, and making what is best out of them; and these two objects are always attainable together, and by the same means; the training which makes men happiest in themselves, also makes them most serviceable to others.

John Ruskin, *The Stones of Venice*, edited by Ernest Rhys, J.M. Dent & Co., 1907, Volume III, page 197

An education which is not religious is atheistic; there is no middle way. If you give to children an account of the world from which God is left out, you are teaching them to understand the world without reference to God. If He is then introduced, He is an excresence. He becomes an appendix to His own creation.

William Temple, *The Hope of a New World*, SCM Press Ltd., 1940, page 12

One person who has mastered life is better than a thousand persons who have mastered only the contents of books, but no one can get anything out of life without God. If I were looking for a master of learning, I should go to Paris to the colleges where the higher studies are pursued, but if I wanted to know about the perfection of life, they could not tell me there.

Meister Eckhart, *Meister Eckhart*, translated by Raymond B. Blakney, Harper & Row, Publishers, Inc., 1941, page 236

Most people live, whether physically, intellectually or morally, in a very restricted circle of their potential being. They *make use* of a very small portion of their possible consciousness, and of their soul's resources in general, much like a man who, out of his whole bodily organism, should get into a habit of using and moving only his little finger. Great emergencies and crises show us how much greater our vital resources are than we had supposed.

William James, *The Letters of William James*, edited by Henry James, Longmans, Green & Co. Ltd., 1926, page 253

Life should be a giving birth to the soul, the development of a higher mode of reality. The animal must be humanised: flesh must be made spirit; physiological activity must be transmuted into intellect and conscience, into reason, justice, and generosity, as the torch is transmuted into life and warmth. The blind, greedy, selfish nature of man must put on beauty and nobleness. This heavenly alchemy is what justifies our presence on the earth: it is our mission and our glory.

Henri Frédéric Amiel, *Amiel's Journal*, translated by Mrs Humphry Ward, Macmillan & Co. Ltd., 1918, page 285

What is a complete human being? Again I shall take the Greek answer to this question. Human beings have bodies, minds and characters. Each of these is capable of what the Greeks called 'virtue' *apetn* or what we might call 'excellence'. The virtue or excellence of the body is health and fitness and strength, the firm and sensitive hand, the clear eye; the excellence of the mind is to know and to understand and to think, to have some idea of what the world is and of what man has done and has been and can be; the excellence of the character lies in the great virtues. This trinity of body, mind and character is man: man's aim, besides earning his living, is to make the most of all three, to have as good a mind, body and character as possible; and a liberal education, a free man's education, is to help him to this; not because a sound body, mind and character help to success, or even because they help to happiness, but because they are good things in themselves, and because what is good is worth while, simply because it is good.

Sir Richard Livingstone, *On Education*, Cambridge at the University Press, 1954, page 61

Educational programmes, educational methods, educational goals and education personnel are involved today in a far-reaching crisis. Educational authorities and those responsible for socialization (family, school, university, but also institutions and businesses) and likewise educational personnel (father, mother, teacher, educator, instructor) find that they are exposed to harsh criticism and impatient accusations from right to left: for some they are too conservative, for others too progressive; for some too political; for others too unpolitical; for some too authoritarian, for others too anti-authoritarian. Perplexity and disorientation are widespread. We can only outline the causes and conditions, symptoms and consequences of this crisis.

In the family: the acceleration of the rate of change in society means that parents not only grow older but often quickly lost touch with the situation. The criteria for educating their children are no longer certain. The result is a lack of understanding and knowledge. There is a profound insecurity which often leads to insistence on the wrong things and thus to disastrous conflicts of authority for children and family.

In school and university: the discrepancy between pretension and reality, between often unrealistic theory and heightened practical expectations and requirements, the conflict of roles between teachers and pupils, professors and students, turn school and university into objects of political-educational controversy between all socially relevant groups and a field of experiment for more and more new educational-didactic projects and plans of study. After a planning euphoria we are now threatened with a planning lethargy, after excessive organization we are faced with disorganization, after the optimism of a future equality of opportunity we are uncertain about the future as a result of increasing restriction of studies; after conjuring up an educational emergency and the exhaustion of the last educational reserves we now have an educational glut and the 'academic proletariat.'

And the young people themselves? At the centre of the conflicts and contradictions of the educational scene, they are reacting increasingly with apathy, indifference and weariness and often enough break down completely. Taken seriously by society as consumers and pampered in their self-awareness also as consumers, at home and in school they are often made to feel irresponsible and dependent. Influenced by adults, by school attendance and the continual rising of the school-leaving age to think in terms of social prestige, they must see how dubious are the criteria of achievement, how remote from life their training has often been, and how uncertain are their future chances of an occupation.

And the adults? Educational virtues, absolutely sacred and unquestioned yesterday, have apparently become obsolete today: adult authority, obedience to older people, subordination to the parents' will, adaptation to the existing order. But now there are some who question not only the contents and methods but the very idea of education. Those who identified education with determination by others, manipulation, imposition of the teacher's will, now go to the other extreme and advocate anti-authoritarian education, absolute self-determination, unrestricted freedom; aggression is to be cultivated, frustrations worked out, instincts satisfied, conflicts encouraged. Relationships are reversed: young people are no longer subject to the will of adults, but the claims of adults are subordinated to the claims, needs and requirements of young people.

A significant trend is emerging. A false conception of authority on both sides, fear and uncertainty in reaction to the others produce an atmosphere of pressure and counter-pressure, of refusal or self-assertion, of stronger destructive tendencies, of brutality and aggression. The school passes on the responsibility to the family and society, society to school and family, family to school and society. There is a vicious circle. What is to be done? Here are some brief suggestions:

The Christian message gives no detailed information as to how the scholastic and vocational training system is to be better and more effectively organized, how curricula are to be worked out, training and educational programmes implemented, educational problems solved, institutions governed and children educated.

But the Christian message has something essential to say about the attitude and approach of the teacher to the child and the child to the teacher, and also about the reason for commitment even in the face of disappointments and failures: that in the light of the person of Jesus education can never be for the sake of my own prestige, repute, interest, but for the sake of the one who is entrusted to me. Education is understood therefore as non-repressive, as mutual service regardless of precedence. This means that the children never exist simply for the sake of the teachers, nor indeed the teachers simply for the sake of the children; that the teachers may never exploit their children, nor indeed the children their teachers; that the teachers may never impose their will in an authoritarian spirit on their children, nor however may the children impose their will in an anti-authoritarian spirit on their teachers. Mutual service regardless of precedence in a Christian spirit means for the teacher unconditional trust, goodness, loving good will, in advance and without any compelling reasons. And in all this he will refuse to let anything deter him.

Hans Küng, *On Being a Christian*, translated by Edward Quinn, William Collins Sons & Co. Ltd., 1977, page 598

EUCHARIST

*'Eucharist'—the sacrament of the Lord's Supper, the Communion,
essential elements being remembrance and thanksgiving.*

I n term time, we have a celebration of the Eucharist in the college chapel every Sunday morning at 8.15 a.m. As is well known, this service gets its name from the Greek word *eucharistia*—meaning thanksgiving—and thanksgiving is one of the most important elements in this Service.

One Sunday I was administering the chalice and the recipient, instead of responding with an 'amen', looked at me straight in the eye and said 'thanks'.

I have often wondered what he had in mind at that precise moment. Was he giving thanks—to Jesus Christ, for his life, death, resurrection, ascension, and for the gift of the Holy Spirit? Or was he giving thanks for life itself—for speech, sight and hearing?—for food, shelter, clothing and his time at university?—for his mind, his imagination, his intellect, his thinking and feeling capacities?—or was he giving thanks for his special gift of being a long-distance runner, who would later represent his county in the Olympics?

I never did find out. This one word 'thanks' can cover such a rich diversity of life. This is also true of the Eucharist. Can anyone say what it is we receive in this sacrament? Is it bread and wine or the body and blood of Christ? Or what about divine attributes such as life, light, joy, truth and love as experienced by Christ? I have come to see all these gifts are included and have come to realize the supreme value of the Eucharist. Thanks to be God for his inexpressible gift.

And he took bread, and when he had given thanks he broke it and gave it to them, saying, 'This is my body which is given for you. Do this in remembrance of me.' And likewise the cup after supper, saying, 'This cup which is poured out for you is the new covenant in my blood.'

Luke 22.19-20

I am the living bread which came down from heaven; if any one eats of this bread, he will live for ever; and the bread which I shall give for the life of the world is my flesh.

John 6.51

As the living Father sent me, and I live because of the Father, so he who eats me will live because of me.

John 6.57

The cup of blessing which we bless, is it not a participation in the blood of Christ? The bread which we break, is it not a participation in the body of Christ? Because there is one bread, we who are many are one body, for we all partake of the one bread.

1 Corinthians 10.16-17

That we should 'take' and 'eat' is an indispensable aid which the sincere Christian cannot omit; but the one thing that matters is that we should 'feed upon him in our hearts.'

William Temple, *Readings in St. John's Gospel*, First and Second Series, Macmillan & Co. Ltd., 1947, page 95

The idea is that you appropriate to yourself and assimilate the essence of his sacrifice, symbolically represented by the bread and wine of the Eucharist. A man who was completely innocent offered himself as a sacrifice for the good of others, including his enemies and became the ransom of the world. It was a perfect act.

Mohandas K. Gandhi, *Non-Violence in Peace & War*, Navajivan Publishing House, 1949, Volume II, page 166

The Prayer of the Chalice
Father, to Thee I raise my whole being, a vessel emptied of self. Accept, Lord, this my emptiness, and so fill me with Thyself—Thy Light, Thy Love, Thy Life—that these Thy precious gifts may radiate through me and overflow the chalice of my heart into the hearts of all with whom I come into contact this day revealing unto them the beauty of Thy Joy and Wholeness and the serenity of Thy Peace which nothing can destroy.

Anon.

I believe that when I take that piece of bread and it becomes part of my frame, it is woven into my nerves and muscles, so that as I do that in faith I receive Jesus Christ, the Bread of Life, who strengthens me and passes into my being; so that I can say, 'I live, yet no longer I, but Christ liveth in me.' And I believe that the sacrament is a vehicle of divine grace and—receiving it in faith and humility and penitence—that new life comes into me.

Francis Glasson, in *Priestland's Progress*, Gerald Priestland, BBC, 1982, page 174

The Eucharist to the Christian is the culminating point of all sacramental rites... For this Sacrament is the constantly repeated act from which the soul draws its spiritual food. Its virtue resides in its repetition; it is repeated again and again, just because it is constantly needed to effect that contact with divine life and power which, in its aspect of communion, is all its meaning. Here the Christian believes that he takes into himself the very life which makes him one with God.

Oliver Quick, *The Christian Sacraments*, Nisbet & Co. Ltd., 1952, pages 185, 186

I do believe that when we address to the Lord our prayer to send down His Holy Spirit upon this bread and wine, it does happen. I have no theory about how it happens. But it happens with the same simple certainty which I would attach to the incarnation. If God could unite Himself to a human flesh and soul, he can unite Himself as completely to this bread and wine. And when we receive communion, I believe that God reaches out to us on the most primitive and simple level. A babe can receive a small particle of bread and a drop of wine, and with it be reached by God.

Anthony Bloom, in *Priestland's Progress*, Gerald Priestland, BBC, 1982, page 185

When we receive the Holy Communion, we express our belief that the mysterious Divine presence, of which we are conscious in prayer (using, once more, the word prayer of all communings of the soul with the unseen spiritual world)—that this mysterious Divine presence is not only God, or the Spirit of God, but 'the Spirit of *Jesus*,' to use a phrase which the Revised Version has restored to our New Testament. We are identifying the living well spring of our faith, the source of our hope and our happiness, the guide and inspirer of our lives, with a historical character who lived nearly two thousand years ago.

W.R. Inge, *Speculum Animae*, Longmans, Green & Co. Ltd., 1911, page 17

Two men stand before some great picture. Both see the same colours and the same lines—one sees beauty, the other sees nothing significant. But the one who sees the beauty does not make it—the artist made it.—And so when you listen to beautiful music, where is the beauty? You do not create it: you do not invent it—you find it. And yet you will not find it unless you have the understanding of music which qualifies you to be sensitive to it. It is the same with beauty everywhere... And so in the Holy Communion Christ offers Himself in all His fullness of holiness and love to be ours, but whether you receive Him depends on the insight of your faith, on how far you are conscious of your need of Him, on how far you are sincere in seeking to be united with Him in His offering of Himself to the Father.

William Temple, *Christian Faith and Life*, SCM Press Ltd., 1963, page 122

The Holy Communion is the Sacrament in and by which we are to remember Him, and in remembering to be united to Him. The culmination of the life of prayer is the reception of the life of God within us, and this is the mystery of the Eucharist. Whether or not it be true, as the mystics of all ages have taught, ... that there is a 'soul centre' which is as it were the natural point of contact with the Divine, an unquenchable spark from the altar in heaven, a principle which does not and cannot consent to sin, and which, as William Law says, 'is so infinite that nothing can satisfy it, or give it any rest, but the infinity of God,' at any rate in this sacrament the 'medicine of immortality' is offered us, and offered in the name and through the mediation of Jesus Christ. 'Whoso eateth my flesh and drinketh my blood hath eternal life.'

W.R. Inge, *Speculum Animae*, Longmans, Green & Co. Ltd., 1911, page 13

The Eucharist is the supreme way in which the people of Christ are, through our Great High Priest, with God with the world around on their hearts.

The author and the agent in the Eucharist is the Word of God. The Word is proclaimed in the scripture lections and in the preaching. Then the same Word, who is Jesus, blesses the loaf and the cup, and invites and commands us.

Jesus the Word feeds us so that we may be increasingly his own Body in the world to share with him in his work of the world's re-creation. He does not feed us in order to draw us away with him into a separated realm of religion, but to draw us into participation with him in the work of moulding the world into his own likeness.

And the meaning of all life is here set forth, since men exist to worship God for God's own sake.

Like the incarnation itself, the Eucharist is the breaking into history of something eternal, beyond history, inapprehensible in terms of history alone.

The supreme question is not what we make of the Eucharist but what the Eucharist is making of us, as (together with the Word) it fashions us into the way of Christ.

Michael Ramsey, in *Gateway to God*, edited by Lorna Kendall, Darton, Longman & Todd, 1988, page 45

So [the Church's] children bring the bread and wine, fruit of the earth and work of human hands, symbols of the offering of ourselves. These are laid upon the altar with our poor lives, each day, each hour... filled with little actions, aspirations, fears, longings, sufferings—all that goes to make up a human span—but in sacrifice. We want these poor earthly things to be an expression of perfect love for the Father.

We give you, dear Lord, all we have and are under the veil of bread and wine. In themselves, as of themselves, they are ineffective, they can never carry us to the Father. Make them into your own offering, your own flight of love which does get there. Transform us into your immolated self.

In Holy Communion we receive back the humble offerings we first presented, not as themselves, but as sacrament of union, of transformation. We eat God and are transformed thereby. Not that we become something marvellous but so that we become nothing but a living response, an act of obedience, a pure burnt-offering. Thus we too will shine with the light of Godhead—but he alone will see it.

Ruth Burrows, *Living Love and Our Father*, Darton, Longman & Todd, 1990, page 142

The symbol of the Eucharist is life and joy. Bread satisfies, wine elates and both produce gladness of heart. The joy of each individual is intensified by the joy of the whole.

In the Eucharist as elsewhere it is only in Christ's glory that we make contact with his death. It is in Christ's glory that we sit down at the table of his sacrifice. He himself is present eating with us and nourishing us at one and the same time.

The Eucharist contains all that God in his love has done for us, it is the memorial of his wonderful works. Creation looks forward to the incarnation and redemption, and the redemption is the outpouring of the Spirit, the beginning of eternal life.

All this is in the Eucharist. Here we eat of the Risen Christ, God's own Son, from whose wounded side the Spirit comes to us giving us the adoption of sons. We go to the Body of Christ to receive the stream of living water, the Spirit and eternal life.

Each day we celebrate the Eucharist, the giving of thanks, taking our divine meal with gladness. Let us ask for the gifts of joy and gratitude that we may delight God in recognizing his marvellous love.

Ruth Burrows, in *The Watchful Heart*, edited by Elizabeth Ruth Obbard, Darton, Longman & Todd, 1988, page 26

EVOLUTION

'Evolution'—opening out (of roll, bud, etc.); appearance (of events etc.) in due succession; evolving, giving off (of gas, heat, etc.); development (of organism, design, argument, etc.); theory of evolution—(that the embryo is not created by fecundation, but developed from a pre-existing form); origination of species by development from earlier forms, not by special creation.

In 1970 I went to Kenya to stay with some friends for a few weeks. We visited several of places of interest including the Samburu Game Reserve, the Masai-Amboseli Game Reserve, and the Tsavo National Park. After this I went on my own to spend a memorable night at Treetops, watching animals in the floodlit area, coming to refresh themselves at the waterhole and the salt lick. Later we climbed almost to Point Lenana on Mount Kenya, followed by an exciting safari to a remote part of Lake Rudolf—now Lake Tekana.

One of the most eye-opening experiences in Kenya was a visit to Olorgesaillie prehistoric site. There we saw hundreds of primitive stone axe-heads, and realized we were standing in one of the first cradles of mankind and civilization. Up to that point I was still naïvely focused on the Middle East and the 'Garden of Eden'. Here, in the heart of Kenya, my eyes were opened to the evidence of evolution on all sides.

In this topic I like the sentence written by Bede Griffiths in which he says the human person is a centre of consciousness which is capable of infinite extension. Link this up with Robert Browning's statement—'man is not Man as yet'—and we get a glimpse of where hope for the future can be found.

Where were you when I laid the foundation of the earth?

Job 38.4

Thine is the day, thine also the night, thou hast established the luminaries and the sun.

Psalm 74.17

... but we shall all be changed.

1 Corinthians 15.51

... we await a Saviour, the Lord Jesus Christ, who will change our lowly body to be like his glorious body...

Philippians 3.21

Progress is
The law of life, man is not Man as yet.

Robert Browning, *The Poetical Works of Robert Browning*, Smith, Elder & Co., 1899, Volume I, 'Paracelsus V', page 70

If we do not develop within ourselves this deeply rooted feeling that there is something higher than ourselves, we shall never find the strength to evolve to something higher... The heights of the spirit can only be climbed by passing through the portals of humility. You can only acquire right knowledge when you have learnt to esteem it... Whoever seeks for higher knowledge, must create it for himself. He must instil it into his soul. It cannot be done by study; it can only be done through life.

Rudolf Steiner, *Knowledge of the Higher Worlds and its Attainment*, Rudolf Steiner Press, 1936, page 18

The last end of man, the ultimate reason for human existence, is unitive knowledge of the divine Ground—the knowledge that can come only to those who are prepared to 'die to self' and so make room, as it were, for God. Out of any given generation of men and women very few will achieve the final end of human existence; but the opportunity for coming to unitive knowledge will, in one way or another, continually be offered until all sentient beings realize Who in fact they are.

Aldous Huxley, *The Perennial Philosophy*, Chatto & Windus Ltd., 1974, page 29

It is always worth while to inquire how far the doctrine of evolution has anything to do with any reasonable notion of progress... If you take an unarmed saint and confront him with a hungry tiger, there will be a struggle for existence culminating in the survival of the fittest, which means, of course, the fittest to survive in those conditions; but it will not be a survival of the ethically best. There is no reason to suppose that the struggle for existence always favours what is ethically admirable any more than there is any reason to suppose that a social order, if it may have the name, characterized by cut-throat competition, will always bring its best citizens to the top.

William Temple, *The Preacher's Theme Today*, SPCK, 1936, page 32

Let every man remember that the destiny of mankind is incomparable and that it depends greatly on his will to collaborate in the transcendent task. Let him remember that the Law is, and always has been, to struggle and that the fight has lost nothing of its violence by being transposed from the material onto the spiritual plane; let him remember that his own dignity, his nobility as a human being, must emerge from his efforts to liberate himself from his bondage and to obey his deepest aspirations. And let him above all never forget that the divine spark is in him, in him alone, and that he is free to disregard it, to kill it, or to come closer to God by showing his eagerness to work with Him, and for Him.

Lecomte du Noüy, *Human Destiny*, Longmans, Green & Co. Ltd., 1947, page 273

To read the gospel with an open mind is to see beyond all possibility of doubt that Jesus came to bring us new truths concerning our destiny: not only a new life superior to that we are conscious of, but also in a very real sense a new physical power of acting upon our *temporal* world.

Through a failure to grasp the exact nature of this power newly bestowed on all who put their confidence in God—a failure due either to a hesitation in face of what seems to us so unlikely or to a fear of falling into illuminism—many christians neglect this earthly aspect of the promises of the Master, or at least do not give themselves to it with that complete hardihood which he nevertheless never tires of asking of us, if only we have ears to hear him. We must not allow timidity or modesty to turn us into poor craftsmen. If it is true that the development of the world can be influenced by our faith in Christ, then to let this power lie dormant within us would indeed be unpardonable.

Pierre Teilhard de Chardin, *Hymn of the Universe*, William Collins Sons & Co. Ltd., 1961, page 143

The human person is a centre of consciousness which is capable of infinite extension. As it grows it becomes more and more integrated with the whole complex of persons who make up humanity.

We become more ourselves as we enter more deeply into relationship with others. We do not lose ourselves but we lose our sense of separation and division.

This is essentially a mystery of love. When two people love one another they do not lose their distinction of person, they become more fully personal.

The whole process of evolution, as Teilhard de Chardin saw it, is a process of personalization. The ultimate goal of humanity is a communion of persons in love.

This is what was revealed in St John's Gospel when Jesus prayed for his disciples 'that they may be one as you, Father, are in me and I in you, that they may be one in us' (John 17.21).

Bede Griffiths OSB, in *The Universal Christ*, edited by Peter Spink, Darton, Longman & Todd, 1993, page 9

Jesus was a man in whom body and soul were pure instruments of the indwelling spirit. In him human destiny has been fulfilled.

Whereas in the universe as we know it there is conflict at every level, and body and soul are in conflict with one another, in Jesus this conflict has been overcome. Body and soul have been restored in unity with the spirit, and a power of unification has been released into the world.

So we are able to see the death of Jesus and the free surrender of his life on the cross to the Father as a cosmic event.

Certain events, that is, the emergence of life on this planet, the awakening of consciousness in man, mark critical changes in the evolution of the world. The death of Jesus was an event of this kind. It marked the point of transition of the human consciousness to the Divine, the point where the human being was totally surrendered, body and soul, to the divine Being. In this sense the death of Jesus can be called 'a redemptive sacrifice'; it is an offering of human nature to the divine which 'redeems', that is, restores human nature to its unity with the divine nature.

Bede Griffiths OSB, in *The Universal Christ*, edited by Peter Spink, Darton, Longman & Todd, 1993, page 4

The theory of evolution provides the basis for two premises which lie at the heart of modern biology. The first is that all living things are related as part of the same family tree, a premise which has recently received spectacular support from molecular biology and the discovery that all known genetic systems are based on the same genetic code. The second is that the most fruitful questions to ask about the ways in which life has developed are in terms of the advantages which particular developments give to their possessors. Advantage, rather than purpose or design, is the key explanatory concept. In this general conceptual sense the theory is now treated as axiomatic.

The details of evolutionary history still contain many areas of uncertainty, and understanding of how evolution actually takes place is still incomplete, though it has advanced greatly in complexity and sophistication since Darwin's day. However, the twin principles of random variation and natural selection remain the pillars on which everything else is built. Since the beginning of this century the principle of random variation has been given precise content through the development of genetics, and latterly through the advances in molecular biology. Natural selection is no longer thought of in terms of crude competition between individuals, but has been broadened to include populations of animals in complex inter-relationships responding in different ways to environmental change. Of particular interest to those concerned about the 'meaning' of the evolutionary process is the recognition that behavioural adaptation may be as important as genetic change in determining the success of an individual species. The idea that the story can be understood wholly in terms of chemistry, i.e. in the progress of 'the selfish gene', is a gross over-simplification.

Current debates about evolution have given some religious believers the mistaken idea that the theory itself is in doubt. So-called 'creation scientists' exploit selected, and often misinterpreted, evidence in the interests of demonstrating that Genesis provides a scientific account of pre-history, a conclusion which study of the history of the documents themselves render highly improbable. Some of their more detailed and technical criticism is focused on the relative lack of fossil evidence for intermediate evolutionary forms. It is important to note, therefore, that for Darwin the fossil record only provided corroborative evidence, and could not be expected to do more on account of its paucity. The three main lines of evidence on which he relied were 1. the experience of animal and plant breeders; 2. the geographical distribution of different species; and 3. the possibilities of classifying species in a reasonable historical sequence. These, extended and refined in countless ways, remain the basis of the theory.

Apart from the problems created for fundamentalists, there were other legitimate reasons for concern among Christians when Darwin's theory was first made public. For example, it stood the teleological argument for the existence of God (i.e. the argument from 'design') on its head. Creatures were seen to be wonderfully adapted to their environment, not because they had been designed that way, but because only well-adapted creatures survived. Modern versions of the teleological argument concentrate, more wisely than earlier ones, on the intelligibility of the universe, an intelligibility to which the theory of evolution itself contributes, thus strengthening belief in the purposiveness of God as the author of a rational process.

Darwin's theory also put in question the unique character and dignity of man. T.H. Huxley's famous exchange with Bishop Wilberforce reached its sharpest point in repartee about Huxley's relationship to the apes. Nowadays it is less difficult for Christians to accept that human distinctiveness does not necessarily have to depend on the belief that humanity had a distinct and separate origin. Just as individual human beings emerge gradually into full personhood through a natural process of growth and development, so the fact that *homo sapiens* evolved through many millions of years does not detract from our present uniqueness. In fact it is a source of wonder and reassurance about the evolutionary process as a whole that it should reach a peak of significance in producing creatures capable of responding to God.

The mechanism of evolution, in particular the element of chance, has always caused difficulties for those who believe that the universe is the work of a loving creator. It is important, therefore, to distinguish between a random process and a process which contains a random element. A completely random process would be by definition meaningless. A process containing a random element, however, in which random possibilities are selected and developed in the light of previous developments and under the pressure of particular circumstances, may be highly purposive. In fact there is good reason to suppose that much creative activity takes place in precisely this way. Creativity entails the exploration of hitherto undreamt of possibilities, and randomization is one of the ways of generating these. In evolutionary terms, chance may thus be an expression of God's super-abundance. In Teilhard de Chardin's words, evolution 'means pervading everything so as to try everything, and trying everything so as to find everything'.

The success of Darwin's theory has led to the wide extension of the concept of evolution into other fields of study. The perception that most things are in process of change and development is one of his legacies. But how and why particular phenomena change, e.g. in cosmic evolution, may bear little relationship to the actual processes of biological evolution. The application of evolutionary concepts to human behaviour, under the title of sociobiology, and the attempt to prescribe human norms in the light of evolutionary development, is a present source of major controversy. Earlier excursions into this field, e.g. social Darwinism, have rightly been discredited.

John Habgood, in *A New Dictionary of Christian Theology*, edited by Alan Richardson and John Bowden, SCM Press Ltd., 1983, page 196

EXPERIENCE

'Experience'—personal observation of or involvement with fact,
event, etc.; knowledge of skill based on this; event that affects one.

T his topic is not about experience of life in general but of experience of 'God' in particular.

I am very fond of St Augustine's 'experience' of God, recorded in his *Confessions,* as it mirrors my own experience. He writes of a Beauty—at once so ancient and so new—and after a long search discovers this Beauty as something within himself. It takes him many years to find this Beauty, as he was outside himself, searching elsewhere. He concludes, 'You were with me, but I was not with you.'

As a young man I was in the world outside myself. I was looking for 'God' and fell upon the lovely things of creation—nature, travel, knowledge, music, and last but not least—people of the opposite sex.

The search for 'God' continued, now focusing on the Church and the scriptures. Although I was getting close I was still outside myself, trying to find 'God' in a hallowed place, or in a book, completed nearly 2,000 years ago.

The penny finally dropped when I discovered Beauty in the depths of myself, and was able to experience this at first hand. Beauty, of course, is only one aspect of this 'inner presence'. There are many other descriptions—Father, Son, Holy Spirit, life, joy, love, truth, goodness, and so on. Experience of this kind is crucial in our quest for faith. Through it we reach an inner conviction of mind, heart and spirit, at one with our deepest intuitions and instincts.

I have learned by divination that the Lord has blessed me because of you.
Genesis 30.27

I have acquired great wisdom ... and my mind has had great experience of wisdom and knowledge.
Ecclesiastes 1.16

Yet he is not far from each one of us, for 'In him we live and move and have our being.'
Acts 17.27-28

... we rejoice in our sufferings, knowing that suffering produces endurance, and endurance produces character, and character produces hope, and hope does not disappoint us, because God's love has been poured into our hearts through the Holy Spirit which has been given to us.
Romans 5.3-5

The essential meaning of religion is not to know God as one knows a friend; it is to become God, for to know Him is to take Him into our inmost self as the fulfilment of that self; and it is only in becoming Him that we know Him.
Anon.

I have learnt to love you late, Beauty at once so ancient and so new! I have learnt to love you late! You were within me, and I was in the world outside myself. I searched for you outside myself and, disfigured as I was, I fell upon the lovely things of your creation. You were with me. But I was not with you.
St Augustine, *Confessions,* translated by R.S. Pine-Coffin, Penguin Books Ltd., 1964, page 231

By religious experience we ought to mean an experience which is religious through and through—an experiencing of all things in the light of the knowledge of God. It is this, and not any moment of illumination, of which we may say that it is self-authenticating; for in such an experience all things increasingly fit together in a single intelligible whole.
William Temple, *Thoughts On Some Problems Of The Day,* Macmillan & Co. Ltd., 1931, page 25

The significant features of the experience are the consciousness of fresh springs of life, the release of new energies, the inner integration and unification of personality, the inauguration of a sense of mission, the flooding of the life with hope and gladness, and the conviction, amounting in the mind of the recipient to certainty, that God is found as an environing and vitalizing presence.

Rufus M. Jones, *Spiritual Reformers in the 16th and 17th Centuries*, Macmillan & Co. Ltd., 1914, page xxi

He comes to us as One unknown, without a name, as of old, by the lake-side, He came to those men who knew Him not. He speaks to us the same word. 'Follow thou me!' and sets us to the tasks which He has to fulfil for our time. He commands. And to those who obey Him, whether they be wise or simple, He will reveal Himself in the toils, the conflicts, the sufferings which they shall pass through in His fellowship, and, as an ineffable mystery, they shall learn in their own experience Who He is.

Albert Schweitzer, *The Quest of the Historical Jesus*, A. & C. Black Ltd., 1954, page 401

People today are not prepared to take their faith from the tradition in which they were born, nor from other people. They want to deduce it from their own experience of life. They do not need theories, but the experience which will be the source of their own interpretation. They are suspicious of anything which seems to escape from life into theory, from experience into doctrine, or from the thing itself into talk about it. The method they want to follow is the inductive one rather than the deductive.

George Appleton, *Journey for a Soul*, William Collins Sons & Co. Ltd., 1976, page 37

The ultimate mystery cannot be named, cannot be properly conceived.

This is the foundation of all theology, this understanding that the ultimate mystery of being, by whatever name it is known, cannot be properly named or conceived. All words which are used about this mystery are signs or symbols of the ineffable and are of value only in so far as they point towards this mystery and enable its presence to be experienced in the 'heart' or the inner 'centre' of the person beyond speech and thought.

This presence cannot be known by the senses or by the rational mind. It is unseen but seeing; unheard but hearing; unperceived but perceiving; unknown but knowing.

Bede Griffiths OSB, in *The Universal Christ*, edited by Peter Spink, Darton, Longman & Todd, 1990, page 21

The challenge to the Church is the same one facing all men and women—to understand that the absolute is the only realism. Not only is it realistic, but it is the only way to come into contact with reality.

The Church cannot effectively proclaim a past experience. It can only proclaim what it is actually experiencing. It can only proclaim what *it is*.

If the gap between what we believe and what we experience makes us inauthentic, our message can convince no one until it has so convinced us that we are transformed by it.

A life that is not based on prayer, a Church that is not based on prayer, a world that is not based on prayer, cannot be a world, a Church or a life that is fully alive.

John Main, in *The Joy of Being*, selected by Clare Hallward, Darton, Longman & Todd, 1987, page 8

What must we do to gain this knowledge of 'That which is...?'

Study, experiment, and live it as far as possible in your ordinary lives until the time comes when you can absorb it into your own rhythm. The grace of Supreme Love will reveal it to you in time. The flow is continuous between the seed and the fruit. What is written in books does not touch the heart of a reader unless he experiences what he learns. What is taught cannot reach the soul of a listener until he lives what he hears. One can no more pass on the Truth than one can acquire it from others ... Nevertheless, there is Life of the heart. Speak to your hearts, speak slowly, clearly, *using no words*. Give birth to that Life that lies concealed therein. Feel it! Know it!'

Lizelle Reymond, *My Life With A Brahmin Family*, translated by Lucy Norton, Rider & Company, 1958, page 177

The spiritual life is a grand experiment which ends in an experience; but it is not merely a leap in the dark; throughout its whole course there is a progressive verification of its fundamental hypothesis, which makes us quite sure that we are on the right road. It is much like climbing a mountain. We are too much occupied with finding our way and securing footholds to think much about the elevation which we have reached; but from time to time we observe that we are nearer the summit, by the larger prospect which has opened around us. For the fuller revelation we look forward. Our world is still in the making, and we are in the making too. We look to the *'Christus futurus'* to interpret the Christ of past history, and to the *homo futurus* to show us what is the meaning of human personality.

W.R. Inge, *Speculum Animae*, Longmans, Green & Co. Ltd., 1911, page 42

These lectures [attended as a trade union organizer] opened up a new world of adventure, a spiritual world—an introduction to the mystery and dynamic force of prayer. Unlike other turns in the road of life, this experience was of slow growth—full of retreat, of backsliding, to use an old evangelical word. I do not think it possible to exaggerate the importance of the discoveries I made about life, and the relation of the self to the unseen world of the Spirit, and yet I find it hard to speak about; these are matters that cannot be taken on trust, they must be individually experienced and have no validity otherwise. In my case, a course of reading brought to me a sense of the *quality* of service given to the world by people like the Lady Julian of Norwich, Catherine of Sienna, the Quaker Saints, Josephine Butler, and that great host of dedicated lives. My everyday trade union work took on a deeper significance. The doing of ordinary everyday things became lit up with that inner light of the Spirit which gave one strength and effectivness; strength to meet defeat with a smile; to face success with a sense of responsibility; to be willing to do one's best without thought of reward; to bear misrepresentation without giving way to futile bitterness. Saint Theresa declared that: 'There are only two duties required of us—the love of God and the love of our neighbour, and the surest sign of discovering whether we observe these duties is the love of our neighbour'; and a great scholar has asserted that this love of God is not an emotion, although that may be experienced, it is a *principle of action*—it reinforces effort, it demands that we *do* something, not merely talk or feel sympathetic, we've got to use the new strength or it will break us.

That is the vital difference between those who drift with the stream, as I did at first, and those who, like the great souls down the ages, inspire, revive, and strengthen the corporate life of their generation.

Margaret Bondfield, in *What Life Has Taught Me*, edited by Sir James Marchant, Odhams Press Ltd., 1948, page 26

FELLOWSHIP

'Fellowship'—friendly association with others, companionship,
brotherhood.

S hortly after I had been ordained I was preaching on a regular basis in Bradford
Cathedral. This was something of an ordeal for me and I found the early years
particularly difficult.

I remember on one occasion having to preach on fellowship, and beforehand was
searching high and low for suitable illustrations. Fortunately the short stories of H.L. Gee
came to my rescue. I found one on fellowship, and it went something like this.

A middle-aged man, a regular attender at his local church, suddenly stopped coming,
and was conspicuous for his absence. After a few weeks the vicar decided to visit him and
find out if anything was the matter. He was cordially invited in and offered a cup of tea.
The two men then sat by the fireside and gazed into a blazing coal-fire in silence. The
vicar was tongue-tied and did not quite know how to tackle this delicate matter. A burning
piece of coal dropped from the fire into the hearth. It flamed for a few seconds and then
went out, becoming grey and dark. The vicar looked at it and then delicately took the
tongs from the coal-scuttle. He gingerly picked up this piece of coal and gently put it back
into the fire. Within a few seconds the piece of coal was glowing again, and a part of the
blazing fire.

The eyes of the two men met, and in a slightly haltering voice, the former attender
said, 'Yes, I see your point. I'll be along to church again next Sunday.'

One of the reasons for our going to church is fellowship, and encouraging others in
the life of faith.

> Iron sharpens iron, and one man sharpens another.
>
> Proverbs 27.17

> Every one helps his neighbour, and says to his brother, 'Take courage!' The craftsman
> encourages the goldsmith, and he who smooths with the hammer him who strikes the anvil,
> saying of the soldering, 'It is good'; and they fasten it with nails so that it cannot be moved.
>
> Isaiah 41.6-7

> May the God of steadfastness and encouragement grant you to live in such harmony with
> one another, in accord with Christ Jesus, that together you may with one voice glorify the
> God and Father of our Lord Jesus Christ.
>
> Romans 15.5-6

> So if there is any encouragement in Christ, any incentive of love, any participation in the
> Spirit, any affection and sympathy, complete my joy by being of the same mind, having the
> same love, being in full accord and of one mind.
>
> Philippians 2.1-2

> Fellowship with Christ is participation in the divine life which finds its fullest expression in
> triumph over death. Life is a larger word than Resurrection but Resurrection is, so to speak,
> the crucial quality of Life.
>
> William Temple, *Readings in St. John's Gospel*, First and Second Series, Macmillan & Co. Ltd., 1947, page 181

No one enters into fellowship with God but one who has given much time to the recollection of Him, for perfect fellowship means that the mind and the understanding have become absorbed in the joy of inward converse with their Lord, as one who talks with his beloved.

Al-Ghazali, in *Al-Ghazali, the Mystic,* Margaret Smith, Luzac & Co., 1944, page 182

Is our fellowship in Christ a reality more profound and effective than our membership of our earthly fellowships—family, school, party, class, nation, race—and able in consequence to unite us in love across all natural divisions and hostilities? Of course not. And the reason is that we do not truly abide in Him.

William Temple, *Readings in St. John's Gospel,* First and Second Series, Macmillan & Co. Ltd., 1947, page 267

The fundamental fact about human life is that God in His love, has entered into fellowship with us; the loftiest hope for human life is that we may, in answering love, enter into fellowship with Him. This is not to be found in the devotional life alone, nor in the practical life alone, but only in the perfect blend of both.

William Temple, *Lent with William Temple,* edited by G.P. Millick Belshaw, A.R. Mowbray & Co. Ltd., 1966, page 7

In the Apostles' Creed Christians confess their faith in a communion of saints, a fellowship of holy, loving people of all generations who have tried to live according to the light they have received. There is a fellowship of saintliness, a kinship of character and dedication, which is not confined to the Christian religion only, but comprises all who live by the highest they know and are glad to recognize a similar dedication in other people.

George Appleton, *Journey for a Soul,* William Collins Sons & Co. Ltd., 1976, page 191

And moreover, in these first words [Our Father], the praying soul accepts once for all its true status as a member of the whole family of man. Our Father. It can never again enter into prayer as a ring-fenced individual, intent on a private relation with God; for this is a violation of the law of Charity. Its prayer must overflow the boundaries of selfhood to include the life, the needs of the race; accepting as a corollary of its filial relation with God a brotherly relation with all other souls however diverse, and at every point replacing 'mine' by 'ours.' This widespreading love, this refusal of private advantage is the very condition of Christian prayer; for that prayer is an instrument of redemptive action, not merely of personal achievement.

Evelyn Underhill, *Abba,* Longmans, Green & Co. Ltd., 1940, page 14

One of the most rewarding experiences of living in a strange land is the experience of being loved not for what we can do, but for who we are. When we become aware that our stuttering, failing, vulnerable selves are loved even when we hardly progress, we can let go of our compulsion to prove ourselves and be free to live with others in a fellowship of the weak. This is a true healing.

Ministry is entering with our human brokenness into communion with others and speaking a word of hope. This hope is not based on any power to solve the problems of those with whom we live, but on the love of God, which becomes visible when we let go of our fears of being out of control and enter into his presence in a shared confession of weakness.

This is a hard vocation. It goes against the grain of our need for self-affirmation, self-fulfillment and self-realization. It is a call to true humility.

Henri J.M. Nouwen, in *Circles of Love,* arrangement by John Garvey, Darton, Longman & Todd, 1990, page 50

The Church of these spiritual Reformers [sixteenth and seventeenth centuries] was a Fellowship, a Society, a Family, rather than a mysterious and supernatural entity. They felt once again, as powerfully perhaps as it was possible in their centuries to feel it, the immense significance of the Pauline conception of the Church as the continued embodiment and revelation of Christ, the communion of saints past and present who live or have lived by the Spirit. Through this spiritual group, part of whom are visible and part invisible, they held that the divine revelation is continued and the eternal Word of God is being uttered to the race. 'The true religion of Christ', as one of these spiritual teachers well puts it, 'is written in the soul and spirit of man by the Spirit of God and the believer is the only book in which God now writes His New Testament.' This Church of the Spirit is always being built. Its power is proportional to the spiritual vitality of the membership, to the measure of apprehension of divine resources, to the depth of insight and grasp of truth, to the prevalence of love and brotherhood, to the character of service, which the members exhibit. It possesses no other kind of power or authority than the power and authority of personal lives formed into a community by living correspondence with God, and acting as human channels and organs of His Life and Spirit. Such a Church can meet new formulations of science and history and social ideals with no authoritative and conclusive word of God which automatically settles the issue. Its only weapons are truth and light, and these have to be continually re-discovered and re-fashioned to fit the facts which the age has found and verified. Its mission is *prophetic*. It does not dogmatically decide what facts must be believed, but it sees and announces the spiritual significance of the facts that are discovered and verified. It was, thus, in their thought a growing, changing, ever-adjusting body—the living body of Christ in the World.

Rufus M. Jones, *Spiritual Reformers in the 16th and 17th Centuries*, Macmillan & Co. Ltd., 1914, page 1

FREEDOM

'Freedom'—personal liberty, non-slavery; independence; liberty of action, right to do; power of self-determination, independence of fate or necessity, freedom of speech and religion, from fear and want.

A s I was approaching the end of schooldays, a brown envelope came through the post, marked 'On Her Majesty's Service'. I was required to attend a medical, prior to call-up for National Service. This was followed by a further letter instructing me to report to Topsham Barracks, Exeter, on a certain date. As soon as I entered the barracks, my personal freedom disappeared for the next two years.

I was a private soldier in the Devons and Dorsets. The first thing I can recall was being shouted at as though I was a complete idiot. This verbal battery continued for the next few weeks during basic training. We were issued with our army kit and ordered to post our civilian clothes home. For our meals we had to form up in ranks outside the barrack-room, and were marched to the cookhouse. On the first full day, we were despatched to the regimental barber, and given haircuts the likes of which we had never seen before. For some inexplicable reason we had to get up at 5 a.m. each day, and got to bed at 11 p.m. completely exhausted.

After eight weeks I went on a WOSB (War Office Selection Board) and was recommended for four months' training at Mons Officer Cadet School in Aldershot. On returning to Topsham Barracks, I picked up six charges in four days. The powers that be had it in for me. Freedom received a further battering. After two years of military service I really came to value freedom.

The Spirit of the Lord God is upon me, because the Lord has anointed me to bring good tidings to the afflicted; he has sent me to bind up the brokenhearted, to proclaim liberty to the captives, and the opening of the prison to those who are bound.

Isaiah 61.1

I will heal their faithfulness; I will love them freely, for my anger has turned from them.

Hosea 14.4

And you will know the truth, and the truth will make you free.

John 8.32

Because the creation itself will be set free from its bondage to decay and obtain the glorious liberty of the children of God.

Romans 8.21

So free we seem, so fettered fast we are!

Robert Browning, *The Poetical Works of Robert Browning*, Volume I, Smith, Elder & Co., 1899, page 524, *Men and Women*, 'Andrea Del Sarto,' l.51

Anything is free when it spontaneously expresses its own nature to the full in activity.

John Macmurray, *Freedom in the Modern World*, Faber & Faber Ltd., 1935, page 101

But what is Freedom? Rightly understood,
A universal licence to be good.

Hartley Coleridge, *The Complete Poetical Works of Hartley Coleridge*, edited by Ramsay Colles, George Routledge & Sons Ltd., 1908, 'Liberty,' page 106

Every man has freedom to do all that he wills, provided he infringes not the equal freedom of any other man.

Herbert Spencer, *Social Statics*, Williams & Norgate, 1892, page 54

The freedom of the heart from all that is other than God is needful if it is to be pre-occupied with the love of Him and the direct experience of Him.

Al-Ghazali, in *Al-Ghazali, The Mystic*, Margaret Smith, Luzac & Co., 1944, page 106

God has laid upon man the duty of being free, of safeguarding freedom of spirit, no matter how difficult that may be, or how much sacrifice and suffering it may require.

Nicolas Berdyaev, *The Fate of Man in the Modern World*, translated by Donald A. Lowrie, SCM Press Ltd., 1935, page 44

Yes! to this thought I hold with firm persistence;
The final word of all that's wise and true:
He only earns his freedom and existence,
Who daily conquers them anew.

Johann Wolfgang von Goethe, *Faust*, translated by Bayard Taylor, Sphere Books Ltd., 1974, page 424, Part 2, Act V. sc.vi. l.11573

When freedom is not an inner idea which imparts strength to our activities and breadth to our creations, when it is merely a thing of external circumstance, it is like an open space to one who is blindfolded.

Rabindranath Tagore, *Creative Unity*, Macmillan & Co. Ltd., 1922, page 133

All creation is for [God] a communication of his very being, that is, he can only create free beings. He can only call into existence beings that he calls upon to make themselves.

Louis Lavelle, in Paul Foulquié, *Existentialism*, translated by Kathleen Raine, Dennis Dobson Ltd., 1947, page 113

If we would have a living thing, we must give that thing some degree of liberty—even though liberty bring with it risk. If we would debar all liberty and all risk, then we can have only the mummy and the dead husk of the thing.

Edward Carpenter, *Love's Coming-Of-Age*, George Allen & Unwin Ltd., 1923, page 108

The coming of the Son of God and the Messiah in His power and glory as the King of the world and as a conqueror would have been the end of the freedom of the human spirit and the realization of the Kingdom of God by means of necessity and compulsion.

Nicolas Berdyaev, *Freedom and the Spirit*, Geoffrey Bles, The Centenary Press, 1935, page 140

Freedom in Christ is not freedom to do what I like, but freedom to be what I am meant to be. It is freedom from all the chains which hold me back from being my true self. It is freedom from all imposed limitations and external pressures. It is to share in Christ's freedom to do God's will, and then to help others find a similar freedom.

George Appleton, *Journey for a Soul*, William Collins Sons & Co. Ltd., 1976, page 181

God compels nobody, for He will have no one saved by compulsion. God has given freewill to men that they may choose for themselves, either the good or the bad. Christ said to His disciples, 'Will ye go away?' as though He would say, 'You are under no compulsion.' God forces no one, for love cannot compel, and God's service is, therefore, a thing of complete freedom.

Rufus M. Jones, *Spiritual Reformers in the 16th and 17th Centuries*, Macmillan & Co. Ltd., 1914, page 22

Our emancipation lies through the path of suffering. We must unlock the gate of joy by the key of pain. Our heart is like a fountain. So long as it is driven through the narrow channel of self it is full of fear and doubt and sorrow; for then it is dark and does not know its end. But when it comes out into the open, on the bosom of the All, then it glistens in the light and sings in the joy of freedom.

Rabindranath Tagore, *Letters to a Friend*, George Allen & Unwin Ltd., 1928, page 80

It may now be very easily conceived what is human freedom, which I define to be this: it is, namely, a firm reality which our understanding acquires through direct union with God, so that it can bring forth ideas in itself, and effects outside itself, in complete harmony with its nature; without, however, its effects being subjected to any external causes, so as to be capable of being changed or transformed by them.

Spinoza, *Short Treatise on God, Man, and His Well-Being*, translated by A. Wolf, Adam and Charles Black, 1910, page 148

My experience in the West, where I have realised the immense power of money and of organised propaganda,—working everywhere behind screens of camouflage, creating an atmosphere of distrust, timidity, and antipathy,—has impressed me deeply with the truth that real freedom is of the mind and spirit; it can never come to us from outside. He only has freedom who ideally loves freedom himself and is glad to extend it to others. He who cares to have slaves must chain himself to them; he who builds walls to create exclusion for others builds walls across his own freedom; he who distrusts freedom in others loses his moral right to it. Sooner or later he is lured into the meshes of physical and moral servility.

Rabindranath Tagore, *Creative Unity*, Macmillan & Co. Ltd., 1922, page 136

Meditation, as the way of life centred faithfully and with discipline on prayer, is our way into the true experience of spirit, of *the* Spirit. Anyone who follows this way soon comes to know for himself that its demand upon us increases with each step we take along the pilgrimage.

As our capacity to receive the revelation increases so too does the natural impulse we feel to make our response, our openness, more generous, more unpossessive.

The strange and wonderful thing is that this demand is unlike any other demand made upon us. Most demands upon us seem to limit our freedom, but this demand is nothing less than an invitation to enter into full liberty of spirit—the liberty we enjoy when we are turned away from self.

To understand this we cannot flinch from the fact that the demand is absolute, and consequently so must be our response.

John Main OSB, in *The Joy of Being*, selected by Clare Hallward, Darton, Longman & Todd, 1989, page 43

What our encounter with India and the East is teaching us is something we should never have forgotten—that the essential Christian experience is beyond the capacity of any cultural or intellectual form to express or contain. This is what St Paul called the 'glorious liberty of the children of God', no restriction.

This experience has to be restored to the heart of the Church if she is to face creatively the challenges before her: the challenge of the renewal of her contemplative religious life, the challenge of restoring unity in the Spirit with all Christian communions, the challenge of embracing non-Christian religions with the universal love of Christ which is already present in the hearts of all people and which she has a special duty to release and identity. To meet these challenges each one of us must be personally rooted in Jesus' personal experience of God and which he shares with us all through his Spirit.

We do not earn this experience or create it from our own resources; it is for us to prepare for the grace of its giving.

John Main OSB, in *The Joy of Being*, selected by Clare Hallward, Darton, Longman & Todd, 1989, page 22

FRIENDSHIP

'Friendship'—the state of being a friend; association of persons as friends; a friendly intimacy, conformity, affinity, correspondence, aptness to unite.

F riendship is very important in all stages of life but particularly so with young people. At the beginning of an academic year with a fresh intake there is always a frenetic rush to make new friends. For some undergraduates this is their first time away from home. A few suffer acutely from homesickness and it takes them time to settle down in a new environment. Most experience bouts of loneliness during their three or four years at university. The learning process involves hours and hours of reading on one's own, and this inevitably cuts people off from one another. Stress and strain inevitably take their toll. Friendship is thus extremely important in this situation.

I can remember one of our female undergraduates coming to see me. She was unhappy and depressed as she had no friends. She was feeling homesick, being away from home for the first time. She came from the north of England and felt a long way from home. She was reading chemistry and had a heavy workload, with lectures, lab work, and essays to be written. She was feeling isolated and lonely and in spare time would sit in her room, waiting for someone to call in for a coffee. So far she had waited in vain. I listened to her carefully and then introduced her to the words of Ralph Waldo Emerson: 'The only way to have a friend is to be one.' She brightened up and went off to visit her neighbours for a coffee. She made some good friendships in her time at Univ. and from that moment never looked back.

Saul and Jonathan were lovely and pleasant in their lives, and in their death they were not divided: they were swifter than eagles, they were stronger than lions.

2 Samuel 1.23 (AV)

A faithful friend is a strong defence: and he that hath found such an one hath found a treasure.

Ecclesiasticus 6.14 (AV)

Greater love has no man than this, that a man lay down his life for his friends. You are my friends if you do what I command you. No longer do I call you servants, for the servant does not know what his master is doing; but I called you friends, for all that I have heard from my Father I have made known to you.

John 15.13-15

Do you not know that friendship with the world is enmity with God?

James 4.4

I am wealthy in my friends.

William Shakespeare, *Timon of Athens*, Act II. sc.ii. l.189

The only way to have a friend is to be one.

Ralph Waldo Emerson, *Essays*, Bernhard Tauchnitz Edition, 1915, page 147, 'Friendship'

A friend may well be reckoned the masterpiece of nature.

Ralph Waldo Emerson, *Essays*, Bernhard Tauchnitz Edition, 1915, page 147, 'Friendship'

The essence of friendship is entireness, a total magnanimity and trust.

Ralph Waldo Emerson, *Essays*, Bernhard Tauchnitz Edition, 1915, page 156, 'Friendship'

To be a strong hand in the dark to another in the time of need.

Hugh Black, *Friendship*, Hodder & Stoughton Ltd., 1897, page 43

Friendship . . . is an union of spirits, a marriage of hearts, and the bond thereof virtue.

William Penn, *Fruits of Silence*, in 'Reflections and Maxims, relating to, The Conduct of Human Life,' A.W. Bennett, 1863, page 23

Friendship requires great communication between friends. Otherwise, it can neither be born nor exist.

St Francis de Sales, *Introduction to the Devout Life*, translated and edited by John K. Ryan, Longmans, Green & Co. Ltd., 1962, page 186

Nor do I question for a moment that Affection is responsible for nine-tenths of whatever solid and durable happiness there is in our natural lives.

C.S. Lewis, *The Four Loves*, William Collins Sons & Co. Ltd., 1981, page 52

A true friend unbosoms freely, advises justly, assists readily, adventures boldly, takes all patiently, defends courageously, and continues a friend unchangeably.

William Penn, *Fruits of Solitude*, in 'Reflections and Maxims, relating to, The Conduct of Human Life,' A.W. Bennett, 1863, page 24

If a man does not make new acquaintance as he advances through life, he will soon find himself alone. A man, Sir, should keep his friendship *in constant repair.*

Samuel Johnson, *Boswell's Life of Johnson*, edited by G.B. Hill, revised by L.F. Powell, Oxford at the Clarendon Press, 1934, Volume I, page 300

That friendship may be at once fond and lasting, there must not only be equal virtue on each part, but virtue of the same kind; not only the same end must be proposed, but the same means must be approved by both.

Samuel Johnson, *The Yale Edition of the Works of Samuel Johnson*, edited by W.J. Bate and Albrecht B. Strauss, Yale University Press, 1969, Volume III, page 341, 'The Rambler,' No. 64

Like everyone else I feel the need of relations and friendship, of affection, of friendly intercourse, and I am not made of stone or iron, so I cannot miss these things without feeling, as does any other intelligent and honest man, a void and deep need. I tell you this to let you know how much good your visit has done me.

Vincent van Gogh, *Dear Theo: An Autobiography of Vincent van Gogh*, edited by Irving Stone, Constable & Co. Ltd., 1937, page 39

I dream'd in a dream I saw a city invincible to the attacks
of the whole of the rest of the earth,
I dream'd that was the new city of Friends,
Nothing was greater there than the quality of robust love, it led the rest,
It was seen every hour in the actions of the men of that city,
And in all their looks and words.

Walt Whitman, *The Complete Poems*, edited by Francis Murphy, Penguin Books Ltd., 1982, 'I Dream'd in a Dream,' l.1

To be honest, to be kind—to earn a little and to spend a little less, to make upon the whole a family happier for his presence, to renounce when that shall be necessary and not be embittered, to keep a few friends, but these without capitulation—above all, on the same grim condition, to keep friends with himself—here is a task for all that a man has of fortitude and delicacy.

Robert Louis Stevenson, Across the Plains, T. Nelson & Sons, Ltd., 1892, page 274

The truest kind of friendship is what we call spiritual friendship. We should desire it for its own intrinsic worth and for the way it reaches into the human heart, rather than for any external reason or because it might bring any worldly advantage.

Indeed, when it comes to fruition, this kind of friendship is its own reward. In the Gospel, Jesus says: 'I have appointed you, that you should go and bring forth fruit'—that is, 'you should love one another'. True friendship increases as it makes itself more perfect: and our sensing that perfection, in all its sweetness, is the 'fruit' that is derived from it.

The spiritual friendship that exists between people of integrity springs out of their common attitude to life, their shared moral outlook and the kind of activities they engage in—in other words, it consists of mutual agreement in matters human and divine, combined with goodwill and practical loving concern.

Aelred of Rievaulx, De spiritu amicitia, 1:45 (adapted)

Speak to us of Friendship.
And he answered, saying:
Your friend is your needs answered.
He is your field which you sow with love and reap with thanksgiving.
And he is your board and your fireside.
For you come to him with your hunger, and you seek him for peace.
When your friend speaks his mind you fear not the 'nay' in your
own mind, nor do you with-hold the 'ay.'
And when he is silent your heart ceases not to listen to his heart;
For without words, in friendship, all thoughts, all desires, all
expectations are born and shared, with joy that is unacclaimed.
When you part from your friend, you grieve not;
For that which you love most in him may be clearer in his
absence, as the mountain to the climber is clearer from the plain.
And let there be no purpose in friendship save the deepening of the spirit.
For love that seeks aught but the disclosure of its own mystery is
not love but a net cast forth: and only the unprofitable is caught.
And let your best be for your friend.
If he must know the ebb of your tide, let him know its flood also.
For what is your friend that you should seek him with hours to kill?
Seek him always with hours to live.
For it is his to fill your need, but not your emptiness.
And in the sweetness of friendship let there be laughter, and sharing of pleasures.
For in the dew of little things the heart finds its morning
and is refreshed.

Kahlil Gibran, The Prophet, William Heinemann Ltd., 1970, page 69

FULFILMENT

'Fulfilment'—develop fully one's gifts and character.

A few years ago I was invited to attend a regimental dinner. The 2nd Battalion of the 2nd King Edward VII's Own Gurkha Rifles was doing a tour of duty in the UK and was stationed at Church Crookham, near Aldershot. The last time they came to England I had the privilege of watching them 'change the guard' at Buckingham Palace. I accepted the invitation, and looked forward to making contact with the battalion again.

The Adjutant of the Officers' Training Corps in Oxford was a serving officer in the 2nd Gurkhas, and offered me a lift to the dinner. During the journey he wondered if there would still be any Gurkhas in the battalion I would know. He mentioned two names. The first I could not remember, but the second—Resambahadur Gurung—had joined my platoon in 1960, and I used to know him well. The Adjutant said he would try to find him on our arrival at Church Crookham.

After about ten minutes Resambahadur Gurung greeted me with a huge grin on his face. We were delighted to see each other. We spent the whole evening catching up on each other's news. He had done rather well. As a Rifleman he had won the Military Medal and had risen rapidly through the ranks. He was now a Gurkha Captain, and shortly would be returning to Nepal for a topmost position— Gurkha Major of the depot in Pokhara.

He talked with pride of his time in the army. He had lived an outdoor life and had travelled widely. He was now looking forward to returning to his own country for a final spell of service, and then retirement on his farm in the hills of Nepal—and the joys of family life. Here was a man who had found fulfilment in his work and in his life.

Thou dost show me the path of life; in thy presence there is fulness of joy, in thy right hand are pleasures for evermore.

Psalm 16.11

For he satisfies him who is thirsty, and the hungry he fills with good things.

Psalm 107.9

Think not that I have come to abolish the law and the prophets; I have not come to abolish them, but to fulfil them. For truly, I say to you, till heaven and earth pass away, not an iota, not a dot, will pass from the law until all is accomplished.

Matthew 5.17-18

For this reason I bow my knees before the Father, from whom every family in heaven and on earth is named, that according to the riches of his glory he may grant you to be strengthened with might through his Spirit in the inner man, and that Christ may dwell in your hearts through faith; that you, being rooted and grounded in love, may have power to comprehend with all the saints what is the breadth and length and height and depth, and to know the love of Christ which surpasses knowledge, that you may be filled with all the fulness of God.

Ephesians 3.14-19

None save God can fill the perfect whole.

P.J. Bailey, Festus, William Pickering, 1839, page 51

Happiness lies in the fulfilment of the spirit through the body.

Cyril Connolly, The Unquiet Grave, Hamish Hamilton, 1945, page 26

The moment one is on the side of life 'peace and security' drop out of consciousness. The only peace, the only security, is in fulfilment.

Henry Miller, The Wisdom of the Heart, New Directions Books, 1941, page 87

It is the sign of a feeble character to seek for a short-cut to fulfilment through the favour of those whose interest lies in keeping it barred—the one path to fulfilment is the difficult path of suffering and self-sacrifice.

Rabindranath Tagore, *Letters to a Friend*, George Allen & Unwin Ltd., 1928, page 88

There is certainly no greater happiness, than to be able to look back on a life usefully and virtuously employed, to trace our own progress in existence, by such tokens as excite neither shame nor sorrow.

Samuel Johnson, *The Yale Edition of the Works of Samuel Johnson*, edited by W.J. Bate and Albrecht B. Strauss, Yale University Press, 1969, Volume III, page 225, 'The Rambler,' No. 41

As long as anyone believes that his ideal and purpose is outside him, that it is above the clouds, in the past or in the future, he will go outside himself and seek fulfillment where it can not be found. He will look for solutions and answers at every point except the one where they can be found—in himself.

Erich Fromm, *Man For Himself*, Routledge & Kegan Paul Ltd., 1975, page 249

Love alone is capable of uniting living beings in such a way as to complete and fulfil them, for it alone takes them and joins them by what is deepest in themselves... Does not love every instant achieve all around us, in the couple or the team, the magic feat,... of 'personalising' by totalising? And if that is what it can achieve daily on a small scale, why should it not repeat this one day on world-wide dimensions?

Pierre Teilhard de Chardin, *The Phenomenon of Man*, William Collins Sons & Co. Ltd., 1982, page 291

Give me fulness of life like to the sea and the sun, to the earth and the air; give me fulness of physical life, mind equal and beyond their fulness; give me a greatness and perfection of soul higher than all things; give me my inexpressible desire which swells in me like a tide— give it to me with all the force of the sea...

My heart has been lifted the higher towards perfection of soul... Fulness of physical life ever brings to me a more eager desire of soul-life.

Richard Jefferies, *The Story of My Heart*, Duckworth & Co., 1923, pages 79, 86

Our own insufficiency is that we live in a fraction of ourselves, in a narrow *I*, in a narrow vision, *in time*, in a belief that the material universe of the moment is *all*. The perfecting of oneself, the attainment of unity, is connected with grasping the idea of pleroma, with a full-filling which must mean, to begin with, an overcoming of our narrow temporal vision—so that now we can understand better why the Hermetist advises the exercise of thinking of the life *as living at all points*, as a movement towards 'eternal life'. But time—life—is only one track through the fullness of things.

Maurice Nicoll, *Living Time*, Vincent Stuart Publishers Ltd., 1952, page 136

It is of the very nature of human love that it cannot be completely satisfied with physical contact or emotional sympathy. It seeks a radical fulfilment in total self-giving.

For some, sexual union is the way to total self-giving and self-discovery. Others may awaken to the ecstasy of love in the presence of nature, like Wordsworth; others may find it in loving service and self-sacrifice.

It is no accident that the mystical experience is sometimes described in terms of sexual union. This is not 'sublimation' in the Freudian sense. Rather it is an opening of human nature to the full dimension of its being.

Whichever way we are destined to take leads to the discovery of the depths of the self, no longer in isolation but in the communion of love for which it was created.

Bede Griffiths OSB, in *The Universal Christ*, edited by Peter Spink, Darton, Longman & Todd, 1993, page 47

It would seem that the amount of destructiveness to be found in individuals is propor-tionate to the amount to which expansiveness of life is curtailed. By this we do not refer to individual frustrations of this or that instinctive desire but to the thwarting of the whole of life, the blockage of spontaneity of the growth and expression of man's sensuous, emotional, and intellectual capacities. Life has an inner dynamism of its own; it tends to grow, to be expressed, to be lived. It seems that if this tendency is thwarted the energy directed towards life undergoes a process of decomposition and changes into energies directed towards destruction. In other words: the drive for life and the drive for destruction are not mutually independent factors but are in a reversed interdependence. The more the drive towards life is thwarted, the stronger is the drive towards destruction; the more life is realized, the less is the strength of destructiveness. *Destructiveness is the outcome of an unlived life.*

Erich Fromm, *The Fear of Freedom*, Routledge & Kegan Paul Ltd., 1961, page 158

The world today is striving to attain a more complete humanity, to enable every man to realize his total personal being in a society which respects the human person. The human person is constituted by its experience both of physical reality in the world to which it belongs and of the social reality of the persons with whom it lives in communion. This whole world therefore of physical and social relationships is included in the sphere of contemplation. This is not to be found in separation from the body and society but in the transfiguration both of the body and of society, by which the total human being achieves its growth to full personal being, 'to mature manhood, to the measure of the stature of the fullness of Christ' (Ephesians 4.13), as St Paul describes it.

Perfect contemplation is attained only through the struggle to achieve the total interpretation of the human personality in all its dimensions. To find fulfilment man has to transcend himself, to discover a dimension of being beyond both the physical and the mental, and where the physical world itself is transfigured and is no more subject to corruption and death. This is the world of the resurrection, the 'new creation' of St Paul.

Bede Griffiths OSB, in *The Universal Christ*, edited by Peter Spink, Darton, Longman and Todd, 1993, page 60

To be happy here on earth we must live a full life. But there is no truly full life for us unless we live at a level above our natural powers as reasoning beings. So, if God is not to make nonsense of His own plan, He must add to our natural powers an extra capacity which will lift us to His own level. And unless we use that extra capacity, we shall not know the fullest life possible to us, nor shall we satisfy certain powers within us if we don't even know they exist. And all this shows that to bother about super-nature, to talk about another level of life than our natural life, is not to trail off into vague abstractions and dreams, but to appreciate our own possibilities. That other level of life is so definite as to belong to one actual Being just as my life belongs to me. What could be more concrete than that? And it is surely the most practical thing in the world to learn about all our powers, all our capabilities. Physiology tells us about our bodies, education exercises our minds, philosophy tells us about our powers of reasoning, art opens up possibilities of enjoying beauty. And now religion comes along and shows us that we have further powers still—the crown of all our natural powers. We shall be losers if we refuse to listen, merely on the ground that they are supernatural powers, for they will still be there whether we choose to recognize them or not. We are definitely refusing to rise to those heights because we are refusing to learn about them. That may take some doing. It takes courage and stamina to climb a mountain, but we cannot see the view from its summit if we stay in the plain. And the view is worth all the effort.

R J. Smith, in Paul Rowntree Clifford, *Man's Dilemma and God's Answer*, broadcast talks, SCM Press Ltd., 1944, page 76

GENIUS

*'Genius'—natural ability, special mental endowments; exalted
intellectual power, instinctive and extraordinary imaginative,
creative, or inventive capacity, person having this.*

One Christmas I went to Arosa (in Switzerland) to look after a church and to take
services for those on skiing holidays. There was just one snag—no organist at the
church—so before a service I would hover near the door and ask those coming in if they
could play the organ.

I remember a family of four, a father, a mother and two children, coming to the
church a few minutes before the service was due to begin. In response to my question the
mother looked at the father and said—'Well, John plays.' I looked at John carefully. He
was sturdily built and had a bushy beard. I thought I recognized him. 'John Ogdon?' I
asked. He smiled, and agreed to play the organ for the service.

I remember seeing this distinguished pianist on television in 1962, when he won the
Tchaikovsky prize in Moscow.

His son manned the bellows, and the carols were played as they had never been
played before. A delighted congregation responded in like manner. Although the organ
was not his natural instrument, John Ogdon took to it as though he had played it all his
life. Genius is easy to recognize.

I wonder if genius is yet another consequence of the divine inbreathing in the
Genesis story of the creation of man. Several quotations in this topic suggest genius is a
gift of God, requiring an appropriate response. I have no doubt John Ogdon was an
extremely gifted pianist, but I imagine it was the hours of practice which enabled him to
become a truly brilliant pianist.

Can we find such a man as this, in whom is the Spirit of God?

Genesis 41.38

I have filled him with the Spirit of God, with ability and intelligence, with knowledge and all
craftsmanship, to devise artistic designs, to work in gold, silver, and bronze, in cutting
stones for setting, and in carving wood, for work in every craft.

Exodus 31.3-5

Each has his own special gift from God, one of one kind and one of another.

1 Corinthians 7.7

Every good endowment and every perfect gift is from above, coming down from the Father
of lights with whom there is no variation or shadow due to change.

James 1.17

Genius is mainly an affair of energy.

Matthew Arnold, *The Complete Prose Works of Matthew Arnold*, Volume III, edited by R.H. Super, *Lectures and Essays in
Criticism*, Ann Arbor, The University of Michigan Press, 1962, 'The Literary Influence of Academics,' page 238

In every man of genius a new strange force is brought into the world.

Havelock Ellis, *Selected Essays*, J.M. Dent & Sons Ltd., 1936, page 111

Geniuses are the luckiest of mortals because what they must do is the same as what they most want to do.

Samuel W.H. Auden, 'Foreword,' *Markings*, Dag Hammarskjöld, Faber & Faber Ltd., 1964, page 17

The true Genius is a mind of large general powers, accidentally determined to some particular direction.

Samuel Johnson, *Lives of the English Poets*, edited by G.B. Hill, Oxford at the Clarendon Press, 1905, Volume I, page 2, 'Cowley'

Men of genius do not excel in any profession because they labour in it, but they labour in it because they excel.

William Hazlitt, *Hazlitt's Characteristics*, Elkin Mathews & Marrot Ltd., 1827, page 123

Time, Place, and Action, may with pains be wrought,
But Genius must be born, and never can be taught.

John Dryden, *The Poems of John Dryden*, edited by James Kinsley, Oxford at the Clarendon Press, 1958, Volume II, page 853, 'To my Dear Friend Mr. Congreve,' l.59

To believe your own thought, to believe that what is true for you in your private heart is true for all men,—that is genius.

Ralph Waldo Emerson, *Essays*, Bernhard Tauchnitz Edition, 1915, page 34, 'Self-Reliance'

Hast thou any notion what a Man of Genius is? Genius is 'the inspired gift of God.' It is the clearer presence of God Most High in a man. Dim, potential in all men; in this man it has become clear, actual.

Thomas Carlyle, *Past and Present*, Ward, Lock & Co. Ltd., page 199

Genius is the unreserved devotion of the whole soul to the divine, poetic arts, and through them to God, deeming all else, even to our daily bread, only valuable as it helps us to unveil the heavenly face of Beauty.

Samuel Palmer, in David Cecil, *Visionary and Dreamer*, Constable & Company Ltd., 1969, page 63

There are two kinds of genius. The first and highest may be said to speak out of the eternal to the present, and must compel its age to understand it; the second understands its age, and tells it what it wishes to be told.

J.R. Lowell, *My Study Windows*, George Routledge & Sons Ltd., 1905, page 383

... a man of genius should be like a growing boy, who is never, never, and never will be a grown up. He must have a new style and new methods, not for fashion's sake, but because he has outgrown the old ways.

J.B. Yeats, *Letters to His Son W.B. Yeats and Others*, Faber & Faber Ltd., 1944, page 228

I know now that revelation is from the self, but from that age-long memorised self, that shapes the elaborate shell of the mollusc and the child in the womb, that teaches the birds to make their nest; and that genius is a crisis that joins that buried self for certain moments to our trivial daily mind.

W.B. Yeats, *Autobiographies*, Macmillan & Co. Ltd., 1966, page 272

Genius is not a single power, but a combination of great powers. It reasons, but it is not reasoning; it judges, but it is not judgement; it imagines, but it is not imagination; it feels deeply and fiercely, but it is not passion. It is neither, because it is all. It is another name for the perfection of human nature, for Genius is not a fact but an ideal. It is nothing less than the possession of all the powers and impulses of humanity, in their greatest possible strength and most harmonious combination; and the genius of any particular man is great in proportion as he approaches this ideal of universal genius.

Edwin P. Whipple, *Literature And Life*. Lectures, John Chapman, 1851, page 81

He felt there, felt amid the stirring of some wonderful new hope within himself, the genius, the unique power of Christianity; in exercise then, as it has been exercised ever since, in spite of many hindrances, and under the most inopportune circumstances. Chastity,—as he seemed to understand—the chastity of men and women, amid all the conditions, and with the results, proper to such chastity, is the most beautiful thing in the world, and the truest conservation of that creative energy by which men and women were first brought into it. The nature of the family, for which the better genius of old Rome itself had sincerely cared, of the family and its appropriate affections—all that love of one's kindred by which obviously one does triumph in some degree over death—had never been so felt before.

Walter Pater, *Marius the Epicurean*, Macmillan & Co. Ltd., 1902, Volume II, page 110

If one listens to the faintest but constant suggestions of his genius, which are certainly true, he sees not to what extremes, or even insanity, it may lead him; and yet that way, as he grows more resolute and faithful, his road lies. The faintest assured objection which one healthy man feels will at length prevail over the arguments and customs of mankind. No man ever followed his genius till it misled him. Though the result were bodily weakness, yet perhaps no one can say that the consequences were to be regretted, for these were a life in conformity to higher principles. If the day and the night are such that you greet them with joy, and life emits a fragrance like flowers and sweet-scented herbs, is more elastic, more starry, more immortal,—that is your success. All nature is your congratulation, and you have cause momentarily to bless yourself. The greatest gains and values are farthest from being appreciated. We easily come to doubt if they exist. We soon forget them. They are the highest reality. Perhaps the facts most astounding and most real are never communicated by man to man. The true harvest of my daily life is somewhat as intangible and indescribable as the tints of morning or evening. It is a little star-dust caught, a segment of the rainbow which I have clutched.

Henry David Thoreau, *Walden*, The New American Library of World Literature, Inc., 1960, page 147

GLORY

'Glory'—exalted renown, honourable fame; resplendent majesty, beauty, or magnificence, imagined unearthly beauty; state of exaltation, prosperity etc.; circle of light round head or figure of deity or saint, aureole, halo.

I n the story of the creation of man in the book of Genesis, God is depicted as fashioning and shaping man in his own image and likeness, and the last thing he does is breathe into man and man becomes a living being. I take this to mean something of the divine glory can be found in ourselves.

If we want to see this fully worked out in a life, we go to the Gospels—to the person of Jesus Christ. In the Prologue of St John's Gospel we find the words—'And the Word became flesh and dwelt among us, full of grace and truth; we have beheld his glory, glory as of the only Son from the Father.'

Jesus spelt out the implications of this verse for us in a crucial passage later on in St John's Gospel—'The glory which thou hast given me I have given to them, that they may be one even as we are one, I in them and thou in me, that they may become perfectly one.'

St Paul picked this up and described it in these terms— 'For it is the God who said, "Let light shine out of darkness," who has shone in our hearts to give the light of the knowledge of the glory of God in the face of Christ. But we have this treasure in earthen vessels...'

In my early twenties I came across someone who had entered into this heritage, and whose features radiated the glory of God. This meeting with glory changed the whole course of my life, and enabled me in turn to find glory in my 'earthen vessel'.

Ascribe to the Lord, O families of the peoples, ascribe to the Lord glory and strength! Ascribe to the Lord the glory due his name; bring an offering, and come before him! Worship the Lord in holy array; tremble before him, all the earth.

1 Chronicles 16.28-30

Declare his glory among the nations, his marvellous works among all the peoples!

Psalm 96.3

And the Word became flesh and dwelt among us, full of grace and truth, we have beheld his glory, glory as of the only Son from the Father.

John 1.14

The glory which thou hast given me I have given to them, that they may be one even as we are one. I in them and thou in me, that they may become perfectly one.

John 17.22-23

The glory of God is a living Man (i.e. a man fully alive).

S. Irenaeus, *Five Books of S. Irenaeus Against Heresies*, translated by the Rev. John Keble, James Parker & Co., 1872, page 369, Book IV

That is what gives Him the greatest glory—the achieving of great things through the weakest and most improbable means.

Thomas Merton, *The Sign of Jonas*, Sheldon Press, 1976, page 76

When one candle is lighted... we light many by it, and when God hath kindled the Life of His glory in one man's Heart he often enkindles many by the flame of that.

Rufus M. Jones, *Spiritual Reformers in the 16th and 17th Centuries*, Macmillan & Co. Ltd., 1914, page 287

What is the freedom of the godly man? Being absolutely nothing to and wanting absolutely nothing for himself but only the glory of God in all his works.

Meister Eckhart, *Meister Eckhart*, Franz Pfeiffer, translated by C. de B. Evans, John M. Watkins, 1956, Volume I, page 287

The noble hart, that harbours vertuous thought,
And is with child of glorious intent,
Can never rest, untill it forth have brought
Th'eternall brood of gloric excellent.

Edmund Spenser, *Spenser's Faerie Queene*, edited by J.C. Smith, Oxford at the Clarendon Press, 1964, page 55, Book 1, Canto V, st.i, l.1

The principle that governs the universe 'became flesh and dwelt among us and we beheld His glory,' and the impression was as of something that shone through Him from beyond— 'glory as of an Only Begotten Son from a Father'; of One who perfectly represented something and who is perfectly united with it.

William Temple, *Christian Faith and Life*, SCM Press Ltd., 1963, page 34

As we become forgetful of ourselves and entirely filled with His glory, the glory of His righteousness and love, we become transformed into His image... from glory to glory and because we are more like Him, we shall do something that is far more truly His will than what we might have planned out for ourselves in an eager and perhaps impatient generosity.

William Temple, *Basic Convictions*, Hamish Hamilton, 1937, page 29

The glory of God illuminates every part of the structure of the Christian faith:
God
    The glory of God is both to rejoice in His works, and to own their absolute dependence upon the Creator.

Incarnation

It was in humiliation that the glory was revealed on earth. The mission of the Lord was at once the descent of one who trod the road of frustration, ignorance, pain and death and the assent of one who was realizing in humiliation a glory which had been His from all eternity.

Atonement

The glory shewn forth on Calvary was a kingly power mightier than the human and cosmic evil which was ranged against it. The prince of this world was defeated and judged: the world was overcome.

Church

The glory which Christians are to grow into and to manifest by the practical response of the Christian life is a glory which is *theirs* already.

Michael Ramsey, *The Glory of God and the Transfiguration of Christ*, Darton, Longman & Todd Ltd., 1967, page 83

A man does not direct all his actions to the glory of God by forming a conception in his mind, or stirring up a strong imagination upon any action, that that must be for the glory of God: it is not thinking of God's glory that is glorifying of Him . . .

We rather glorify God by entertaining the impressions of His glory upon us, than by communicating any kind of glory to Him. Then does a good man become the tabernacle of God, wherein the divine Shechinah does rest, and which the Divine glory fills, when the frame of his mind and life is wholly according to that idea and pattern which he receives from the mount. We best glorify Him when we grow most like to Him: and we then act most for His glory, when a true spirit of sanctity, justice, meekness, &c., runs through all our actions; when we so live in the world as becomes those that converse with the great Mind and Wisdom of the whole world with that Almighty Spirit that made, supports, and governs all things with that Being from whence all good flows, and in which there is no spot, stain, or shadow of evil; and so, being captivated and overcome by the sense of the Divine loveliness and goodness, we endeavour to be like Him, and conform ourselves, as much as may be, to Him.

John Smith the Platonist, *Select Discourses*, Cambridge at the University Press, 1859, page 417

The Priestly writer seems to have taken over the conception of the *glory of Yahweh* from Ezekiel. The glory was veiled from human sight, except on the rarest occasions, by the cloud. The cloud, which was over the tent and not at the door of it, was the visible sign of Yahweh's presence; but the presence itself was veiled by it. The 'glory of God' is, in effect, the term used to express that which men can *apprehend*, originally by sight, of the presence of God on earth. It was Ezekiel who first used it and described by it the brilliant appearance of God when he came to renew the prophet's call to prophesy amongst the exiles in Babylon after the fall of Jerusalem. It was a second inaugural vision (the first was experienced on Palestinian soil) in which Ezekiel saw God. In describing what he saw in detail, when he comes to the divine majesty seated on the throne he says: 'This was the appearance of the likeness of the glory of God' (Ezek. 1.28). Later we are told that Ezekiel saw the glory of God move out of the Temple eastward to the Mount of Olives, presumably on the way to Babylon where his people were exiled (Ezek.11.23). *Glory* (Heb. *Kabod*) seems to have been a peculiarly happy word to choose, not only for its Hebrew antecedents, but for the way in which its equivalent in translations could readily take over the new Hebrew content. Its primary meaning is that of weight and substance. A man of wealth is a man of substance, of *kabod*. His external appearance and bearing would, in nine cases out of ten, reflect his wealth, and also be called *kabod*. His wealth and dignity demanded and compelled respect and honour from his fellows, and this too was called glory or honour (*kabod*). Hence weight, substance, wealth, dignity, noble bearing and honour all contributed to its meaning. To these fundamental meanings Ezekiel added that of brightness, the dominant element in the chariot vision . . . the word and idea were taken up by the Priestly writer (Ezekiel himself was a priest) to whom we owe the description of it as 'like devouring fire on the top of the mount in the eyes of the children of Israel' (Exod.24.17). In P (the Priestly writer) the idea is used in two ways. First, the appearance of the glory established the fact of Yahweh's presence on the mount and later in the sanctuary

(Exod.24.16f., 29.43, 40.34f.); and, second, it vindicated the rights of Moses and Aaron when the people murmured against them (Exod.16.10, Num.14.10, 16.19,42, 20.6). To God's enemies it was an ominous appearance, verily a *devouring* fire. Outside Ezekiel and P it is found in Zechariah (2.5), Isaiah (24.23, 59.19, 60.1f., all late passages) and Psalms 97.6, 102.16). In the non-priestly passages there is a notable reorientation. The glory is no longer conceived as an actualized or potential experience in this life but as an element in the messianic age.

This new direction of thought came to stay, and glory slowly became eschatological, so that in the New Testament we find it as an integral part of the life of the Kingdom of God, both realized now and expected in the future. The actual and the eschatological elements come together with dynamic certainty in the person of Jesus Christ. The *doxa* (glory) of God, who dwells in light unapproachable (1 Tim.6.16), shone about the shepherds when Christ's birth was announced. On earth the glory of God was made known in him, and men apprehended through him the presence of God. At death he was 'glorified' and sat down at the right hand of God, thus pioneering in a path that men of faith might tread after him and through him share in the glory of God. Henceforth vision of Christ came in the same form as did formerly the vision of God (Acts 22.6,7): the glory of Christ is identifiable with the glory of God. It is in the face of Christ that the light of the knowledge of the glory of God shines in our hearts with creative power (11 Cor.4.6).

Throughout the New Testament Christ is presented as the glory of God made visible on earth to those whose eyes are opened to see it; but it is perhaps in the Fourth Gospel that this conception is most strongly stressed. Behind the Johannine *doxa* (Gk., glory) we must recollect the full biblical richness of the word, as we have described it above, 'We beheld his *doxa*, glory as of the only-begotten from the Father' (John 1.14). The miracles of Christ manifested his *doxa* (2.11). His *doxa* is not the glory of men but of God (5.41, 17.5,22). The great high-priestly prayer of Jesus (John 17) is dominated by the idea of *doxa*, and the entire Passion of Jesus is presented to us as his 'glorification' (17.1): he goes to the cross not as a helpless martyr to his agony, but as a victorious king to his crowning. In the Passion and Resurrection of Christ the utter glory of God is revealed.

L.H. Brockington, in *A Theological Word Book of the Bible*, edited by Alan Richardson, SCM Press Ltd., 1975, page 175

GOD WITHIN

*'God within'—a belief that primarily or in the first instance, God is
to be found in the depths of our being.*

One of our female undergraduates came to see me and asked if I would prepare her for baptism and confirmation. After an affirmative response we met for an hour a week and I put her through a course of formal instruction.

She was duly baptized and confirmed, and by way of follow-up, joined a reflection group. She valued the period of silence and found the discussion enlightening. She felt the group experience a good way of growing in the faith. Not only did this facilitate 'the daily increase' but she was able to learn much from the other members of the group. When the vacation came she asked me to lend her some material so she could reflect at home on her own.

When she returned to college next term we noticed a profound change in her. She was relaxed, cheerful and brimming over with life. She had found one of the topics— 'God Within'—especially helpful. The words of the Master in Herman Hesse's *The Glass Bead Game* had particularly hit home: 'The deity is within *you*, not in ideas and books. Truth is lived, not taught.'

She went on to explain what had happened to her. Initially she had come to a belief in God through ideas and books. The outcome was a belief in a creed, culminating in a belief in Jesus Christ as revealed in the Gospels.

She now came to see this was essentially a belief in a God 'outside herself'. Herman

Hesse's words triggered off a belief in the 'God within'. She was now able to experience God at first hand, Father, Son and Holy Spirit, and found this exhilarating.

As God lives, who has taken away my right, and the Almighty, who has made my soul bitter; as long as my breath is in me, and the spirit of God is in my nostrils; my lips will not speak falsehood, and my tongue will not utter deceit. Far be it from me to say that you are right; till I die I will not put away my integrity from me. I hold fast my righteousness, and will not let it go; my heart does not reproach me for any of my days.

Job 27.2-6

God is our refuge and strength, a very present help in trouble.

Psalm 46.1

In him we live and move and have our being.

Acts 17.28

God is love, and he who abides in love abides in God, and God abides in him.

1 John 4.16

I myself believe that the evidence for God lies primarily in inner personal experiences.

William James, *Pragmatism*, Longmans, Green & Co. Ltd., 1943, page 109

The name of this infinite and inexhaustible depth and ground of all being is *God.*

Paul Tillich, *The Shaking of the Foundations*, SCM Press Ltd., 1949, page 57

Where the creature ends, there God begins to be. God only asks that you get out of his way, in so far as you are creature, and let him be God in you.

Meister Eckhart, *Meister Eckhart*, translated by Raymond B. Blakney, Harper & Row, Publishers, Inc., 1941, page 127

Christian education has done all that is humanly possible; but it has not been enough. Too few people have experienced the divine image as the innermost possession of their own souls.

C.G. Jung, *Psychological Reflections*, selected and edited by Jolande Jacobi, Routledge & Kegan Paul Ltd., 1953, page 308

To get at the core of God at his greatest, one must first get into the core of himself at his least, for no one can know God who has not first known himself. Go to the depths of the soul, the secret place of the Most High, to the roots, to the heights; for all that God can do is focussed there.

Meister Eckhart, *Meister Eckhart*, translated by Raymond B. Blakney, Harper & Row, Publishers, Inc., 1941, page 246

Remember how Saint Augustine tells us about his seeking God in many places and eventually finding Him within himself. Do you suppose it is of little importance that a soul which is often distracted should come to understand this truth and to find that, in order to speak to its Eternal Father and to take its delight in Him, it has no need to go to Heaven or to speak in a loud voice? However quietly we speak, He is so near that He will hear us: we need no wings to go in search of Him but have only to find a place where we can be alone and look upon Him present within us.

St Teresa of Avila, *The Complete Works of St Teresa of Jesus*, translated by E. Allison Peers, Sheed & Ward Ltd., 1978, Volume II, Way of Perfection, page 114

'Oh, if only it were possible to find understanding,' Joseph exclaimed. 'If only there were a dogma to believe in. Everything is contradictory, everything tangential; there are no certainties anywhere. Everything can be interpreted one way and then again interpreted in the opposite sense. The whole of world history can be explained as development and progress and can also be seen as nothing but decadence and meaninglessness. Isn't there any truth? Is there no real and valid doctrine?' The Master had never heard him speak so fervently. He walked on in silence for a little, then said: 'There is truth, my boy. But the doctrine you desire, absolute, perfect dogma that alone provides wisdom, does not exist. Nor should you long for a perfect doctrine, my friend. Rather, you should long for the perfection of yourself. The deity is within *you*, not in ideas and books. Truth is lived, not taught. Be prepared for conflicts, Joseph Knecht—I can see they have already begun.'

Herman Hesse, *The Glass Bead Game*, translated by Richard and Clara Winston, Penguin Books Ltd., 1979, page 79

The Gospel tells us that the kingdom of God is within us first of all. If we cannot find the kingdom of God within us, if we cannot meet God within, in the very depth of ourselves, our chances of meeting Him outside ourselves are very remote. When Gagarin came back from space and made his remarkable statement that he never saw God in Heaven, one of our priests in Moscow remarked, 'If you have not seen Him on earth, you will never see Him in Heaven.' This is also true of what I am speaking about. If we cannot find a contact with God under our own skin, as it were, in this very small world which I am, then the chances are very slight that even if I meet Him face to face, I will recognise Him. St John Chrysostom said, 'Find the door of your heart, you will discover it is the door of the kingdom of God.' So it is inward that we must turn, and not outward—but inward in a very special way. I am not saying that we must become introspective. I don't mean that we must go inward in the way one does in psychoanalysis or psychology. It is not a journey into my *own* inwardness, it is a journey *through* my own self, in order to emerge from the deepest level of self into the place where He is, the point at which God and I meet.

Anthony Bloom, *School for Prayer*, Darton, Longman & Todd, 1970, page 19

There is a young man,
who lives in a world of progress.
He used to worship a God
who was kind to him.
This God had a long white beard,
He lived in the clouds,
but all the same
He was close to the solemn child
who had secretly
shut Him up, in a picture book.
But now,
the man is enlightened.
Now he has been to school,
and has learned to kick a ball,
and to be abject
in the face of public opinion.
He knows too,
that men are hardly removed from monkeys.
You see, he lives in the light
of the twentieth century.
He works, twelve hours a day,
and is able to rent a room,
in a lodging house,
that is not a home.
At night he hangs
a wretched coat
up on a peg on the door
and stares
at the awful jug and basin,
and goes to bed
And the poor coat,
worn to the man's shape,
round-shouldered and abject,

watches him, asleep,
dreaming of all
the essential
holy things,
that he cannot hope to obtain
for two pounds ten a week.
Very soon
he will put off his body,
like the dejected coat
that he hates.
And his body will be
worn to the shape
of twelve hours' work a day
for two pounds ten a week.
If he had only known
that the God in the picture book,
is not an old man in the clouds
but the seed of life in his soul,
the man would have lived.
And his life would have flowered
with the flower of limitless joy.
But he does not know,
and in him
the Holy Ghost
is a poor little bird
in a cage,
who never sings,
and never opens his wings,
yet never, never
desires to be gone away.

Caryll Houselander, 'The Young Man,' in *Let There Be God*, compiled by T.H. Parker and F.J. Teskey, The Religious Education Press Ltd., 1968, page 123

GOOD

'Good'—virtue; positive or comparative excellence; benevolence, kindness, generosity; what is good in a thing, its essence or strength.

I have recently been thinking about some words of Jesus in St Mark's Gospel. To the question—'Good Teacher, what must I do to inherit eternal life?'—Jesus replied, 'Why do you call me good? No one is good but God alone.'

Perhaps there is something more than modesty in this brief reply. I wonder if Jesus wanted to reveal to the rich young ruler the source of his goodness—one of the divine attributes in the depths of his being. In his final advice to the wealthy young man he recommended him to 'go, sell what you have, and give to the poor, and you will have treasure in heaven; and come, follow me'.

Link this up with another verse—'The good man out of the good treasure of his heart produces good'—and this might lead to a deeper understanding of the nature of 'good' and 'goodness'. We might even come to see this as yet another consequence of the divine inbreathing in the Genesis story of the creation of man.

St John's Gospel gives a further slant on the nature of 'good' and 'goodness'. In a certain passage Jesus described himself as 'the good shepherd'. The good shepherd was a tough character, carrying a heavy burden of responsibility. He spent endless days in the mountains looking after the village flock. Often this involved sleepless nights, keeping a vigilant eye on the sheep, protecting them from wild animals, thieves and robbers, sometimes laying down his life for the sheep. For Jesus 'good' and 'goodness' was not a passive concept, but meant activity and costly involvement, right in the thick of life.

And God saw everything that he had made, and behold, it was very good.
Genesis 1.31

Thus says the Lord: 'Stand by the roads, and look, and ask for the ancient paths, where the good way is; and walk in it, and find rest for your souls.'
Jeremiah 6.16

I am the good shepherd. The good shepherd lays down his life for the sheep.
John 10.11

He went about doing good.
Acts 10.38

Be good yourself and the world will be good.
Hindu proverb

I am larger, better than I thought,
I did not know I held so much goodness.
Walt Whitman, *The Complete Poems*, edited by Francis Murphy, Penguin Books Ltd., 1982, page 181, 'Song of the Open Road,' section 5, l.60

Goodness is a special kind of truth and beauty. It is truth and beauty in human behaviour.
H.A. Overstreet, *The Enduring Quest*, Jonathan Cape Ltd., 1931, page 174

Loving-kindness is the better part of goodness. It lends grace to the sterner qualities of which this consists.
W. Somerset Maugham, *The Summing Up*, Bernhard Tauchnitz, 1938, page 242

Look around the Habitable World, how few
Know their own Good; or knowing it, pursue.
John Dryden, *The Poems of John Dryden*, Oxford at the Clarendon Press, 1958, Volume II, page 720, *The Satires of Juvenal*, 'The Tenth Satyr,' l.1

Good, the more
Communicated, more abundant grows.
John Milton, *The Poetical Works of John Milton*, edited by the Rev. H.C. Beeching, Oxford at the Clarendon Press, 1900, page 274, *Paradise Lost*, Book V, l.71

[Goodness] needeth not to enter into the soul, for it is there already, only it is unperceived.
Theologia Germanica, translated by Susanna Winkworth, Stuart & Watkins Ltd., 1966, page 48

Anyone who proposes to do good must not expect people to roll stones out of his way, but must accept his lot calmly if they even roll a few more upon it.
Albert Schweitzer, *Out of My Life and Thought*, Henry Holt and Company Inc., 1949, page 92

There is but one unconditional commandment, which is that we should seek incessantly, with fear and trembling, so to vote and to act as to bring about the very largest total universe of good which we can see.
William James, *The Will To Believe*, Longmans, Green & Co. Ltd., 1904, page 209

He lived in a continuous enjoyment of God and perpetually drew nearer to the Centre of his soul's rest and always stayed God's time of advancement. His spirit was absorbed in the business and employment of becoming perfect in his art and profession—which was the art *of being a good man.*

Rufus M. Jones, said of John Smith, in *Spiritual Reformers in the 16th and 17th Centuries*, Macmillan & Co. Ltd., 1914, page 308

And when we come to think of it, goodness *is* uneventful. It does not flash, it glows. It is deep, quiet, and very simple. It passes not with oratory, it is commonly foreign to riches, nor does it often sit in the places of the mighty: but may be felt in the touch of a friendly hand or the look of a kindly eye.

David Grayson, *Adventures in Contentment*, Andrew Melrose, Ltd., 1946, page 192

The Father was all in all to the Son, and the Son no more thought of his own goodness than an honest man thinks of his honesty. When the good man sees goodness, he thinks of his own evil: Jesus had no evil to think of, but neither does he think of his goodness; he delights in his Father's. 'Why callest thou me good?'

George Macdonald, *Unspoken Sermons*, Second Series, Longmans, Green & Co. Ltd., 1885, page 6

Those people work more wisely who seek to achieve good in their own small corner of the world and then leave the leaven to leaven the whole lump, than those who are for ever thinking that life is vain unless one can act through the central government, carry legislation, achieve political power and do big things.

Herbert Butterfield, *Christianity and History*, G. Bell & Sons Ltd., 1949, page 104

He said to Judas, when he betrayed Him: 'Friend, wherefore art thou come?' Just as if He had said: 'Thou hatest Me and art Mine enemy: yet I love thee and am thy friend....' As though God in human nature were saying: 'I am pure, simple Goodness, and therefore I cannot will, or desire, or rejoice in, or do or give anything but goodness. If I am to reward thee for any evil and wickedness, I must do it with goodness, for I am and have nothing else.'

Theologia Germanica, translated by Susanna Winkworth, Stuart & Watkins Ltd., 1966, page 87

And what rule do you think I walked by? Truly a strange one, but the best in the whole world. I was guided by an implicit faith in God's goodness: and therefore led to the study of the most obvious and common things. For thus I thought within myself: God being, as we generally believe, infinite in goodness, it is most consonant and agreeable with His nature, that the best things should be the most common. For nothing is more natural to infinite goodness, than to make the best things most frequent and only things worthless scarce.

Thomas Traherne, *Centuries*, The Faith Press Ltd., 1969, page 138

I am so sure of God's guiding hand, and I hope I shall never lose that certainty. You must never doubt that I am travelling my appointed road with gratitude and cheerfulness. My past life is replete with God's goodness, and my sins are covered by the forgiving love of Christ crucified. I am thankful for all those who have crossed my path, and all I wish is never to cause them sorrow, and that they like me will always be thankful for the forgiveness and mercy of God and sure of it.

With every power for good to stay and guide me,
comforted and inspired beyond all fear,
I'll live these days with you in thought beside me,
and pass, with you, into the coming year.
The old year still torments our hearts, unhastening:
the long days of our sorrow still endure:
Father, grant to the soul thou hast been chastening
that thou hast promised, the healing and the cure.

Should it be ours to drain the cup of grieving
even to the dregs of pain, at thy command,
we will not falter, thankfully receiving
all that is given by thy loving hand.

Dietrich Bonhoeffer, *Letters and Papers from Prison*, edited by Eberhard Bethge, translated by R.H. Fuller, SCM Press Ltd., 1953, page 185

GRACE

'Grace'—unmerited favour of God, divine regenerating, inspiring
and strengthening influence, condition (also state of grace) of being
so influenced; divinely given talent.

O nce a year the Gurkhas celebrate a big religious festival called Dashera. On the final night the whole battalion gathers together in a huge open-sided hut (donated by Lord Nuffield) and there is feasting, singing, dancing, sketches and role playing, throughout the night. At ten o'clock the following morning the battalion's weapons are assembled, and a specially selected Gurkha officer (noted for his strength) beheads a bullock—usually in one stroke of a double-handed kukri. The blood of the bullock is then sprinkled over the weapons—a blessing for the coming year.

I arrived at the battalion during Dashera, and was intrigued by this ceremony. I particularly enjoyed watching one of the Gurkha dancers. He was brilliant. His sense of rhythm and timing was perfect, and he made it all look so easy. The only word to describe his dancing was *graceful.* This man seemed to me to possess a divinely given talent, and he certainly stole the show in the all-night session. I can still see him dancing in my mind's eye, thirty-six years after the event.

This is only one manifestation of *grace* and there are many others. I still value the simple definition of *grace* I learnt as a child—'God's love in action'—but one of my favourite descriptions is given by Daniel D. Williams. 'The power of grace always remains God's power, but it becomes operative in man and thus fulfills, sustains, and renews human nature.'

The older I get the more I value God's grace.

Moses said, 'I pray thee, show me thy glory.' And he said, 'I will make all my goodness pass before you, and will proclaim before you my name "The Lord"; and I will be gracious to whom I will be gracious, and will show mercy on whom I will show mercy.'

Exodus 33.18-19

Therefore the Lord waits to be gracious to you; therefore he exalts himself to show mercy to you. For the Lord is a God of justice; blessed are all those who wait for him.

Isaiah 30.18

And from his fulness have we all received, grace upon grace.

John 1.16

My grace is sufficient for you, for my power is made perfect in weakness.

2 Corinthians 12.9

When once our grace we have forgot,
Nothing goes right.

William Shakespeare, *Measure for Measure*, Act IV. sc.iv. l.31

God gives His gifts where He finds the vessel empty enough to receive them.

C.S. Lewis, *Williams and The Arthuriad*, Oxford University Press, 1948, page 156

The power of grace always remains God's power but it becomes operative in man and thus fulfils, sustains, and renews human nature.

Daniel D. Williams, in *A Dictionary of Christian Ethics*, edited by John Macquarrie, SCM Press Ltd., 1967, page 139

Grace is not something other than God, imparted by Him; it is the very Love of God (which is Himself) approaching and seeking entry to the soul of man.

William Temple, *Nature, Man and God*, Macmillan & Co. Ltd., 1934, page 485

If you knew how to annihilate self-interest and cast out all affection for the created world, then I would come, and my grace would well up abundantly within you.

Thomas à Kempis, *The Imitation of Christ*, translated by Betty I. Knott, William Collins Sons & Co. Ltd., 1979, page 175

This gift is from God and not of man's deserving. But certainly no one ever receives such a great grace without tremendous labour and burning desire.

Richard of Saint-Victor, *Selected Writings on Contemplation*, translated by Clare Kirchberger, Faber & Faber Ltd., 1957, page 111

But O! th'exceeding grace
Of highest God, that loves his creatures so,
And all his works with mercy doth embrace.

Edmund Spenser, *Spenser's Faerie Queene*, edited by J.C. Smith, Oxford at the Clarendon Press, 1964, page 258, Book 2, Canto VIII, st.i, l.5

Let nobody presume upon his own powers for such exaltation or uplifting of the heart or ascribe it to his own merits. For it is certain that this comes not from human deserving but is a divine gift.

Richard of Saint-Victor, *Selected Writings on Contemplation*, translated by Clare Kirchberger, Faber & Faber Ltd., 1957, page 205

O Lord, I need your grace so much if I am to start anything good, or go on with it, or bring it to completion. Without grace, I have no power to do anything—but nothing is beyond my powers, if your grace gives strength to me.

Thomas à Kempis, *The Imitation of Christ*, translated by Betty I. Knott, William Collins Sons & Co. Ltd., 1979, page 202

I am aware
Of my own unworthiness,
But I am certain
Of Thy boundless grace.

Al-Ansari, *The Persian Mystics*, translated by Sardar Sir Jogendra Sing, John Murray Ltd., 1939, page 51

No one is suddenly endowed with all graces, but when God, the source of all grace, helps and teaches a soul, it can attain this state by sustained spiritual exercises and wisely ordered activity. For without His especial help and inner guidance no soul can reach a state of perfection.

Walter Hilton, *The Ladder of Perfection*, translated by Leo Sherley-Price, Penguin Books Ltd., 1957, page 146

If and when a horror turns up you will then be given Grace to help you. I don't think one is usually given it in advance. 'Give us our daily bread' (not an annuity for life) applies to spiritual gifts too; the little *daily* support for the *daily* trial. Life has to be taken day by day and hour by hour.

C.S. Lewis, *Letters of C.S. Lewis*, edited by W.H. Lewis, Geoffrey Bles Ltd., 1966, page 250

Whoso walks in solitude,
And inhabiteth the wood,
Choosing light, wave, rock, and bird,
Before the money-loving herd,
Into that forester shall pass,
From these companions, power and grace.

Ralph Waldo Emerson, *The Works of Ralph Waldo Emerson*, edited by George Sampson, George Bell & Sons Ltd., 1906, Volume V, *Poems*, 'Woodnotes,' page 37

For the Goodness of God is the highest prayer, and it cometh down to the lowest part of our need. It quickeneth our soul and bringeth it on life, and maketh it for to waxen in grace and virtue. It is nearest in nature and readiest in grace: for *it* is the same grace that the soul seeketh, and ever shall seek till we know verily that He hath us all in Himself enclosed.

Lady Julian of Norwich, *Revelations of Divine Love*, edited by Grace Warrack, Methuen & Co. Ltd., 1949, page 13

The means of grace are arteries to convey the Spirit to us.
Well may we hope if we use them well, that he will come unto us, to inform us by his holy word, to sanctify us by prayer, to comfort us in the sacraments.
These three, prayer, the word and the sacraments are a little trinity which God will bless.
A complete obedience in the conscientious use of his means never went away empty.

Thomas Traherne, in *Landscapes of Glory*, edited by A.M. Allchin, Darton, Longman & Todd, 1989, page 32

Grace, *charis*, in its Greek religious usage means 'divine gift' or 'favor.' Thus a 'grace' was a quality or power usually bestowed by the gods, a quality that could be exhibited by a mortal. The English word 'graceful' reflects this meaning.
Here as in so many cases the Christians used the Greek word in such a way as to make it express a special meaning in the context of the biblical understanding of the relationship of God and humanity. The foundation of the New Testament meaning of grace is given in the Hebrew *hesed*. God's mercy and love through which he overcomes and redeems the sin of his covenanted people. The Septuagint usually renders *hesed* by *eleos*, pity. There is evidence, however, that there was an increasing tendency in the Hellenistic period to use *charis*. Thus the way is prepared for the New Testament use of *charis* to express the specific redemptive action of God in Jesus Christ. Grace thus means the divine forgiveness of sin constituting the new creation, and it also means the power of God communicated to those who enter upon the new life of faith, hope, and love. Thus Paul says, we 'are justified by his grace as a gift, through the redemption which is in Christ Jesus' (Rom.3.24), where grace is the quality and power of the divine action which redeems human beings from sin. Paul also speaks of grace as the continuing action of God which enables the Christian to live the new life. 'God is able to provide you with every blessing (grace) in abundance.' (2 Cor.9.8). Thus also the writer of the letter to the Hebrews appeals to his hearers to have grace whereby we may serve God acceptably with reverence and godly fear (Heb.12.28).

Daniel D. Williams, in *A New Dictionary of Christian Ethics*, edited by James F. Childress and John Macquarrie, SCM Press Ltd., 1986, page 254

Defined in psychological terms, grace is something other than our self conscious personal self, by which we are helped. We have experience of three kinds of such helps—animal grace, human grace and spiritual grace. Animal grace comes when we are living in full accord with our own nature on the biological level—not abusing our bodies by excess, not interfering with the workings of our indwelling animal intelligence by conscious cravings and aversions, but living wholesomely and laying ourselves open to the 'virtue of the sun and the spirit of the air.' The reward of being thus in harmony with Tao or Logos in its physical and physiological aspects is a sense of well-being, an awareness of life as good, not for any reason, but just because it is life. There is no question, when we are in a condition of animal grace, *propter vitam vivendi perdere causas*, for in this state there is no distinction between the reasons for living and life itself. But, of course, the fullness of animal grace is reserved for animals. Man's nature is such that he must live a self-conscious life in time, not in a blissful sub-rational eternity on the hither side of good and evil.

Consequently animal grace is something he knows only spasmodically in an occasional holiday from self-consciousness, or as an accompaniment to other states, in which life is not its own reward but has to be lived for a reason outside itself.

Human grace comes to us either from persons, or from social groups, or from our own wishes, hopes and imaginings projected outside ourselves and persisting somehow in the psychic medium in a state of what may be called second-hand objectivity. We have all had experience of the different types of human grace. There is, for example, the grace which, during childhood, comes from mother, father, nurse or beloved teacher. At a later stage we experience the grace of friends; the grace of men and women morally better and wiser than ourselves; the grace of the *guru*, or spiritual director. Then there is the grace which comes to us because of our attachment to country, party, church or other social organization—a grace which has helped even the feeblest and most timid individuals to achieve what, without it, would have been impossible. And finally there is the grace which we derive from our ideals, whether low or high, whether conceived of in abstract terms or bodied forth in imaginary personifications. To this last type, it would seem, belong many of the graces experienced by the pious adherents of the various religions. The help received by those who devotedly adore or prayer to some personal saint, deity or Avatar is often, we may guess, not a genuinely spiritual grace, but a human grace, coming back to the worshipper from the vortex of psychic power set up by repeated acts (his own and other people's) of faith, yearning and imagination.

Spiritual grace cannot be received continuously or in its fullness, except by those who have willed away their self-will to the point of being able truthfully to say, 'Not I, but God in me.' There are, however, few people so irremediably self-condemned to imprisonment within their own personality as to be wholly incapable of receiving the graces which are from instant to instant being offered to every soul. By fits and starts most of us contrive to forget, if only partially, our preoccupation with 'I,' 'me,' 'mine,' and so become capable of receiving, if only partially, the graces which, in that moment, are being offered us.

Spiritual grace originates from the divine Ground of all being, and it is given for the purpose of helping man to achieve his final end, which is to return out of time and selfhood to that Ground. It resembles animal grace in being derived from a source wholly other than our self-conscious, human selves; indeed, it is the same thing as animal grace, but manifesting itself on a higher level of the ascending spiral that leads from matter to the Godhead. In any given instance, human grace may be wholly good, inasmuch as it helps the recipient in the task of achieving the unitive knowledge of God; but because of its source in the individualized self, it is always a little suspect and, in many cases, of course, the help it gives is help towards the achievement of ends very different from the true end of our existence.

Aldous Huxley, *The Perpetual Philosophy*, Chatto & Windus Ltd., 1947, page 191

GREATNESS

'Greatness'—of remarkable ability, genius, intellectual or practical qualities, loftiness or integrity of character.

At school one of my favourite subjects was history, and in the sixth form we undertook a study of the life of Napoleon and the Napoleonic Wars. He was, our history master felt, one of the greatest men of all time—a military genius.

Recently I came across a record of Napoleon's 'Conversation with General Bertrand at St. Helena.' To my delight I discovered Napoleon himself had made some interesting remarks on greatness.

He is recorded as having said several great men— 'Alexander, Caesar, Charlemagne and myself founded empires. But on what did we rest the creations of our genius? Upon force. Jesus Christ alone founded his empire upon love; and at this hour, millions of men would die for him.'

He added that 'everything in Christ astonishes me. His spirit overawes me, and his will confounds me ... the nearer I approach, the more carefully I examine, everything is above me; everything remains grand,—of a grandeur which overpowers. His religion is a revelation from an intelligence which certainly is not that of man. There is a profound originality which has created a series of words and of maxims before unknown. Jesus borrowed nothing from our science. One can absolutely find nowhere, but in him alone, the imitation or the example of his life.'

In the life of Jesus we find all the qualities mentioned in the dictionary definition of greatness—remarkable ability, genius, intellectual and practical qualities, and a loftiness or integrity of character. His greatness continues to inspire those of us who worship him.

Behold, the Lord our God has shown us his glory and greatness.

Deuteronomy 5.24

Thine, O Lord, is the greatness, and the power, and the glory, and the victory, and the majesty; for all that is in the heavens and in the earth is thine; thine is the kingdom, O Lord; and thou art exalted as head above all. Both riches and honour come from thee, and thou rulest over all. In thy hand are power and might; and in thy hand it is to make great and to give strength to all.

1 Chronicles 29.11-12

But Jesus called them to him and said, 'You know that the rulers of the Gentiles lord it over them, and their great men exercise authority over them. It shall not be so among you; but whoever would be great among you must be your servant, and whoever would be first among you must be your slave; even as the Son of man came not to be served but to serve, and to give his life as a ransom for many.

Matthew 20.25-28

... that the God of our Lord Jesus Christ, the Father of glory, may give you a spirit of wisdom and of revelation in the knowledge of him, having the eyes of your hearts enlightened, that you may know what is the hope to which he has called you, what are the riches of his glorious inheritance in the saints, and what is the immeasurable greatness of his power in us who believe, according to the working of his great might.

Ephesians 1.17-19

Great Hopes make great Men.

Thomas Fuller, M.D., *Gnomologia*, 1732, Dublin, page 67, No.1759

Great souls care only for what is great.

Henri Frédéric Amiel, *Amiel's Journal*, translated by Mrs Humphry Ward, Macmillan & Co. Ltd., 1918, page 137

Great men are the guide-posts and landmarks in the state.

Edmund Burke, *Speeches and Letters on American Affairs*, J.M. Dent & Sons Ltd., 1961, page 51

Nothing great or new can be done without enthusiasm.

Dr Harvey Cushing, in *Dialogues of Alfred North Whitehead*, as recorded by Lucien Price, Max Reinhardt, 1954, page 47

It is a rough road that leads to the heights of greatness.

Seneca, *Epistulae Morales*, Richard M. Gummere, William Heinemann, Volume II, page 285

All great gifts are one-sided and pretty well exclude the others.

Theodor Haecker, *Journal in the Night* translated by Alexander Dru, Harvill Press Ltd., 1950, page 37

No great man lives in vain. The History of the world is but the Biography of great men.

Thomas Carlyle, *Sartor Resartus*, 'Lectures on Heroes,' Chapman & Hall Ltd., 1840, page 206

Great Truths are portions of the soul of man;
Great souls are portions of Eternity.

> J.R. Lowell, *The Poetical Works of James Russell Lowell*, Ward, Lock & Co. Ltd., 1911, page 110, Sonnet No. 6

And I smiled to think God's greatness flowed around our incompleteness,—
Round our restlessness, His rest.

> E.B. Browning, *Elizabeth Barrett Browning's Poetical Works*, Smith, Elder, & Co., 1873, Volume II, page 82, 'Rhyme of the Duchess May,' st. xi

Man's Unhappiness, as I construe, comes of his Greatness; it is because there is an Infinite in him, which with all his cunning he cannot quite bury under the Finite.

> Thomas Carlyle, *Sartor Resartus*, Ward, Lock & Co. Ltd., lxxx, page 127

Greatness after all, in spite of its name, appears to be not so much a certain size as a certain quality in human lives. It may be present in lives whose range is very small.

> Phillips Brooks, *Sermons*, Richard D. Dickinson, 1879, page 14

Greatness is a spiritual condition worthy to excite love, interest, and admiration and the outward proof of possessing greatness is that we excite love, interest, and admiration.

> Matthew Arnold, *The Complete Prose Works of Matthew Arnold*, Volume V, *Culture and Anarchy*, edited by R.H. Super, Ann Arbor, The University of Michigan Press, 1965, 'Sweetness and Light,' page 96

It is difficult to achieve greatness of mind and character where our responsibility is diminutive and fragmentary, where our whole life occupies and affects an extremely limited area.

> Rabindranath Tagore, *Letters to a Friend*, George Allen & Unwin Ltd., 1928, page 90

Altogether it will be found that a quiet life is characteristic of great men, and that their pleasures have not been of the sort that would look exciting to the outward eye.

> Bertrand Russell, *The Conquest of Happiness*, George Allen & Unwin Ltd., 1984, page 49

Great men are the true men, the men in whom Nature has succeeded. They are not extraordinary—they are in the true order. It is the other species of men who are not what they ought to be.

> Henri Frédéric Amiel, *Amiel's Journal*, translated by Mrs Humphry Ward, Macmillan & Co. Ltd., 1918, page 112

All things that we see standing accomplished in the world are properly the outer material result, the practical realisation and embodiment, of Thoughts that dwelt in the Great Men sent into the world.

> Thomas Carlyle, *Sartor Resartus*, 'Lectures on Heroes,' Chapman & Hall Ltd., 1840, page 185

The heights by great men reached and kept
Were not attained by sudden flight,
But they, while their companions slept,
Were toiling upward in the night.

> Henry Wadsworth Longfellow, *The Poetical Works of Longfellow*, Humphrey Milford, Oxford University Press, 1913, page 299, 'The Ladder of St. Augustine,' st.x, l.1

The greatest man is he who chooses the Right with invincible resolution, who resists the sorest temptations from within and without, who bears the heaviest burdens cheerfully, who is calmest in storms and most fearless under menace and frowns, whose reliance on truth, on virtue, on God is most unfaltering and is this a greatness, which is apt to make a show, or which is most likely to abound in conspicuous station?

> William E. Channing, *Self-Culture*, Dutton and Wentworth, Printers, 1838, page 9

He alone deserves the appellation of great, who either achieves great things himself, or teaches how they may be achieved; or who describes with suitable dignity the great achievements of others. But those things only are great, which either make this life of ours happy, or at least comfortable and agreeable as far as is consistent with honesty, or which lead to another and a happier life.

John Milton, *The Works of John Milton*, Columbia University Press, 1933, Volume VIII, page 95, 'Second Defence of the People of England'

It seems that there is a general rule in the moral universe which may be formulated 'The higher, the more in danger.' The 'average sensual man' who is sometimes unfaithful to his wife, sometimes tipsy, always a little selfish, now and then (within the law) a trifle sharp in his deals, is certainly, by ordinary standards, a 'lower' type than the man whose soul is filled with some great Cause, to which he will subordinate his appetites, his fortune, and even his safety. But it is out of the second man that something really fiendish can be made; an Inquisitor, a Member of the Committee of Public Safety. It is great men, potential saints, not little men, who become merciless fanatics. Those who are readiest to die for a cause may easily become those who are readiest to kill for it.

C.S. Lewis, *Reflections on the Psalms*, Geoffrey Bles Ltd., 1958, page 28

GROWING

*'Growing'—increasing in size, height, quality, degree, power etc.,
advancing to maturity, reaching full size.*

I am very fond of two parables which have helped me to understand something of the nature of growing.

The first is the parable of a grain of mustard seed. To the rhetorical question—'What is the kingdom of God like? And to what shall I compare it?'—Jesus answered: 'It is like a grain of mustard seed which a man took and sowed in his garden; and it grew and became a tree, and the birds of the air made nests in its branches.'

A grain of mustard seed is so small it can hardly be seen by the naked eye, and yet it grows to a fair-sized bush, out of all proportion to the original seed. Growing in the kingdom of God is like this, as many of us have been discovering.

The second parable is similar, this time about a grain of wheat. Some Greeks wished to see Jesus. In the company of his disciples Jesus spoke to them a weighty saying: 'Truly, truly, I say to you, unless a grain of wheat falls into the earth and dies, it remains alone; but if it dies, it bears much fruit.'

The grain of wheat does not completely die when sown. The outer case perishes but this lets in the nutrients of the soil which stimulate growth from the centre of the seed. The seed takes root, the stem emerges, and growing begins, leading to much fruit. As before, growing in the kingdom of God is similar to this—out of all proportion to that small grain of wheat.

Visions of Grace contains many 'seeds' of the kingdom of God. Growing comes through reflection, individually or in a group. Abundant growing is the usual consequence.

But I am like a green olive tree in the house of God. I trust in the steadfast love of God for ever and ever.

Psalm 52.8

The righteous flourish like the palm tree, and grow like a cedar in Lebanon. They are planted in the house of the Lord, they flourish in the courts of our God. They still bring forth fruit in old age, they are ever full of sap and green.

Psalm 92.12-14

And he said, 'With what can we compare the kingdom of God, or what parable shall we use for it? It is like a grain of mustard seed, which, when sown upon the ground, is the smallest of all the seeds on earth; yet when it is sown it grows up and becomes the greatest of all shrubs, and puts forth large branches, so that the birds of the air can make nests in its shade.

Mark 4.30-32

And now I commend you to God and to the word of his grace, which is able to build you up and to give you the inheritance among all those who are sanctified.

Acts 20.32

Big oaks from little acorns grow.

Anon.

Why stay we on the earth unless to grow?

Robert Browning, The Poetical Works of Robert Browning, Volume I, Smith, Elder & Co., 1899, page 543, Men and Women, 'Cleon,' l.114

All growth that is not towards God
Is growing to decay.

George Macdonald, Within and Without, Longman, Brown, Green, and Longmans, 1855, page 16

To regret one's own experience is to arrest one's own development. To deny one's own experience is to put a lie into the lips of one's own life. It is no less than a denial of the soul.

Oscar Wilde, The Works of Oscar Wilde, edited by G.F. Maine, William Collins Sons & Co. Ltd., 1948, De Profundis, page 860

A child-like man is not a man whose development has been arrested; on the contrary, he is a man who has given himself a chance of continuing to develop long after most adults have muffled themselves in the cocoon of middle-aged habit and convention.

Aldous Huxley, Music At Night, Chatto & Windus Ltd., 1970, page 332

I would finally just like to advise you to grow through your development quietly and seriously; you can interrupt it in no more violent manner than by looking outwards, and expecting answer from outside to questions which perhaps only your innermost feeling in your most silent hour can answer.

Rainer Maria Rilke, Letters to a Young Poet, translation and commentary by Reginald Snell, Sidgwick and Jackson, 1945, page 13

All the growth of the Christian is the more and more life he is receiving. At first his religion may hardly be distinguishable from the mere prudent desire to save his soul but at last he loses that very soul in the glory of love, and so saves it; self becomes but the cloud on which the white light of God divides into harmonies unspeakable.

George Macdonald, Unspoken Sermons, Second Series, Longmans, Green & Co. Ltd., 1885, page 173

Let us not say
'Spite of this flesh to-day
I strove, made head, gained ground upon the whole!'
As the bird wings and sings,
Let us cry 'All good things
Are ours, nor soul helps flesh more, now, than flesh helps soul.'

Robert Browning, The Poetical Works of Robert Browning, Volume I, Smith, Elder & Co., 1899, page 581, Dramatis Personae, 'Rabbi Ben Ezra,' st.xii, l.1

In this strange life we grow through adversity rather than through success. The greatest lessons we have to learn are those concerned with loss, not gain. Although worldly wisdom emphasises the importance of winning the race to success and affluence, the spiritual path teaches us how to become good and gracious losers. The man who seeks his life will lose it when he dies, but the man who is prepared to lose everything he possesses for the sake of righteousness, enters a new field of experience that is completely at variance with anything he had previously glimpsed.

Martin Israel, *The Pain That Heals*, Hodder & Stoughton Ltd., 1981, page 9

God does not offer Himself to our finite beings as a thing all complete and ready to be embraced. For us He is eternal discovery and eternal growth. The more we think we understand Him, the more He reveals Himself as otherwise. The more we think we hold Him, the further He withdraws, drawing us into the depths of Himself. The nearer we approach Him through all the efforts of nature and grace, the more He increases, in one and the same movement, His attraction over our powers, and the receptivity of our powers to that divine attraction.

Pierre Teilhard de Chardin, *Le Milieu Divin*, William Collins Sons & Co. Ltd., 1960, page 131

There are no short-cuts. There are no crash courses. There is no instant mysticism. It is simply the gentle and gradual change of direction. The change of heart that comes is to stop thinking of yourself and to be open to God, to the wonder of him, to the glory of him and to the love of him.

There are many spiritual 'techniques' that promise 'instant' results. Any technique of prayer is by definition impatient—a disposable method, used until it produces a desired effect, then dropped and taken up again when we want more.

A technique is a goal-oriented thing, necessary if we are involved in learning how to drive a car or grow roses but disastrous if we are learning the way of unlearning, the way of prayer.

A technique in the realm of spirit intensifies our self-centredness. Meditation, in the Christian tradition, is so much more than a technique. It is to be understood as a discipline. It is a discipline in the richest and most positive sense of the word: a learning, a discipleship.

Does it make us think more about ourselves or less about ourselves? That is the Christian touchstone.

John Main OSB, in *The Joy of Being*, selected by Clare Hallward, Darton, Longman & Todd, 1989, page 33

From the beginning of history the Body of Christ, which is the Body of a true humanity, has been growing age by age and every religion has contributed to its growth.

There is one self who has become incarnate in humanity. Humanity in the total course of history is the body of this self.

What becomes of the individual self in this knowledge of the one self? Without doubt the individual loses all sense of separation from the one and enters into the experience of total unity, but the individual still exists. As in nature every element is a unique reflection of the one reality, so every human being is a unique centre of consciousness in the universal consciousness.

Every person grows as he opens himself to the totality of personal being which is found in the supreme person.

This is what is expressed in the doctrine of the mystical Body of Christ. This Body embraces all humanity in the unity of the one person of Christ. This is described by St Augustine as follows: 'There is only one Christ loving himself.'

Bede Griffiths OSB, in *The Universal Christ*, edited by Peter Spink, Darton, Longman & Todd, 1993, page 11

Victorious living does not mean freedom from temptation. *Nor does it mean freedom from mistakes.* We are personalities in the making, limited and grappling with things too high for us. Obviously we, at our very best, will make many mistakes. But these mistakes need not be sins. Our actions are the result of our intentions and our intelligence. Our intentions may be very good, but because the intelligence is limited the action may turn out to be a mistake—a mistake, but not necessarily a sin. For sin comes out of a wrong intention.

Therefore the action carries a sense of incompleteness and frustration, but not of guilt. Victorious living does not mean perfect living in the sense of living without a flaw, but it does mean adequate living and that can be consistent with many mistakes. *Nor does it mean maturity.* It does mean a cleansing away of things that keep from growth, but it is not full growth. In addition to many mistakes in our lives, there will be many immaturities. Purity is not maturity. This Gospel of ours is called the Way. Our feet are on that Way, but only on that Way, we have not arrived at the goal.

Nor does it mean that we may not occasionally lapse into a wrong act which may be called a sin. At that point we may have lost a skirmish, but it doesn't mean we may not still win the battle. We may even lose a battle and still win the war. One of the differences between a sheep and a swine is that when a sheep falls into a mud hole it bleats to get out, while the swine loves it and wallows in it. In saying that an occasional lapse is consistent with victorious living I am possibly opening the door to provide for such lapses. This is dangerous and weakening. There must be no such provision in the mind. There must be an absoluteness about the whole thing. But nevertheless, victorious living can be consistent with occasional failure.

E. Stanley Jones, *Victorious Living*, Hodder & Stoughton Ltd., 1941, page 78

HAPPINESS

'Happiness'—(of person or circumstance) being lucky, fortunate, contented with one's lot.

W hen I was on the staff of Bradford Cathedral, the diocese (of Bradford) celebrated its fiftieth anniversary. As part of the celebrations the bishop decreed every parish in the diocese would produce a wooden model of their church building, and these were to be put on display in the City Hall on a certain day. A model of the cathedral was required as centrepiece, and the provost gave me specifications, and asked me to produce a model in two months' time.

No volunteers were forthcoming, so I got down to work on my next day off. First of all I took a good long look at the cathedral and kept this image in my mind's eye. Next, I bought some balsa wood and glue, and a special knife. I tentatively started the construction process and was soon completely absorbed in what I was doing. The hours sped by and I made good progress.

A week later I resumed work on the model of the cathedral. I got up early and worked from dawn to dusk. I was enjoying myself now, particularly as the model was beginning to take shape. Another week went by. On the next day off I was up early and worked steadily throughout the day. This time I managed to finish the basic construction. All that was needed now were stained glass windows and interior lighting.

Looking back on this experience, I was extremely happy during the building of this model. This has led me to believe one of the main ways of finding happiness lies in creativity, though there are other suggestions in the material of this topic.

Satisfy us in the morning with thy steadfast love, that we may rejoice and be glad all our days.

Psalm 90.14

Happy the people to whom such blessings fall! Happy the people whose God is the Lord!

Psalm 144.15

... that we should keep in mind the words of the Lord Jesus, who himself said, 'Happiness lies more in giving than in receiving.'

Acts 20.35 (NEB)

Behold, we call those happy who were steadfast.

James 5.11

Happiness is neither without us nor within us. It is in God, both without us and within us.

Blaise Pascal, *Pensées*, translated by W.F. Trotter, Random House Inc., 1941, page 154

In every part and corner of our life, to lose oneself is to be gainer; to forget oneself is to be happy.

Robert Louis Stevenson, *Memories & Portraits*, Chatto & Windus Ltd, 1887, page 48

Look inwards, for you have a lasting fountain of happiness at home that will always bubble up if you will but dig for it.

Marcus Aurelius, *The Meditations of Marcus Aurelius*, translated by Jeremy Collier, Walter Scott, page 116

A happy life must be to a great extent a quiet life, for it is only in an atmosphere of quiet that true joy can live.

Bertrand Russell, *The Conquest of Happiness*, George Allen & Unwin Ltd., 1984, page 52

Happiness is more than anything that serene, secure, happy freedom from guilt.

Henrik Ibsen, *Rosmersholm*, translated and edited by James Walter McFarlane, Oxford University Press, 1960, Volume VI, page 349, Act III

The happy people are those who are producing something; the bored people are those who are consuming much and producing nothing.

W.R. Inge, in *The Wit and Wisdom of Dean Inge*, compiled by Sir James Marchant, Longmans, Green & Co. Ltd., 1927, page 55

Wherein lies happiness? In that which becks
Our ready minds to fellowship divine,
A fellowship with essence.

John Keats, *The Poems of John Keats*, edited by E. de Selincourt, Methuen & Co. Ltd. 1907, page 70, 'Endymion,' Book I, l.777

I have come to know happy individuals, by the way, who are happy only because they are whole. Even the lowliest, provided he is whole, can be happy and in his own way perfect.

Johann Wolfgang von Goethe, *Wisdom and Experience*, selections by Ludwig Curtius, translated and edited by Hermann J. Weigand, Routledge & Kegan Paul Ltd., 1949, page 213

A happiness that is sought for ourselves alone can never be found: for a happiness that is diminished by being shared is not big enough to make us happy.

Thomas Merton, *No Man is an Island*, Burns & Oates Ltd., 1974, page 1

Happy the Man, and happy he alone,
He, who can call to day his own:
He, who secure within, can say
Tomorrow do thy worst, for I have liv'd to day.

John Dryden, *The Poems of John Dryden*, edited by James Kinsley, Oxford at the Clarendon Press, 1958, Volume I, page 436, *Horace*, Ode 29, Book III, st.viii, l.65

True happiness is of a retired nature, and an enemy to pomp and noise: it arises, in the first place, from the enjoyment of one's self; and in the next, from the friendship and conversation of a few select companions.

Joseph Addison, *The Works of Joseph Addison*, edited and published by Henry G. Bohn, 1856, Volume II, page 264

If we were to ask the question: 'What is human life's chief concern?' one of the answers we should receive would be: 'It is happiness.' How to gain, how to keep, how to recover happiness, is in fact for most men at all times the secret motive of all they do, and of all they are willing to endure.

William James, *The Varieties of Religious Experience*, William Collins Sons & Co. Ltd., 1974, page 92

Is not making others happy the best happiness? To illuminate for an instant the depths of a deep soul... is to me a blessing and a precious privilege. There is a sort of religious joy in helping to renew the strength and courage of noble minds. We are surprised to find ourselves the possessors of a power of which we are not worthy, and we long to exercise it purely and seriously.

Henri Frédéric Amiel, *Amiel's Journal*, translated by Mrs Humphry Ward, Macmillan & Co. Ltd., 1918, page 239

Happiness is nothing else, as we usually describe it to ourselves, but the enjoyment of some chief good: and therefore the Deity is so boundlessly happy, because it is every way one with its own immense perfection and every thing so much the more feelingly lives upon happiness, by how much the more it comes to partake of God, and to be made like Him... And, as it is impossible to enjoy happiness without a fruition of God so it is impossible to enjoy Him without an assimilation and conformity of our natures to Him in a way of true goodness and godlike perfection.

John Smith the Platonist, *Select Discourses*, Cambridge at the University Press, 1859, page 150

A sentence that I harped on years ago, and one that used to comfort me—so well—was this, 'What I do thou knowest not now, but thou shalt know hereafter.' That saying has always been a perfect treasure to me; I have never been able to get along without it.

A happy life is not built up of tours abroad and pleasant holidays, but of little clumps of violets noticed by the roadside, hidden away almost so that only those can see them who have God's peace and love in their hearts in one long continuous chain of little joys; little whispers from the spiritual world; little gleams of sunshine on our daily work... So long as I have stuck to Nature and the New Testament I have only got happier and happier every day.

Edward Wilson, in *Edward Wilson of the Antarctic*, George Seaver, John Murray Ltd, 1935, page 71

At its highest level... happiness is the ecstasy which mystics have inadequately described. At more humdrum levels it is human love; the delights and beauties of our dear earth, its colours and shapes and sounds; the enchantment of understanding and laughing, and all other exercise of such faculties as we possess; the marvel of the meaning of everything, fitfully glimpsed, inadequately expounded, but ever-present.

Such is happiness: not compressible into a pill; not translatable into a sensation; lost to whoever would grasp it to himself alone; not to be gorged out of a trough, or torn out of another's body, or paid into a bank, or driven along on an autoroute, or fired in gun-salutes, or discovered in the stratosphere. Existing, intangible, in every true response to life, and absent in every false one; propounded through the centuries in every noteworthy word and thought and deed; expressed in art and literature and music; in vast cathedrals and tiny melodies; in everything that is harmonious, and in the unending heroism of imperfect men reaching after perfection.

Malcolm Muggeridge, *Muggeridge Through the Microphone*, edited by Christopher Ralling, BBC, 1967, page 64

There are various ways of being happy, and every man has the capacity to make his life what it needs to be for him to have a reasonable amount of peace in it. Why then do we persecute ourselves with illusory demands, never content until we feel we have conformed to some standard of happiness that is not good for us only, but for *everyone*? Why can we not be content with the secret gift of happiness that God offers us, without consulting the rest of the world? Why do we insist, rather, on a happiness that is approved by the magazines and TV? Perhaps because we do not believe in a happiness that is given to us for nothing. We do not think we can be happy with a happiness that has no price tag on it. If we are fools enough to remain at the mercy of the people who want to sell us happiness, it will be impossible for us ever to be content with anything. How would they profit if we became content? We would no longer need their new product. The last thing the salesman wants is for the buyer to become content. You are of no use in our affluent society unless you are always just about to grasp what you never have.

Thomas Merton, *Conjectures of a Guilty Bystander*, Burns & Oates Ltd., 1968, page 84

Fundamental happiness depends more than anything else upon what may be called a friendly interest in persons and things. A friendly interest in persons is a form of affectionateness, but not the form which is grasping and possessive and seeking always an emphatic response. This latter form is very frequently a source of unhappiness. The kind that makes for happiness is the kind that likes to observe people and finds pleasure in their individual traits, that wishes to afford scope for the interests and pleasures of those with whom it is brought into contact without desiring to acquire power over them or to secure their enthusiastic admiration. The person whose attitude towards others is genuinely of this kind will be a source of happiness and a recipient of reciprocal kindness. His relations with others, whether slight or serious, will satisfy both his interests and his affections; he will not be soured by ingratitude, since he will seldom suffer it and will not notice it when he does.

The same idiosyncrasies which would get on another man's nerves to the point of exasperation will be to him a source of gentle amusement. He will achieve without effort results which another man, after long struggles, will find to be unattainable. Being happy in himself, he will be a pleasant companion, and this in turn will increase his happiness. But all this must be genuine; it must not spring from an idea of self-sacrifice inspired by a sense of duty. A sense of duty is useful in work, but offensive in personal relations. People wish to be liked, not to be endured with patient resignation. To like many people spontaneously and without effort is perhaps the greatest of all sources of personal happiness. I spoke also of what I call a friendly interest in things. This phrase may perhaps seem forced; it may be said that it is impossible to feel friendly to things. Nevertheless, there is something analagous to friendliness in the kind of interest that a geologist takes in rocks, or an archeologist in ruins, and this interest ought to be an element in our attitude to individuals or societies. It is possible to have an interest in things which is hostile rather than friendly. A man might collect facts concerning the habitats of spiders because he hated spiders and wished to live where they were few. This kind of interest would not afford the same satisfaction as the geologist derives from his rocks. An interest in impersonal things, though perhaps less valuable as an ingredient in everyday happiness than a friendly attitude towards our fellow creatures, is nevertheless very important. The world is vast and our powers are limited. If all our happiness is bound up entirely in our personal circumstances it is difficult not to demand of life more than it has to give. And to demand too much is the surest way of getting even less than is possible. The man who can forget his worries by means of a genuine interest in, say, the Council of Trent, or the life history of stars, will find that, when he returns from his excursion into the impersonal world, he has acquired a poise and calm which enable him to deal with his worries in the best way, and he will in the meantime have experienced a genuine even if temporary happiness. The secret of happiness is this: let your interests be as wide as possible, and let your reactions to the things and persons that interest you be as far as possible friendly rather than hostile.

Bertrand Russell, *The Conquest of Happiness*, George Allen & Unwin Ltd., Unwin Paperbacks, 1978, page 120

HEART

'Heart'—the seat of feeling, understanding, and thought. The seat of one's inmost thoughts and secret feelings; one's inmost being.

When I was chaplain *to* University College, London, I used to run a chaplaincy house in Woburn Square. Ten students lived in this house, plus the black cat, 'Satan'. They stayed for a year and then moved on to other accommodation, being replaced by a new intake. Living under the same roof for six years, I came to know the students well and learnt a thing or two about the heart.

One year a promising Brazilian artist, studying at The Slade School of Art (a part of University College, London), came to live in our chaplaincy house. She was extremely gifted, not only as a budding artist, but also as a brilliant pianist.

Occasionally in the evenings, when her art work had not been going particularly well, she would have a session on the piano. She would start with a few simple scales, and these would become more complex, building up to a terrific crescendo. The house throbbed and vibrated as she opened up her heart and gave vent to her feelings of frustration and creativity. I half-listened to the music and came to understand something of what she was going through.

The practices of reflection, meditation and contemplation help us to understand the inner thoughts and feelings of the heart. For many years I have kept a journal (or spiritual diary). I greatly enjoy mulling over a quotation, working out a variety of thoughts and feelings which come to the surface during this disciplined time of silence. I have come to regard this as a 'listening' form of prayer in which the heart is fully engaged.

You shall love the Lord your God with all your heart, and with all your soul, and with all your might.

Deuteronomy 6.5

The Lord sees not as man sees; man looks on the outward appearance, but the Lord looks on the heart.

1 Samuel 16.7

Out of the abundance of the heart the mouth speaks.

Matthew 12.34

Did not our hearts burn within us while he talked to us on the road, while he opened to us the scriptures?

Luke 24.32

It is the heart which experiences God, and not the reason.

Blaise Pascal, *Pensées*, translated by W.F. Trotter, Random House Inc., 1941, page 95

Man *becomes* man only by the intelligence, but he *is* man by the heart.

Henri Frédéric Amiel, *Amiel's Journal*, translated by Mrs Humphry Ward, Macmillan & Co. Ltd., 1918, page 12

The 'heart' in the biblical sense is not the inner life, but the whole man in relation to God.

Dietrich Bonhoeffer, *Letters and Papers from Prison*, edited by Eberhard Bethge, translated by R.H. Fuller, SCM Press Ltd., 1967, Second Revised Edition, page 192

Go to your bosom,
Knock there, and ask your heart what it doth know.

William Shakespeare, *Measure For Measure*, Act II, sc.ii. l.136

Better to have the poet's heart than brain,
To feel than write.

George Macdonald, *Within and Without*, Longman, Brown, Green, and Longmans, 1855, page 93

His heart was as great as the world, but there was no room in it to hold the memory of a wrong.

Ralph Waldo Emerson, *The Works of Ralph Waldo Emerson*, edited by George Sampson, George Bell & Sons Ltd., 1906, Volume III, *Society and Solitude: Letters and Social Aims: Addresses*, page 350

Ye whose hearts are fresh and simple,
Who have faith in God and Nature.

Henry Wadsworth Longfellow, *The Poetical Works of Longfellow*, Humphrey Milford, Oxford University Press, 1913, page 203, *Hiawatha*, 'Introduction,' l.88

The logic of the heart is usually better than the logic of the head, and the consistency of sympathy is superior as a rule for life to the consistency of the intellect.

Randolph Bourne, *Youth and Life*, Constable & Co. Ltd., 1913, page 244

And about feelings: all feelings are pure which gather you and lift you up; a feeling is impure which takes hold of only one side of your being and so distorts you.

Rainer Maria Rilke, *Letters to a Young Poet*, translation by Reginald Snell, Sidgwick & Jackson, 1945, page 41

Do not cry out to God
Your own heart is the source
from which He flows unceasingly
unless you stop its course.

Angelus Silesius, *The Book of Angelus Silesius*, translated by Frederick Franck, Wildwood House Ltd., 1976, page 120

True conviction springs from the heart. As the real seat of conscience, it is a far more reliable judge than the understanding of what is permissible and what is not. The latter, for all its subtlety and discernment, is likely to miss the central point.

Johann Wolfgang von Goethe, *Wisdom and Experience*, selections by Ludwig Curtius, translated and edited by Hermann J. Weigand, Routledge & Kegan Paul Ltd., 1949, page 133

It is a fine thing to establish one's own religion in one's heart, not to be dependent on tradition and second hand ideals. Life will seem to you, later, not a lesser, but a greater thing. This which is a great torment now, will be a noble thing to you later on.

D.H. Lawrence, *The Letters of D.H. Lawrence*, edited by James T. Boulton, Cambridge University Press, 1979, Volume I, page 256

The heart has its reasons, which reason does not know. We feel it in a thousand things. I say that the heart naturally loves the Universal Being, and also itself naturally, according as it gives itself to them; and it hardens itself against one or the other at its will. You have rejected the one, and kept the other. Is it by reason that you love yourself?

Blaise Pascal, *Pensées*, translated by W.F. Trotter, Random House Inc., 1941, page 95

Yet if, putting aside for the moment all conventions and custom, one will look quietly within himself, he will perceive that there are most distinct and inviolable inner forces, binding him by different ties to different people, and with different and inevitable results according to the quality and the nature of the affection bestowed—that there is in fact in that world of the heart a kind of cosmical harmony and variety, and an order almost astronomical.

Edward Carpenter, *Love's Coming-of-Age*, George Allen & Unwin Ltd., 1923, page 176

The heart is to be understood here, not in its ordinary meaning, but in the sense of the 'inner man.' We have within us an inner man, according to the Apostle Paul, or a hidden man of the heart, according to the Apostle Peter. It is the God-like spirit that was breathed into the first man, and it remains with us continuously, even after the Fall. It shows itself in the fear of God, which is founded on the certainty of God's existence, and in the awareness of our complete dependence on Him, in the stirrings of conscience and in our lack of contentment with all that is material.

Theophan the Recluse, in *The Art of Prayer, An Orthodox Anthology*, compiled by Igumen Chariton of Valamo, translated by E. Kadloubovsky and E.M. Palmer, edited by Timothy Ware, Faber & Faber Ltd., 1973, page 191

The Kingdom of Heaven is among us and we must be open to it now. As St Peter says, we must be alive in the Spirit and become fully alive with the life of God. As Christians we must never settle for less.

Christian life is not a question of just getting through our lives; every word of the New Testament suggests to us that it is of supreme importance that we live our lives in a state of continuous expansion of heart and spirit, growing in love and becoming more firmly rooted in God.

Above all, know from your own heart, from your own experience, that you were created for infinite expansion of spirit. Every act of faith is a step into the infinite expansion of God.

John Main OSB, in *The Joy of Being*, selected by Clare Hallward, Darton, Longman & Todd, 1989, page 60

We are what we see; we create what we see; our rank in the scale of being is determined by the objects of our interest and love. There is absolutely no other way of rising in the scale of being, of realizing our true destiny, of filling our allotted place in the chain of spiritual life, than by ascending in heart and mind to the spiritual world, having our conversation there, setting our affections on things above... We can transcend the limitations of our finite existence; we can live the life of the hidden man of the heart. Such a life is not foreign to the nature of the soul. The way to it is by love and yearning, which are natural to the soul when she sees glimpses of her father's house, and the home from which she has been exiled.

W.R. Inge, *The Awakening of the Soul*, edited by Prebendary A.F. Judd, A.R. Mowbray & Co. Ltd., 1959, pages 30, 26

HOLINESS

*'Holiness'—being consecrated, sacred; state of belonging to,
commissioned by, devoted to, God; state of high moral excellence.*

A t the end of every academic year at University College, London, a group of twenty of
us would go on a pilgrimage. One year we decided to make for Holy Island (or
Lindisfarne Island), two miles off the Northumberland coast. We hired a minibus and
drove to Hexham, and from then onwards walked to Holy Island, sleeping at night on
church hall floors en route. Each day we walked about sixteen miles, whilst the minibus
transported our luggage and equipment to the next destination—another hard church
hall floor. We took it in turns to cook the evening meal, and usually had a short service
before settling down for the night.

We timed our arrival at Holy Island well, and were able to cross the causeway at low
tide, without any difficulty. We then made for a small island, off Holy Island. Here lay the
ruins of a little chapel, at one time frequented by St Cuthbert when he needed peace and
quiet. We clambered over the rocks before an incoming tide, and formed a small circle
within the secluded ruined walls of the chapel. In the evening sun and with the sound of
water lapping all around us we had a quiet celebration of Holy Communion to mark the
climax of our pilgrimage.

We could well understand why St Cuthbert had chosen this site for some peace and
quiet. When the tide was in, this small island was entirely cut off from Holy Island. We
quickly sensed the special atmosphere of this sacred and holy place. For a few precious
moments we had a strange awareness of the numinous, and then had to make a hasty
retreat to beat the tide.

> You shall be holy; for I the Lord your God am holy.
> Leviticus 19.2

> Worship the Lord in the beauty of holiness.
> 1 Chronicles 16.29 (AV)

Since we have these promises, beloved, let us cleanse ourselves from every defilement of
body and spirit, and make holiness perfect in the fear of God.
2 Corinthians 7.1

… and be renewed in the spirit of your minds, and put on the new nature, created after the
likeness of God in true righteousness and holiness.
Ephesians 4.23-24

> There is no true Holiness, without Humility.
> Thomas Fuller, M.D., *Gnomologia*, 1732, Dublin, page 214, No. 4924

There is nothing holier, in this life of ours, than the first consciousness of love,—the first
fluttering of its silken wings.
Henry Wadsworth Longfellow, *Hyperion*, George Routledge & Sons Ltd., 1887, page 215

A true love to God must begin with a delight in his holiness, and not with a delight in any
other attribute: for no other attribute is truly lovely without this.
Jonathan Edwards, *A Treatise concerning Religious Affections*, Chalmers and Collins, 1825, page 323

Think of a white cloud as being holy, you cannot love it but think of a holy man within the
cloud, love springs up in your thoughts, for to think of holiness distinct from man is
impossible to the affections.
William Blake, *The Complete Writings of William Blake*, edited by Geoffrey Keynes, Oxford University Press, 1974, page
90, 'Annotations to Swedenborg's Divine Love,' page 12

The measure of your holiness is proportionate to the goodness of your will. Consider then how good your will is, and the degree of your holiness will be clear to you. For every one is as holy, as he is good of heart.

John of Ruysbroeck, *The Seven Steps of the Ladder of Spiritual Love*, translated by F. Sherwood Taylor, Dacre Press, 1942, page 15

He that sees the beauty of holiness, or true moral good, sees the greatest and most important thing in the world, which is the fulness of all things, without which all the world is empty... Unless this is seen, nothing is seen that is worth the seeing; for there is no other true excellency or beauty.

Jonathan Edwards, *A Treatise concerning Religious Affections*, Chalmers and Collins, 1825, page 349

Our progress in holiness depends on God and ourselves—on God's grace and on our will to be holy. We must have a real living determination to reach holiness. 'I will be a saint' means I will despoil myself of all that is not God; I will strip my heart of all created things; I will live in poverty and detachment; I will renounce my will, my inclinations, my whims and fancies, and make myself a willing slave to the will of God.

Mother Teresa of Calcutta, in Malcolm Muggeridge, *Something Beautiful for God*, William Collins Sons & Co. Ltd., 1983, page 66

The primary characteristic of the Church is neither its missionary enterprise which is the essence of Apostolicity, nor its universal scope which is its Catholicity, but the fact that it is constituted by the redeeming act of God in Christ and is sustained by the indwelling divine Spirit, or in short its Holiness. And the first way in which it is called to be itself is neither through missionary extension nor through influence upon national life but through inward sanctification.

William Temple, *Citizen and Churchman*, Eyre & Spottiswoode Ltd., 1941, page 98

All human love is a holy thing, the holiest thing in our experience. It is the chief mode of initiation into the mysteries of the divine life, the most direct point of contact with the nature of our Creator. 'He prayeth best who loveth best.' Pure affection 'abides' in a sense in which nothing else abides. It is rooted in the eternal, and cannot be destroyed by any of the changes and chances of mortal life. It is a relation between immortal spirits, which in the eternal world are united together solely by likeness of nature so that death not only makes no break in the ties of pure affection, but liberates it from adventitious obstacles which at present only impede its free action and dull its radiance. When we know even as we are known, we shall know our friends and be known by them, to a degree which we cannot even imagine now.

W.R. Inge, *Speculum Animae*, Longmans, Green & Co. Ltd., 1911, page 50

The idea of *holiness* finds a new emphasis in the early Church. In the new covenant the role of the 'holy nation' is now taken over by the Christians; they are the *ecclesia* of God, they are called to be holy, they are the elect race, the holy nation, the people for God's possession (1 Peter 2.9).

The use of *hoi hagioi*, the holy ones, as the normal description of the Christians, brings out the new and overwhelming emphasis upon holiness in Christianity.

So life in the Spirit is holiness.

Possessing holiness in the call of God and in the Spirit of holiness, the Church grows along the way of Christ's holiness. Unity, holiness, truth; as the prayer of our Great High Priest is indivisible, so the fulfilment is indivisible too. It is useless to think that we can look for unity in Christ's name unless we are looking no less for holiness in his obedience and for the realization of the truth which he has revealed.

All the while Christ the Head of the Church goes on in his mercy using the Church, divided though it be, to make known his truth and unity and to lead many in the way of saintliness.

Michael Ramsey, in *Gateway to God*, edited by Lorna Kendall, Darton, Longman & Todd, 1988, page 57

It is very important for the comprehension of holiness to understand that it has two poles: *God* and the *World*. Its source, its fulcrum and its content is God; but its point of impact, the place into which it is born, where it develops and also where it is expressed in terms of Christ's salvation, is the world, this ambiguous world which, on the one hand, was created by God and is the object of such love that the Father gave His only-begotten Son for its salvation, and on the other hand, has fallen into the slavery of evil. This pole of holiness which relates to the world therefore has two aspects: a vision of the world as God willed it, as He loves it, and at the same time an asceticism which requires us to disengage ourselves from the world and free the world from the grip of Satan.

This second element, this battle which is our vocation, is part and parcel of holiness. The Desert Fathers, the ascetics of early times, did not flee from the world in the sense in which modern man sometimes tries to escape its grip in order to find a haven of security, they set out to conquer the Enemy in battle. By the grace of God, in the power of the Spirit, they were engaging in combat.

Anthony Bloom, *God and Man*, Darton, Longman & Todd, 1971, page 73

All holiness is God's holiness in us: it is a holiness that is participation and, in a certain way, more than participation, because as we participate in what we can receive from God, we become a revelation of that which transcends us. Being a limited light we reveal the light. But we should also remember that in this life in which we are striving towards holiness, our spirituality should be defined in very objective and precise terms. When we read books on spirituality or engage in studying the subject, we see that spirituality, explicitly or implicitly, is repeatedly defined as an attitude, a state of soul, an inner condition, a type of interiority and so on. In reality, if you look for the ultimate definition and try to discover the inner core of spirituality, you find that spirituality does not consist in the states of soul that are familiar to us, but that it is the presence and action of that holy spirit in us, by us and through us in the world. It is not fundamentally a matter of the way in which we express it.

There is an absolute objectivity both to holiness and to the spirituality which is expressed in it. Spirituality is that of the Spirit; didn't St Paul tell us that it is the holy Spirit who teaches us to say: 'Abba, Father'? Doesn't he mean that it is the holy Spirit, God Himself, who shapes in us the knowledge of God? And, furthermore, there is no other holiness than that of God; it is as the Body of Christ that we can participate in holiness, in Christ and in the Holy Spirit.

Anthony Bloom, *God and Man*, Darton, Longman & Todd, 1971, page 93

HOPE

'Hope'—expectation and desire combined (of thing, of doing, that);
feeling of trust.

A few weeks after joining the 2nd Gurkhas in Singapore I was appointed cross country running officer. We used to train early in the morning and late in the evening to avoid the heat of the day. On level ground I was more than able to hold my own, but when it came to hills I was completely outclassed. The Gurkhas have very strong legs, developed from living in the mountains of Nepal. This enabled them to go up hills quickly and come down equally quickly, without falling over. This was a physical impossibility for me— much to their amusement.

One evening we went on a training run. We were running over level ground, keeping together as a group. When we were a considerable distance from the barracks our star runner tripped over a root, and fell badly on the side of a monsoon drain. To my great horror a great gash appeared just below his knee and blood was gushing out of this huge cut.

I had not been faced with this sort of situation before and was hoping against hope I would do the right thing. Before I could work out what to do, the group beat me to it and took spontaneous action—a consequence of their training. One of them pinched the gash with his fingers and held them there, stopping the flow of blood. The others formed a human stretcher and carried him back to the barracks on their shoulders. We headed straight for the medical centre, and the doctor did the rest.

Sometimes we find ourselves in seemingly impossible situations. It is then that we fall back on hope and pray that the right course of action will present itself.

Why are you so cast down, O my soul, and why are you disquieted within me? Hope in God; for I shall again praise him, my help and my God.
Psalm 42.5

But I will hope continually, and will praise thee yet more and more.
Psalm 71.14

May the God of hope fill you with all joy and peace in believing, so that by the power of the Holy Spirit you may abound in hope.
Romans 15.13

Therefore gird up your minds, be sober, set your hope fully upon the grace that is coming to you at the revelation of Jesus Christ.
1 Peter 1.13

Hope in action is charity, and beauty in action is goodness.
Miguel de Unamuno, *The Tragic Sense of Life in Men and in Peoples*, Macmillan & Co. Ltd., 1921, page 203

Hope is itself a species of happiness, and, perhaps, the chief happiness which this world affords.
Samuel Johnson, *Boswell's Life of Johnson*, edited by G.B. Hill, revised by L.F. Powell, Oxford at the Clarendon Press, 1934, Volume I, page 368

To hope till Hope creates
From its own wreck the thing it contemplates.
Percy Bysshe Shelley, *The Poetical Works of Percy Bysshe Shelley*, edited by H. Buxton Forman, George Bell & Sons Ltd., 1892, Volume III, page 257, *Prometheus Unbound*, Act IV, l.573

I live on hope and that I think do all
Who come into this world.
Robert Bridges, *Poetical Works of Robert Bridges*, Humphrey Milford, Oxford University Press, 1913, page 218, Sonnet: 'The Growth of Love,' st.lxiii, l.1

So, when dark thoughts my boding spirit shroud,
Sweet Hope, celestial influence round me shed.
John Keats, *The Poems of John Keats*, edited by E. de Selincourt, Methuen & Co. Ltd., 1907, page 19, 'To Hope,' concluding lines

Hope springs eternal in the human breast:
Man never is, but always to be blest.
Alexander Pope, *An Essay on Man*, introduction by Henry Morley, Cassell and Company Ltd., 1905, Epistle I, page 18

The virtue of hope is an orientation of the soul towards a transformation after which it will be wholly and exclusively love.
Simone Weil, *Gateway to God*, edited by David Raper, with the collaboration of Malcolm Muggeridge and Vernon Sproxton, William Collins Sons & Co. Ltd., 1974, page 131

Anything that is found to stimulate hope should be seized upon and made to serve. This applies to a book, a film, a broadcast, or a conversation with someone who can impart it.
Hubert van Zeller, *Considerations*, Sheed & Ward Ltd., 1974, page 100

Christian Hope is the consecration of desire, and desire is the hardest thing of all to consecrate. That will only happen as you begin to think how lovely the life according to Christ is.
William Temple, *Christian Faith and Life*, SCM Press Ltd., 1963, page 44

Hope like the gleaming taper's light
Adorns and cheers our way
And still as darker grows the night
Emits a brighter ray.

Oliver Goldsmith, *Collected Works of Oliver Goldsmith*, edited by Arthur Friedman, Oxford at the Clarendon Press, 1966, Volume IV, page 222, *The Captivity*, Act II. l.135

Know then, whatever cheerful and serene
Supports the mind, supports the body too.
Hence the most vital movement mortals feel
Is Hope; the balm and life-blood of the soul.

John Armstrong, *The Art of Preserving Health*, 1756, Book IV, page 54

Hope to the last... Always hope;... Never leave off hoping; it don't answer... Don't leave a stone unturned. It's always something to know you've done the most you could. But don't leave off hoping, or it's no use doing anything. Hope, hope, to the last!

Charles Dickens, *Nicholas Nickleby*, The Gresham Publishing Company, 1904, page 528

For if you find hope in the ground of history, you are united with the great prophets who were able to look into the depth of their times, who tried to escape it, because they could not stand the horror of their visions, and who yet had the strength to look to an even deeper level and there to discover hope.

Paul Tillich, *The Shaking of the Foundations*, SCM Press Ltd., 1949, page 59

The ability to hope is the greatest gift that God could make to man.

When man is endowed with hope, he overcomes the obstacles in which he is ensnared.

When man hopes, he dies already seeing his body in the resurrection light.

When man hopes, he overcomes fear, understands the purpose of ordeal, puts his trust in God, believes in things which are impossible, feels God's presence in the darkness, begins to pray. Abraham's hope is one of the wonders of mankind, and the hope of the martyrs is the radiance of the Church.

Hope is born when man experiences the abyss of his helplessness, as Israel did in Babylon, as Jeremiah when lowered into the prison cistern, as Jesus on the Cross.

And now I approach Jesus Forsaken with greater understanding. In him, I see all the world's suffering concentrated, the redemptive fire of mankind in evolution, the key to love's greatest secret.

Carlo Carretto, *Summoned by Love*, translated by Alan Neame, Darton, Longman & Todd, 1977, page 116

Those with hope do not get tangled up with concerns of how their wishes will be fulfilled. So, too, their prayers are not directed toward the gift, but toward the one who gives it. Their prayers might still contain just as many desires, but ultimately it is not a question of having a wish come true but of expressing an unlimited faith in the giver of all good things...

Hope is based on the premise that the other gives only what is good. Hope includes an openness by which you wait for the other to make his loving promise come true, even though you never know when, where or how this might happen.

The person who prays with hope might still ask for many things; he or she might ask for everything, and very concretely, like nice weather or an advancement. This concreteness is even a sign of authenticity. For if you ask only for faith, hope, love, freedom, happiness, modesty, humility, etc., without making them concrete... you probably haven't really involved God in your real life. But if you pray in hope, all those concrete requests are merely ways of expressing your unlimited trust in him who fulfills all his promises, who holds out for you nothing but good, and who wants for himself nothing more than to share his goodness with you.

Henri J.M. Nouwen, in *Circles of Love*, arrangement by John Garvey, Darton, Longman & Todd, 1990, page 33

HUMILITY

*'Humility'—the faculty of being humble, or having a lowly opinion of oneself;
meekness, lowliness, humbleness; the opposite of pride or haughtiness.*

William Temple once wrote, 'The source of humility... is the habit of realizing the presence of God.' I wonder if humility provides us with another illustration of the outworking of the Genesis story of the creation of man.

As we have seen, two truths come out of this story. First, God is depicted as fashioning and shaping man in his own image and likeness and the last thing he does is breathe into man and man becomes a living being. Secondly, that which is fashioned and shaped in the image and likeness of God is taken from the dust of the earth. Hence man has something akin to a divine potential along with his 'earthiness' and 'creatureliness'. Sadly he has tended to centre himself on the earthy and creaturely, ignoring his rich divine inheritance.

If we want to see this fully and correctly worked out in a life we go to the person of Jesus Christ. As Jesus went through life he discovered something of the divine in his own nature—Father, Holy Spirit, life, light, truth, joy, love and so on. He centred himself on this divine side of his nature and accepted the earthy and creaturely in a subservient yet equally vital role. As he went through life he developed the habit of realizing the presence of God, and his life became for us a true pattern of humility. John the Baptist got the message with his retort—'He must increase, I must decrease.' What Christ experienced, we can all in some measure also experience—*if we have humility.* We, too, must develop his habit of realizing the presence of God.

O Lord, thou wilt hear the desire of the meek; thou wilt strengthen their heart, thou wilt incline thy ear.
Psalm 10.17

The fear of the Lord is instruction in wisdom, and humility goes before honour.
Proverbs 15.33

He has filled the hungry with good things, and the rich he has sent empty away.
Luke 1.53

Put on then, as God's chosen ones, holy and beloved, compassion, kindness, lowliness, meekness, and patience, forbearing one another and, if one has a complaint against another, forgiving each other; as the Lord has forgiven you, so you also must forgive.
Colossians 3.12-13

Show yourself humble in all things.
Thomas à Kempis, *The Imitation of Christ*, translated by Betty I. Knott, William Collins Sons & Co. Ltd., 1979, page 150

True humility is contentment.
Henri Frédéric Amiel, *Amiel's Journal*, translated by Mrs Humphry Ward, Macmillan & Co. Ltd., 1918, page 46

Humility like darkness reveals the heavenly lights.
Henry David Thoreau, *Walden*, The New American Library of World Literature, Inc., 1960, page 218

He that is humble, ever shall
Have God to be his Guide.
John Bunyan, *The Pilgrim's Progress*, J.M. Dent & Sons, 1964, page 237

True humility,
The highest virtue, mother of them all.
Alfred, Lord Tennyson, *The Poems of Tennyson*, edited by Christopher Ricks, Longmans, Green & Co. Ltd., 1969, page 1674, No.471, 'The Holy Grail,' 1.445

The Holy Ghost flows into the soul as fast as she is poured forth in humility and so far as she has gotten the capacity. He fills all the room he can find.

Meister Eckhart, *Meister Eckhart*, Franz Pfeiffer, translated by C. de B. Evans, John M. Watkins, 1956, Volume I, page 158

There must be feelings of humility, not from nature, but from penitence, not to rest in them, but to go on to greatness.

Blaise Pascal, *Pensées*, translated by W.F. Trotter, Random House Inc., 1941, page 169

You will find Angling to be like the virtue of humility, which has a calmness of spirit, and a world of other blessings attending upon it.

Izaak Walton, *The Compleat Angler*, Macmillan & Co. Ltd., 1906, page 37

O Saviour pour upon me thy Spirit of meekness & Love!
Annihilate the Selfhood in me: be thou all my life!
Guide thou my hand, which trembles exceedingly upon the rock of ages.

William Blake, *The Complete Writings of William Blake*, edited by Geoffrey Keynes, Oxford University Press, 1974, page 623, *Jerusalem*, Ch.1, Plate 5, l.21

If thou wouldst become a pilgrim on the path
Of love
The first condition is
That thou become as humble as dust
And ashes.

Al-Ansari, *The Persian Mystics*, translated by Sardar Sir Jogendra Sing, John Murray Ltd., 1939, page 39

Humility does not rest, in final count, upon bafflement and discouragement and self-disgust at our shabby lives, a brow-beaten, dog-slinking attitude. It rests upon the disclosure of the consummate wonder of God, upon finding that only God counts, that all our self-originated intentions are works of straw...

Humility rests upon a holy blindness, like the blindness of him who steadily looks into the sun. For wherever he turns his eyes on earth, there he sees only the sun. The God-blinded soul sees nought of self.

Thomas Kelly, *A Testament of Devotion*, Hodder & Stoughton Ltd., 1943, page 54

I am sure it is no easier to pray than it is to create music or write a poem; it must be as hard to do as it is to build a bridge, or to discover a great scientific principle, or to heal the sick, or to understand another human being. It is surely as important as these to man in his search for his role in the universal scheme of things...

To pray... It is so necessary and so hard. Hard not because it requires intellect or knowledge or a big vocabulary or special technics but because it requires of us humility. And that comes, I think, from a profound sense of one's brokenness, and one's need. Not the need that causes us to cry, 'Get me out of this trouble, quick!' but the need that one feels every day of one's life—even though one does not acknowledge it—to be related to something bigger than one's self, something more alive than one's self, something older and something not yet born, that will endure through time.

Lillian Smith, *The Journey*, The Cresset Press, 1955, page 40

Humility, therefore, does not consist in forever trying to abase ourselves and renounce the dignity which God gives us and demands of us because we are his children not his slaves. Humility as we see it in his saints is not born solely of their awareness of sin, because even a sinner can bring to God a broken and contrite heart and a word of forgiveness is enough to blot out all evil from the past and the present.

The humility of the saints comes from the vision of the glory, the majesty, the beauty of God. It is not even a sense of contrast that gives birth to their humility, but the consciousness that God is so holy, such a revelation of perfect beauty, of love so striking that the only thing they can do in his presence is to prostrate themselves before him in an act of worship, joy and wonder. When the great experience of the overwhelming love that

God has for us came to St Teresa, she was struck to her knees, weeping in joy and wonder; when she arose she was a new person, one in whom the realisation of God's love left her 'with a sense of unpayable debt'. This is humility—not humiliation.

Anthony Bloom, *Meditations on a Theme*, A.R. Mowbray and Co. Ltd., 1972, page 68

Every person, when he first applies himself to the exercise of the virtue of humility, must... consider himself as a learner, that is to learn something that is contrary to former tempers and habits of mind, and which can only be got by daily and constant practice.

He has not only as much to do as he that has some new art or science to learn, but he has also a great deal to unlearn: he is to forget and lay aside his own spirit, which has been a long while fixing and forming itself; he must forget and depart from abundance of passions and opinions, which the fashion, and vogue, and spirit of the world, has made natural to him. He must lay aside his own spirit; because as we are born in sin, so in pride, which is as natural to us as self-love, and continually springs from it. And this is one reason why Christianity is so often represented as a new birth, and a new spirit.

He must lay aside the opinions and passions which he has received from the world; because the vogue and fashion of the world, by which we have been carried away as in a torrent, before we could pass right judgements of the value of things is, in many respects, contrary to humility; so that we must unlearn what the spirit of the world has taught us, before we can be governed by the spirit of humility...

To abound in wealth, to have fine houses, and rich clothes,... to be beautiful in our persons, to have title of dignity, to be above our fellow creatures,... to overcome our enemies with power, to subdue all that oppose us, to set out ourselves in as much splendour as we can, to live highly and magnificently, to eat, and drink, and delight ourselves in the most costly manner, these are the great, the honourable, the desirable things, to which the spirit of the world turns the eyes of all people. And many a man is afraid of standing still, and not engaging in the pursuit of these things, lest the same world should take him for a fool...

This is the mark of Christianity: you are to be dead, that is, dead to the spirit and temper of the world, and live a new life in the Spirit of Jesus Christ.

William Law, *A Serious Call to a Devout and Holy Life*, J.M. Dent & Co. Ltd., 1898, page 255

The source of humility... is the habit of realising the presence of God. Humility does not mean thinking less of yourself than of other people, nor does it mean having a low opinion of your own gifts. It means freedom from thinking about yourself one way or the other at all. It may be quite right that a man conscious of certain powers given him by God should desire the opportunities to exercise those powers for God. It may be quite right that under certain circumstances a man should insist that he is more capable than another man of doing something that must be done. No one would select as an example of humility the elder Pitt but there was nothing contrary to humility in his alleged declaration to the Duke of Devonshire: 'I know that I can save this country and I know that no one else can'. He knew the political life of the time pretty well; he was conscious of power in himself, and in a few years he showed that he was right in what he said of himself; only if he set about his task in his own interest or for self-glorificatiion did he fail in humility.

Humility means that you feel yourself, as a distinct person, out of count, and give your whole mind and thought to the object towards which they are directed, to God himself in worship and to the fulfilment of His will in Christian love; and humility, in that sense, is quite plainly a source of effectiveness. The humility which consists in being a great deal occupied about yourself, and saying you are of little worth, is not Christian humility. It is one form of self-occupation, and a very poor and futile one at that; but real humility makes for effectiveness because it delivers a man from anxiety, and we all know that in all undertakings, from the smallest to the greatest, the chief source of feebleness is anxiety. If you once begin to wonder whether you are going to catch the ball you will drop it, but if you just catch it without thinking about anything but catching it—not, above all, of what other people are going to think of you—probably you will hold it. That goes through everything, from such a simple act to the greatest. But there is nothing big enough to hold a man's soul in detachment from the centre of himself through all the occupations of life except the majesty of God and his love; and it is in worship, worship given to God because He is God, that man will most learn the secret of real humility.

William Temple, *Christ in His Church*, Macmillan & Co. Ltd., 1925, page 145

I

IDEALS

'Ideals'—one's highest conceptions; things embodying an idea; things existing only in idea; the visionary, relating to, consisting of, ideas; perfect types; actual things as standards for imitation.

M y ideals are in *Visions of Grace*, and the other books which make up the *Visions* series. In these books are a large number of ideals, but they find their focus in the person of Jesus Christ. He is seen both as an historical character, and because of the resurrection and the coming of the Holy Spirit, as a *presence* to be found in us and around us in our day and age. A verse from the New Testament, which is valuable to me, speaks 'of Christ in whom are hid all the treasures of wisdom and knowledge'.

These ideals have been collected from a wide variety of sources. The foundation is made up of several hundred verses from the Bible, culminating in the Gospels and the Epistles. To these have been added ideals coming from poets, playwrights, novelists, philosophers, theologians, historians, scientists, artists, musicians, statesmen, politicians, economists, and psychologists.

Christ's life was a perfect fusion of theory and practice, and the lives of the great saints, who have lived out his ideals, have shown a similar balance. Their insights in turn have also been added to these anthologies.

Visions of Grace can be used to grow in these ideals. The book itself acts as a skeleton or a framework of faith. Add to this the practice of reflection in which we 'read, mark, learn and inwardly digest' the contents, and it will not be long before the mind and the feelings are triggered off, and ideals assimilated. This has already been the experience of young and old alike.

For I will proclaim the name of the Lord. Ascribe greatness to our God! 'The Rock, his work is perfect; for all his ways are justice. A God of faithfulness and without iniquity, just and right is he.'

Deuteronomy 32.3-4

Set up waymarks for yourself, make yourself guideposts, consider well the highway, the road by which you went. Return, O virgin Israel, return to these your cities.

Jeremiah 31.21

If you would be perfect, go, sell what you possess and give to the poor, and you will have treasure in heaven; and come, follow me.

Matthew 19.21

Brethren, I do not consider that I have made it my own; but one thing I do, forgetting what lies behind and straining forward to what lies ahead, I press on toward the goal for the prize of the upward call of God in Christ Jesus.

Philippians 3.13-14

The Ideal is in thyself, the Impediment too is in thyself: thy condition is but the stuff thou art to shape that same Ideal out of.

Thomas Carlyle, *Sartor Resartus*, Ward, Lock & Co. Ltd., page 131

The highest flights of charity, devotion, trust, patience, bravery to which the wings of human nature have spread themselves have been flown for religious ideals.

William James, *The Varieties of Religious Experience*, William Collins Sons & Co. Ltd., 1974, page 258

If one advances confidently in the direction of his dreams, and endeavours to live the life which he has imagined, he will meet with a success unexpected in common hours.

Henry David Thoreau, *Walden*, The New American Library of World Literature, Inc., 1960, page 215

For the idealist living wholly with people occupied with the concrete, existence is not merely lonely, but fatiguing. It is as though he or she were for ever talking a foreign language.

L. Falconer, in *The Note Books of a Woman Alone*, edited by M.G. Ostle, J.M. Dent & Sons Ltd., 1935, page 228

In reverence for life my knowledge passes into experience… My life carries its own meaning in itself. This meaning lies in my living out the highest idea which shows itself in my will-to-live, the idea of reverence for life. With that for a starting-point I give value to my own life and to all the will-to-live which surrounds me, I persevere in activity, and I produce values.

Albert Schweitzer, *The Philosophy of Civilization*, Part II, *Civilization and Ethics*, translated by C.T. Campion, A. & C. Black Ltd., Third English Editon, revised by Mrs C.E.B. Russell, 1946, page xvii

The ideals which have lighted my way, and time after time have given me new courage to face life cheerfully, have been Kindness, Beauty, and Truth. Without the sense of kinship with men of like mind, without the occupation with the objective world, the eternally unattainable in the field of art and scientific endeavours, life would have seemed to me empty. The trite objects of human efforts—possessions, outward success, luxury—have always seemed to me contemptible.

Albert Einstein, *Ideas and Opinions*, Souvenir Press (Educational & Academic) Ltd., 1973, page 9

The essential nature of the will-to-live is determination to live itself to the full. It carries within it the impulse to realize itself in the highest possible perfection. In the flowering tree, in the strange forms of the medusa, in the blade of grass, in the crystal; everywhere it strives to reach the perfection with which it is endowed. In everything that exists there is at work an imaginative force, which is determined by ideals. In us beings who can move about freely and are capable of pre-considered, purposive working, the craving for perfection is given in such a way that we aim at raising to their highest material and spiritual value both ourselves and every existing thing which is open to our influence. How this striving originated within us, and how it has developed, we do not know, but it is given with our existence. We must act upon it, if we would not be unfaithful to the mysterious will-to-live which is within us.

Albert Schweitzer, *The Philosophy of Civilization*, translated by C.T. Campion, Third English Edition, revised by Mrs E.B. Russell, Part II, *Civilization and Ethics*, A. & C. Black Ltd., 1946, page 213

Today there is an increased number of people who cherish communism as their ideal, but the type of communism thus coming into existence is woefully defective. Russia has established a Soviet-organised communism. But in order to carry out communism genuinely, there is no other way than for every man to return his possessions to God first of all. It is very important to give all our property back to God to whom everything belongs. Unless each of us has sufficient devotion to restore all things to God before we cry, 'Workers, unite!' communism can never be a success. I do not believe that communism restricted to a single country can be called real and valid. To be real, communism must be changed into a God-centred undertaking. There is no other way to accomplish it. I often think that thieves maintain a kind of communism, too; that is, among themselves. So it can be said that there are two brands of communism: the God-centred type, and the thief type. It goes without saying that every genuine communist is seeking for God first of all. Paul dwelt on this condition. He expressed it in very marvellous words. According to him, Jesus Christ became poor, though he was rich, so that all men might be enriched through his poverty.

If this ideal should be put into practice, heaven would descend upon earth. Dwelling upon this idea led Paul furthermore to declare that all men are made equal.

Toyohiko Kagawa, Meditations, translated by Jiro Takenaka, Harper Brothers, 1950, No.44

It is innocence that is full and experience that is empty.
It is innocence that wins and experience that loses.
It is innocence that is young and experience that is old.
It is innocence that grows and experience that wanes.
It is innocence that is born and experience that dies.
It is innocence that knows and experience that does not know.
It is the child who is full and the man who is empty,
Empty as an empty gourd and as an empty barrel:
That is what I do with that experience of yours.
Now then, children, go to school.
And you men, go to the school of life.
Go and learn,
How to unlearn.

Charles Péguy, Basic Verities, translated by Ann and Julian Green, Kegan Paul, Trench, Trubner & Co. Ltd., 1943, page 223

Devotion and the Role of Ideals

We must have some passionate devotion to give us the necessary drive of life. If that passionate devotion is given to established and accepted ideals, we cannot seek and find the new possibilities that arise with changing conditions. Where, then, shall we find an object of passionate devotion? Such an object is that order of value which enters into our present state of existence, but which also includes the highest possibilities of value however unknown and undefined by us as yet. Without such a devotion, we maintain, maturity is not attained, the art of living is not mastered, and the way is blocked that leads to the good life in our present age of science, machinery, and industry when all things are changing so rapidly.

There are two ways in which we can deal with the socially accepted ideals, these achieved structures of value and known possibilities. We can live with them as though they were final, as though they were the supreme good, as though there were nothing on beyond them to seek and explore, or we can use them not as final goods, not as our home and resting place, but as merely torches and trails, leading on. In other words, there are two ways of life according to what we make supreme. We may give our highest allegiance to the socially accepted ideals, the known possibilities, the goods achieved, while the unknown possibilities are for us mere nebulosity and dreamland. Or, on the other hand, we may give our supreme loyalty to this realm of meanings yet to be achieved, these possible structures of value not yet defined and mastered, while the known possibilities and socially accepted ideals are for us mere tools and instruments to be used in this highest devotion. This is the contrast between religion forever on the defensive and in peril and religion invincible.

The Invincibility of Devotion to the Good

Why does dedication to the supreme and unknown good engender a striving so invincible? For three reasons. First, because the object of devotion which then inspires the striving is invaluable, being the best there is in all reality actual and possible, and hence worth everything that may be endured or given. Second, because it is not irrevocably identified with any known object or undertaking, there all being more or less tentative and exploratory; hence failure or disaster to any of these does not blot out from life the star of value which leads on. Third, under the dominance of such a devotion all experience becomes a seeking of this highest value, an adoration of it and a reaching after it. Hence all experience becomes a way of experiencing the best there is in all reality. Even failure of any specific enterprise, even pain and all medium of experience in which we seek for and reach after the supreme good, are ways of experiencing this object of our supreme devotion.

Henry Nelson Wieman, in The Choice is Always Ours, edited by Dorothy Berkley Phillips, Harper & Row, Publishers, Inc.,
1960, page 84

IMAGINATION

'Imagination'—imagining, mental faculty forming images of external objects not present to the senses; creative faculty of the mind.

L ate one evening I went down to the porter's lodge in University College, Oxford. The door leading out to High Street suddenly opened and an undergraduate came in, looking somewhat shaken. 'Bill,' he said, 'I have just had my mind blown. Can I come and talk to you please?' I immediately invited him back to my rooms, put the kettle on, and gave him a cup of tea.

He had been to see a film called *The Shining*, and it had greatly affected him. I listened carefully as he tried to communicate to me what he had been through. He ended up making me promise to come and see the film with him the following evening.

Once in the pew I was thoroughly absorbed in the film and found it came to an end far too quickly. We returned to my rooms to talk it through over a cup of coffee. I knew my undergraduate friend was reputed to have 'a Rolls Royce mind', but now I also witnessed a powerful imagination in action. He quickly revealed to me the underlying plot, not immediately obvious to a casual film-goer like myself. He then slipped his imagination into top gear and made scores and scores of connections which I had not been able to fathom. However at that point I was able to engage my imagination and make a contribution. We must have gone on for two or three hours—an exciting and stimulating experience.

Not surprisingly he went into television when he left University College. In the many programmes he has produced, he has already made an excellent use of his imagination.

. . . know the God of your father, and serve him with a whole heart and with a willing mind; for the Lord searches all hearts, and understands every plan and thought.

1 Chronicles 28.9

. . . out of my understanding a spirit answers me.

Job 20.3

Be transformed by the renewal of your mind.

Romans 12.2

Whereas the aim of our charge is love that issues from a pure heart and a good conscience and sincere faith.

1 Timothy 1.5

Imagination is the eye of the soul.

Joseph Joubert, *Pensées and Letters*, George Routledge & Sons Ltd., 1928, page 48

The great instrument of moral good is the imagination.

Percy Bysshe Shelley, *The Prose Works of Percy Bysshe Shelley*, edited by H. Buxton Forman, Reeves & Turner, 1880, Volume III, page 111, 'A Defence of Poetry'

Imagination and fiction go to make up more than three-quarters of our real life.

Simone Weil, *Gravity and Grace*, Routledge & Kegan Paul Ltd., 1952, page 50

Imagination grows by exercise and contrary to common belief is more powerful in the mature than in the young.

W. Somerset Maugham, *The Summing Up*, Bernhard Tauchnitz, 1938, page 131

It is the marriage of the soul with Nature that makes the intellect fruitful, that gives birth to imagination.

Henry David Thoreau, *The Journal of Henry D. Thoreau*, edited by Bradford Torrey and Francis H. Allen, Houghton Mifflin Company, Boston, The Riverside Press, 1949, Volume II, page 413

There are no days in life so memorable as those which vibrated to some stroke of the imagination.

Ralph Waldo Emerson, *The Conduct of Life, Nature, and Other Essays*, J.M. Dent & Sons Ltd., 1911, page 298

Only in men's imagination does every truth find an effective and undeniable existence. Imagination, not invention, is the supreme master of art as of life.

Joseph Conrad, *A Personal Record*, J.M. Dent & Sons Ltd., 1923, page 25

What is it that we ask of our ideal audience? It is imagination. And is not all our writing a profession of belief in the powers of the imagination?

Katherine Mansfield, in Anthony Alpers, *Katherine Mansfield*, Jonathan Cape Ltd., 1954, page 296

I am certain of nothing but the holiness of the heart's affections, and the truth of Imagination. What the Imagination seizes as Beauty must be Truth, whether it existed before or not.

John Keats, *The Works of John Keats*, edited by H. Buxton Forman, Reeves & Turner, 1883, Volume III, page 90, Letter to Benjamin Bailey

But how entirely I live in my imagination; how completely depend upon spurts of thought, coming as I walk, as I sit; things churning up in my mind and so making a perpetual pageant, which is to be my happiness.

Virginia Woolf, *A Writer's Diary*, edited by Leonard Woolf, The Hogarth Press, 1953, page 67

The primary IMAGINATION I hold to be the living Power and prime Agent of all human Perception, and as a repetition in the finite mind of the eternal act of creation in the infinite I AM.

Samuel Taylor Coleridge, *Coleridge, Select Poetry & Prose*, edited by Stephen Potter, The Nonesuch Press, 1817, page 246, *Biographia Literaria*, Chapter XIII

The virtue of the Imagination is its reaching, by intuition and intensity of gaze (not by reasoning, but by its authoritative opening and revealing power), a more essential truth than is seen at the surface of things.

John Ruskin, *Modern Painters*, George Allen & Sons, 1911, Volume II, page 201, Part III, section 2, ch. 3, No. 29

He realised in the entire sphere of human relations that imaginative sympathy which in the Sphere of Art is the sole secret of creation. He understood the leprosy of the leper, the darkness of the blind, the fierce misery of those who live for pleasure, the strange poverty of the rich.

Oscar Wilde, *The Works of Oscar Wilde*, edited by G.F. Maine, William Collins Sons & Co. Ltd., 1948, *De Profundis*, page 867

The imagination—the divinest of mental faculties—is God's self in the soul. All our other faculties seem to me to have the brown touch of earth on them but this one carries the very livery of heaven. It is God's most supernal faculty, interpreting to us the difference between the material and the immaterial, and the difference between the visible and the invisible; teaching us how to take material and visible things and carry them up into the realm of the invisible and the immaterial, and how to bring down immaterial and invisible things, and embody them in visible and material symbols;—and so being God's messenger and prophet, standing between our soul and God's.

Henry Ward Beecher, *Royal Truths*, Alexander Strahan & Co., 1862, page 47

The more we come to depend on the images offered to us by those who try to distract us, entertain us, use us for their purposes, and make us conform to the demands of a consumer society, the easier it is for us to lose our identity. These imposed images actually make us into the world which they represent, a world of hatred, greed, manipulation and oppression. But when we believe that we are created in the image of God himself and come to realize that Christ came to let us reimagine this, then meditation and prayer can lead us to our true identity.

Latin America offers us the image of the suffering Christ. The poor we see every day, the stories about deportation, torture and murder we hear every day, and the undernourished children we touch every day, reveal to us the suffering Christ hidden within us. When we allow this image of the suffering Christ within us to grow into its full maturity, then ministry to the poor and oppressed becomes a real possibility; because then we can indeed hear, see and touch him within us as well as among us. This prayer becomes ministry and ministry becomes prayer. Once we have seen the suffering Christ within us, we will see him whenever we see people in pain. Once we have seen the suffering Christ among us, we will recognize him in our innermost self.

Henri J.M. Nouwen, in *Circles of Love*, arrangement by John Garvey, Darton, Longman & Todd, 1990, page 51

(1) The faculty of creative thought. (2) Vain or false thinking.

In popular thought, as well as in philosophy, imagination has often been equated with fantasy as either sustained deluded flight from reality or as, in a biblical context, the source of human wrongdoing (Gen.8.21: 'For the imagination of a man's heart is evil from his youth'). Before consideration of other accounts of the term 'imagination', it may be relevant to note that while fantasy as persistent escapism may be psychologically undesirable, in proper dosage and in appropriate applications, it may be eminently commendable. For example, it is an essential feature of the seeing of visions which Joel (2.28) characterizes as one of the gifts of God's spirit, and of the idealism without which both persons and nations spiritually perish. It is endemic to the writing of romantic sages which have achieved so much popularity, both in their own right (as in J.R.R. Tolkien's *The Lord of the Rings*) and as religious allegories (as in C.S. Lewis's *Narnia* stories). It is psychologically healthy also as a means of relief in times of stress, but becomes pathologically dangerous when it assumes control of the individual's thought and action, to the exclusion of all realism.

A strong case has been made, however, in recent years for regarding imagination, not as a special faculty of the mind (as was the case in medieval epistemology, reflected recently in Mary Warnock's descriptions of it as 'a power of the mind'), certainly not as agency for evil in the human heart, but as the human mind working in certain specifiable ways, which it is now possible to enumerate.

1. Imagination is the human mind in heightened sensitivity and openness to, and perceptiveness of, features in the world of nature and in persons, which the ordinary observer passes without noticing. Artistic imagination is able to detect in a landscape, in the sky or in the sea, colours and formations, which others notice only when their attention is drawn to them; or in the sitter for a portrait insights into aspects of character which are denied to most casual observers. Such qualities of imagination are seen in Jesus' relationship to persons of his day, and in the Christian ethic they constitute the virtues of care and concern for human need and suffering.

2. Imagination is *selective* from the mass of material with which the human mind is confronted, and out of which it concentrates upon salient, and significant features. The Old Testament prophets seized upon this occasion or that in the past history of the nation, to demonstrate to Israel that God was working out his purpose of salvation for them. From the literature of Israel, Jesus selected such themes as redemptive ransom, the suffering servant, the concept of Kingdom, to be the load-bearing topics of his *kerygma*, or message. In less exalted contexts, ordinary people select parts of their lives as the most meaningful for them, and organize their emotions and their motivation around them.

3. Accordingly, imagination has a special *interpretative* role to play, using selected topics, points in human existence, as the basis of understanding the rest of life, and even wider spans of history. It does so by establishing analogies, and imagination so employed plays a central part in poetry, and in the enrichment of human experience which poetry achieves.

4. One of the very obvious elements in imagination is its *constructive* and *creative* features. These are in evidence in the arts, but are equally apparent in the scientific constructions of Einstein, in the dogmatic and philosophical works of Tillich or Barth, as in choice of paradigms and models which the expert in any field employs to advance his discipline (Barbour 1974).

5. Imagination has to be recognized further as having a very important *cognitive* role to play in our intellectual lives. There are certain things that we would not know about the world around us, about other persons, about ourselves, about God, the Bible and doctrine, had we—or more precisely, those into whose labours we have entered—not employed the imagination. Mary Warnock's contribution to the study of imagination is to demonstrate that imagination is one imagination, whether perceiving the world about us and the music and so on. It has to be affirmed that imagination therefore must not be thought of as adding characteristics to reality which do not actually exist, but rather as cognizing dimensions of reality which are hidden from the unimaginative.

6. It would be wrong to give an unduly intellectualistic account of imagination, for it also has an *empathetic* role to play. It is the medium whereby we project ourselves into a situation, not only cognitively, but affectively and emotionally, so that the plight and suffering of others is not only understood but, being understood, also moves us to effective action. 'Identification', now a key concept in much philosophy of counselling and caring requires imagination as its enabling condition.

7. Imagination is not intended solely to further personal emotion, motivation or ambition, however laudable. It has a specifically *communicative* role to fulfil. It is the responsibility of the artist, the poet, or the dramatist, to make others feel as they do about a certain subject, and, to achieve this end, they must not only have the experience themselves: they have to create the media for this appreciation of it, which will place others where they are, so that these others see with their eyes, hear with their ears, and feel with their hearts. The differentia between the genius and the commonplace lies at the points not just of experiental depth, but also of communicative capacity.

8. There is a function of imagination in relation to time which is worth noting, namely, its *contemporanizing* function, treating the past as present. R.G. Collingwood noted it in relation to history (*The Idea of History*, 1946) when he said that historical knowledge is the imaginative re-enactment of the past, rethinking the thoughts of historical agents. The notion might equally have been applied to Kierkegaard's theme that all Christians are contemporary disciples of Jesus Christ. Imagination is the medium through which the events of the gospels are, for faith, regarded as happening in the category of past-as-present.

9. A not dissimilar role which imagination plays is its *conspatializing* function, making the absent-as-present. J.P. Sartre often discussed the way in which, through imagination, a portrait of an absent friend creates his presence for me. In the 'global village' of the modern world, peoples 5,000 miles absent are, through imagination, present in their hunger and deprivation. Our neighbour, however distantly absent, is as near as our next-door neighbour.

10. Finally, Iris Murdoch says that the imagination creates what she calls 'our-world' wherein appear our system of values, our principles, our prejudices, or religious commitments, as well as our fantasies and delusions. Some of this world we create for ourselves, actively or by re-action; some of it, we might wish to say, through the incoming grace of God; but, on the human side, the structure is formed and the tone set by our imagination. It is the framework within which our decisions are made, our ambitions determined and in most general terms, our lives are 'lived'.

J. McIntyre, in *A Dictionary of Pastoral Care*, edited by Alastair V. Campbell, SPCK, 1987, page 126

IMMORTALITY

'Immortality'—state of being undying, divine, unfading, incorruptible, constant, long-lasting.

I n my early twenties I went on a memorable holiday to Lake Como in northern Italy. I stayed in the lakeside resort of Menaggio, and was accommodated in a lovely old house called the Villa D'Este. It belonged to the family I was staying with.

The grounds were spacious and went down to the edge of the lake. Although there was a large swimming pool near the house we preferred to swim in the lake. The water was cooler and more refreshing.

Life was idyllic. We swam, sunbathed, read, and ate big juicy peaches. The scenery was magnificent. Behind us were the mountains. In front of us was a variety of trees, a profusion of brightly coloured flowers, all backed up with a clear blue sky and the heat of a merciless sun. Wordsworth's Ode, 'Intimations of Immortality' came to mind. Youthful thoughts and imaginings took over. Life was so good at this particular moment I wished it could go on for ever.

After these idle musings, we had a change of scene and went to Verona. We ambled round the city looking at Roman remains. After a visit to an art gallery we made our way to the ancient amphitheatre. Here, teams of men were pushing vast pieces of scenery into place for an evening performance of *Nabucco*. We bought tickets and after some pasta made our way to our seats.

In this venue *Nabucco* was spectacular, especially with camels on stage, and acoustically the deep rich music of Verdi floated up on all sides. The ancient story and the slightly ruined amphitheatre reminded us again of immortality.

The afflicted shall eat and be satisfied; those who seek him shall praise the Lord! May your hearts live for ever!

Psalm 22.26

God created man to be immortal, and made him to be an image of his own eternity.

Wisdom of Solomon 2.23 (AV)

If the Spirit of him who raised Jesus from the dead dwells in you, he who raised Christ Jesus from the dead will give life to your mortal bodies also through his Spirit which dwells in you.

Romans 8.11

Lo! I tell you a mystery. We shall not all sleep, but we shall all be changed, in a moment, in the twinkling of an eye, at the last trumpet. For the trumpet will sound, and the dead will be raised imperishable, and we shall be changed. For this perishable nature must put on the imperishable, and this mortal nature must put on immortality.

1 Corinthians 15.51-53

The blazing evidence of immortality is our dissatisfaction with any other solution.

Ralph Waldo Emerson, *The Heart of Emerson's Journals*, edited by Bliss Perry, Constable & Co. Ltd., 1927, page 270

I believe in the immortality of the soul, not in the sense in which I accept the demonstrable truths of science, but as a supreme act of faith in the reasonableness of God's work.

John Fiske, *The Destiny of Man*, Macmillan & Co. Ltd., 1884, page 116

Our Creator would never have made such lovely days and have given us the deep hearts to enjoy them, above and beyond all thought, unless we were meant to be immortal.

Nathaniel Hawthorne, *Mosses From An Old Manse*, William Paterson, 1883, page 30

The belief of immortality is impressed upon all men, and all men act under an impression of it, however they may talk, and though, perhaps, they may be scarcely sensible of it.

Samuel Johnson, *Boswell's Life of Johnson*, edited by G.B. Hill, revised by L.F.Powell, Oxford at the Clarendon Press, 1934, Volume II, page 358

If you were to destroy the belief in immortality in mankind, not only love but every living force on which the continuation of all life in the world depended, would dry up at once.

Fyodor Dostoyevsky, *The Brothers Karamazov*, translated by David Magarshack, Penguin Books Ltd., 1963, Volume I, page 77

Cold in the dust this perished heart may lie,
But that which warmed it once shall never die!
That spark unburied in its mortal frame,
With living light, eternal, and the same.

Thomas Campbell, *The Pleasures of Hope*, edited by Henry Morley, George Routledge & Sons, Ltd., 1892, page 50

It is only true goodness and virtue in the souls of men, that can make them both to know and love, believe and delight themselves in their own immortality... His soul being purged and enlightened by true sanctity, is more capable of those divine irradiations, whereby it feels itself in conjunction with God... it knows that Almighty love which it lives by, to be stronger than death... It knows that God will never forsake His own life which He hath quickened in it ... those breathings and gaspings after an eternal participation of Him are but the energy of His own breath within us.

John Smith the Platonist, *Select Discourses*, Cambridge at the University Press, 1859, page 102

If the soul is really immortal, what care should be taken of her, not only in respect of the portion of time which is called life, but of eternity. And the danger of neglecting her from this point of view does indeed appear to be awful. If death had only been the end of all, the wicked would have had a good bargain in dying, for they would have been happily quit not only of their body, but of their own evil together with their souls. But now, inasmuch as the soul is manifestly immortal, there is no release or salvation from evil except the attainment of the highest virtue and wisdom.

Socrates, in *The Dialogues of Plato*, translated by B. Jowett, Oxford at the Clarendon Press, 1875, Volume I, page 488, 'Phaedo,' 107

It must be so—Plato, thou reason'st well!—
Else whence this pleasing hope, this fond desire,
This longing after immortality?
Or whence this secret dread, and inward horror,
Of falling into nought? Why shrinks the soul
Back on herself, and startles at destruction?
'Tis the divinity that stirs within us;
'Tis heaven itself, that points out an hereafter,
And intimates eternity to man.
Eternity! thou pleasing, dreadful thought!

Joseph Addison, *The Works of Joseph Addison*, notes by Richard Hurd, edited and published by Henry G. Bohn, 1856, Volume I, *Cato*, Act V, page 220

As to the supreme form of soul that is within us, we must believe that God has given it to each of us as a guiding genius—even that which we say, and say truly, dwells in the summit of our body and raises us from earth towards our celestial affinity, seeing we are of no earthly, but of heavenly growth: since to heaven, whence in the beginning was the birth of our soul, the diviner part attaches the head or root of us and makes our whole body upright. Now whoso is busied with appetites or ambitions and labours hard after these, all the thoughts of his heart must be altogether mortal and so far as it is possible for him to become utterly mortal, he falls no whit short of this; for this is what he has been fostering. But he whose heart has been set on the love of learning and on true wisdom, and has chiefly exercised this part of himself, this man must without fail have thoughts that are immortal and divine, if he lay hold upon the truth and so far as it lies in human nature to possess immortality, he lacks nothing thereof; and seeing that he ever cherishes the divinest part and keeps in good estate the guardian spirit that dwells in him, he must be happy above all.

Plato, *The Timaeus of Plato*, edited by F.D. Archer-Hind, Macmillan & Co. Ltd., 1888, page 337, 90A

'I cannot see what harm would come of letting us know a little—as much at least as might serve to assure us that there was more of *something* on the other side.'—'Just this ... that, their fears allayed, their hopes encouraged from any lower quarter, men would, as usual, turn away from the fountain to the cistern of life… That there are thousands who would forget God if they could but be assured of such a tolerable state of things beyond the grave as even this wherein we now live, is plainly to be anticipated from the fact that the doubts of so many in respect of religion concentrate themselves nowadays upon the question whether there is any life beyond the grave; a question which… does not immediately belong to religion at all. Satisfy such people, if you can, that they shall live, and what have they gained? A little comfort perhaps—but a comfort not from the highest source, and possibly gained too soon for their well-being. Does it bring them any nearer to God than they were before? Is he filling one cranny more of their hearts in consequence?'

George Macdonald, *Thomas Wingfold, Curate*, Chatto & Windus Ltd., 1883, page 486

INFLUENCE

'Influence'—affecting character and destiny of person; action insensibly exercised upon, ascendancy, moral power (over, with persons, etc); thing, person, exercising power.

A reflection group had just begun. The four participants were sipping their tea and hot chocolate, and Hobnob biscuits were on hand, invitingly poised. Several topics were put forward but the group finally settled for the Bible. The material was circulated, and the period of silence got under way.

After twenty-five minutes I asked them if they had finished. One person needed to mull over the last quotation, so we fell back into silence for a couple of minutes. We then started the discussion part of the reflection group.

I began this with the usual question. 'Who was it who chose this topic?' One person indicated it was his choice. I asked him if he had a reason for choosing the Bible. 'Yes,' he said, 'when I was twelve we had a speaker at school from the Gideons who spoke to us about the Bible. The man who gave the talk was not at all pushy, but at the end of the talk we were each given a Bible and invited to read it from time to time. At the front of this Bible I found a programme of the New Testament, advising the reader to tackle a few verses each day, completing the New Testament in a two-year period. I have followed this daily discipline and now have read the New Testament three times. I think it has been a great influence in my life. It has helped me to keep things in perspective and lead a balanced life. I was just interested in seeing what these quotations had to say about the Bible.' In the discussion which followed the influence of the Bible continued to progress—a little bit further.

The Lord our God be with us, as he was with our fathers; may he not leave us or forsake us; that he may incline our hearts to him, to walk in all his ways, and to keep his commandments, his statutes, and his ordinances, which he commanded our fathers.

1 Kings 8.57-58

O Lord, the God of Abraham, Isaac, and Israel, our fathers, keep for ever such purposes and thoughts in the hearts of thy people, and direct their hearts towards thee.

1 Chronicles 29.18

One who heard us was a woman named Lydia, from the city of Thyatira, a seller of purple goods, who was a worshipper of God. The Lord opened her heart to give heed to what was said by Paul.

Acts 16.14

... he being dead yet speaketh.

Hebrews 11.4 (AV)

Blessed influence of one true loving human soul on another!

George Eliot, *Scenes of Clerical Life, Janet's Repentance*, Oxford University Press, 1909, page 369

A teacher affects eternity; he can never tell where his influence stops.

Henry Adams, *The Education of Henry Adams*, Constable & Co. Ltd., 1919, page 300

You can exert no influence if you are not susceptible to influence.

C.G. Jung, *Modern Man in Search of a Soul*, translated by W.S. Dell and Cary F. Baynes, Kegan Paul, Trench, Trubner & Co. Ltd., 1933, page 57

God must act and pour in as soon as he finds that you are ready.

Meister Eckhart, *Meister Eckhart*, translated by Raymond B. Blakney, Harper & Row, Publishers, Inc., 1941, page 121

No life
Can be pure in its purpose or strong in its strife
And all life not be purer and stronger thereby.

Owen Meredith, *Lucile*, Longmans, Green & Co. Ltd., 1893, Part II, Canto vi, section 40, page 333

Thou art the framer of my nobler being;
Nor does there live one virtue in my soul,
One honourable hope, but calls thee father.

Samuel Taylor Coleridge, *The Poetical Works of Samuel Taylor Coleridge*, edited by James Dykes Campbell, Macmillan & Co. Ltd., 1893, page 401, 'Zapolya,' sc.i. l.73

It is certainly often sad and depressing when one tries to effect something in life by one's words and sees in the end that one has effected nothing; but that the person in question obstinately perseveres in his opinion; but on the other hand there is something great in the fact that the other person, and in the same way everyone, is a world unto himself, has his holy of holies into which no strange hand can penetrate.

Søren Kierkegaard, *The Journals of Søren Kierkegaard*, a selection edited and translated by Alexander Dru, Oxford University Press, 1938, page 25

Whose powers shed round him in the common strife,
Or mild concerns of ordinary life,
A constant influence, a peculiar grace;
But who, if he be called upon to face
Some awful moment to which Heaven has joined
Great issues, good or bad for human kind,
Is happy as a Lover; and attired
With sudden brightness, like a Man inspired;
And, through the heat of conflict, keeps the law
In calmness made, and sees what he foresaw.

William Wordsworth, *The Poetical Works of William Wordsworth*, edited by E. de Selincourt and Helen Darbishire, Oxford at the Clarendon Press, 1958, Volume IV, page 87, 'Character of a Happy Warrior,' l.45

We can influence and direct others as we desire their good, but only when they are convinced, with the shrewd sense that all creatures have, that our motives are clean, our statements true, that we do seek their good, and not our advancement and elevation as their essential benefactors. All of us are individual spirits created to evolve into a common union. If we have made ourselves to grow, so that we are advanced some stages beyond the average intensity of individualism, we can directly influence those who wish to grow, and who are feeling the natural need to grow, in that direction. The spirit and character which is already advanced in constant creativeness, in wide compassion and unceasing illumination, knowing what life means and how to attain that meaning—such a spirit not only influences those among whom it is—but its influence spreads radioactively, telepathetically, and the limits of its force cannot be set, because the source on which it is drawing is itself illimitable. Being, therefore, is all, and doing merely the symptom and sign of being, as body is the appearance of spirit.

Anon.

Ask yourselves, Who are the people who have really helped me? You will find, I think, that they have been laymen more often than clergymen, women perhaps more often than men; that the occasions have been most trivial, that the words spoken and things done have been slight and unpremeditated. They have been sidelights upon the person's character, peeps into the inner life of one whom God hides privily by His own presence from the provoking of all men whose mind is kept in perfect peace because it is stayed on God; of one who sees God because his heart is pure. It is the sudden sting of self-reproach, the shame of the contrast, the longing to be like such an one, to see things as he sees them, that sticks in a man's mind, and sends him to his knees as soon as he is alone. Sometimes when such a man or woman dies, we learn for the first time, not without surprise, what he or she has been to many. Such persons have laid up a rich store of gratitude by being what God has helped them to be. A character can never be refuted or ignored; disinterestedness is always interesting.

W.R. Inge, Personal Religion and the Life of Devotion, Longmans, Green & Co. Ltd., 1924, page 72

Nothing is more important in the early stages of the spiritual life than to resist that 'temptation of beginners,' the reformation of others. 'Let us look at our own faults, and not at other people's ... We ought not to insist on everyone following in our footsteps, nor to take upon ourselves to give instructions in spirituality when, perhaps, we do not even know what it is.' (St. Theresa) ... 'when people begin to have pleasure in the rest and the fruit of prayer, they will have everyone else to be very spiritual also. To desire this is not wrong, but to try to bring it about may not be right, except with great discretion and great reserve, without any appearance of teaching.' She gives an illustration from her own experience, for she had made others endeavour to pray, only to find that they contrasted what she said of the blessedness of prayer with her lack of virtue, in spite of her prayer. 'And thus, during many years, only three persons were the better from what I said to them; but now that our Lord has made me stronger in virtue, in the course of two or three years, many persons have profited.'

Bede Frost, The Art of Mental Prayer, Philip Allan & Co. Ltd., 1935, page 89

When I look back upon my early days I am stirred by the thought of the number of people whom I have to thank for what they gave me or for what they were to me. At the same time I am haunted by an oppressive consciousness of the little gratitude I really showed them while I was young. How many of them have said farewell to life without my having made clear to them what it meant to me to receive from them so much kindness and so much care! Many a time have I, with a feeling of shame, said quietly to myself over a grave the words which my mouth ought to have spoken to the departed, while he was still in the flesh.

For all that, I think I can say with truth that I am not ungrateful, I did occasionally wake up out of that youthful thoughtlessness which accepted as a matter of course all the care and kindness that I experienced from others, and I believe I became sensitive to my duty in this matter just as early as I did to the prevalence of suffering in the world. But down to my twentieth year, and even later still, I did not exert myself sufficiently to express the gratitude which was really in my heart. I valued too low the pleasure felt at receiving real proofs of gratitude. Often, too, shyness prevented me from expressing the gratitude that I really felt.

Albert Schweitzer, Memoirs of Childhood and Youth, translated by C.T. Campion, George Allen & Unwin Ltd., 1924, page 87

INSPIRATION

'Inspiration'—drawing in of breath; divine influence, sudden happy idea; inspiring principle.

Inspiration plays a very important role in *Visions of Grace*. We recall the Genesis story of the creation of man. After God fashioned and shaped man in his own image and likeness he breathed into man and man became a living being.

What is depicted in this story is God 'inspiring' man; God 'breathing into' man. As we have tried to point out elsewhere inspiration is multi-faceted and mysterious. Many words are used to describe it—God, Jesus Christ, Holy Spirit, life, light, truth, joy, grace, love, and so on.

I came across an interesting illustration of inspiration whilst sitting in my rooms in Univ. On the same staircase was an American graduate, reading for an honours degree in modern history. His grandfather and great uncle had both been eminent theologians. Unlike his forbears he was not an overtly religious person, but from time to time came to evensong, and occasionally would drop in to my rooms for a chat and a coffee.

When he returned to the States he became a journalist. After three years working on a provincial newspaper, he came back to England on holiday, and popped in to see me. After sharing a few pleasantries he said, 'You know, Bill, I have come to realize Oxford is a very spiritual place.' I was taken aback by this observation and expressed my feelings that Oxford is spiritually dead. 'No, no,' he said, 'I do not mean the current generation of Fellows and students. I think *the Spirit is in the walls.*'

The penny dropped. I saw exactly what he meant. Oxford is an inspirational place. The Spirit is, indeed, in the walls.

The Spirit of the Lord speaks by me, his word is upon my tongue.

2 Samuel 23.2

But it is the spirit in a man, the breath of the Almighty, that makes him understand. It is not the old that are wise, nor the aged that understand what is right. Therefore I say, 'Listen to me; let me also declare my opinion.'

Job 32.8-10

When they deliver you up, do not be anxious how you are to speak or what you are to say; for what you are to say will be given to you in that hour; for it is not you who speak, but the Spirit of your Father speaking through you.

Matthew 10.19-20

And you became imitators of us and of the Lord, for you received the word in much affliction, with joy inspired by the Holy Spirit.

1 Thessalonians 1.6

When God intends doing some act of great charity in us, by us, or with us, first, He proposes it by inspiration; secondly, we are pleased with it; and thirdly, we give our full consent to it.

St Francis de Sales, *Introduction to the Devout Life*, translated and edited by John K. Ryan, Longmans, Green & Co. Ltd., 1962, page 92

Perpetual Inspiration, therefore, is in the Nature of the Thing as necessary to a Life of Goodness, Holiness, and Happiness, as perpetual Respiration of the Air is necessary to animal life.

William Law, *The Spirit of Love*, full text, edited by Sidney Spencer, James Clarke & Co. Ltd., 1969, page 206

What but God?
Inspiring God! who, boundless spirit all,
And unremitting energy, pervades,
Adjusts, sustains, and agitates the whole.

James Thomson, *The Seasons and The Castle of Indolence*, edited by J. Logie Robertson, Oxford at the Clarendon Press,
1891, 'Spring,' 1.852, page 54

Those divinely possessed and inspired have at least the knowledge that they hold some
greater thing within them though they cannot tell what it is; from the movements that stir
them and the utterances that come from them they perceive the power, not themselves,
that moves them.

Plotinus, *The Enneads*, translated by Stephen Mackenna, Faber & Faber Ltd., 1956, page 396

Now, this continual knocking of Christ at the door of the heart sets forth the case or nature
of a continual, immediate divine inspiration within us; it is always with us, but there must be
an opening of the heart to it; and though it is always there, yet it is only felt and found by
those who are attentive to it, depend upon, and humbly wait for it.

William Law, *Selected Mystical Writings of William Law*, edited by Stephen Hobhouse, Rockliff, 1948, page 219

Thou, my all!
My theme! my inspiration! and my crown!
My strength in age! my rise in low estate!
My soul's ambition, pleasure, wealth! my world!
My light in darkness! and my life in death!
My boast thro' time! bliss thro' eternity!
Eternity, too short to speak thy praise,
Or fathom thy profound of love to man!

Edward Young, *Night Thoughts*, Thomas Nelson, 1841, page 59

Sometimes, when I have come to my work empty, I have suddenly become full, ideas being
in an invisible manner showered upon me, and implanted in me from on high; so that
through the influence of divine inspiration I have become filled with enthusiasm, and have
known neither the place in which I was nor those who were present, nor myself, nor what I
was saying, nor what I was writing, for then I have been conscious of a richness of
interpretation, an enjoyment of light, a most keen-sighted vision, a most distinct view of
the objects treated, such as would be given through the eyes from the clearest exhibition.

Philo, in *The Philosophy of Plotinus*, W.R. Inge, Longmans, Green & Co. Ltd., 1918, Volume II, page 154

Already I am wavering in my absolute determination to shut myself up daily, wherever I am
and in whatever external circumstances, for so-and-so many hours for my work's sake. I do
not know whether it will really come now or whether I am just making the appropriate
gestures, but remain unfilled... Have I not known ever since I was in Russia, and with such
great conviction, that prayer and its time and its reverent and unstinted gestures were the
condition of God and of his return to all those who barely expect it, who only kneel down
and stand up and are suddenly filled to the brim? So will I kneel down and stand up, daily,
alone in my room, and will keep holy all that befalls me: even what has *not* come, even
disappointment, even desertion. There is no poverty that is not fullness could we but
accept it gravely and worthily, and not surrender or yield it up to bitterness...

Rainer Maria Rilke, *Selected Letters of Rainer Maria Rilke*, translated by R.F.C. Hull, Macmillan & Co. Ltd., 1946, page 98

It is by long obedience and hard work that the artist comes to unforced spontaneity and
consummate mastery. Knowing that he can never create anything on his own account, out
of the top layers, so to speak, of his personal consciousness, he submits obediently to the
workings of 'inspiration'; and knowing that the medium in which he works has its own self-
nature, which must not be ignored or violently overridden, he makes himself its patient
servant and, in this way, achieves perfect freedom of expression. But life is also an art, and

the man who would become a consummate artist in living must follow, on all the levels of his being, the same procedure as that by which the painter or the sculptor or any other craftsman comes to his own more limited perfection.

Aldous Huxley, *The Perennial Philosophy*, Chatto & Windus Ltd., 1974, page 135

The Greek sculptor who wrought his statue, and, when it was finished, fell on his knees before it, felt that its beauty was no mere creation of his own, but something heavenly. Milton's passionate prayer to the celestial muse was not a poetic convention. And to Wordsworth what in literary phrase is named the consciousness of genius was in truth the consciousness of dependence upon, union with, and devotion to, the spirit of thought and love which manifests itself in nature and is more fully revealed in the thought and love of humanity. The man who is conscious of genius is generally a little man of talent. Men of genius are more often intensely conscious of their own littleness, and of the immeasurable heights above them. Here again we find the paradox of inspiration—that the greater the spiritual activity within a man, the less is he able to ascribe this activity to himself. And this fact, however paradoxical, is the root of religion...

In truth the man of genius (or rather the spirit which expresses itself in him under the limitations which belong to his individuality and diminish his greatness) is the main factor in human progress. Be his sphere that of religion, or science, or art, or of practice in morals or politics or even industry, he comes, and something as yet unrevealed breaks into the light. That which he brings, the new insight, begins its work upon the world, often, alas, in pain and conflict, struggling through clouds, and losing, as it conquers them and brightens on the general mind, much of the ineffable purity and radiance of its dawn. But even so it does its work. Like a stream from a mountain spring his idea divides and spreads. Slowly it distributes itself along the hundred channels of minds less original, and then along the thousand channels of minds less original still, till it has irrigated and fertilized a country or a continent, meeting again and again with like streams of influence from other springs, mixing with them and acquiring from its union a new virtue and a continued life. We *are* in our spiritual substance the spirits of the great dead.

A.C. Bradley, *A Miscellany*, Macmillan & Co. Ltd., 1931, page 235

INTELLECT

'Intellect'—faculty of knowing and reasoning; understanding;
persons collectively, of good understanding.

I n the early 1970s the choir of the University Church of Christ the King (London) went on a tour of East-Coast America. I was fortunate in being a member of that group.

We sang first of all in New York, at the Cathedral Church of St John the Divine, and Trinity Church, Wall Street. We then travelled northwards to give a concert at Storrs University, before moving on to New Haven, to sing in the main chapel at Yale. We partly retraced our steps to Baltimore, and then headed for Washington, singing in the 'President's Church', and ending up with a service in the National Cathedral.

Several of us had a special interest in student counselling, and took every opportunity of meeting experts in this field. At Baltimore we visited a down-town hospital. The hospital was going through a difficult time, financially and administratively, and had just called in a 'high-flyer' from Harvard to sort out these problems. Crucial decisions were needed to set the hospital on its feet again.

We met him for a few minutes and he gave us a brief analysis of the situation. He paused and asked if we had any questions. He then went on to give an outline of proposals to rescue the hospital. He was brilliant—a sharp bright man of enormous intellect. His clear lucid mind had immediately identified the causes of the problems. Not only did he understand them in full, but at one and the same time, spontaneously thought out practical ways to resolve them—a true intellectual in action.

A wise man is mightier than a strong man, and a man of knowledge than he who has strength.

Proverbs 24.5

For wisdom is a loving spirit.

Wisdom of Solomon 1.6 (AV)

Behold, I send you out as sheep in the midst of wolves; so be wise as serpents and innocent as doves.

Matthew 10.16

... gird up your minds.

1 Peter 1.13

Opinion is ultimately determined by the feelings, and not by the intellect.

Herbert Spencer, *Social Statics*, Williams & Norgate, 1892, page 244

The greater intellect one has, the more originality one finds in men. Ordinary persons find no difference between men.

Blaise Pascal, *Pensées*, translated by W.F. Trotter, Random House Inc., 1941, page 6

When Man has arrived at a certain ripeness of intellect any one grand and spiritual passage serves him as a starting-post towards all 'the two-and-thirty Palaces.'

John Keats, *The Works of John Keats*, edited by H. Buxton Forman, Reeves & Turner, 1883, Volume III, page 117, Letter to J. H. Reynolds, l.10

For no creature, howsoever rational and intellectual, is lighted of itself, but is lighted by participation of eternal Truth.

St Augustine, *An Augustine Synthesis*, arranged by Erich Przywara, SJ, Sheed & Ward Ltd., 1945, page 21

We must shut the eye of sense, and open that brighter eye of our understandings, that other eye of the soul, (as the philosopher calls our intellectual faculty,) ... 'which indeed all have, but few make use of.'

John Smith the Platonist, *Select Discourses*, Cambridge at the University Press, 1859, page 16

The uncertainty, however, lies always in the intellectual region, never in the practical. What Paul cares about is plain enough to the true heart, however far from plain to the man whose desire to understand goes ahead of his obedience.

George Macdonald, *Unspoken Sermons*, Third Series, Longmans, Green & Co. Ltd., 1889, page 43

The mind will never unveil God to man. God is only found at a certain point on the road of experience. He speaks to man through his heart and when that happens man knows, and he never again questions the love of God.

Grace Cooke, *Spiritual Unfoldment*, The White Eagle Publishing Trust, 1961, page 113

How often does the weak will obscure the clear call of conscience by resort to intellectual 'difficulties!' Some of these are real enough but some are sheer self-protection against the exacting claim of the holy love of God.

William Temple, *Readings in St. John's Gospel*, First and Second Series, Macmillan & Co. Ltd., 1947, page 68

We should not pretend to understand the world only by the intellect; we apprehend it just as much by feeling. Therefore the judgement of the intellect is, at best, only the half of truth, and must, if it be honest, also come to an understanding of its inadequacy

C.G. Jung, *Psychological Types*, translated by H. Godwin Baynes, Kegan Paul, Trench, Trubner & Co. Ltd., 1946, page 628

The longest way to God
the indirect
lies through the intellect
Here is my journey's end
and here its start.

Angelus Silesius, *The Book of Angelus Silesius*, translated by Frederick Franck, Wildwood House Ltd., 1976, page 104

All these intellectual attitudes would have short shrift if Christianity had remained what it was, a communion, if Christianity had remained what it was, a religion of the heart. This is one of the reasons why modern people understand nothing of true, real Christianity, of the true, real history of Christianity and what Christendom really was.

Charles Péguy, *Basic Verities*, translated by Ann and Julian Green, Kegan Paul, Trench, Trubner & Co. Ltd., 1943, page 115

It often seems to me when listening to the talk of clever people that they are in effect saying, 'Unless I understand, unless I am let into all the secrets of the Creator, I shall refuse to believe in him at all.' I am sure that such an attitude, even if it be unconscious, creates a strong barrier between man and his understanding of his true position.

Anyone with the most elementary knowledge of physics knows that there are sounds which are too high in pitch for us to hear, and forms of light which are quite invisible to the human eye... Yet for some curious reason we find it very difficult to believe that there may be sense higher than our sense, reason above our reason, and a total purpose quite beyond our comprehension. It seems to me perfectly possible that there may be supra-human wisdom, and we might well assume an attitude of wholesome humility when we reflect upon our relative insignificance. Can we not accept the suggestion that there are facts, even 'scientific' facts, which we can never know because we are incapable of understanding them? Can we not be persuaded to believe that specks of consciousness on this little planet cannot, in all reasonableness, be thought of as accurate critics of the total purpose behind creation?

J.B. Phillips, *God Our Contemporary*, Hodder & Stoughton Ltd., 1961, page 54

Perhaps the most dangerous by-product of the Age of Intellect is the unconscious growth of the idea that the human brain can solve the problems of the world. Even on the low level of practical affairs this is patently untrue. Any small human activity, the local bowls club or the ladies' luncheon club, requires for its survival a measure of self-sacrifice and service on the part of the members. In a wider national sphere, the survival of the nation depends basically on the loyalty and self-sacrifice of the citizens. The impression that the situation can be saved by mental cleverness, without unselfishness or human self-dedication, can only lead to collapse. Thus we see that the cultivation of the human intellect seems to be a magnificent ideal, but only on condition that it does not weaken unselfishness and human dedication to service. Yet this, judging by historical precedent, seems to be exactly what it does do. Perhaps it is not the intellectualism which destroys the spirit of self-sacrifice—the least we can say is that the two, intellectualism and the loss of a sense of duty, appear simultaneously in the life-story of the nation. Indeed it often appears in individuals, that the head and the heart are natural rivals. The brilliant but cynical intellectual appears at the opposite end of the spectrum from the emotional self-sacrifice of the hero or the martyr. Yet there are times when the perhaps unsophisticated self-dedication of the hero is more essential than the sarcasm of the clever.

Sir John Glubb, *The Fate of Empires and Search For Survival*, William Blackwood & Sons Ltd., 1978, page 13

JOY

'Joy'—pleasurable emotion due to well-being or satisfaction; the feeling or state of being highly pleased; exultation of spirit, gladness, delight.

I wonder if joy can be seen as another illustration of the Genesis story of the creation of man. In that story a seed or a spark of divine joy is 'breathed into' man.

The Psalmist, by instinct or intuition, knew this by feel. In Psalm 16 he spoke of his experience of the divine in very positive terms: 'Thou dost show me the path of life; in thy presence there is fullness of joy, in thy right hand are pleasures for evermore.'

Jesus was no stranger to joy. Could it be that he found joy in the depths of his own being? Two verses suggest this a distinct possibility. In St John's Gospel he is recorded as having said to his disciples: 'These thing I have spoken to you, that my joy may be in you, and that your joy may be full.' Later in the same Gospel, as he approached the cross, he extended this to include the world: 'But now I am coming to thee; and these things I speak in the world; that they may have my joy fulfilled in themselves.' We also remember the 'good and faithful servant' was bidden to 'enter into the joy of your master.'

The Apostle Paul (no stranger to joy) encouraged the Philippians to 'Rejoice in the Lord always'; and, as if this was not enough, added, 'again I say, Rejoice'.

Joy has not been a stranger to our experience during the last two thousand years. Many of us are able to sympathize with those words of Samuel Taylor Coleridge: 'Joy rises in me, like a summer's morn.'

Thou dost show me the path of life, in thy presence there is fulness of joy, in thy right hand are pleasures for evermore.

Psalm 16.11

The gladness of the heart is the life of man, and the joyfulness of a man prolongeth his days.

Ecclesiasticus 30.22 (AV)

These things I have spoken to you, that my joy may be in you, and that your joy may be full.

John 15.11

But now I am coming to thee; and these things I speak in the world, that they may have my joy fulfilled in themselves.

John 17.13

Joy rises in me, like a summer's morn.

Samuel Taylor Coleridge, *Coleridge's Poetical Works*, edited by Ernest Hartley Coleridge, Oxford University Press, 1978, page 340, 'A Christmas Carol,' st.viii, l.47

Joy is prayer—Joy is strength—Joy is love . . . A joyful heart is the normal result of a heart burning with love.

Mother Teresa of Calcutta, in *Something Beautiful for God*, Malcolm Muggeridge, William Collins Sons & Co. Ltd., 1983, page 68

How good is man's life, the mere living! how fit to employ
All the heart and the soul and the senses for ever in joy!

Robert Browning, *The Poetical Works of Robert Browning*, Smith, Elder & Co., 1899, Volume I, page 275, 'Saul,' st.ix, l.21

This glory and honour wherewith man is crowned ought to affect every person that is grateful, with celestial joy: and so much the rather because it is every man's proper end and sole inheritance.

Thomas Traherne, *Centuries*, The Faith Press Ltd., 1969, page 150

There are some people who have the quality of richness and joy in them and they communicate it to everything they touch. It is first of all a physical quality; then it is a quality of the spirit. With such people it makes no difference if they are rich or poor: they are really always rich because they have such wealth and vital power within them that they give everything interest, dignity, and a warm colour.

Thomas Wolfe, *The Web and the Rock*, The Sun Dial Press, 1940, page 377

Joy is everywhere; it is in the earth's green covering of grass; in the blue serenity of the sky; in the reckless exuberance of spring; in the severe abstinence of grey winter; in the living flesh that animates our bodily frame; in the perfect poise of the human figure, noble and upright; in living; in the exercise of all our powers; in the acquisition of knowledge; in fighting evils; in dying for gains we can never share. Joy is there everywhere.

Rabindranath Tagore, *Sadhana*, Macmillan & Co. Ltd., Indian Edition, 1930, page 116

Given reasonable health and freedom from anxiety, the world is for most people a good place to live in, with much of interest, beauty and wonder. Contact with other people can bring friendship, co-operation, humour and enjoyment. Given the faith that the world is God's creation and that each man is made in the image of God in a unique and personal way, our enjoyment becomes increasingly right and satisfying. Add to this the availability of divine grace for every difficulty and opportunity, and our enjoyment becomes almost mandatory.

George Appleton, *Journey for a Soul*, William Collins Sons & Co. Ltd., 1976, page 39

Life in the dimension of Spirit is a mystery rooted in the joy of being.
    The wonderful beauty of prayer is that the opening of our heart is as natural as the opening of a flower. To let a flower open and bloom it is only necessary to let it be, so if we simply *are*, if we become and remain still and silent, our heart cannot but be open, the Spirit cannot but pour through into our whole being. It is this we have been created for.
    Our meditation teaches us that we have to put our whole heart into this work of the Spirit if we are genuinely to respond to the call to leave the shallows and enter into the deep, direct knowledge that marks a life lived in the mystery of God.
    The call of Jesus is to worship God who is Spirit 'in Spirit and in Truth'.
    These words of Jesus which we have perhaps listened to as an injunction should now be heard as a declaration of liberty.

John Main OSB, in *The Joy of Being*, selected by Clare Hallward, Darton, Longman & Todd, 1989, page 42

We have an instinctive drive towards seeking a sense of well-being in whatever way we conceive of it. Unchecked by reason it is likely to lead us to immediate satisfactions of one kind or another.
    Hope is a similar drive which puts us in motion towards the attainment of our desired objective; we feel it is there to be had, that we have a right to it.
    When our well-being is threatened we are afraid; we dread feeling 'unwell', unhappy, insecure, miserable, unattractive, downcast... We fear all that is inimical to what we conceive of as our happiness. When we lack the sense of well-being, we grieve.
    But our true happiness lies in God and all our energy must be poured into surrendering to his will, not dissipated on things which eventually pall.

We must learn to make God our only joy and satisfaction, fearing only to miss him, to disappoint him; sad only for his grief.

This will not come easily, it must be struggled for.

Ruth Burrows, in *The Watchful Heart*, edited by Elizabeth Ruth Obbard, Darton, Longman & Todd, 1988, page 36

Joy in the Lord. It is the joy experienced by those who, come what may, are beginning to know God, to enjoy God in his beauty and loveliness, and to be exposed to his energies...

It is not only the joy of a sure faith that God reigns supreme; it is the joy of a practical fellowship with one who is himself joy and pours joy into lives which are united with him...

Our joy is the joy of those who are forgiven and forgiving. Lose hold on the realities of penitence and forgiveness in your life, and it will not be surprising if the joy which is your privilege begins to fade.

To have joy in God means knowing that God is our country, our environment, the air we breath. 'God is the country of the soul,' said St Augustine. Living in that country, we do not turn away from the griefs of our present environment—indeed, we may expect a greater sensitivity to these—but we are in the perspective of God, of heaven, of eternity.

Michael Ramsey, *The Christian Priest Today*, SPCK, 1972, page 90

Joy belongs, not only to those who have been called home, but also to the living, and no one shall take it from us. We are one with them in this joy, but never in sorrow. How shall we be able to help those who have become joyless and fearful unless we ourselves are supported by courage and joy? I don't mean by this something fabricated, compelled, but something given, free. Joy dwells with God; it descends from him and seizes spirit, soul and body, and where this joy has grasped a man it grows greater, carries him away, opens closed doors. There is a joy which knows nothing of sorrow, need and anxiety of the heart; it has no duration, and it can only drug one for the moment. The joy of God has been through the poverty of the crib and the distress of the cross; therefore it is insuperable, irrefutable. It does not deny the distress where it is, but finds God in the midst of it, indeed precisely there; it does not contest the most grievous sin, but finds forgiveness in just this way; it looks death in the face; yet finds life in death itself.

Dietrich Bonhoeffer, *True Patriotism*, William Collins Sons & Co. Ltd., 1965, page 189

Many people hardly believe anymore in the possibility of a truly joy-filled life. They have more or less accepted life as a prison and are grateful for every occasion that creates the illusion of the opposite; a cruise, a suspense novel, a sexual experience, or a few hours in a heightened state of consciousness. This is happiness in the house of fear, a happiness which is 'made in the world' and thus is neither lasting nor deeply satisfying...

The joy that Jesus offers his disciples is his own joy, which flows from his intimate communion with the One who sent him. It is a joy that does not separate happy days from sad days, successful moments from moments of failure, experiences of honour from experiences of dishonour, passion from resurrection. This joy is a divine gift that does not leave us during times of illness, poverty, oppression or persecution. It is present even when the world laughs or tortures, robs or maims, fights or kills. It is truly ecstatic, always moving us away from the house of fear into the house of love, and always proclaiming that death no longer has the final say, though its noise remains loud and its devastation visible. The joy of Jesus lifts up life to be celebrated.

Henri J.M. Nouwen, *In the House of the Lord*, Darton, Longman & Todd, 1994, page 64

Joy is the triumph of *life*; it is the sign that we are living our true life as spiritual beings. We are sent into the world to become something and to make something. The two are in practice so closely connected as to be almost inseparable. Our personality expands by creativeness, and creates spontaneously as it expands. Joy is the signal that we are spiritually alive and active. Wherever joy is, creation has been; and the richer the creation, the deeper the joy...

A great work of art, or a great scientific discovery, gives greater joy to its maker than a work of merely technical or mechanical skill...

Joy was a characteristic of the Christian community so long as it was growing, expanding, and creating healthfully. The time came when the Church ceased to grow, except externally in wealth, power and prestige; and these are mere outward adornments, or hampering burdens, very likely. They do not imply growth, or creativeness...

God sent us into the world to create something, and to enrich our own personality in the process. In our wrestling with intractable material, we have to draw on what is *above* ourselves. We have to rely on God's help to make anything worth making. And in drawing upon this power above ourselves, we take this higher power *into* ourselves; we raise ourselves above ourselves. This is how creativeness and inner growth mutually condition each other.

I want you to think earnestly of the witness which Joy on the one hand, and its antithesis, Boredom, on the other, bear to the duty and happiness of creative work, that is to say, real work, on however small a scale. The happy people are those who are producing something; the bored people are those who are consuming much and producing nothing... God punishes the useless by giving them pleasure without joy; and very wearisome they find it...

Joy will be ours, in so far as we are genuinely interested in great ideas outside ourselves. When we have once crossed the charmed circle and got outside ourselves, we shall soon realise that all true joy has an eternal and Divine soul and goal. We are immortal spirits, set to do certain things in time; were it not so, our lives would lack any rational justification. The joy of achievement is the recognition of a task understood and done. It is done, and fit to take its place—however lowly a place—in the eternal order... To do our duty in our own sphere, to try to create something worth creating, as our life's work, is the way to understand what joy is in this life, and by God's grace to earn the verdict: 'Well done, good and faithful servant; enter into the joy of thy Lord.'

W.R. Inge, *Personal Religion and the Life of Devotion*, Longmans, Green & Co. Ltd., 1924, page 64

KINDNESS

'Kindness'— the quality or habit of being kind; kind feeling; affection, love.

When I went into the army to do National Service we were first of all put through basic training. This involved twelve weeks of 'square bashing' (drill on the barracks' square), and learning 'weaponcraft' (i.e. how to fire our rifles). Many hours were spent in cleaning our 'top kit' (webbing equipment) and learning the delicate art of 'bulling our boots' (i.e. with spit and polish). After basic training we were to be posted to Cyprus.

In the seventh week I appeared before a panel and was recommended to attend a WOSB—a War Office Selection Board. If I passed this hurdle I would go to Mons Officer Cadet School in Aldershot for four months' training. After that, all being well, I would be commissioned.

I remember going to a very cold barracks for the WOSB, somewhere in a remote part of Hampshire. For three days we were put through a series of tests. One of these involved scaffolding poles and a piece of string. We were required to get a squad of men and equipment over a nearby stream—dry. The only trouble was, the scaffolding poles were not long enough. This was designed to test our powers of initiative and leadership.

On the third day I was summoned to see the colonel. My papers were laid out before him. 'I notice your eyesight is not A1. Regulations restrict you to the Pays Corps or the Pioneer Corps.' He looked at me intently. 'How keen are you to go into an Infantry Regiment?' I looked him straight in the eye and said, 'Very keen, Sir.' He said, 'Okay, we'll see what we can do.'

His act of kindness changed the whole course of my life.

He who despises his neighbour is a sinner, but happy is he who is kind to the poor.
Proverbs 14.21

Thus says the Lord of hosts. Render true judgments, show kindness and mercy each to his brother.
Zechariah 7.9

Love your enemies, and do good, and lend, expecting nothing in return; and your reward will be great, and you will be sons of the Most High; for he is kind to the ungrateful and the selfish.
Luke 6.35

What wisdom can you find that is greater than kindness?
Jean Jacques Rousseau, *Emile* or *Education*, translated by Barbara Foxley, J.M. Dent & Sons Ltd., 1911, page 43

There is a grace of kind listening, as well as a grace of kind speaking.
F.W. Faber, *Spiritual Conferences*, Thomas Richardson & Son, 1859, page 40

Kindness is the principle of tact, and respect for others the first condition of *savoir-vivre*.
Henri Frédéric Amiel, *Amiel's Journal*, translated by Mrs Humphry Ward, Macmillan & Co. Ltd., 1918, page 16

'Twas a thief said the last kind word to Christ:
Christ took the kindness and forgave the theft.

Robert Browning, *The Poetical Works of Robert Browning*, Smith, Elder, & Co., 1910, Volume 11, page 128, *The Ring and the Book*, Part VI, l.869

My feeling is that there is nothing in life but refraining from hurting others, and comforting those that are sad.

Olive Schreiner, *The Letters of Olive Schreiner*, edited by S.C. Cronwright-Schreiner, T. Fisher Unwin Ltd., 1924, page 48

Life is short, and we have never too much time for gladdening the hearts of those who are travelling the dark journey with us. Oh, be swift to love, make haste to be kind!

Henri Frédéric Amiel, *Amiel's Journal*, translated by Mrs Humphry Ward, Macmillan & Co. Ltd., 1918, page 146

On that best portion of a good man's life,
His little, nameless, unremembered, acts
Of kindness and of love.

William Wordsworth, *The Poetical Works of William Wordsworth*, edited by E. de Selincourt, Oxford at the Clarendon Press, 1944, Volume II, page 260, 'Lines composed a few miles above Tintern Abbey', l.33

I expect to pass through this world but once; any good thing therefore that I can do, or any kindness that I can show to any fellow-creature, let me do it now; let me not defer or neglect it, for I shall not pass this way again.

Attributed to Stephen Grellet

Be kind and merciful. Let no one ever come to you without coming away better and happier. Be the living expression of God's kindness: kindness in your face, kindness in your eyes, kindness in your smile, kindness in your warm greeting.

Mother Teresa of Calcutta, in *Something Beautiful For God*, Malcolm Muggeridge, William Collins Sons & Co. Ltd., 1983, page 69

More skilful in self-knowledge, even more pure,
As tempted more; more able to endure,
As more exposed to suffering and distress;
Thence, also, more alive to tenderness.

William Wordsworth, *The Poetical Works of William Wordsworth*, edited by E. de Selincourt and Helen Darbishire, Oxford at the Clarendon Press, 1958, Volume IV, page 87, 'Character of a Happy Warrior,' l.23

Kind thoughts are rarer than either kind words or kind deeds. They imply a great deal of thinking about others. This in itself is rare. But they imply also a great deal of thinking about others without the thoughts being criticisms. This is rarer still.

F.W. Faber, *Spiritual Conferences*, Thomas Richardson & Son, 1859, page 22

When we have been absorbed in great music, I do not think we generally feel particularly charitable to the people we meet outside. They seem to be of a coarser fibre than that into which we have been entering. That could never be true of our worship if it has really been worship of God, not some indulgence of our own spiritual emotion, but the concentration of mind, heart and will on Him. You will be full of kindness for everybody as you go out from such worship.

William Temple, *Christian Faith and Life*, SCM Press Ltd., 1963, page 28

All ordinary violence produces its own limitations, for it calls forth an answering violence which sooner or later becomes its equal or its superior. But kindness works simply and perseveringly; it produces no strained relations which prejudice its working; strained relations which already exist it relaxes. Mistrust and misunderstanding it puts to flight, and it strengthens itself by calling forth answering kindness. Hence it is the furthest-reaching and the most effective of all forces. All the kindness which a man puts out into the world works on the heart and the thoughts of mankind, but we are so foolishly indifferent that we are never in earnest in the matter of kindness. We want to topple a great load over, and yet will not avail ourselves of a lever which would multiply our power a hundred-fold

Albert Schweitzer, *Memoirs of Childhood and Youth*, translated by C.T. Campion, George Allen & Unwin Ltd., 1924, page 103

But that men should be so condemned or so favoured as to be released from responsibility for self-devotion as men to men, the ethic of reverence for life will not allow to be legitimate. They demand that every one of us in some way and with some object shall be a human being for human beings. To those who have no opportunity in their daily work of giving themselves in this way, and have nothing else that they can give, it suggests their sacrificing something of their time and leisure, even if of these they have but a scanty allowance. It says to them, find for yourselves some secondary activity, inconspicuous, perhaps secret. Open your eyes and look for a human being, or some work devoted to human welfare, which needs from some one a little time or friendliness, a little sympathy, or sociability, or labour. There may be a solitary or an embittered fellow-man, an invalid or an inefficient person to whom you can be something. Perhaps it is an old person or a child. Or some good work needs volunteers who can offer a free evening or run errands. Who can enumerate the many ways in which that costly piece of working capital, a human being, can be employed? More of him is wanted everywhere! Search, then, for some investment for your humanity, and do not be frightened away if you have to wait, or to be taken on trial. And be prepared for disappointments. But in any case, do not be without some secondary work in which you give yourself as a man to men. It is marked out for you, if you only truly will to have it...

Thus do the true ethics speak to those who have only a little time and a little human nature to give. Well will it be with them if they listen, and are preserved from becoming stunted natures because they have neglected this devotion of self to others.

Albert Schweitzer, *The Philosophy of Civilization*, translated by C.T. Campion, third English edition, revised by Mrs Charles E.B. Russell, Part II, *Civilization and Ethics*, A. & C. Black Ltd., 1946, page 256

LEADERSHIP

*'Leadership'—direction given by going in front, example,
encouragement by doing thing.*

I wonder if Jesus as revealed in the Gospels is the greatest leader we have ever seen? At the age of thirty he had fully worked out what was meant for him to be made in the image and likeness of God. In these thirty years he discovered the Father in the depths of his being, the Holy Spirit, life, light, truth, joy, love and so on. In his sojourn in the wilderness, led by the Spirit, He worked out his strategy and then came proclaiming the kingdom of God, inviting those around him to enter the kingdom of God, and discover 'the pearl of great price' in the depths of their being. The essence of his teaching is 'the kingdom of God is within you' and 'I came that they may have life and have it abundantly.' By this he meant a superabundance of life.

In his short life, theory and practice were fused together in a unity. In the Gospels we find the greatest spiritual and moral teaching of all time. The essence of his ethical teaching lay in the two great commandments: 'You shall love the Lord your God with all your heart, and with all your soul, and with all your mind, and with all your strength . . . and you shall love your neighbour as yourself.' This was simplified in a new commandment: 'Love one another; even as I have loved you.'

His choice of the twelve disciples was a master-stroke and made a way for the continuance of his work and ministry. His concern for the individual revealed a depth of compassion second to none and issued in healing. His sacrificial death on the cross, his subsequent resurrection, and the coming of the Holy Spirit, sealed his leadership for all time.

Choose able men from all the people, such as fear God, men who are trustworthy and who hate a bribe.

Exodus 18.21

The Lord hath wrought great glory by them through his great power from the beginning. Such as did bear rule in their kingdoms, men renowned for their power, giving counsel by their understanding, and declaring prophecies: Leaders of the people by their counsels, and by their knowledge of learning meet for the people, wise and eloquent in their instructions.

Ecclesiasticus 44.2-4 (AV)

But Jesus called them to him and said, 'You know that the rulers of the Gentiles lord it over them, and their great men exercise authority over them. It shall not be so among you; but whoever would be great among you must be your servant, and whoever would be first among you must be your slave.

Matthew 20.25-27

Never flag in zeal, be aglow with the Spirit, serve the Lord.

Romans 12.11

The real leader has no need to lead—he is content to point the way.

Henry Miller, *The Wisdom of the Heart*, New Directions Books, 1941, page 46

In the simplest terms, a leader is one who knows where he wants to go, and gets up and goes.

John Erskine, *The Complete Life*, Andrew Melrose Ltd., 1945, page 134

There are men, who, by their sympathetic attractions, carry nations with them, and lead the activity of the human race.

Ralph Waldo Emerson, *The Conduct of Life, Nature and Other Essays*, J.M. Dent & Sons Ltd., 1911, page 175

He that would govern others, first should be
The master of himself.

Philip Massinger, *The Plays of Massinger*, Alfred Thomas Crocker, 1868, *The Bondman*, page 102, Act I. sc.iii.

The fire of God
Fills him: I never saw his like: there lives
No greater leader.

Alfred, Lord Tennyson, *The Poems of Tennyson*, edited by Christopher Ricks, Longmans, Green & Co. Ltd., 1969, page 1629, *Idylls of the King*, No.470, 'Lancelot and Elaine,' l.314

No man is great enough or wise enough for any of us to surrender our destiny to. The only way in which any one can lead us is to restore to us the belief in our own guidance.

Henry Miller, *The Wisdom of the Heart*, New Directions Books, 1941, page 122

We that had loved him so, followed him, honoured him,
Lived in his mild and magnificent eye,
Learned his great language, caught his clear accents,
Made him our pattern to live and to die!

Robert Browning, *The Poetical Works of Robert Browning*, Smith, Elder & Co., 1899, Volume I, page 249, 'The Lost Leader,' st.i, l.12

... Christian leadership is accomplished only through service. This service requires the willingness to enter into a situation, with all the human vulnerabilities a man has to share with his fellow man. This is a painful and self-denying experience, but an experience which can indeed lead man out of his prison of confusion and fear. Indeed, the paradox of Christian leadership is that the way out is the way in, that only by entering into communion with human suffering can relief be found ...

... every Christian is constantly invited to overcome his neighbour's fear by entering into it with him, and to find in the fellowship of suffering the way to freedom.

Henri J.M. Nouwen, *The Wounded Healer*, Doubleday, 1979, page 77

A leader of his people, unsupported by any outward authority: a politician whose success rests neither upon craft nor the mastery of technical devices, but simply on the convincing power of his personality; a victorious fighter who has always scorned the use of force; a man of wisdom and humility, armed with resolve and inflexible consistency, who has devoted all his strength to the uplifting of his people and the betterment of their lot; a man who has confronted the brutality of Europe with the dignity of the simple human being, and thus at all times risen superior.

Generations to come, it may be, will scarce believe that such a one as this ever in flesh and blood walked upon this earth.

Albert Einstein, written of Mahatma Gandhi, in *Ideas and Opinions*, Souvenir Press (Educational & Academic) Ltd., 1973, page 7

However dedicated men may be, the success of their work inevitably depends on the quality of their leaders. I am convinced that the key to leadership lies in the principle: 'He that is greatest among you, let him be as the younger and he that is chief, as he that doth serve.' Leadership should not bring privileges, but duties. No man should ask his subordinates to do more than he does himself. If work begins at eight in the morning, the top man should be there on time. If the workers snatch a quick lunch in a cafeteria, the directors should do the same, and not absent themselves for two hours to eat at a restaurant. Everyone should enjoy his or her daily work. Enjoyment depends on personal relations. It is the duty of the senior men to make their subordinates happy by knowing them personally and by producing a spirit of comradeship and of mutual pride in the work. Warm personal relationships can be used by senior men to discuss with their subordinates the progress of the work, their mutual achievements and the difficulties which lie ahead. Such intercourse and exchange of confidences foster a sense of comradeship and team-work.

Sir John Glubb, *The Fate of Empires and Search for Survival*, William Blackwood & Sons Ltd., 1978, page 39

'It's a pity that the leaders of the Church are so rotten.' Yes, indeed. It is a worse pity that, when leaders are picked, there is only you to pick them from!

But what is the leadership which the human race needs? It is the leading of the human race into fellowship with the Creator, so as to reflect him in all human affairs. This leadership is the role of the *whole* Christian Church. 'As the soul is in the body, so are the Christians in the world.'

Within the Church, this leadership is shared by different people in different roles. There are the prophets. God raises them up with particular insight into the divine will and purpose in human affairs. The prophet has eyes which see what the rest of us do not see.

There are statesmen. These are practical people with the gift of carrying out particular implications of the divine will in this or that situation.

There are all the members of the Church. They all share in the task of leading the human race the right way; of healing that derangement of the relation of creatures to their Creator by which humanity is poisoned. Each will look to his or her own share in that derangement.

What is it in *me* that must be put right?

Michael Ramsey, *Through the Year with Michael Ramsey*, edited by Margaret Duggan, Hodder & Stoughton Ltd., 1975, page 173

LIFE

'Life'—period from birth to death, birth to the present time, or present time to death; energy, liveliness, vivacity, animation; vivifying influence, active part of existence.

At the age of twenty-four I was at the crossroads of life. A choice of career had to be made in the next few months. I was soon to sit 'Schools' (the Oxford name for Finals) for a law degree, and my time at Oxford would come to an end shortly afterwards.

I thought carefully about going into the family firm of lawyers. The material rewards were promising. The firm was well-established and relatively secure. Being a solicitor was still regarded as 'respectable' and carried a certain amount of status in the community. I would be in a position to get married and have a family, etc. The omens were promising.

As I was musing over this possibility, I discerned a certain selfishness of outlook. I was thinking primarily of myself and my own comfort and security. The cost of this would be considerable; forty years working in an office; for five and a half days a week; for fifty weeks a year. This did not seem to me a sufficient justification of life.

About this time I made a spiritual commitment—to live the Christian *life* at all costs. I had just come to see the spiritual dimension as the most important thing in life. Before long an inner voice challenged my integrity: 'Come on, Bill, if living this Christian spiritual life is so important to you, shouldn't you be actively engaged in spreading it?'

A vital question had been asked. Money, comfort and status were set aside as I made a bid for life itself.

Then the Lord God formed man of dust from the ground, and breathed into his nostrils the breath of life; and man became a living being.

Genesis 2.7

For he who finds me finds life and obtains favour from the Lord, but he who misses me injures himself.

Proverbs 8.35

If anyone thirst, let him come to me and drink. He who believes in me, as the scripture has said, 'Out of his heart shall flow rivers of living water.'

John 7.38

I came that they may have life, and have it abundantly.

John 10.10

Creative life is always on the yonder side of convention.

C.G. Jung, *Psychological Reflections*, selected and edited by Jolande Jacobi, Routledge & Kegan Paul Ltd., 1953, page 185

The mystery of life is not a problem to be solved; it is a reality to be experienced.

J.J. van der Leeuw, *The Conquest of Illusion*, Alfred A. Knopf, 1928, page 9

Life is its own journey; pre-supposes its own change and movement, and one tries to arrest them at one's eternal peril.

Laurens van der Post, *Venture to the Interior*, Penguin Books Ltd., 1968, page 124

Reflect that life, like ev'ry other blessing,
Derives its value from its use alone.

Samuel Johnson, *The Yale Edition of the Works of Samuel Johnson*, edited by E.L. McAdam Jr., with George Milne, Yale University Press, 1964, Volume VI, *Poems*, page 162, 'Irene,' Act III. sc.viii. l.28

Is life so wretched? Isn't it rather your hands which are too small, your vision which is muddied? You are the one who must grow up.

Dag Hammarskjöld, *Markings*, translated by Leif Sjoberg and W.H. Auden, Faber & Faber Ltd., 1964, page 63

To live as fully, as completely as possible, to be happy and again to be happy is the true aim and end of life. 'Ripeness is all.'

Llewelyn Powys, *Impassioned Clay*, Longmans, Green & Co. Ltd., 1931, page 94

What makes our lives worth while is stretching towards God who is love and truth. That we reach out beyond our capacity is at once our pain, our adventure, our hope.

Hubert van Zeller, *Considerations*, Sheed & Ward Ltd., 1974, page 69

After all it is those who have a deep and real inner life who are best able to deal with the 'irritating details of outer life.'

Evelyn Underhill, *The Letters of Evelyn Underhill*, edited by Charles Williams, Longmans, Green and Co., 1947, page 219

The web of our life is of a mingled yarn, good and ill together; our virtues would be proud if our faults whipp'd them not, and our crimes would despair if they were not cherish'd by our virtues.

William Shakespeare, *All's Well That Ends Well*, Act IV. sc.iii. l.68

We live in deeds, not years; in thoughts, not breaths;
In feelings, not in figures on a dial.
We should count time by heart-throbs. He most lives
Who thinks most; feels the noblest; acts the best.

P.J. Bailey, *Festus*, William Pickering, 1839, page 62

The true spiritual goal of life is the formation of a rightly fashioned will, the creation of a controlling personal love, the experience of a guiding inward Spirit, which keep the awakened soul steadily approximating the perfect Life which Christ has revealed.

Rufus M. Jones, *Spiritual Reformers in the 16th and 17th Centuries*, Macmillan & Co. Ltd., 1914, page 38

People are always blaming their circumstances for what they are. I don't believe in circumstances. The people who get on in this world are the people who get up and look for the circumstances they want, and, if they can't find them, make them.

George Bernard Shaw, *The Complete Plays of Bernard Shaw*, Paul Hamlyn, 1965, page 75, *Mrs. Warren's Profession*, Act II

Man is a journey out of animal individuality to the human significance which is personality, and on to the life of God... Man is able, 'even here and now, vividly to conceive... the timeless character... of his own spirit,' and of God, and of his experience of God who penetrates his own spirit.

Friedrich von Hügel, in Joseph P. Whelan, SJ, *The Spirituality of Friedrich von Hügel*, William Collins Sons & Co. Ltd., 1971, page 48

You have striven so hard, and so long, to *compel* life. Can't you now slowly change, and let life slowly drift into you. Surely it is even a greater mystery and preoccupation even than willing, to let the invisible life steal into you and slowly possess you.

D.H. Lawrence, *The Selected Letters of D.H. Lawrence*, edited by Diana Trilling, Farrar, Straus & Cudahy, 1958, page 210

Not a May-Game is this man's life; but a battle and a march, a warfare with principalities and powers. No idle promenade through fragrant orange-groves and green flowery spaces, waited on by coral Muses and rosy Hours: it is a stern pilgrimage through burning sandy solitudes, through regions of thick-ribbed ice.

Thomas Carlyle, *Past and Present*, Ward, Lock & Co. Ltd., page 198

If you don't know what man was made for, neither do you know what man can do. You don't know the heights to which he can rise, the fullness of living of which he is capable or the happiness which can come his way. The whole thing means a tremendous difference here and now, the difference of knowing what life really can be.

R.L. Smith, in Paul Rowntree Clifford, *Man's Dilemma and God's Answer*, broadcast talks, SCM Press Ltd., 1964, page 73

A man contains all that is needful to his government within himself. He is made a law unto himself. All real good or evil that can befall him must be from himself... The purpose of life seems to be to acquaint a man with himself. He is not to live to the future as described to him, but to live to the real future by living the real present. The highest revelation is that God is in every man.

Ralph Waldo Emerson, *The Heart of Emerson's Journals*, edited by Bliss Perry, Constable & Co. Ltd., 1927, page 79

People 'died' all the time in their lives. Parts of them died when they made the wrong kind of decisions—decisions against life. Sometimes they died bit by bit until finally they were just living corpses walking around. If you were perceptive you could see it in their eyes; the fire had gone out... But you always knew when you made a decision against life. When you denied life you were warned. The cock crowed, always, somewhere inside you. The door clicked and you were safe inside—safe and dead.

Anne Morrow Lindbergh, *The Steep Ascent*, Chatto & Windus Ltd., 1945, page 57

I do know that trying to be open to things that are good, and beautiful, and true, wherever they are to be found, brings to me a strength that is greater than my own. This is fortified by seeking out and finding reassurance from 'good deeds in a naughty world,' which encourages the belief that goodness, courage, generosity and heroism are possible. This remains true even when such virtues are partially disclosed. There have been many lives like those of St. Francis, Gandhi and Schweitzer, which have shown how great is the human potential for heroic living.

George H. Gorman, *Introducing Quakers*, Friends Home Service Committee, 1969, page 22

There are real ends in life, and they are all in that realm which belongs to us in virtue of our spiritual and intellectual capacities, and not of our animal capacities.

They all belong to the realm, for example, either of knowledge, or appreciation of beauty, or friendship, or family affection or loyalties, and courage, and love and joy and peace. They are all, in fact, in the wider sense of the term part of the fruit of the spirit; and those, and those only, are real ends. The whole economic sphere is concerned with means to those ends; and it must be judged, not primarily by its efficiency within itself, by its effectiveness in promoting the maximum output and the like; but primarily in the light of the question whether it is fostering the attainment of the real ends by the greatest number of people. We may take as our slogan, if you like 'Fullness of Personality in the widest possible Fellowship.'

William Temple, The Church Looks Forward, Macmillan & Co. Ltd., 1944, page 117

We too must have life in ourselves. We too must, like the Life himself, live. We can live in no way but that in which Jesus lived, in which life was made in him. That way is, to give up our life. This is the one supreme action of life possible to us for the making of life in ourselves. Christ did it of himself, and so became light to us, that we might be able to do it in ourselves, after him, and through his originating act. We must do it ourselves, I say. The help that he has given and gives, the light and the spirit—working of the Lord, the spirit, in our hearts, is all in order that we may, as we must, do it ourselves. Till then we are not alive; life is not made in us. The whole strife and labour and agony of the Son with every man, is to get him to die as he died. All preaching that aims not at this, is a building of wood and hay and stubble.

George Macdonald, Unspoken Sermons, Third Series, Longmans, Green & Co. Ltd., 1889, page 20

When we pray 'Thy Kingdom come' we are inviting God to come and do in us all he wants to do. We are affirming that we want him to be our God and Father, to love us into fullness of life. We are praying that his great plan of love for his creation be accomplished. Nothing else can satisfy the human hearts he has made for himself . . .

We are utterly confident that the Father wants to give us his kingdom (Luke 12.32) and that he will leave no stone unturned to do so. There is therefore no need for strain or anxiety. There is no mysterious art to be mastered, it is all there before us at each moment. What God asks of us we can always accomplish. There is nothing to be afraid of. It is not a chancy thing that might not come off.

Be happy to feel that you cannot control your life, that there is so much in you that you seem unable to cope with. Trust yourself to him, take each moment as it comes, for each moment holds him. Let him have the say, let him take charge, even though you are left feeling no one is in charge.

Dispossession of self is the reverse side of God-possession.

Ruth Burrows, Living Love and Our Father, Darton, Longman & Todd, 1990, page 130

LIGHT

'Light'—mental illumination, elucidation, enlightenment, vivacity
in a person's face, especially in the eyes, illumination of the soul by
divine truth.

V isitors entering the chapel of University College, Oxford, can be excused for thinking it dark and gloomy. Enter the main body of the chapel and witness the beauty of the seventeenth-century van Linge windows. Notice how the darkness accentuates the colours in these painted windows, works of art in themselves, and the college's most valuable possession.

From time to time we have baptisms in the college chapel. Those baptized are either undergraduates, or the offspring of old members recently married in the chapel. Each light (one hundred in all) is switched on for these services, and all of our sixty-two candles are lit. This creates a wonderful atmosphere—the chapel bathed in light.

Before the service I say a few words about baptism. Water is used for cleansing, but the main emphasis of this service is on spiritual rebirth. I begin with the Genesis story of the creation of man, the divine inbreathing, and the divine life to be found in the depths of our being. This seed or spark of divine life is catalysed or triggered off in a baptism 'in the name of (nature of) the Father, and of the Son, and of the Holy Spirit'. After the signing of the cross, the candidate for baptism (or a godparent) is given a lighted candle, symbolic of Christ 'the light of the world' entering the life of the newly baptized person. A reminder of Christ's words is given: 'You are the light of the world... Let your light so shine before men that they may see your good works and give glory to your Father who is in heaven.'

Light dawns for the righteous, and joy for the upright in heart.

Psalm 97.11

My son, keep your father's commandment, and forsake not your mother's teaching... For the commandment is a lamp and the teaching a light, and the reproofs of discipline are the way of life.

Proverbs 6.20,23

In him was life, and the life was the light of men. The light shines in the darkness, and the darkness has not overcome it.

John 1.4-5

I am the light of the world; he who follows me will not walk in darkness, but will have the light of life.

John 8.12

I am aware of something in myself *whose shine is my reason.* I see clearly that something is there, but what it is I cannot understand. But it seems to me, that, if I could grasp it, I should know all truth.

Meister Eckhart, *Meister Eckhart*, translated by Raymond B. Blakney, Harper & Row, Publishers, Inc., 1941, page 101

Christ the Light of the World shines first upon the soul, and then from within the soul upon the path of life. He does not illumine our way while leaving us unconverted; but by converting us He illumines our way.

William Temple, *Readings in St. John's Gospel*, First and Second Series, Macmillan & Co. Ltd., 1947, page 179

Hast never come to thee an hour,
A sudden gleam divine, precipitating, bursting all these bubbles, fashions, wealth?
These eager business aims—books, politics, art, amours,
To utter nothingness?

Walt Whitman, *The Complete Poems*, edited by Francis Murphy, Penguin Books Ltd., 1982, page 303, 'Hast Never Come to Thee an Hour,' l.1

And I said to the man who stood at the gate of the year:
'Give me a light that I may tread safely into the unknown.'
And he replied: 'Go out into the darkness and put your hand into the hand of God.
That shall be to you better than light and safer than a known way.'

Louise M. Haskins, *God Knows* (quoted by King George VI in a Christmas Broadcast, 25 December 1939)

This opening of the spiritual eyes is that glowing darkness and rich nothingness of which I spoke earlier. It may be called: Purity of soul and spiritual rest, inward stillness and peace of conscience, refinement of thought and integrity of soul, a lively consciousness of grace... the tasting of heavenly joys, the ardour of love and brightness of light, the entry into contemplation and reformation of feeling.

Walter Hilton, *The Ladder of Perfection*, translated by Leo Sherley-Price, Penguin Books Ltd., 1957, page 223

There is a Light in man which shines into his darkness, reveals his condition to him, makes him aware of evil and checks him when he is in the pursuit of it; gives him a vision of righteousness, attracts him towards goodness, and points him infallibly toward Christ from whom the Light shines. This Light is pure, immediate, and spiritual. It is of God, in fact it is God immanently revealed.

Rufus M. Jones, *Spiritual Reformers in the 16th and 17th Centuries*, Macmillan & Co. Ltd., 1914, page 345

The world may be in darkness but this should not upset us. Christ is the light of the world. If we bring this truth into the context of our own experience we must know that light inaccessible has invited us to enter into this light. He has asked us not merely to reflect it but to *be* it. Otherwise his words 'you are the light of the world, the city seated on a hill, the salt of the earth' are no more than an oratorical flourish. Jesus did not go in for oratorical flourishes.

Hubert van Zeller, *Considerations*, Sheed & Ward Ltd., 1974, page 51

But I will now show a little more distinctly, what this *Pearl of Eternity* is. First, It is the *Light* and *Spirit* of God within Thee, which has hitherto done Thee but little Good, because all the Desire of thy Heart has been after the Light and Spirit of this World. Thy Reason, and Senses, thy Heart and Passions, have turned all their Attention to the poor Concerns of this Life, and therefore thou art a Stranger to this Principle of Heaven, this Riches of Eternity within Thee. For as God is not, cannot be truly found by any Worshippers, but those who worship Him in *Spirit* and in *Truth*, so this Light and Spirit, though always within us, is not, cannot be found, felt, or enjoyed, but by those whose whole Spirit is turned to it.

William Law, *The Spirit of Prayer*, full text, edited by Sidney Spencer, James Clarke & Co. Ltd., 1969, page 45

I do not believe that we can put into anyone ideas which are not in him already. As a rule there are in everyone all sorts of good ideas, ready like tinder. But much of this tinder catches fire, or catches it successfully, only when it meets some flame or spark from outside, i.e., from some other person. Often, too, our own light goes out, and is rekindled by some experience we go through with a fellow-man. Thus we have each of us cause to think with deep gratitude of those who have lighted the flames within us. If we had before us those who have thus been a blessing to us, and could tell them how it came about, they would be amazed to learn what passed over from their life into ours.

Albert Schweitzer, *Memoirs of Childhood and Youth*, translated by C.T. Campion, George Allen & Unwin Ltd, 1924, page 90

Now the Lord God hath opened to me by his invisible power how that every man was enlightened by the divine light of Christ; and I saw it shine through all, and that they that believed in it came out of condemnation and came to the light of life and became children of it, but they that hated it, and did not believe in it, were condemned by it, though they made a profession of Christ. This I saw in the pure openings of the Light without the help of any man, neither did I then know where to find it in the Scriptures; though afterwards, searching the Scriptures, I found it. For I saw in that Light and Spirit which was before Scripture was given forth, and which led the holy men of God to give them forth, that all must come to that Spirit, if they would know God, or Christ, or the Scriptures aright, which they that gave them forth were led and taught.

George Fox, *The Journal of George Fox*, a revised edition by John L. Nickalls, Cambridge at the University Press, 1952, page 33

The Bride lives in light, surrounded by it, penetrated by it from every angle. Because it is unimpeded, naked, full, circumambient, it is essentially formless, like an atmosphere.

For most of us light can get at us here and there, now from this angle, now from that, and more persistently as we progress. But for the Bride the inflow of light is total.

She always sees God, always loves him in the multiple concrete demands of every day. She is never 'not there', never unprepared.

Hers is real, solid virtue; a habit that is the effect of great, constant love. 'I do always the things that please him.' Hers is inviolable strength, not as from herself, for she remains poor and weak, as well she knows, but from the God who possesses her and communicates to her his own strength. She lives by his life, his virtue, his wisdom, his love; hence her utter security.

She has chosen to abandon all for his sake... So now God assumes full care of her, holds her in his arms, feeds her with all good things and takes her into his deepest secrets.

Ruth Burrows, in *The Watchful Heart*, edited by Elizabeth Ruth Obbard, Darton, Longman & Todd, 1988, page 60

Christ walked in the full light of God, we only have flashes of it. Hence, whereas Christ knew when His day was coming, we cannot know. Christ's life was marred by no error of judgement, because He had full light. Our lives are full of errors of judgement because our sight is dim, so that we often cannot see what is our right path. If we have put our earthly life in God's hands—that is to say, if we are ready to die today, as we should be—we can have absolutely no fear, no matter what happens. For I know that once having given myself to God, to be in His hand a mere tool on earth, a tool with which some good work may be done while I live,—having once and for all done away with my own free-will and having put God's will in its place,—I know that no power of earth can do me any harm till God's day comes...

So I live, knowing that I am in God's hands, to be used to bring others to Him, if He so wills by a long life full of work, or to die tomorrow if He wills, having done nothing worth mentioning... We must do what we can and leave the rest to Him... My trust is in God, so that it matters not what I do nor where I go.

Edward Wilson, in *The Faith of Edward Wilson*, George Seaver, John Murray Ltd., 1949, page 43

LISTENING

'Listening'—making effort to hear something, hearing person speaking with attention; giving ear to (person or sound or story).

One of my favourite quotes on listening is a short sentence from Martin Buber's book *I and Thou*: 'He [God] cannot be seen, but he can be listened to.'

The Old Testament prophets were great listeners. Take, for instance, Elijah. He tried to find God in the wind, in the earthquake and in the fire. We are told the Lord was not to be found there, but rather in 'a still small voice'.

Jesus was a great listener. He spent nights in prayer, and sometimes was up early in the morning, a great while before day. In the quiet and stillness of these times, He would be able to listen. When active he listened to his disciples and to those who came to him for healing. On the mount of transfiguration a voice came out of the cloud and advised the disciples to listen: 'This is my beloved Son; listen to him.'

Søren Kierkegaard suggests we learn to 'listen' when reading the scriptures: 'When thou readest God's Word, then in everything that thou readest, constantly to say to thyself, "It is I that am addressed, to me this is spoken."'

I have found an important part of reflection lies in listening. As we mull over the contents of *Visions of Grace*, we might put into practice some words of an anonymous writer: 'Listen to the meaning beneath the words.' When reflecting I have found it helpful to have a pen and paper on hand, and write down thoughts and feelings which come to me. Listening then becomes a valuable experience and helps us on our journey of faith.

And the Lord came and stood forth, calling as at other times, 'Samuel! Samuel!' And Samuel said, 'Speak, for thy servant hears.'

1 Samuel 3.10

O that my people would listen to me, that Israel would walk in my ways!

Psalm 81.13

He who has ears to hear, let him hear.

Matthew 11.15

Behold, I stand at the door and knock; if any one hears my voice and opens the door, I will come in to him and eat with him, and he with me.

Revelation 3.20

Give us grace to listen well.

John Keble, *The Christian Year*, edited by Ernest Rhys, J.M. Dent & Sons Ltd., 1914, page 72

By listening it is possible to bring a man's soul into being.

Anon., heard on the radio

Basically the answer is simple, very simple. We need only listen to what Jesus has told us. It's enough to listen to the Gospel and put into practice what it tells us.

Carlo Carretto, *Letters from the Desert*, translated by Rose Mary Hancock, Darton, Longman & Todd, Orbis Books, 1972, page 40

Difficult as it is really to listen to someone in affliction, it is just as difficult for him to know that compassion is listening to him.

Simone Weil, *Waiting on God*, translated by Emma Craufurd, William Collins Sons & Co. Ltd., 1974, page 106

If we knew how to listen to God, we should hear him speaking to us. For God does speak. He speaks in his Gospel; he speaks also through life—that new Gospel to which we ourselves add a page each day.

Michel Quoist, *Prayers of Life*, translated by Anne Marie de Commaile and Agnes Mitchell Forsyth, Gill and Macmillan Ltd., 1963, page 2

The boy Samuel was told by Heli to pray: 'Speak, Lord, for your servant listens.' He was not instructed to say: 'Listen, Lord, for your servant speaks.' If we listened more we would learn more about spirit and truth ... and in turn would be better able to worship in spirit and in truth.

Hubert van Zeller, *Considerations*, Sheed & Ward Ltd., 1974, page 88

Listening to oneself is so difficult because this art requires another ability, rare in modern man: that of being alone with oneself ...

Listening to the feeble and indistinct voice of our conscience is difficult also because it does not speak to us directly but indirectly and because we are often not aware that it is our conscience which disturbs us. We may feel only anxious (or even sick) for a number of reasons which have no apparent connection with our conscience.

Erich Fromm, *Man For Himself*, Routledge & Kegan Paul Ltd., 1975, page 161

The most useful service we can do for anybody, says Laubach, is to link him with God. Our prayers to do this need not be long prayers. Laubach is a great advocate of the 'flash prayer', made whenever the thoughts of somebody else comes to mind: linking him immediately with the thought of God! ...

Most of us, in our praying, devote far less time and attention to 'waiting upon God'—to the listening side of prayer—than we devote to the incessantly active and vocal form of praying that most of us indulge in. We ought ... to give more time to listening to God than we do to speaking to Him.

Dr Cyril H. Powell, *Secrets of Answered Prayer*, Arthur James Ltd., 1958, pages 114, 123

There is a great need today for hearts that listen. Martin Israel assures us that we do not have to rely upon ourselves alone when trying to solve the problems with which we are confronted. He says, 'When we are able to listen in silence to the life story of another person and not respond with our own wisdom, a greater wisdom, that of the Holy Spirit who is the Advocate, will flow from our lips and will lead both that other person and ourselves into truth. From the lips of silence proceeds wisdom the Word of God, from the hushed heart flows love.'

Elizabeth Bassett, *The Bridge is Love*, Darton, Longman & Todd Ltd., 1981, page 93

So many Christians have lost touch with their own tradition of prayer. We no longer benefit as we should from the wisdom and experienced counsel of the great masters of prayer. All these masters have agreed that in prayer it is not we ourselves who are taking the initiative. We are not talking to God. We are listening to His word within us. We are not looking for Him; it is He who has found us. Walter Hilton expressed it very simply in the fourteenth century. He wrote, 'You, yourself, do nothing, you simply allow him to work in your soul!' (*The Scale of Perfection*, Book 11, Ch.24). The advice of St Theresa was in tune with this. She reminds us that all we can do in prayer is to dispose ourselves; the rest is in the power of the Spirit who lead us.

These teachers (Walter Hilton and St Theresa) have the same experience of prayer as that which led St Paul to write that 'we do not even know how to pray, but the Spirit prays within us' (Rom 8.26) ... He was not writing to specialists in prayer, but to husbands, wives, butchers and bakers.

John Main OSB, *Word into Silence*, Darton, Longman & Todd, 1980, page 50

At this point let us call to mind one very important thing: prayer is not so much a matter of talking as listening; contemplation is not watching but being watched.

On the day when we realize this, we will have entered finally into possession of the truth, and prayer will have become a living reality. To be watched by God: that is how I would define contemplation, which is passive rather than active, more a matter of silence than of words, of waiting rather than of action.

What am I before God?

What can I do to be worthy of his revelation?

If he shuts, no one opens, and if he opens, no one shuts. He is the active principle of love, he is before all, he is the one who makes within me his own prayer, which then becomes my prayer.

I do not know what has happened or is happening within you, but I do know what has happened and is happening within myself, and I can tell you this: that it was he who sought me in the first place, and it is he who continues to seek me.

Carlo Carretto, *In Search of the Beyond*, translated by Sarah Fawcett, Darton, Longman & Todd, 1975, page 76

The phrase taught by old Eli to the boy Samuel, 'Speak, Lord, for thy servant hears' (1 Sam 3.9), expresses a fundamental attitude of the soul which knows by faith that its God wants to communicate with it direct. Thus the soul is constantly listening out for every appeal from God, on the watch for every breath of the Spirit, 'Blessed ... are those who hear the word of God and keep it' (Luke 11.28). But the word speaks to us only when all things are wrapped in a profound silence. Give me, O Lord, a heart that listens, for the Word does not use many words (Mt 6.7). When the Lord, who is uncreated Wisdom, takes possession of a soul, he does not cry or lift up his voice (Is 42.2), but rather he is silent in his love (Zeph 3.17). He who listens to him dwells secure (Prov 1.33). All we have to do is to listen in our heart to the silence of God until our heart is purified in this silence and the Lord can give it wisdom (Prov 2.6), that gift of Wisdom which transforms silence into savour and enables us to delight in the uncreated savour which is the Spirit.

Encountering our fellow men

However, this heart that listens is not something that is relevant only at the deep level of our life with God. It is equally necessary in other fields and, first and foremost, in that of our human relationships ... In some obscure way, it is this kind of listening heart that all our fellow men look for in us.

In very many cases, the sick and the poor have a greater need for a heart that listens than for medicine or food. But do we not somehow sense this mute appeal even among those who are closest to us? Each one has his own cross to carry and burden to bear. At times, the heaviest burden of all may well be the demands of etiquette, the need to keep up appearances, to present to the world what we may describe as the 'social I' quite distinct from the real 'me' from whom no one can escape. Even when the 'inner man is being renewed every day through the Spirit' (2 Cor 4.16; Ep 3.16), all the rind of the 'outer man' still clings to him like a shell or prison. And he cries out without managing to make himself heard, though all he really needs is to have near him a heart that listens ... this alone would probably enable him to open his own heart. If we once release our real selves, we are in a position to fulfil them in the true sense and make them really exist.

Carrying one another's burdens

Every one of our fellow men is in search of a heart ready to listen to him in such a way that he will no longer be *another* human being. Let us then try to give this kind of welcome, to pay him that depth of attention which comes from the bottom of the heart so that he will be at ease with us as he is with himself. So often the eyes of those who surround him and even of those closest to him are like so many distorting mirrors; instead, let him find in us a heart so clear and transparent that the refraction index, so to speak, is nil. 'Bear one another's burdens' (Gal 6.2). We are so very weak that we are often unable to bear any one else's burden. However we can always at least relieve him of his load by letting him pour it out into us. All we have to do is to listen with our heart. It is not simply a question of exchanging confidences, though this may well come into it. It is a question of an interior welcome at a deep level, of a heart so full of fellow feeling as to be on the alert for all that is best, and frequently most hidden and unexpressed, in all those with whom we come into contact. A silence impregnated with love, which listens in charity to the groans of the sufferer, is often far more effective than words of comfort...

The apostolate

When it comes to the active apostolate, how very damaging a certain desire to proclaim the truth and spread the light can prove to be. Very often we are merely projecting ourselves, proclaiming our own truth, spreading our own light, our own little store of knowledge and, in doing so, we make our victim a present of an intolerable burden. What is he to do with it? He has his own problems, his own perplexities, his own experiences which are not ours; he simply does not know what to do with all the surplus we heap on to him. A reply is only called for when a question has been asked—and even then only when the question has matured and the questioner is ready to listen to what we have to say. We must approach our neighbour with reverence, in a sense kneeling before him, with that listening heart which love alone can give. Only by means of this silence and transparency in us will he be able to find the light. By thus opening out our arms to him in the depths of our heart, we shall ensure that our own response offers him precisely that truth which he can assimilate.

There is no richer teaching on this subject than the words of Christ: 'I have yet many things to say to you, but you cannot bear them now' (Jn 16.12). The end is near. He is just about to leave his apostles for ever. He, the Word of God, who has come to cast fire upon the earth and whose one wish is that it were already kindled (cf. Lk 12.49), sees that in spite of all the love and care that he has put into their training, the apostles are not ready to receive what he has yet to give. He does not insist. He entrusts it all to the Holy Spirit. What a lesson for our impatience, for that projection of ourselves which we keep on directing at others instead of just listening in a constant attitude of openness and ready welcome!

Sister Jeanne D'Arc OP, *The Listening Heart*, translated by Sister Mary John OP, Geoffrey Chapman, 1968, page 14

LITERATURE

'Literature'—literary culture; realm of letters, writings of country or period; writings whose value lies in beauty of form or emotional effect.

I once went on a camping holiday with my young sister on the Continent. Our ultimate destination was a beach in what was then Yugoslavia but we planned to take our time over the journey and visit places of interest en route. My sister was reading English at university at the time, so she rounded up some novels and off we went.

We did not get very far before our Mini broke down—on the M1 near Luton. The garage mechanics were amused to learn our destination was Yugoslavia and jokingly placed bets on how far we would get. As it turned out the rest of the journey was trouble-free.

We soon got into a leisurely routine. We enjoyed a brief sojourn in Paris. In Switzerland we camped in the Lauterbrunnen valley and visited the high-altitude village of Mürren. By now we were both deeply absorbed in novels and for me Tolstoy's *Anna Karenina* was compulsive reading. Various times during the day were set aside for the books.

We moved on to Cortina and witnessed the splendour of the Dolomites. As we approached Venice we faced a mini-crisis. We had read all our books. Luck was on our side and we replenished our supplies in Venice. After a couple of days we moved on to Yugoslavia and camped near a beach. The next few days were spent sun-bathing, swimming and reading. All too soon we retraced our steps via Innsbruck and Salzburg. On this holiday I discovered something of the truth of Carlyle's words: 'Literature is the Thought of thinking Souls.'

Of making many books there is no end, and much study is a weariness of the flesh.
Ecclesiastes 12.12

Seek and read from the book of the Lord.
Isaiah 34.16

For whatever was written in former days was written for our instruction, that by steadfastness and by the encouragement of the scriptures we might have hope.
Romans 15.4

But as for you, continue in what you have learned and have firmly believed, knowing from whom you learned it, and how from childhood you have been acquainted with the sacred writings which are able to instruct you for salvation through faith in Christ Jesus.
2 Timothy 3.14-15

Literature is the Thought of thinking Souls.
Thomas Carlyle, *The Works of Thomas Carlyle*, Chapman and Hall Ltd., 1899, *Critical and Miscellaneous Essays*, Volume IV, page 83

He (Shakespeare) was the man who of all Modern, and perhaps Ancient Poets, had the largest and most comprehensive soul.
John Dryden, *The Works of John Dryden*, general editor, H.T. Swedenberg, Jr., University of California Press, 1971, Volume XVII, *Prose 1668–1691*, page 55, 'Essay of Dramatic Poesy,' 1.20

Of all literary pleasures, the reading of a poem is the highest and purest. Only pure lyric poetry can sometimes achieve the perfection, the ideal form wholly permeated by life and feeling, that is otherwise the secret of music.
Herman Hesse, *Reflections*, selected from his books and letters by Volker Michels, translated by Ralph Manheim, Jonathan Cape Ltd., 1977, page 109

Books are the treasured wealth of the world and the fit inheritance of generations and nations ... Their authors are a natural and irresistible aristocracy in every society, and, more than kings or emperors, exert an influence on mankind!
Henry David Thoreau, *Walden*, The New American Library of World Literature, Inc., 1960, page 74

To me it seems that the novels of Dostoievski derive almost the whole of their power and value from the fact that they are interpretations of life in its heights and its depths ... I do indeed regard them as among the greatest masterpieces with which I am acquainted, and I think that they show an interpretation of the real meaning both of human life and of the Christian religion in its dealing with human life, of which I know no equal in fiction or other literature.
William Temple, *The Resources and Influences of English Literature*, National Book Council, 1943, page 17

It is chiefly through books that we enjoy intercourse with superior minds, and these invaluable means of communication are in the reach of all. In the best books, great men talk to us, give us their most precious thoughts, and pour their souls into ours. God be thanked for books. They are the voices of the distant and the dead, and make us heirs of the spiritual life of past ages. Books are the true levellers. They give to all, who will faithfully use them, the society, the spiritual presence of the best and greatest of our race.

William E. Channing, *Self-Culture*, Dutton and Wentworth, Printers, 1838, page 40

Woe betide that nation whose literature is interrupted by the interference of force. This is not simply a violation of the 'freedom of the press': it is the locking-up of the national heart, the carving-up of the national memory. Such a nation does not remember itself, it is deprived of its spiritual unity, and although its population supposedly have a common language, fellow-countrymen suddenly stop understanding each other. Mute generations live out their lives and die without telling their story either to their own or a future generation. If such geniuses as Akhmatova or Zamyatin are walled up alive for the duration of their lives, if they are condemned to create in silence until the grave, without hearing any response to what they have written, then this is not just their own personal misfortune but the deep tragedy of the whole nation—and, too, a threat to the whole nation. And in certain cases it is a danger for the whole of mankind, too: when the whole of history ceases to be understood because of that silence.

Alexander Solzhenitsyn, '*One Word of Truth...*', The Nobel Speech on Literature 1970, The Bodley Head, 1972, page 16

It has been said by some that there is no religion in Shakespeare, or, what is the same thing, no element of the divine in his view of the world. To this it may be said, there is the same element of the divine which is to be seen in the world itself. Shakespeare's purpose is to give a section of the real world that we may read the whole world by it. He does not moralise himself, but lets the picture speak. But a poet may do much without moralising. He may indicate the presence of two elements, destiny, or what Christians call providence, and free-will, not always harmonising—for this would not be true—but always present, and therefore urging a wish for solution, which can only be found finally in a right view of God and of man. Next, he may indicate how moral faults and weaknesses bring catastrophes in good characters—irresolution in Hamlet, jealousy in Othello, parental partiality in Lear, etc. Further, he may make us prefer, like Cato, to share the lot of the good man in adversity rather than that of the bad man in success, to love the right and hate the wrong, whatever circumstances surround them. And lastly, he may give such views of man's nature as exalt our conceptions of it, admiring without deifying it in some of its aspects, condemning without despising it in others. Besides, there may be the introduction of touches of Christian truth, which make us feel that the heart of the author was with the speaker:—
    'Those holy fields
    Over whose acres walk'd those blessed feet
    Which, fourteen hundred years ago, were nail'd
    For our advantage on the bitter cross.'
King Henry IV, Part I, Act I. sc.i.

John Ker, *Thoughts for Heart and Life*, David Douglas, 1888, page 62

Just as words have two functions—information and creation—so each human mind has two personalities, one on the surface, one deeper down. The upper personality has a name. It is called S.T. Coleridge, or William Shakespeare, or Mrs. Humphry Ward. It is conscious and alert, it does things like dining out, answering letters, etc., and it differs vividly and amusingly from other personalities. The lower personality is a very queer affair. In many ways it is a perfect fool, but without it there is no literature, because, unless a man dips a bucket down into it occasionally he cannot produce first-class work. There is something general about it. Although it is inside S.T. Coleridge, it cannot be labelled with his name. It has something in common with all other deeper personalities, and the mystic will assert that the common quality is God, and that here, in the obscure recesses of our being, we near the gates of the Divine. It is in any case the force that makes for anonymity. As it came from the depths, so it soars to the heights, out of local questionings; as it is general to all men, so the works it inspires have something general about them, namely beauty. The poet wrote the poem no doubt, but he forgot himself while he wrote it, and we forget him while we read. What is so wonderful about great literature is that it transforms the man who reads it towards the condition of the man who wrote, and brings to birth in us also the creative impulse. Lost in the beauty where he was lost, we find more than we ever threw away, we reach what seems to be our spiritual home, and remember that it was not the speaker who was in the beginning but the Word.

E.M. Forster, *Anonymity. An Enquiry*, Leonard and Virginia Woolf at the Hogarth Press, 1925, page 16

LONELINESS

'Loneliness'—dejection at the consciousness of being alone; having a feeling of solitariness, dreariness.

Some years ago I went on sabbatical leave. A friend kindly lent me a farmhouse cottage in a remote hamlet on the Cumbrian fells. The nearest village was three miles away. My plan for this period of leave was to work on *Visions of Hope* and *Love*.

At first I greatly enjoyed the peace and quiet, and being able to work without anyone making demands on me was a great privilege. In the evenings I lit a log-fire in the sitting room and caught up on some reading.

After a few weeks a feeling of loneliness crept up on me. I began to realize I was missing my friends and companions at University College. Shortly after this realization I was feeling extremely isolated and dejected. I remember one morning bemoaning the fact I had a voice and no one to talk to, eyes and no one to look at, only scores of sheep in the surrounding fields.

The radio proved to be invaluable, and I made a quick trip back to college to retrieve a music centre. I visited a nearby farmhouse, and the farmer and his wife and family welcomed me in, and made me feel at home. I also went further afield and kept in touch with some elderly friends in the village. In my isolation I came to value reflection more and more.

Loneliness is a great source of human suffering today and afflicts both young and old alike. The breakdown of society and the competitive nature of modern living bring about feelings of isolation difficult to combat. One antidote to loneliness is an acquisition of wholeness in which we become happy in ourselves, and learn to relate well with those around us.

I lie awake, I am like a lonely bird on the housetop.

Psalm 107.7

For if they fall, one will lift up his fellow; but woe to him who is alone when he falls and has not another to lift him up. Again, if two lie together, they are warm; but how can one be warm alone?

Ecclesiastes 4.10-11

And in the morning, a great while before day, he rose and went out to a lonely place, and there he prayed.

Mark 1.35

I am not alone, for the Father is with me.

John 16.32

And lifting up mine eyes, I found myself
Alone, and in a land of sand and thorns.

Alfred, Lord Tennyson, *The Poems of Tennyson*, edited by Christopher Ricks, Longmans, Green & Co. Ltd., 1969, page 1673, *The Idylls of the King*, No.471, 'The Holy Grail,' l.375

Loneliness is bred of a mind that has grown earthbound. For the spirit has its homeland, which is the realm of the meaning of all things.

Antoine de Saint-Exupéry, *The Wisdom of the Sands*, translated by Stuart Gilbert, Hollis & Carter, 1952, page 224

When you close your doors and make darkness within, remember never to say that you are alone: you are not alone, God is within.

Epictetus, *The Stoic and Epicurean Philosophers*, edited by Witney J. Oates, Random House, Inc., 1940, page 251

We are born helpless. As soon as we are fully conscious we discover loneliness. We need others physically, emotionally, intellectually; we need them if we are to know anything, even ourselves.

C.S. Lewis, *The Four Loves*, William Collins Sons & Co. Ltd., 1960, page 7

Our language has wisely sensed those two sides of man's being alone. It has created the word 'loneliness' to express the pain of being alone. And it has created the word 'solitude' to express the glory of being alone.

Paul Tillich, *The Eternal Now*, SCM Press Ltd., 1963, page 11

The knowledge of the ever-present Christ can reach down into the hidden depths and assure lonely modern man that he is not alone. More than that; it can draw him out of his loneliness to the rediscovery of the human race.

Stephen Neill, *The Church and Christian Union*, Oxford University Press, 1968, page 279

Essentially loneliness is the knowledge that one's fellow human beings are incapable of understanding one's condition and therefore are incapable of bringing the help most needed. It is not a question of companionship—many are ready to offer this and companionship is certainly not to be despised—but rather one of strictly sharing, of identifying. No two human beings can manage this, so to a varying extent loneliness at times is the lot of all.

Hubert van Zeller, *Considerations*, Sheed & Ward Ltd., 1974, page 18

That Jesus was lonely is indisputable. Not only during his agony in the garden when his friends failed him, not only at every stage of his passion when again he had to endure his sufferings alone, not only when on the cross and he felt himself to be deserted by his Father, but also throughout his life when he looked for understanding and hardly ever met with it. If he allowed loneliness to be his lot, was it not to invite the lonely to unite their lot with his?

Hubert van Zeller, *Considerations*, Sheed & Ward Ltd., 1974, page 18

In fact, we have developed a phobia of being alone; we prefer the most trivial and even obnoxious company, the most meaningless activities, to being alone with ourselves; we seem to be frightened at the prospect of facing ourselves. Is it because we feel we would be such bad company? I think the fear of being alone with ourselves is rather a feeling of embarrassment, bordering sometimes on terror at seeing a person at once so well known and so strange, we are afraid and run away.

Erich Fromm, *Man For Himself*, Routledge & Kegan Paul Ltd., 1975, page 161

Yes: I am alone on earth: I have always been alone . . . Do not think you can frighten me by telling me that I am alone. France is alone; and God is alone; and what is my loneliness before the loneliness of my country and my God? I see now that the loneliness of God is His strength: what would He be if He listened to your jealous little counsels? Well, my loneliness shall be my strength too; it is better to be alone with God: His friendship will not fail me, nor His counsel, nor His love. In His strength I will dare, and dare, and dare, until I die.

George Bernard Shaw, *The Complete Plays of Bernard Shaw*, Paul Hamlyn Ltd., 1965, page 989, *Saint Joan*, sc.v

... I would like to voice loudly and clearly what might seem unpopular and maybe even disturbing: The Christian way of life does not take away our loneliness; it protects and cherishes it as a precious gift. Sometimes it seems as if we do everything possible to avoid the painful confrontation with our basic human loneliness, and allow ourselves to be trapped by false gods promising immediate satisfaction and quick relief.

But perhaps the painful awareness of loneliness is an invitation to transcend our limitations and look beyond the boundaries of our existence. The awareness of loneliness might be a gift we must protect and guard because our loneliness reveals to us an inner emptiness that can be destructive when misunderstood, but filled with promise for him who can tolerate its sweet pain.

Henri J.M. Nouwen, *The Wounded Healer*, Doubleday, 1979, page 84

We live in a society in which loneliness has become one of the most painful human wounds. The growing competition and rivalry which pervade our lives from birth have created in us an acute awareness of our isolation. This awareness has in turn left many with a heightened anxiety and an intense search for the experience of unity and community. It has also led people to ask anew how love, friendship, brotherhood and sisterhood can free them from isolation and offer them a sense of intimacy and belonging. All around us we see the many ways by which the people of the western world are trying to escape this loneliness...

But the more I think about loneliness, the more I think that the wound of loneliness is like the Grand Canyon—a deep incision in the surface of our existence which has become an inexhaustible source of beauty and self-understanding.

Henri J.M. Nouwen, *The Wounded Healer*, Doubleday, 1979, page 83

When loneliness is among the chief wounds of the minister, hospitality can convert that wound into a source of healing. Concentration prevents the minister from burdening others with his pain and allows him to accept his wounds as helpful teachers of his own and his neighbour's condition. Community arises where the sharing of pain takes place, not as a stifling form of self-complaint, but as a recognition of God's saving promises...

Our loneliness and isolation has become so much a part of our daily experience, that we cry out for a Liberator who will take us away from our misery and bring us justice and peace.

To announce, however, that the Liberator is sitting among the poor and that the wounds are signs of hope and that today is the day of liberation, is a step very few can take. But this is exactly the announcement of the wounded healer: 'The master is coming—not tomorrow, but today, not next year, but this year, not after all our misery has passed, but in the middle of it, not in another place but right here where we are standing.'

Henri J.M. Nouwen, *The Wounded Healer*, Doubleday, 1979, page 94

When we are impatient, when we want to give up our loneliness and try to overcome the separation and incompleteness we feel, too soon, we easily relate to our human world with devastating expectations. We ignore what we already know with a deep-seated, intuitive knowledge—that no love or friendship, no intimate embrace or tender kiss, no community, commune or collective, no man or woman, will ever be able to satisfy our desire to be released from our lonely condition...

Many marriages are ruined because neither partner was able to fulfill the often hidden hope that the other would take his or her loneliness away. And many celibates live with the naïve dream that in the intimacy of marriage their loneliness will be taken away.

When the minister lives with these false expectations and illusions he prevents himself from claiming his own loneliness as a source of human understanding, and is unable to offer any real service to the many who do not understand their own suffering.

Henri J.M. Nouwen, *The Wounded Healer*, Doubleday, 1979, page 84

LONGING

'Longing'—yearn, wish vehemently, for thing to do.

K enya is a beautiful country. I have visited friends there on two occasions and thoroughly enjoyed our safaris in game parks. During my first stay I went to Treetops, and stayed up all night to watch wild animals come to the salt lick and waterhole. For those who have never been there, the area around Treetops is spotlighted at night, so there is an excellent view of animals coming to seek refreshment. During the night a number of gazelles came to drink water, and I was reminded of the words of the Psalmist: 'As a hart longs for flowing streams, so longs my soul for thee, O God.'

This set me off thinking about longing. I recalled to mind my youth. I saw this as a time in life of intense longing—for meaning, for purpose, for companionship, for sex, for a spouse, for sporting achievement, for success, for a career, for money, for security—for God perhaps?

In my early twenties I had been influenced by the book *Edward Wilson of the Antarctic*, written by George Seaver, and in particular by the quotation in this section. I remember also reading a passage from *A Grief Observed* by C.S. Lewis, in which he described how he and his wife had feasted on every aspect of love, yet both were aware of a want for something besides each other, a quite different kind of want. St Augustine took me one stage further in my quest with his words: 'You made us for yourself and our hearts find no peace until they rest in you.' I wonder if we have something akin to a home-sickness, namely 'a God-sickness'. This I take to be a longing for the divine, best satisfied by experiencing the presence of God.

As a hart longs for flowing streams, so longs my soul for thee, O God.
Psalm 42.1

My soul yearns for thee in the night, my spirit within me earnestly seeks thee.
Isaiah 26.9

Truly, I say to you, many prophets and righteous men longed to see what you see, and did not see it, and to hear what you hear, and did not hear it.
Matthew 13.17

Here indeed we groan, and long to put on our heavenly dwelling, so that by putting it on we may not be found naked. For while we are still in this tent, we sigh with anxiety; not that we would be unclothed, but that we would be further clothed, so that what is mortal may be swallowed up by life. He who has prepared us for this very thing is God, who has given us the Spirit as a guarantee.
2 Corinthians 5.2-5

The thing we long for, that we are
For one transcendent moment.
J.R. Lowell, *The Poetical Works of James Russell Lowell*, Ward, Lock & Co. Ltd., 1911, page 94, 'Longing'

If there was one that I could trust and love and be so bound up with that he or she could share with me and understand my joys and my love, and my passion for beauty, for colour, for form, for pure joy in nature,—if he or she could enter into my thoughts and feel with me,—if my sorrow, my pain, my doubts, my unspoken thoughts and hopes and fancies and longings—my life and my love—if only—

If I could find such a one, shouldn't I bring every joy, every delight, every pain, every sorrow, every passion, every love to be shared and to open the whole before that one: I know that I should: but there exists not the person on earth with whom lies the power of even to a small extent feeling with me in one of the smallest of my joys. Now and again one can truly say that one has felt with another, in joy or pain, in love or sorrow. But it is only now and again, and for years the heart hungers in between.

Edward Wilson, in *Edward Wilson of the Antarctic*, George Seaver, John Murray Ltd., 1935, page 46

Life is a search for this 'something,' a search for something or someone to give meaning to our lives, to answer the question, who am I, why am I here, what is the purpose of my life?

I believe that this great need we all feel is caused by a longing which cannot be satisfied by the usual goals we set ourselves in this journey of life. Even when they have been achieved they so often fall short of our hopes and expectations. The longed-for objective is not something which can be possessed, it cannot be held or kept, can only be fleetingly glimpsed as it comes and goes.

It can only be hinted at, referred to obliquely; indescribable in words, it can only be felt, and all we know of it is that it is what we are looking for. The promise of it is there in our love for another person. In the glory of a sunrise or sunset, the silver path of the moon on the sea, the sad haunting cry of sea-birds, the touching protective courage of a wild thing for its young or its mate. In the mountains and the streams, in the flowers and the forests, in the sufferings and sorrows of mankind as well as in the joys and the laughter.

This longing is all bound up with memories too, it carries its light like a will-o'-the-wisp through the scents and sounds and sights which suddenly bring back to us the magical moments when we were very young and in love with life. But it is also there, playing its part in the despair and the sorrowing and the regrets and the remorse. Sadly it seems that this yearning can become misdirected into channels which lead to drugs or drink or other excesses for excitement to assuage the longing when it has not been recognised for what it is.

There are countless ways in which the longing can be expressed, by poets and painters, musicians and dancers, and by so many of those whose talent is for living and loving in awe and worship.

Perhaps the whole of life is concerned with this yearning. Nothing can be left out, but it carries us on into death and beyond when we dare to hope that we shall come face to face with the source of all our longing.

Elizabeth Bassett, *The Bridge is Love*, Darton, Longman & Todd, 1981, page 31

Men turn to prayer in the extremity of their fears, or anxieties, or helplessness before the perils of their day, and of all human existence. But they also turn to prayer because of the almost universal and unquenchable yearning they have for God, and for that fullness of life to be found in knowing, loving and serving Him.

This hunger for God will be described by every generation in its own language. In the seventeenth century, Henry Scougal, that bright and gentle young Scot, expressed it in saying, 'The glorious things spoken of heaven may make even the carnal heart in love with it.' For some modern minds, the statement of the psychologist, C.G. Jung, may be more intelligible: 'Everyone's ultimate aim and strongest desire lie in developing the fullness of human existence that is called personality'—a goal, as he points out, to be realized through the establishment of a personal relation between the human personality and a Power outside itself. Dorothy Day, a distinguished Catholic laywoman, speaks experientially of this hunger, as she knew it even in her childhood, by quoting the words of Kiriloff, in Dostoevsky's novel *The Possessed*: 'All my life I have been haunted by God.' In every generation, this interior restlessness, this mingling of impassioned longing with the intimation of bright hope, rekindles the inward being in men and women, until they move out to seek Him by whom that being, and that hunger, first were given us.

Nor is this longing after God confined to high moments of ecstasy and vision. A young man sitting down to plan and dream for his future—his career, his marriage, his achievement of professional success and social status—may appear to be thinking in quite material terms. Income, prospects, and connections may seem to be the centre of his anticipation and his calculation as to how they are to be achieved and employed. Yet even as he speaks of these practical considerations, the light in his eyes and the nuance of his voice betrays a larger, unguessed hope, whose aura flames about his dreams.

John L. Casteel, *Rediscovering Prayer*, Hodder & Stoughton Ltd., 1955, page 13

'Follow your longing, and it will lead you to God.'

More and more as I work with patients, I realize the need of teaching them how to turn inwards, to discover the inward world, to meditate and give the Divine in them a chance to grow. This is the most urgent need for young and old, men and women, people of all classes. It is not true that as we turn inward our outward adaptation and success will be hindered; on the contrary I have found even in young people, and particularly in older ones, that only in the measure that they attended to their inner life did the outward adaptation become at last possible. There is an urge in the soul for inward life; and as modern education and the exigencies of life claim outgoing only, there is disturbance. We have no schools or training for the inward life, and we cannot simply take up oriental systems; they do not fit us.

Many advocate that by will power one should concentrate on one line of thought and make every effort to exclude other invading thoughts. I do not think that this way would have been possible for me, and I felt very grateful to Professor Jung who, during psychological work with me, taught me another way which led to parallel results. If my thoughts were horses, I could either be their master, commanding them to go at my will to a certain place, or I could take an expectant attitude, hold the reins loosely, let the horses take the initiative and go where they please. Professor Jung found that if we hold on to the reins (remain awake and observe our thoughts while they take the initiative), they lead us by a logic of their own to new discoveries. I have experienced this for many years and have come to a source of inner knowledge which I know will lead me always, deeper, to new treasures.

I once heard Professor Jung say: 'Always follow your longing and it will lead you to God, even if at the beginning it seems to turn another way.' I followed this principle with my patients and it has proved sound. If I follow a person's deepest longing, although it may seem to lead to human love, to amusement, or to other things, as we go deeper, following the thread of that longing, we come to the inner life, to the sanctuary of the Divine.

Anon., in *The Choice is Always Ours*, edited by Dorothy Berkley Phillips, Harper & Row, Publishers, Ltd., 1960, page 208

LOVE

'Love'—warm affection, attachment, liking, or fondness. In its deepest expression, a self-sacrificial form of love as exemplified in the life of Christ.

I wonder if love shows us another aspect of the Genesis story of the creation of man. In the divine inbreathing, a seed or a spark of the love of God was 'breathed into' man, and man became a living being.

If we want to see this fully worked out in a life we go to the person of Jesus Christ. At the height of his ministry, on being questioned by a scribe, he came out with one of his deepest beliefs: 'You shall love the Lord your God with all your heart, and with all your soul, and with all your mind, and with all your strength ... You shall love your neighbour as yourself.'

I imagine Jesus was speaking out of his own experience. Here was someone who was prepared to love God with all his inner being; heart, soul, mind and strength. This was to be balanced with an outer love to neighbour (which included everyone in the immediate vicinity) and was further balanced by a true and genuine love of self. In a sentence in St John's Gospel he confirmed the source of his love: 'As the Father has loved me, so have I loved you; abide in my love. If you keep my commandments, you will abide in my love, just as I have kept my Father's commandments and abide in his love.'

The two commandments were simplified into one: 'A new commandment I give to you, that you love one another; even as I have loved you.' Jesus lived out this 'new commandment' to the very end, to the cross: 'Greater love hath no man than this, that a man lay down his life for his friends.'

I love those who love me, and those who seek me diligently find me.
Proverbs 8.17

If your enemy is hungry, give him bread to eat; and if he is thirsty, give him water to drink.
Proverbs 25.21

You shall love the Lord your God with all your heart, and with all your soul, and with all your mind, and with all your strength . . . You shall love your neighbour as yourself.
Mark 12.30-31

Make love your aim.
1 Corinthians 14.1

Whoever lives true life, will love true love.
E.B. Browning, *Elizabeth Barrett Browning's Poetical Works*, Smith, Elder & Co., 1873, Volume V, page 39, *Aurora Leigh*, First Book

By love may He be gotten and holden; but by thought never.
The Cloud of Unknowing, John M. Watkins, 1956, page 77

We are all born for love . . . It is the principle of existence and its only end.
Benjamin Disraeli, *Sybil or The Two Nations*, Peter Davies, 1927, page 354

For love is but the heart's immortal thirst
To be completely known and all forgiven.
Henry Van Dyke, *Music and Other Poems*, Hodder & Stoughton Ltd., 1904, Sonnet: 'Love,' page 51

You give but little when you give of your possessions.
It is when you give of yourself that you truly give.
Kahlil Gibran, *The Prophet*, William Heinemann Ltd., 1970, page 24

Love is rarer than genius itself.—And friendship is rarer than love.
Charles Péguy, *Basic Verities*, translated by Ann and Julian Green, Kegan Paul, Trench, Trubner & Co. Ltd., 1943, page 51

The greatest thing that can happen to any human soul is to become utterly filled with love; and self-sacrifice is love's natural expression.
William Temple, *Christian Faith and Life*, SCM Press Ltd., 1963, page 106

Love . . . is the supreme badge of any true Christianity, and the traits of the beatitudes in a person's life are a surer evidence that he belongs in Christ's family, than is the fact that he holds current opinions on obscure questions of belief.
Rufus M. Jones, *Spiritual Reformers in the 16th and 17th Centuries*, Macmillan & Co. Ltd., 1914, page 96

That love shall in the end, as it is now in the eternal verities, be all in all, must remain for him [the Christian] a postulate not of knowledge but of faith. And that too is well, since faith is possible for all men, and knowledge is not.
L.W. Grensted, *The Philosophical Implications of Christianity*, Oxford at the Clarendon Press, 1930, page 17

Love is eager, sincere and kind; it is glad and lovely; it is strong, patient and faithful; wise, long-suffering and resolute; and it never seeks its own ends, for where a man seeks his own ends, he at once falls out of love.
Thomas à Kempis, *The Imitation of Christ*, translated by Betty I. Knott, William Collins Sons & Co. Ltd., 1979, page 118

Would'st thou learn thy Lord's meaning in this thing? Learn it well: Love was His meaning. Who shewed it thee? Love. What shewed He thee? Love. Wherefore shewed it He? For Love. Hold thee therein and thou shalt learn and know more in the same.
Lady Julian of Norwich, *Revelations of Divine Love*, edited by Grace Warrack, Methuen & Co. Ltd., 1949, page 202

I always think that the best way to know God is to love many things. Love a friend, a wife, something, whatever you like, but one must love with a lofty and serious intimate sympathy, with strength, with intelligence, and one must always try to know deeper, better, and more.

Vincent van Gogh, *Dear Theo: An Autobiography of Vincent van Gogh*, edited by Irving Stone, Constable & Co. Ltd., 1937, page 44

Love is the cosmic energy that flames from the constellations and is concealed in the abyss of the atom; is whispered by the Holy Spirit in the heart, and placarded before men's eyes upon the Cross. It offers to us all that it has, and demands from us all that we can give.

Bishop Lumsden Barkway, in the introduction of *An Anthology of the Love of God*, Evelyn Underhill, edited by Bishop Barkway and Lucy Menzies, A.R. Mowbray & Co. Ltd., 1953, page 23

Love once kindled in the soul, is the mother of all heroic actions; love knows how to abound and overflow—the man who has lighted his life from Christ's love is constant in trials, patient in sufferings, courageous in assaults, prudent in difficulties, victorious and triumphant in action.

Rufus M. Jones, *Spiritual Reformers in the 16th and 17th Centuries*, Macmillan & Co. Ltd., 1914, page 334

Love all God's creation, the whole of it and every grain of sand. Love every leaf, every ray of God's light! Love the animals, love the plants, love everything. If you love everything, you will perceive the divine mystery in things. And once you have perceived it, you will begin to comprehend it ceaselessly more and more every day.

Fyodor Dostoyevsky, *The Brothers Karamazov*, translated by David Magarshack, Penguin Books Ltd., 1963, volume I, page 375

To make Love the ruling power of my life, the only power. To be kind, gentle, considerate and unselfish, to let nothing stand in the way of doing everyone a good turn, never to consider myself and my own feelings, but only other people's. To put myself out to any extent for the sake of others, especially for the sake of those who are not attractive.

Edward Wilson, in *The Faith of Edward Wilson*, George Seaver, John Murray Ltd., 1949, page 15

True love's the gift which God has given
To man alone beneath the heaven: ...
It is the secret sympathy,
The silver link, the silken tie,
Which heart to heart, and mind to mind,
In body and in soul can bind.

Sir Walter Scott, *The Poems and Plays of Sir Walter Scott*, J.M. Dent & Sons Ltd., 1911, Volume I, 'The Lay of the Last Minstrel', page 393

Love is the best motivation and finally the only valid one. It is dynamic and strong; the secret of moral force. At its highest it also seems to be indivisible. If we truly loved anything—whether it be music, plants, mountains or primitive peoples—we would love all. And the precondition of all love is the escape from egoism. Preoccupation with the false self has to give way to love of the true self.

Without that, our new and unprecedented destructive powers will sooner or later eliminate our species.

Ronald Higgins, *The Seventh Enemy*, Hodder & Stoughton Ltd., 1978, page 274

Since love will thrust in itself as the greatest of all principles; let us at last willingly allow it room. I was once a stranger to it, now I am familiar with it as a daily acquaintance. It is the only heir and benefactor of the world. It seems it will break in everywhere, as that without which the world could not be enjoyed. Nay as that without which it would not be worthy to be enjoyed; for it was beautified by love, and commandeth the love of the donor to us. Love is a phoenix that will revive in its own ashes, inherit death, and smell sweetly in the grave

Thomas Traherne, *Centuries, Poems and Thanksgivings*, edited by H.M. Margoliouth, Oxford at the Clarendon Press, 1958, IV.61

Be very sure that all are placed in the exact position in earth life where they are most needed and where they will have opportunities for doing the most good. The unknown man or woman may contribute more to the advancement of the human race than one whose name is in everyone's mouth. The whole purpose of spiritual unfoldment is for the individual man so to train himself that he becomes a more powerful centre from which the love of God can radiate. Then he no longer hankers after the wonderful things that the 'I' can do. Instead he desires only that through him a greater love may be breathed forth into life.

Grace Cooke, *Spiritual Unfoldment*, The White Eagle Publishing Trust, 1961, page 16

In the world everything is problematic except one thing: charity, love. Love alone is not a problem for him who lives it.

I can only say, 'Live love, let love invade you. It will never fail to teach you what you must do...'

I repeat again St Augustine's words: 'Love and do as you will.' Don't worry about what you ought to do. Worry about loving... Loving, you will listen to the Voice. Loving you will find peace.

Love is the fulfillment of the law and should be everyone's rule of life; in the end it's the solution to every problem, the motive for all good.

Carlo Carretto, *Letters from the Desert*, translated by Rose Mary Hancock, Darton, Longman & Todd, 1972, page 24

It is our conviction that the central message of the New Testament is that there is really only one prayer and that is the prayer of Christ.

It is a prayer that continues in our hearts day and night. I can describe it only as the stream of love that flows constantly between Jesus and his Father. This stream of love is the Holy Spirit.

Again it is our conviction that it is the most important task for any fully human life that we should become as open as possible to this stream of love. We have to allow this prayer to become our prayer, to enter into the experience of being swept out of ourselves into this wonderful prayer of Jesus—this great cosmic river of love.

In order for us to do this we must learn a way that is a way of silence and stillness, and this by a discipline that is most demanding.

It is as though we have to create a space within ourselves that will allow this higher consciousness—a consciousness of the prayer of Jesus—to envelop us in this powerful mystery.

John Main OSB, *Moment of Christ*, Darton, Longman & Todd, 1984, page x

These two properties are in it (love), that it can attempt all and suffer all. And the more it suffers the more it is delighted, and the more it attempteth the more it is enriched, for it seems that all love is so mysterious, that there is something in it which needs expression, and can never be understood by any manifestation, (of itself, in itself;) but only by mighty doings and sufferings. This moved God the Father to create the world, and God, the Son to die for it. Nor is this all. There are many other ways in which it manifests itself as well as these; there being still something infinite in it behind. In its laws, in its tenderness, in its provisions, in its caresses, in its joys as well as in its hazards, in its honours as well as in its cares nor does it ever cease till it has poured out itself in all its communications.

Thomas Traherne, *Centuries, Poems and Thanksgivings*, edited by H.M. Margoliouth, Oxford at the Clarendon Press, 1958, IV.62

As St John tells us, no man has ever seen God, but we can all experience God whenever and wherever we encounter love. Jesus continues to communicate his presence to us in every way that people relate to one another in love.

Because meditation leads us into the experience of love at the centre of our being, it makes us more loving people in our ordinary lives and relationships.

You discover in the silence that you are loved and that you are lovable. It is the discovery that everyone must make in their lives if they are going to become fully themselves, fully human. The first step in personhood is to allow ourselves to be loved. To know ourselves loved is to have the depths of our own capacity to love opened up.

This condition of whole-hearted openness to love is the condition to which you and I and every human being is called. It demands everything. But in the end all you will lose are your limitations. So may we 'attain to fullness of being, the fullness of God himself' (Eph 3.19).

John Main OSB, in *The Joy of Being*, selected by Clare Hallward, Darton, Longman & Todd, 1989, page 48

For it is God's love that warms me in the sun and God's love that sends the cold rain. It is God's love that feeds me in the bread I eat and God that feeds me also by hunger and fasting.

It is the love of God that sends the winter days when I am cold and sick, and the hot summer when I labour and my clothes are full of sweat: but it is God who breathes on me with light winds off the river and in the breezes out of the wood. His love spreads the shade of the sycamore over my head and sends the water-boy along the edge of the wheat field with a bucket from the spring, while the labourers are resting and the mules stand under the tree.

It is God's love that speaks to me in the birds and streams; but also behind the clamour of the city God speaks to me in His judgements, and all of these things are seeds sent to me from His will . . .

My food is the will of Him who made me and who made all things in order to give Himself to me through them.

Thomas Merton, *New Seeds of Contemplation*, Burns & Oates Ltd., 1962, page 14

Most people understand love to mean simply love between the sexes. It does mean this, but also much more. On the deepest level, love is an instinctive force present in every person from birth to death. It is a profound urge to preserve and extend life by means of union with another living force, and it expresses itself through an exchange of energy that mutually strengthens and rejuvenates.

Love is born when the child rests in its mother's arms. From this beginning, love grows until it includes the love of family and friends, of school and country, and ultimately of all the world. Love also means love of self. This is an aspect often ignored, yet it is of basic importance—for without healthy self-love, one cannot love anyone else. Love also means love of God, a love that sustains us when human relationships crumble.

Love is all of one piece—from the love of mother and child to the love of sweethearts, husbands and wives, and friends. It is present, too, in the labourer's devotion to his work, in the teacher's solicitude for her pupils, in the physician's dedication to his art. All that heals, cultivates, protects, and inspires—all this is a part of love.

To say that one will perish without love does not mean that everyone without adequate love dies. Many do, for without love the will to live is often impaired to such an extent that a person's resistance is critically lowered and death follows. But most of the time, lack of love makes people depressed, anxious and without zest for life. They remain lonely and unhappy without friends or work they care for, their life a barren treadmill, stripped of all creative action and joy.

Smiley Blanton, *Love or Perish*, The World's Work (1913) Ltd., 1957, page 8

MARRIAGE

'Marriage'—the relation between married persons—intimate union.

A young couple came to see me for marriage preparation. At the time I prepared couples for marriage by going through the wedding service, drawing out the meaning in considerable detail. On this particular occasion we were still on the first page when a terrific row broke out between the couple. A fundamental difference had surfaced which resulted in the 'bride' storming out of the room, flinging her engagement ring behind her. This marked the end of their relationship and made me feel very guilty. Fortunately there was a happy outcome—both married different spouses later on.

As a result of this experience I changed my way of preparing couples for marriage. Instead I gave the couple a copy of the latest booklet published by the Church, and asked them to take it away and read it. When I next saw them I asked them how they had found it. To my dismay they said, 'Ooh, it is not very good is it?'

A new technique was called for. I now decided to lend couples a copy of *Visions of Love* and encouraged them to reflect on 'Marriage' in their own time. In this way they can share their hopes and expectations of marriage, and develop their unique relationship. My hope is having reflected on 'Marriage' they move on to other topics and take the practice of reflection into their married life.

Reflection is akin to meditation, and allows a spiritual dimension to enter a relationship. This can facilitate the adage: 'The couple that prays together, stays together'—and greatly enrich a marriage relationship—'till death us do part'.

Let them marry whom they think best; only, they shall marry within the family of the tribe of their father.
Numbers 36.6

In three things I was beautified, and stood up beautiful both before God and men: the unity of brethren, the love of neighbours, a man and a wife that agree together.
Ecclesiasticus 25.1 (AV)

But from the beginning of creation, 'God made them male and female.' 'For this reason a man shall leave his father and mother and be joined to his wife, and the two shall become one flesh.' So they are no longer two but one flesh. What therefore God has joined together, let not man put asunder.
Mark 10.6-9

The husband should give to his wife her conjugal rights, and likewise the wife to her husband. For the wife does not rule over her own body, but the husband does; likewise the husband does not rule over his own body, but the wife does.
1 Corinthians 7.3-5

None can be eternally united who have not died for each other.
Coventry Patmore, *The Rod, the Root and the Flower*, The Grey Walls Press Ltd., 1950, page 215, 'Aphorisms and Extracts'

Being married is something that takes everything you've got.
Henrik Ibsen, *The League of Youth*, edited and translated by James Walter McFarlane and Graham Orton, Oxford University Press, 1963, Volume IV, page 99, Act IV

Love is a glass which shatters if you hold it too tightly or too loosely.
Russian proverb

It takes patience to appreciate domestic bliss; volatile spirits prefer unhappiness.
George Santayana, *The Life of Reason*, Archibald Constable & Co., 1905, Volume II, 'Reason in Society,' page 45

Love does not cause suffering: what causes it is the sense of ownership, which is love's opposite.
Antoine de Saint-Exupéry, *The Wisdom of the Sands*, translated by Stuart Gilbert, Hollis & Carter, 1952, page 152

I... chose my wife as she did her wedding gown, not for a fine glossy surface, but such qualities as would wear well.
Oliver Goldsmith, *Collected Works of Oliver Goldsmith*, edited by Arthur Friedman, Oxford at the Clarendon Press, 1966, Volume IV, page 18, *The Vicar of Wakefield*, Ch.1, l.8

Suitability helps the security of a marriage, but spirituality, by calling for mutual self-sacrifice, ensures it.
Hubert van Zeller, *Considerations*, Sheed & Ward Ltd., 1974, page 94

Life has taught us that love does not consist in gazing at each other but in looking outward together in the same direction.
Antoine de Saint-Exupéry, *Wind, Sand and Stars*, translated by Lewis Galantière, William Heinemann Ltd., 1939, page 268

When marrying, one should ask oneself this question: Do you believe that you will be able to converse well with this woman into your old age?
Friedrich Nietzsche, *The Portable Nietzsche*, translated by Walter Kaufmanm, Penguin Books Ltd., 1976, page 59

Love is a recent discovery, and requires a new law. Easy divorce is the vulgar solution. The true solution is some undiscovered security for true marriage.
Coventry Patmore, *The Rod, the Root and the Flower*, The Grey Walls Press Ltd., 1950, page 51, 'Aurea Dicta,' cxxxv

Seldom, or perhaps never, does a marriage develop into an individual relationship smoothly and without crises; there is no coming to consciousness without pain.
C.G. Jung, *Contributions to Analytical Psychology*, translated by H.G. and Cary F. Baynes, Kegan Paul, Trench, Trubner & Co. Ltd., 1928, page 193

Unless marriage is thought of in terms of supernatural vocation even the natural side of it will be incomplete. The material and physical will outweigh the natural and spiritual.
Hubert van Zeller, *Considerations*, Sheed & Ward Ltd., 1974, page 93

Affection, companionship, common interests, mutual respect and enduring devotion: these are the temporal elements in a good marriage. Temporal elements have their eternal dimension.
Hubert van Zeller, *Considerations*, Sheed & Ward Ltd., 1974, page 94

Marriage is a terrifying responsibility. Marriage is a unique wholeness and completeness and having a best friend to confide in, to hurt, a friend who will understand, argue, fight, but still make love and be friends.
A young housewife

Love is not getting, but giving; not a wild dream of pleasure, and a madness of desire—oh, no, love is not that—it is goodness, and honour, and peace, and pure living—yes, love is that; and it is the best thing in the world, and the thing that lives longest.
Henry Van Dyke, *Little Rivers*, David Nutt, 1903, page 132

Affinity of nature founded on worship of the same ideal, and perfect in proportion to perfectness of soul, is the only affinity which is worth anything. True love is that which ennobles the personality, fortifies the heart, and sanctifies the existence. And the being we love must not be mysterious and sphinx-like, but clear and limpid as a diamond; so that admiration and attachment may grow with knowledge.

Henri Frédéric Amiel, *Amiel's Journal,* translated by Mrs Humphry Ward, Macmillan & Co. Ltd., 1918, page 284

Only in marriage can human beings fully know one another—the miracle of feeling, touching, seeing another's personality—and this is as wonderful and as unique as the mystic's knowledge of God. It is for this reason that before marriage man hovers about life, observes it from without; only in marriage does he plunge into it, entering it through the personality of another. This joy of knowledge and real life gives us that feeling of achieved plenitude and satisfaction for which we are richer and wiser.

Father Yelchaninov, in *A Treasury of Russian Spirituality,* edited by G.P. Fedatov, Sheed & Ward Ltd., 1977, page 446

Love, indeed, is an affair of maturity. I don't believe that a man, in this country, can love before forty or a woman before thirty- five. They may marry before that and have children; and they will love their children, but very rarely each other. I am thinking now of love at its highest rating, as that passion which is able to lift a man to the highest flight of which the soul is capable here on earth—a flight, mind you, which it may take without love, as the poet's takes it, or the musician's, but which the ordinary man's can only take by means of love.

Maurice Hewlett, in *The Note Books of a Woman Alone,* edited by M.G. Ostle, J.M. Dent & Sons Ltd., 1935, page 228

Marriage and prayer are intimately related in Paul's vision of the Christian life.

In both prayer and marriage the call is to full selfhood by loss of self in the other. The giving of self must become total. Both prayer and marriage are creative of life because of the generosity and faith that enable us to lay down our lives in love.

I suppose it wouldn't be an exaggeration to say that one of the principal causes of the breakdown of so many marriages is a lack of the spirit of obedience.

No word in the religious vocabulary is so much misunderstood by our contemporaries as 'obedience'. Obedience is nothing else than the capacity to listen to the other. We stray from God when we lose this attentiveness and no amount of talking or thinking about God can truly substitute for this openness to him. The Latin root of 'obedience' is *ob-audire*, to hear, to listen. We are to be listeners.

Obedience here is in essence sensitivity, deep sensitivity to the other, to the others. The readiness to think, in the first place, of the other and not of oneself.

As you know, it is impossible for us to love one another unless we serve one another.

John Main OSB, in *The Joy of Being,* selected by Clare Hallward, Darton, Longman & Todd, 1989, page 14

Marriage is the beginning and the pinnacle of all culture. It makes the savage gentle, and it gives the most cultivated the best occasion for demonstrating his gentleness. It has to be indissoluble: it brings so much happiness that individual instances of unhappiness do not come into account. And why speak of unhappiness at all? Impatience is what it really is, ever and again people are overcome by impatience, and then they like to think themselves unhappy. Let the moment pass, and you will count yourself happy that what has so long stood firm still stands. As for separation, there can be no adequate grounds for it. The human condition is compounded of so much joy and so much sorrow that it is impossible to reckon how much a husband owes a wife or a wife a husband. It is an infinite debt, it can be paid only in eternity. Marriage may sometimes be an uncomfortable state. I can well believe that, and that is as it should be. Are we not also married to our conscience, and would we not often like to be rid of it because it is more uncomfortable than a husband or a wife could ever be?

Johann Wolfgang von Goethe, *Elective Affinities,* translated by R.J. Hollindale, 1971, Penguin Books Ltd., 1982, page 89

People get from books the idea that if you have married the right person you may expect to go on 'being in love' for ever. As a result, when they find they are not, they think this proves they have made a mistake and are entitled to a change—not realising that, when they have changed, the glamour will presently go out of the new love just as it went out of the old one. In this department of life, as in every other, thrills come at the beginning and do not last . . .

Let the thrill go—let it die away— go on through that period of death into the quieter interest and happiness that follow—and you will find you are living in a world of new thrills all the time. But if you decide to make thrills your regular diet and try to prolong them artificially, they will all get weaker and weaker, and fewer and fewer, and you will be a bored, disillusioned old man for the rest of your life. It is because so few people understand this that you find many middle-aged men and women maundering about their lost youth, at the very age when new horizons ought to be appearing and new doors opening all round them. It is much better fun to learn to swim than to go on endlessly (and hopelessly) trying to get back the feeling you had when you first went paddling as a small boy.

C.S. Lewis, Mere Christianity, William Collins Sons & Co. Ltd., 1961, page 97

And what of Marriage? . . .
And he answered saying:
You were born together, and together you shall be for evermore.
You shall be together when the white wings of death scatter your days.
Aye, you shall be together even in the silent memory of God.
But let there be spaces in your togetherness.
And let the winds of the heavens dance between you.
Love one another, but make not a bond of love:
Let it rather be a moving sea between the shores of your souls.
Fill each other's cup but drink not from one cup.
Give one another of your bread but eat not from the same loaf.
Sing and dance together and be joyous, but let each one of you be alone,
Even as the strings of a lute are alone though they quiver with the same music.
Give your hearts, but not into each other's keeping.
For only the hand of Life can contain your hearts.
And stand together yet not too near together:
For the pillars of the temple stand apart,
And the oak tree and the cypress grow not in each other's shadow.

Kahlil Gibran, The Prophet, William Heinemann Ltd., 1970, page 16

What are the facts and principles upon which monogamy rests?

Male and female—the differences of gender belongs to many parts of nature as well as humanity. It links humanity with nature, and also serves humanity's divine goal, which reaches far beyond nature. The delicate division of gifts and qualities leaves man eager for woman, and woman eager for man. Eros, or love, is the desire of the one for the other, as one feels incomplete without the other; it is a desire to possess and be possessed. Venus is the pleasurable act in which union is expressed; it serves Eros, and Eros craves for it.

But Eros and Venus together do not exhaust the meaning of man and woman in their togetherness. Man and woman are selves, they are persons; they bring to one another a wealth of thoughts, actions, interests, concerns, and these are to become the stuff of the unity between them, without individuality disappearing. What monogamy does is not only unite Eros and Venus to one another, but unite them both within the whole realm of unities in which man and woman can be joined.

Thus is it that these are linked with Philia (friendship), the whole range of comradeship in life, together with all that this involves, and as God is the giver and God is the goal, there comes also within the relationship of man and woman the Agape (the word which is usually translated as 'love' in the New Testament, especially in 1 Cor. 13) which is the divine self-giving kind of love without which the rest may go astray. Such is monogamy. Its emergence in history, its interior depth, and its stable continuance require the sacrifice of a great restraint.

Michael Ramsey, Through the Year with Michael Ramsey, edited by Margaret Duggan, Hodder & Stoughton Ltd., 1975,
page 93

MATERIALISM

'Materialism'—opinion that nothing exists but matter and its movements and modifications; that consciousness and will are wholly due to material agency; tendency to lay stress on material aspects of objects.

I lived in Bloomsbury for nine years, whilst chaplain *to* University College, London. I enjoyed living there, and at the time felt it was a most exciting area in which to live and work. Occasionally the noise of traffic and vehicle fumes would get me down. In summer the heat and crass materialism tended to depress me, but the college had spacious sports grounds at Shenley, and a short visit out there usually proved to be most refreshing.

A colleague of mine owned a Labrador dog called Arthur. I used to see him taking Arthur for a walk down Gower Street. Poor old Arthur looked thoroughly miserable, his head bowed low, his ears drooping and his tail dangling between his legs. There were hardly any trees in the area apart from in the squares, and grassy patches were almost non-existent. I suspect 'materialism' got him down too.

This was confirmed some time later. My colleague and I ordered a minibus one Saturday and took a dozen students (plus Arthur) out in to the country, south of London. We selected a delectable heath, dotted with small bushes, miles from anywhere.

Arthur was truly amazing. As soon as the minibus doors were opened he shot out and leaped over bushes in a most extraordinary fashion, absolutely delighted with his newly found freedom. He ran and ran until he was exhausted.

I shall always be grateful to Arthur, who unconsciously revealed to me some of the detrimental effects of materialism.

… man does not live by bread alone, but that man lives by everything that proceeds out of the mouth of the Lord.

Deuteronomy 8.3

Behold, thou hast made my days a few handbreadths, and my lifetime is as nothing in thy sight. Surely every man stands as a mere breath! Surely man goes about as a shadow! Surely for nought are they in turmoil; man heaps up, and knows not who will gather!

Psalm 39.5-6

For what will it profit a man, if he gains the whole world and forfeits his life? Or what shall a man give in return for his life?

Matthew 16.26

No man can serve two masters; for either he will hate the one and love the other, or he will be devoted to the one and despise the other. You cannot serve God and mammon.

Luke 16.13

Happily for our blessedness, the joy of possession soon palls.

George Macdonald, *Wilfred Cumbermede*, Hurst and Blackett, Publishers, 1872, page 170

It is preoccupation with possessions, more than anything else, that prevents men from living freely and nobly.

Bertrand Russell, *Principles of Social Reconstruction*, George Allen & Unwin Ltd., 1971, page 162

High thinking is inconsistent with complicated material life based on high speed imposed on us by Mammon worship. All the graces of life are possible only when we learn the art of living nobly.

Mohandas K. Gandhi, *Non-Violence in Peace & War*, Navajivan Publishing House, 1949, Volume II, page 121

We consume, as we produce, without any concrete relatedness to the objects with which we deal; we live in a world of things, and our own only connection with them is that we know how to manipulate or to consume them.

Erich Fromm, *The Sane Society*, Routledge & Kegan Paul Ltd., 1956, page 134

No country has had a more splendid succession of inspiring teachers, whether poets, philosophers, or men of letters. The idealistic tradition in England is much older and more deeply rooted in the national character than our temporary and partly accidental addiction to material success. In proportion as our people can be taught to interest themselves in those treasures of the soul, in which one man's gain is not another man's loss, and which are increased by being shared with others, we may hope that the bitterness and narrowness of economic strife may be assuaged, and that something like a really harmonious civilization may come in sight.

W.R. Inge, *England*, Ernest Benn Ltd., 1926, page 289

We must begin to organise our industry with the supply of need as the primary aim and the making of profits as entirely incidental. This is a return to the 'natural order' as it exists in the mind of the Creator; but of course it is a reversal of the order natural to the selfishness of men! The Church cannot say how it is to be done; but it is called to say that it must be done, and to demand of those upon whom the change will impose sacrifices that they accept those with goodwill in the name of fellowship and service.

There the Church stops, and the State, moved by its citizens and by the Christian impulse communicated through them from the Church, takes up the task. There is room for abundance of divergent opinions.

William Temple, *Citizen and Churchman*, Eyre & Spottiswoode, 1941, page 84

The art of living is not best understood by highly industrialized communities, where men are too busy to think, and where the cult of efficiency makes them reluctant to waste time, as they put it, by considering whether their standards of value correspond with the nature of things and with their own best selves. But we ought not to evade these questions. For it is an unpleasant reflection that the same motives which make big business hostile to sensual gratifications must make it antagonistic to all the higher interests of life— to art, science, philosophy, and religion. For all these are in one way like drink—they 'make men desire fewer things.' A philosopher was once asked by a vulgar fellow whether his philosophy had ever brought him in any money. The answer, intended to be intelligible to the questioner, was: 'It has saved me a great many expenses.' Consumptionism plainly has no use for philosophy!

W.R. Inge, *Lay Thoughts of a Dean*, G.P. Putnam's Sons, 1926, page 194

For in our age all men are separated into self-contained units, everyone crawls into his own hole, everyone separates himself from his neighbour, hides himself away and hides away everything he possesses, and ends up by keeping himself at a distance from people and keeping other people at a distance from him. He accumulates riches by himself and thinks how strong he is now and how secure, and does not realize, madman that he is, that the more he accumulates the more deeply does he sink into self-destroying impotence. For he is used to relying on himself alone and has separated himself as a self-contained unit from the whole. He has trained his mind not to believe in the help of other people, in men and mankind, and is in constant fear of losing his money and the rights he has won for himself. Everywhere today the mind of man has ceased, ironically, to understand that true security of the individual does not lie in isolated personal efforts but in general human solidarity. But an end will most certainly come to this dreadful isolation of man, and everyone will realize all at once how unnaturally they have separated themselves from one another. Such will be the spirit of the time, and everyone will be surprised at having remained so long in darkness and not having seen the light. And then the sign of the Son of Man will appear in the heavens . . . But till then we must still keep the banner flying and, even if he has to do it alone, a man has to set an example at least once and draw his soul out of its isolation and work for some great act of human intercourse based on brotherly love, even if he is to be regarded as a saintly fool for his pains. He has to do so that the great idea may not die...

Fyodor Dostoyevsky, *The Brothers Karamazov*, translated by David Magarshack, Penguin Books Ltd., 1963, page 357

MERCY

'Mercy'—loving kindness and forgiveness.

A n incident happened on our holiday on the Continent, whilst travelling out to 'Yugoslavia'. I was driving at the time, and my young sister was navigating. We had somehow lost our way and were struggling to get out of Paris in our Mini. Just as we felt we were making progress a young *mademoiselle* crossed the road in front of us on what looked to be a pedestrian crossing. She was taking her time, making the most of her elegance. This was too much for my sister. She leaned over and gave the young lady a long loud blast on the horn.

My memory is now hazy on the exact sequence of events. Somehow the young lady finished up on our bonnet, kicking her legs in the air, and giving us a furious exposé of bad language. A long loud blast of a gendarme's whistle rent the air, and he appeared at my side window, wagging his finger at me. 'Oh, gosh,' I thought, 'where's my wallet.' A large spot fine seemed imminent.

My sister reacted with commendable speed. The gendarme was greeted with a rapid confession it was her fault. I have never seen her grovel so quickly before—and in a foreign language too. She then gave him an irresistible battery of fluttering eye-lashes. The poor young man was immediately smitten and completely won over. I gave a sigh of relief and thankfully put my wallet away.

The gendarme, all smiles and kindness, then gave my sister instructions as to how to get out of Paris, and we left him consoling the young *mademoiselle*. We had seen forgiveness and mercy in action, and I, for one, was relieved at the outcome.

Have mercy on me, O God, according to thy steadfast love.
Psalm 51.1

As a father pities his children, so the Lord pities those who fear him.
Psalm 103.13

And his mercy is on those who fear him from generation to generation.
Luke 1.50

Be merciful, even as your Father is merciful.
Luke 6.36

Who will not mercie unto others shew
How can he mercy ever hope to have?
Edmund Spenser, *Spenser's Faerie Queen*, edited by J.C. Smith, Oxford at the Clarendon Press, 1964, page 322, Bk.VI, Canto I, st.xlii, l.1

Wilt thou draw near the nature of the gods?
Draw near them then in being merciful;
Sweet mercy is nobility's true badge.
William Shakespeare, *Titus Andronicus*, Act I. sc.i. l.118

For Mercy has a human heart,
Pity a human face,

And Love, the human form divine,
And Peace, the human dress.

William Blake, *The Complete Writings of William Blake*, edited by Geoffrey Keynes, Oxford University Press, 1974, page 117, *Songs of Innocence*, 'The Divine Image,' st.iii, l.9

Does it never come into your mind to fear, lest He should demand of you why you had not exercised towards your brother a little of that mercy, which He, Who is your Master, so abundantly bestows upon you?

F. de la M. Fénelon, *Letters and Reflections of Fénelon*, edited by B.W. Randolph, A.R. Mowbray & Co. Ltd., 1906, page 128

Teach me to feel another's Woe;
To hide the Fault I see;
That Mercy I to others show,
That Mercy show to me.

Alexander Pope, *The Poems of Alexander Pope*, Volume VI, *Minor Poems*, edited by Norman Ault, compiled by John Butt, Methuen & Co. Ltd., 1954, page 148, 'The Universal Prayer,' st.10, l.37

Then did I see the Saviour over me
Spreading his beams of love & dictating the words of this mild song . . .
I am not a God afar off, I am a brother and friend;
Within your bosoms I reside, and you reside in me:
Lo! we are One, forgiving all Evil, Not seeking recompense.

William Blake, *The Complete Writings of William Blake*, edited by Geoffrey Keynes, Oxford University Press, 1974, page 622, *Jerusalem*, Ch 1, Plate 4, ll.4,16

I saw soothfastly that our Lord was never wroth, nor ever shall be. For He is God: Good, Life, Truth, Love, Peace; His Charity and His Unity suffereth Him not to be wroth. For I saw truly that it is against the property of His Might to be wroth, and against the property of His Wisdom, and against the property of His Goodness.

Lady Julian of Norwich, *Revelations of Divine Love*, edited by Grace Warrack, Methuen & Co. Ltd., 1949, page 97

God is the author of all tender-heartedness and goodness. Misericors—a heart always inclined to another in compassion, a pitiful heart. A heart that is always good—that is, wishing good to another. Wherever we meet these qualities, there, we can be sure, is God.

We have to be perfect as our Father is perfect, and especially as he is perfect in these qualities.

Let me look at my heart. Is it unfailingly tender towards others? Unfailingly bent on their good? Or do I see that there is a lot of hardness there?

Am I perhaps kind to some, but not to others? Kind at some times but not always? Not when I am upset, put out, hurt . . .? Do I wish well to others only when their good doesn't conflict with what I think is mine?

God is the fount of tender-heartedness and goodness. Ask him for the grace to drink deeply of this fountain. Want these God-like qualities with all your heart. Seize the opportunities each day offers to exercise them, no matter how much it costs pride and self-interest.

Ruth Burrows, *Living Love and Our Father*, Darton, Longman & Todd, 1990, page 35

The words 'Be ye perfect, even as your Father which is in heaven is perfect,' coming immediately after the words 'Your Father which is in heaven, who maketh his sun to rise on the evil and on the good, and sendeth rain on the just and on the unjust' imply a whole doctrine which, as far as I know, is not developed anywhere. For Christ cites as the supreme characteristic of God's justice precisely what is always brought forward (example of Job) with the object of accusing him of injustice, namely, that he favours the good and the wicked indifferently.

There must have been in Christ's teaching the notion of a certain virtue attaching to indifference, similar to that which may be found in Greek stoicism and Hindu thought. These words of Christ remind one of the supreme cry uttered by Prometheus: 'Heaven by whom for all the common light revolves ....'

(Moreover, this light and this rain also possess probably a spiritual significance, that is to say, that all—both in Israel and outside it, both in the Church and outside it—have grace showered upon them *equally*, although the majority reject it.)

That is absolutely contrary to the current conception whereby God arbitrarily sends down more grace on one man, less on another man, like some capricious sovereign; and that on the pretext that he does not owe it to any man! He owes it to his own infinite goodness to give to every creature good in all its fulness. We ought rather to believe that he showers continually on each one the fulness of his grace, but that we consent to receive it to a greater or lesser extent. In purely spiritual matters, God grants all desires. Those that have less have asked for less.

Simone Weil, *Gateway to God*, edited by David Raper, with the collaboration of Malcolm Muggeridge and Vernon Sproxton, William Collins Sons & Co. Ltd., 1974, page 137

From the Old Testament onwards, there are two related but distinct aspects of mercy, the divine and the human, the theological and the moral. It is a word which traditionally describes both an attitude (even *the* attitude) of God to man and a disposition which should characterize human dealings. On the former side, it is bound up with consideration like God's justice; on the latter, it is a basic moral duty. But the two aspects, though distinct, are related and intertwined. Thus, the mercy (or 'steadfast love' or 'loving kindness' as it is commonly rendered in recent versions of the Old Testament) which should mark human relationships marks, in the first place, God's relationship with human beings. And in so far as human creatures exercise justice on God's behalf, they are confronted with the question of the bounds of mercy. In the Bible, the two aspects are bound together in the deeper setting of the covenant. As this links not only God and his people but his people among themselves, so the character of the covenant is stamped on them all by virtue of their status within it. In other words, the moral aspect flows from the theological, the human from the divine. And in the Old Testament, the overwhelmingly dominant use relates to the divine side.

This pattern, established in the Old Testament, gives a unity to Christian ideas about mercy. Nevertheless, there are shifts of emphasis related to wider movements of thought and sensibility. The Old Testament roots of the term give it a central and characteristically practical role. It is central in that it is one of the commonest words (Hebrew *hesed*; Greek *eleos*) used to describe the disposition of faithful kindness with which God regards his people (Ps.138.8; Jer.33.11) and the obligation of helpfulness they should feel for each other (Micah 6.8; Judg.1.24); practical in that the attitude is expected to find expression in deeds (Isa.63.7; Zech.7.9). The strength which inheres in this quality is highlighted when it is contrasted with the Stoic idea of *eleos*, where it is seen as an emotion of weakness in that it involves a departure from strict equity into partiality.

The New Testament uses of the word are in line with Old Testament practice, as passages like Matt.9.13, 18.33; Luke 10.37 make plain. However, while it is not a prominent New Testament term, it is brought into the Christian scheme of things. Thus, the saving act of God in and through Christ is seen as the crowning expression of his mercy, as resulting in both the establishment of the new Jew-Gentile church (Rom.9.23; 11.30-32; I Peter 2.10) and in the call of the individual (I Cor.7.25; II Cor.4.1). And the expected consummation may also be described in terms of mercy (Matt.5.7; II Tim.1.18).

It is thus one of a number of words for the gracious, outgoing and dynamic purpose of God for man's salvation, fulfilled in Christ. Its biblical tone is therefore predominantly personal; yet associations of law and justice, so commonly providing a framework of imagery for man's relations with God, were there from the start, and they came to the fore in so far as Christian life came to be seen in such terms, especially in Latin Christianity. Mercy (Latin *misericordia*) now appeared as the clemency which men must hope to receive from God, in mitigation of the condemnation which was his entitlement and his doom.

J.L. Houlden, in *A New Dictionary of Christian Theology*, edited by Alan Richardson and John Bowden, SCM Press Ltd., 1983, page 356

MIND

*'Mind'—direction of thoughts or desires; way of thinking and feeling,
seat of consciousness; thought, volition, and feeling; person as
embodying mental qualities.*

H enri Matisse once said the essential thing is to put oneself in a frame of mind which
is close to that of prayer. This is what I mean by reflection. In reflection we use our
minds, feelings and emotions, our instinct, intuition, imagination, discernment, our
experience of life, and the experience of life of others. Hence all these quotations in
Visions of Grace. In short, the whole of our inner being is brought into play in reflection.

Add to this Joseph Conrad's insight on the mind from his book *The Heart of
Darkness* that 'the mind of man is capable of anything—because everything is in it, all the
past as well as all the future'—and we come to see what a valuable tool the mind is. But
how do we best engage the mind in reflection, as described above?

I imagine this will vary from person to person. My own experience is keeping a
journal or a spiritual diary. If I was to reflect on the section 'Mind', I would open my diary,
and begin by writing down all my thoughts and feelings on the first quotation, Psalm 64:6.
This would probably take me an hour, and then I would move on to the second quotation
from the Wisdom of Solomon, and work slowly through the rest of the section. I have
always been amazed at what comes out in reflection. I am reminded of the astonished
words of an undergraduate who began to reflect in this way. His discovery was: 'Gosh, I
actually have a mind that can think.' He then went on from strength to strength.

> For the inward mind and heart of a man are deep!
>
> Psalm 64.6

> ... the mind that museth upon many things.
>
> Wisdom of Solomon 9.15 (AV)

> Then he opened their minds to understand the scriptures.
>
> Luke 24.45

For who has known the mind of the Lord so as to instruct him? But we have the mind of
Christ.

1 Corinthians 2.16

Only engage, and then the mind becomes heated;
Begin, and then the task will be completed.

Anon.

The mind of man is capable of anything—because everything is in it, all the past as well as
all the future.

Joseph Conrad, *Heart of Darkness*, included in *Youth, a Narrative & Two Other Stories*, J.M. Dent & Sons Ltd., 1923,
page 96

The mind grows always by intercourse with a mind more mature than itself. That is the
secret of all teaching.

William Temple, *Christian Faith and Life*, SCM Press Ltd., 1963, page 36

Our minds are finite, and yet even in these circumstances of finitude we are surrounded by
possibilities that are infinite, and the purpose of human life is to grasp as much as we can
out of that infinitude.

Alfred North Whitehead, *Dialogues of Alfred North Whitehead*, as recorded by Lucien Price, Max Reinhardt, 1954, page 160

The life of Christ is not simply a thing written. It is a thing lived. My sanctification lies in re-living this life in the context of my own life. It lies in identifying myself with the mind of Christ which is primarily the mind of love.

Hubert van Zeller, *Considerations*, Sheed & Ward Ltd., 1974, page 67

Man is distinguished from the animals by possessing, among other things, a conscious mind, with the ability to think, reason, remember, imagine, understand and express himself. He is not just mind, nor is mind just a machine that he uses. It is a vital part of man's personality but not the whole of it. It needs to be brought under the inspiration and guidance of God.

George Appleton, *Journey for a Soul*, William Collins Sons & Co. Ltd., 1976, page 18

The mind of man is meant to be a microcosm of the mind of God. This was shown supremely, in terms of a human life, in Jesus Christ. We therefore need to study the records of that divine and human life, recognizing the faith of the writers but reaching back as far as possible to the life itself. Also, by communion with the ever-living, ever-present Christ, we can experience direct, intuitive contact and illumination.

George Appleton, *Journey for a Soul*, William Collins Sons & Co. Ltd., 1976, page 19

I call that mind free which jealously guards its intellectual rights and powers, which calls no man master, which does not content itself with a passive or hereditary faith, which opens itself to light whencesoever it may come, which receives new truth as an angel from heaven, which, whilst consulting others, inquires still more of the oracle within itself, and uses instructions from abroad not to supersede but to quicken and exalt its own energies.

William E. Channing, *The Complete Works of William Ellery Channing*, 'Spiritual Freedom,' Routledge & Sons, 1884, page 166

The great spiritual teachers of all religions have themselves practised and taught mind-fulness.

To be mindful is to live in the present moment, not to be imprisoned in the past nor anticipating a future that may never happen.

When we are fully aware of the present, life is transformed and strain and stress disappear.

So much of modern life is a feverish anticipation of future activity and excitement. We have to learn to step back from this into the freedom and possibility of the present.

Bede Griffiths OSB, in *The Universal Christ*, edited by Peter Spink, Darton, Longman & Todd, 1993, page 12

Of all things that militate against the spiritual life, none is more disastrous and far-reaching in its effect than the divorce of thought from devotion. We have built a high wall between intellect and spirit. The divine precept which bids us love God with all our mind seems to many to have but little connection with thought...

And where that understanding is exercised upon the things of God, there the will begins to energise toward the Divine and love bursts into flame. Meditation begets a deep yearning; apprehension and adhesion march together. We understand with the heart; we love with the mind.

E. Herman, *The Touch of God*, James Clarke & Co. Ltd., 1926, page 31

Our epoch is scientifically and technically minded. We want first of all to understand and to know and we believe in reason. And so we try to do the same in understanding religious ideas. But religious ideas are always and everywhere symbolic truths. They can never be understood in a rational way alone. They are, as symbols, both rational and irrational; they are paradoxical. They unite psychical facts of the conscious and unconscious mind. Though they appeal to our reason and knowledge, they have contents which we cannot yet know because they are only in the making. Religion is in its essence symbolic and every religious symbol, when it originated, was an experience surpassing conscious knowledge. When a religion becomes established, symbols are worked out into dogmas. The Roman

Catholic Church understands even the dogma to be a symbolic truth. 'The dogma unites knowing and not knowing, something which is intelligible and something which is unintelligible, a clarity and at the same time a mystery.'

One of the most valuable achievements of Professor Jung is to have re-opened the way to symbolic thinking. By this he has led us to understand religious ideas of every race and time. He also helps the modern individual either to understand his own religion in a deeper and more vital way or to find and to experience symbols which come to him from the depths of the unconscious, from that creative psyche which has always been the mother of all the things and ideas which move humanity. The symbols which are born in someone with the help of psychology are individual, but at the same time universal, because they derive from that layer in man which is common to all. Thus the individual is enriched by an inner creative life with mankind in a more vital way than merely rational and conscious efforts could achieve. He may not adhere to a given church or creed, but the Christian spirit which should unite all mankind cannot be denied to him.

Toni Wolff, in *The Choice is Always Ours*, edited by Dorothy Berkley Phillips, Harper & Row, Publishers, Inc., 1960, page 196

I had learned, it seemed, that a spiritual progress was possible to man, by which out of the discordant elements of his being—the desire of the Heart and the knowledge of the Mind—a harmony was created. This harmony was a new kind of being, and it had been called by Jesus and Eckhart and Keats, the Soul. This Soul was at once a new condition of the total human being and a faculty of knowledge. It was aware of the universe as a harmony, and of itself as a part of that harmony; and this awareness was a joyful awareness. This was the ground of the mystical faith that the Soul was consubstantial with God. God, in this mystical sense, was the inseparable counterpart of the Soul; and the Soul, in the process and very moment of becoming aware of its own self-existence, became also aware of the existence of an omnipresent God of which itself was, as it were, a focus of self-knowledge.

This strange and simple process was the 'rebirth' which Jesus had taught, and which was the central mystery of all high religion. It could occur in complete independence of any particular religion; it was the outcome of an internecine conflict between the desire of the Heart and the knowledge of the Mind...

This conflict between Heart and Mind, between feeling and knowledge, was obviously independent of religion, in any ordinary sense of the word. It was simply incidental to humanity. Man, being man was bound to endure this conflict. If he did not endure it, he was less than man, in the sense that he was turning away from something which it was his duty as a man to look upon...

Some drugged themselves with a religion which assured them that the desires of the Heart would be realized, and that death was only the doorway to life; some sought forgetfulness in busy plans for the amelioration of human circumstance; some sought to live in the moment. But there were always a few on whom these opiates failed to work. By some queer destiny the conflict was forced upon them. Heart and Mind in them insisted each upon its rights, and the claims could not be reconciled. There was a deadlock in the centre of their being, and they passed steadily into a condition of isolation, inanition, abandonment and despair. Their inward division was complete.

Then came, out of that extreme and absolute division, a sudden unity. A new kind of consciousness was created in them. Mind and Heart, which had been irreconcilable enemies, became united in the Soul, which loved what it knew. The inward division, which had divided the human being also from the universe of his knowledge, was healed; in a single happening, man became one in himself and one with all that was without him. He knew that he was called upon to play his part in the harmony revealed to him.

This was the great secret of religion; but only because it was the great secret of life. Men who learned and obeyed it, became different. They were a new kind of men.

John Middleton Murry, *God*, Jonathan Cape Ltd., 1929, page 69

MONEY

*'Money'—current coin; property viewed as convertible into money;
coin in reference to its purchasing power.*

I wonder if we might look at money in the context of the Genesis story of the creation of man—of man being made in the image and likeness of God. Firstly, there is the divine inbreathing. Secondly, that which was fashioned and shaped in the image and likeness of God was taken from the dust of the earth, giving us an earthy and creaturely side to our nature. These two sides of our nature need to be integrated and held in balance.

In this modern age, many of us have lost sight of being made in the image and likeness of God. Instead we believe man to be no more than a sophisticated animal, and tend to centre ourselves on ourselves; i.e. on the earthy and creaturely side of our nature. A consequence is that the acquisition of money becomes supremely important, at the cost of realizing our true nature.

I do not want to condemn money because it is important, and none of us can get by without it. Instead I prefer to go for balance, perspective and proportion. In the divine inbreathing we have a rich resource of divine life, latent in the depths of our being, which needs to be drawn out and integrated with the earthy and creaturely side of our nature to produce a rich quality of life. This can be done by the practice of reflection.

If we realize this enormous gift of divine wealth in our lives money finds its rightful place, along with a rich quality of life. What we see going on in the world is a highly competitive struggle for money and material wealth. This is strange when we already possess a unique source of wealth in the depths of our being, given to us without charge.

He who loves money will not be satisfied with money; nor he who loves wealth, with gain; this also is vanity.

Ecclesiastes 5.10

Bread is made for laughter, and wine gladdens life, and money answers everything.

Ecclesiastes 10.19

Do not lay up for yourselves treasures on earth, where moth and rust consume and where thieves break in and steal, but lay up for yourselves treasures in heaven, where neither moth nor rust consumes and where thieves do not break in and steal. For where your treasure is, there will be your heart also.

Matthew 6.19-21

But those who desire to be rich fall into temptation, into a snare, into many senseless and hurtful desires that plunge men into ruin and destruction. For the love of money is the root of all evils; it is through this craving that some have wandered away from the faith and pierced their hearts with many pangs.

1 Timothy 6.9-10

Great Wealth and Content seldom live together.

Thomas Fuller, M.D., *Gnomologia*, published in Dublin, 1732, page 68

Money—money, like everything else—is a deception and a disappointment.

H.G. Wells, *Kipps*, Thomas Nelson and Sons, 1909, page 260

Ill fares the land, to hastening ills a prey,
Where wealth accumulates, and men decay.

Oliver Goldsmith, *Collected Works of Oliver Goldsmith*, edited by Arthur Friedman, Oxford at the Clarendon Press, 1966, Volume IV, page 289, 'The Deserted Village,' l.51

Money is human happiness in the abstract: he, then, who is no longer capable of enjoying human happiness in the concrete devotes himself utterly to money.

Arthur Schopenhauer, in *A Certain World*, W.H. Auden, Faber & Faber Ltd., 1971, page 266

The two things which, of all others, most want to be under a strict rule, and which are the greatest blessings both to ourselves and others, when they are rightly used, are our time and our money. These talents are continual means and opportunities of doing good.

William Law, *A Serious Call to a Devout and Holy Life*, J.M. Dent & Co. Ltd., 1898, page 88

We have not driven home upon men His clear intuition that though, if wealth comes, it ought to be accepted and used as an opportunity, yet it must be recognised as rather a snare to the spiritual life than an aim which the Christian may legitimately set before himself to pursue.

William Temple, *Christian Faith and Life*, SCM Press Ltd., 1963, page 131

Selecting jobs for the pseudo independence that higher pay seems to offer, instead of for autonomous reasons—i.e., the job offering deepest satisfaction because it has intrinsic meaning for the person and adds to his self-respect—is likewise due to neurotic tendencies, namely the unrecognized equation of money with true status. Here, too, the outer security (what money can buy) is accepted in lieu of inner security; the impersonal coin of exchange is given more relevance than the particular product of one's labour. Matters are, of course, much worse when not even a semblance of freedom exists in choosing occupations.

Bruno Bettelheim, *The Informed Heart*, Thames and Hudson, 1960, page 82

If we look at the Gospels with a firm intention to discover the *emphasis* of Christ's morality, we shall find that it did not lie at all along the lines laid down by the opinion of highly placed and influential people. Disreputable people who knew they were disreputable were gently told to 'go and sin no more'; the really unparliamentary language was reserved for those thrifty, respectable, and sabbatarian citizens who enjoyed Caesar's approval and their own. And the one and only thing that ever seems to have roused the 'meek and mild' Son of God to a display of outright physical violence was precisely the assumption that 'business was business.' The money-changers in Jerusalem drove a very thriving trade, and made as shrewd a profit as any other set of brokers who traffic in foreign exchange; but the only use Christ had for these financiers was to throw their property down the front steps of the temple.

Dorothy L. Sayers, *Unpopular Opinions*, Victor Gollancz Ltd., 1946, page 10

Can a rich man be saved? Can a rich society be saved? We must first notice that the Christian gospel has never said that material abundance was in itself evil. The Old Testament constantly reiterated that abundance was the fruit that came of following the ways of the Lord; the Son of Man ate and drank with sinners and publicans, though he had nowhere to lay his head and the Church has constantly prayed for abundance and prosperity for its members and their societies.

The evils of riches, to the Christian, are the evils of distraction (the distraction that keeps men from thinking about God), the evils of a false dependence on the created order, and a would-be security that fails to take account of the inevitable fragility of human destiny on this earth. They are spiritual evils, not material evils, and it may be that they lead men to inadequate, not excessive, appreciation and enjoyment of the glories of the material universe; we tend to use, and abuse, material things, rather than to enjoy them.

D.L. Munby, *God and the Rich Society*, Oxford University Press, 1961, page 55

There does not appear to be any doubt that money is the agent which causes the decline of the strong, brave and self-confident people. The decline in courage, enterprise and a sense of duty is, however, gradual.

The first direction in which wealth injures the nation is a moral one. Money replaces honour and adventure as the objective of the best young men. Moreover, men do not normally seek to make money for their country or their community, but for themselves. Gradually, and almost imperceptibly, the Age of Affluence silences the voice of duty. The object of the young and the ambitious is no longer fame, honour or service, but cash.

Education undergoes the same gradual transformation. No longer do schools aim at producing brave patriots ready to serve their country. Parents and students alike seek the educational qualifications which will command the highest salaries. The Arab moralist, Ghazali (1058–1111), complains in these very same words of the lowering of objectives in the declining Arab world of his time. Students, he says, no longer attend college to acquire learning and virtue, but to obtain qualifications which will enable them to grow rich. The same situation is everywhere evident among us in the West today.

Sir John Glubb, *The Fate of Empires and Search for Survival*, William Blackwood & Sons Ltd., 1978, page 10

The Bible does not teach that the possession of wealth is evil in itself, but that cupidity, greed and the desire to become rich are sources of spiritual danger and of social misery. 'The love of money is a root of all kinds of evil' (1 Tim.6.10). Rich men are almost always bad men: so the prophets had discovered. Perhaps the simple eudaemonism of the older Hebrew point of view contributed to this result, for had it not long been taught that the possession of wealth was evidence of the divine favour (e.g. Ps.1.3f)? Against such a view the Book of Job protests, and the Psalmists generally are perplexed by the success of the wicked and the misfortune of the godly (e.g. Pss.37,49,73; cf. Job 21.7ff.). Worldly success leads to pride, self-esteem and contempt for the unsuccessful, as well as to lust for even greater riches and power. Thus, in the Psalms the expression 'the poor' had acquired a sort of religious significance, and may often almost be equated with 'the godly' (*Hasidim*)—the humble as contrasted with the arrogant rich, those who trust in God as against those who trust in their material wealth. It is important that we should understand that the words 'poor' and 'rich' have in many contexts a religious and an ethical content rather than an economic one. This meaning is carried over into the New Testament, and underlies such sayings of Jesus as 'Blessed are ye poor' (Luke 6.20), which Matthew rightly paraphrases as 'poor in spirit' (5.3). Jesus means 'the poor' in the sense in which the term is used as a technical expression in later Jewish literature, as denoting the class of pious, hard-working, humble folk who look to God for redemption and who do not put their trust in political schemes or material prosperity: theirs, says Jesus, is the Kingdom of God. In the situation of Jesus' own day, the 'rich' would be represented by the wealthy Sadducean high-priestly families, a worldly set of men who made a splendid profit out of their control of the Temple; while the 'poor' would be simple, devout folk—whether in the lower priestly classes (like Simeon in Luke 2.25—'righteous and devout, looking for the consolation of Israel') or in the rank and file of the working-class (like the family or the disciples of Jesus themselves). But the distinction between the two classes was religious rather than economic: Joseph of Arimathaea, though a rich man (Matt.27.57), was 'a good man and a righteous', (Luke 23.50). The publicans, who were Jesus' 'friends', were wealthy men, and Zacchaeus promised to give up only *half* his goods (Luke 19.8)! It was not so much the possession of riches as one's attitude towards them and the use which one makes of them which was the special object of Jesus' teaching; and this is true of the biblical teaching as a whole. Jesus does not condemn private property, nor is he a social reformer in any primary sense; he is concerned with men's motives and hearts: 'Make purses which wax not old, a treasure in heaven which faileth not... for where your treasure is, there will your heart be also' (Luke 12.33f.). He did not call the rich man who built larger barns a wicked capitalist but a fool; his folly consisted in thinking that his wealth was a permanent and ultimate source of satisfaction: 'a man's life consisteth not in the abundance of his possessions' (Luke 12.16-21). In the parable of Dives and Lazarus the point of the condemnation of Dives lies not so much in the fact that he was rich as in the fact that he had regarded his riches as his 'good things' (Luke 16.25): it is to be noted that when Lazarus dies he rests in Abraham's bosom—and Abraham was the very type of the wealthy Jew (cf. Gen.13.2)! Jesus teaches indifference to possessions: 'Consider the ravens...', etc. (Luke 12.22-34); anxiety about food and clothing betrays lack of faith in God: trust in riches is practical atheism. He teaches his disciples to look to God for their daily bread (Luke 11.3). It is because they have such a tempting alternative to trust in God that rich men are in mortal danger. One rich man at least was counselled by Jesus to give away all that he had (Mark 10.17-22); when he refused, Jesus said: 'How hardly shall they that have riches enter into the Kingdom of God' (17.23), but he explains to the amazed disciples that he really means 'those that trust in riches' (17.24). 'Who then can be saved?' ask the disciples. All of us have a defective faith in God; we all trust in our 'riches', whatever they may be, to some extent. No one can be saved by human effort, however rich or poor he may be, says Jesus, in effect; but happily things which are impossible with men are possible with God (17.27). Jesus repeats the usual Jewish emphasis on the value of *ALMSGIVING* (Luke 12.33), an activity which presupposes the institution of private property; and again he stresses the factor of motive as being of greater importance than the sum involved (Matt.6.2-4, Luke 21.1-4). The New Testament bears plenty of evidence that the apostolic church possessed at least some well-to-do members, and was willing to accept their gifts and their hospitality and support. The use of the word 'communism' in connexion with the spontaneous and voluntary act of sharing in the early Jerusalem church is highly misleading, in view of the modern associations of that word (Acts 2.44f., 4 34-7); the experiment does not seem to have been copied elsewhere, and some scholars have held it to have been in part responsible for that state of economic distress which necessitated Paul's collections from his Gentile churches. More significant is Jesus' own poverty and renunciation of worldly goods; he and his disciples used a common purse and were supported by the voluntary offerings of a wider circle of disciples and well-wishers. It is Jesus himself who embodies the biblical ideal of 'the poor man' who trusts only in God, and herein lies the real theological significance of his poverty: 'Ye know the grace of our Lord Jesus Christ, that, though he was rich, yet for your sakes he became poor, that ye through his poverty might become rich' (II Cor.8.9; cf.6.10).

Alan Richardson, in *A Theological Word Book of the Bible*, edited by Alan Richardson, SCM Press Ltd., 1975, page 168

MUSIC

'Music'—art of combining sounds with a view to beauty of form and expression of emotion; sounds so produced.

M usic has always been important to me. When I was appointed chaplain to University College, London, I joined the Music Society and sang in the college choir. This proved to be a good way of meeting and getting to know students. During the term we had a rehearsal each week and put on a concert at the end of term. Once a year we performed an opera—usually a work not previously performed in Britain— hiring professional singers for the solo parts, with the college choir forming the chorus.

I have fond memories of these operas. I can remember one performance when I was in the wings, and the tenors were on stage in full throttle. One tenor at the back of the stage was dangerously close to the curtain. He was so engrossed in singing he failed to notice an umbrella handle coming under the curtain, deftly coiling itself round his ankle, until it was too late. A tug of war took place. I think it was his agonized facial expression, half bent on survival and half concentrating on the music, which was so hilariously funny.

The performance continued on course until the last scene. With only two minutes to go the soprano heroine was building up to the climax. Suddenly without warning the final curtain came down, due to a faulty signal. Her singing stopped and gave way to a peculiar howling noise. At this point the curtain was hurriedly whisked up to expose her lying on the stage floor, beating the floor with her fists in rage. Suddenly she looked up and peered into the bemused eyes of the entire audience of the Collegiate Theatre. How my sides ached at the end of that opera.

Praise the Lord with the lyre, make melody to him with the harp of ten strings! Sing to him a new song, play skilfully on the strings, with loud shouts.

Psalm 33.2-3

He put a new song in my mouth, a song of praise to our God.

Psalm 40.3

... but be filled with the Spirit, addressing one another in psalms and hymns and spiritual songs, singing and making melody to the Lord with all your heart.

Ephesians 5.18-19

Let the word of Christ dwell in you richly, teach and admonish one another in all wisdom, and sing psalms and hymns and spiritual songs with thankfulness in your hearts to God.

Colossians 3.16

Music is a higher revelation than all wisdom and philosophy.

J.W.N. Sullivan, *Beethoven*, Jonathan Cape Ltd., 1931, page 13

Organ playing... is the manifestation of a will filled with a vision of eternity.

C.M. Widor, in *Music in the Life of Albert Schweitzer*, selections from his writings translated and edited by Charles R. Joy, A. & C. Black Ltd., 1953, page 157

Who hears music, feels his solitude
Peopled at once.

Robert Browning, *The Poetical Works of Robert Browning*, Smith, Elder & Co., 1899, Volume I, page 631, 'Balaustion's Adventure'

The soul continues as an instrument of God's harmony, a tuned instrument of divine joy for the Spirit to strike on.

William Law, *Selected Mystical Writings of William Law*, edited by Stephen Hobhouse, Rockliff, 1948, page 246

Music, the greatest good that mortals know,
And all of heaven we have below.

Joseph Addison, *The Works of Joseph Addison*, edited and published by Henry G. Bohn, 1856, Volume I, 'A Song for St. Cecilia's Day,' page 21

But God has a few of us whom he whispers in the ear;
The rest may reason and welcome: 'tis we musicians know.

Robert Browning, *The Poetical Works of Robert Browning*, Smith, Elder & Co., 1899, Volume I, page 580, *Dramatis Personae*, 'Abt Vogler,' st.xi, l.12

There is no truer truth obtainable
By Man than comes of music.

Robert Browning, *The Poetical Works of Robert Browning*, Smith, Elder & Co., 1910, Volume II, page 726, 'Parleyings with Certain People,' with Charles Avison, st.vi., l.2

See deep enough, and you see musically; the heart of Nature *being* everywhere music, if you can only reach it.

Thomas Carlyle, *Sartor Resartus*, 'Lectures on Heroes,' Chapman & Hall Ltd., 1840, page 247

The language of tones belongs equally to all men, and that melody is the absolute language in which a musician addresses every heart.

Richard Wagner, *Beethoven*, translated by Edward Dannreuther, William Reeves, 1880, page 1

It is in Music, perhaps, that the soul most nearly attains the great end for which, when inspired by the Poetic Sentiment, it struggles—the creation of supernal Beauty.

Edgar Allan Poe, *The Portable Poe*, selected and edited by Philip Van Doren Stern, Penguin Books Ltd., 1973, page 574, 'The Poetic Principle'

Yea, music is the Prophets' art;
Among the gifts that God hath sent,
One of the most magnificent!

Henry Wadsworth Longfellow, *The Writings of Henry Wadsworth Longfellow*, Riverside Edition, George Routledge & Sons Ltd., 1886, Volume VII, page 295, *Christus: A Mystery*, Part III, Interlude 2

Who is there that, in logical words, can express the effect music has on us? A kind of inarticulate unfathomable speech, which leads us to the edge of the Infinite, and lets us for moments gaze into that!

Thomas Carlyle, *Sartor Resartus*, 'Lectures on Heroes,' Chapman & Hall Ltd., 1840, page 247

For even that vulgar and Taverne Musicke, which makes one man merry, another mad, strikes me into a deepe fit of devotion, and a profound contemplation of the first Composer; there is something in it of Divinity more than the eare discovers.

Sir Thomas Browne, *The Works of Sir Thomas Browne*, edited by Geoffrey Keynes, Faber & Faber Ltd., 1964, Volume I, *Religio Medici*, page 84

Preposterous ass, that never read so far
To know the cause why music was ordain'd!
Was it not to refresh the mind of man
After his studies or his usual pain?

William Shakespeare, *The Taming of the Shrew*, Act III. sc.i. l.9

Musical training is a more potent instrument than any other, because rhythm and harmony find their way into the secret places of the soul, on which they mightily fasten, imparting grace, and making the soul graceful of him who is rightly educated, or ungraceful of him who is ill-educated.

Plato, *The Republic of Plato*, translated by B. Jowett, Oxford at the Clarendon Press, 1881, page 85, Bk.III, 401D

I lost myself in a Schubert Quartet at the end of a Crowndale Road concert, partly by ceasing all striving to understand the music, partly by driving off intruding thoughts, partly feeling the music coming up inside me, myself a hollow vessel filled with sound.

Joanna Field, *A Life of One's Own*, Chatto & Windus Ltd., 1934, page 29

[Music] is a principal means of glorifying our merciful Creator, it heightens our devotion, it gives delight and ease to our travails, it expelleth sadness and heaviness of spirit, preserveth people in concord and amity, allayeth fierceness and anger; and lastly, is the best physic for many melancholy diseases.

Henry Peacham, *The Compleat Gentleman*, Da Capo Press, Theatrum Orbis Terrarum, 1968, page 104

Now, what is music? This question occupied me for hours before I fell asleep last night. Music is a strange thing. I would almost say it is a miracle. For it stands halfway between thought and phenomenon, between spirit and matter, a sort of nebulous mediator, like and unlike each of the things it mediates—spirit that requires manifestation in time, and matter that can do without space. We do not know what music is.

Heinrich Heine, in *Pleasures of Music*, edited by Jacques Barzun, Michael Joseph Ltd., 1952, page 268

Musical order, as recognized and evaluated by our mind, is not an end in itself. It is an image of a higher order which we are permitted to perceive if we proceed one step further to the sixth degree on our scale of musical assimilation: if we put our enjoyment of such knowledge ('enjoyment, the weight of the soul!') into the side of the balance that tends towards the order of the heavens and towards the unification of our soul with the divine principle.

Paul Hindemith, *A Composer's World*, Harvard University Press, distributed in Great Britain by Geoffrey Cumberlege, Oxford University Press, 1952, page 4

Music seems to say something but we can never put into words just what it is saying. It seems to take us beyond words. The composer Mahler once wrote, 'As long as my

---

experience can be summed up in words, I write no music about it; my need to express myself musically... begins at the door which leads into the "other world"—the world in which things are no longer separated by space and time.' And a contemporary Christian, Ulrich Simon, has stated the same thought in these words, 'For me the D minor quartet and the G minor quintet of Mozart evoke in every bar the truth about God, but I do not know how to express the truth. Perhaps it is a *musical* truth, for what do words like *tragic* and *searing* mean even if I related them to my chosen bars, themes and developments?

'Rather these empty words are fulfilled by the music. We owe everything to Mozart because he has revealed the priority of music in theology.' Music, then, seems to lead us into another world, to make us aware of the spiritual dimension, in a way words so often fail to do.

Richard Harries, *Prayers of Grief and Glory*, Lutterworth Press, 1979, page 86

You say, you should like to know my way of composing, and what method I follow in writing works of some extent. I can really say no more on this subject than the following; for I myself know no more about it, and cannot account for it. When I am, as it were, completely myself, entirely alone, and of good cheer—say, travelling in a carriage, or walking after a good meal, or during the night when I cannot sleep; it is on such occasions that my ideas flow best and most abundantly. *Whence* and *how* they come, I know not; nor can I force them. Those ideas that please me I retain in memory, and am accustomed, as I have been told, to hum them to myself...

All this fires my soul, and, provided I am not disturbed, my subject enlarges itself, becomes methodised and defined, and the whole, though it be long, stands almost complete and finished in my mind, so that I can survey it, like a fine picture or a beautiful statue, at a glance. Nor do I hear in my imagination the parts *successively*, but I hear them, as it were, all at once. What a delight this is I cannot tell! All this inventing, this producing, takes place in a pleasing lively dream. Still the actual hearing of the *tout ensemble* is after all the best. What has been thus produced I do not easily forget, and this is perhaps the best gift I have my Divine Maker to thank for.

Edward Holmes, *The Life of Mozart*, Chapman & Hall Ltd., 1845, page 317, letter written by Mozart

NATURE

*'Nature'—physical power causing phenomena of material world,
these phenomena as a whole.*

W hilst chaplain of University College, Oxford, I received an invitation to officiate at a wedding near San Francisco.

The bridegroom was a former Rhodes Scholar at Univ. and I had come to know him well as he was a member of one of my reflection groups during his time in Oxford.

The wedding was planned to take place out of doors in a vineyard in the hills overlooking the campus of Stanford University. The bride had studied there for an MBA and between them the couple had chosen an ideal setting for their wedding and reception. The result was a ceremony never to be forgotten.

During my short stay in San Francisco I walked across the Golden Gate Bridge, and visited Fisherman's Wharf, Alcatraz, and other tourist spots.

Having put these behind me I devoted the rest of my time to seeing some of nature's spectacles. I first went to Muir Woods, and walked amongst huge redwood trees. Some of these were over 300 feet high, fifteen feet in diameter, and over 2,000 years old. Earlier in the week delegates celebrating the fiftieth anniversary of the founding of the United Nations had come to Muir Woods to pray for the peace of the world.

I then went on a one-day visit to Yosemite National Park. The snow in the surrounding mountains was still melting and a huge volume of water cascaded down the waterfalls. The granite mountains formed an impressive backcloth to the waterfalls. To quote a guidebook, in Yosemite National Park I was 'captivated by the symphony Nature is continually playing'.

But ask the beasts, and they will teach you; the birds of the air, and they will tell you; or the plants of the earth, and they will teach you; and the fish of the sea will declare to you. Who among all these does not know that the hand of the Lord has done this? In his hand is the life of every living thing and the breath of all mankind.

Job 12.7-10

The earth is the Lord's and the fulness thereof, the world and those who dwell therein; for he has founded it upon the seas, and established it upon the rivers.

Psalm 24.1-2

Men, why are you doing this? We also are men, of like nature with you, and bring you good news, that you should turn from these vain things to a living God who made the heaven and the earth and the sea and all that is in them. In past generations he allowed all the nations to walk in their own ways; yet he did not leave himself without witness, for he did good and gave you from heaven rains and fruitful seasons, satisfying your hearts with food and gladness.

Acts 14.15-17

He is the image of the invisible God, the first-born of all creation; for in him all things were created, in heaven and on earth, visible and invisible, whether thrones or dominions or principalities or authorities—all things were created through him and for him. He is before all things, and in him all things hold together.

Colossians 1.15-17

The course of nature is the art of God.

Edward Young, *Night Thoughts*, Thomas Nelson, 1841, page 229

Nature stamped us in a heavenly mould.

Thomas Campbell, *The Pleasures of Hope*, edited by Henry Morley, George Routledge & Sons Ltd., 1892, page 30

All things are artificiall, for Nature is the Art of God.

Sir Thomas Browne, *The Works of Sir Thomas Browne*, edited by Geoffrey Keynes, Faber & Faber Ltd, 1964, Volume I, *Religio Medici*, page 26

Joy in looking and comprehending is nature's most beautiful gift.

Albert Einstein, *Ideas and Opinions*, Souvenir Press (Educational & Academic) Ltd., 1973, page 28

Laws of nature are God's thoughts thinking themselves out in the orbits and the tides.

Charles H. Parkhurst, *The Pattern in the Mount and Other Sermons*, R.D. Dickinson, 1890, page 14

Those who honour Nature well, who teach that she can speak on everything, even on Theology.

Blaise Pascal, *Pensées*, translated by W.F. Trotter, Random House Inc., 1941, page 12

Nature is but a name for an effect,
Whose cause is God.

William Cowper, *The Poetical Works of Cowper*, edited by H.S. Milford, Oxford University Press, 1950, page 224, 'The Task,' Book VI, l.224

Nature is full of genius, full of divinity; so that not a snowflake escapes its fashioning hand.

Henry David Thoreau, *The Journal of Henry D. Thoreau*, edited by Bradford Torrey and Francis H. Allen, Houghton Mifflin Company, Boston, The Riverside Press, 1949, Volume VIII, page 88

Nature has some perfections to show that she is the image of God, and some defects to show that she is only his image.

Blaise Pascal, *Pensées*, translated by W.F. Trotter, Random House Inc., 1941, page 190

Come forth into the light of things,
Let Nature be your Teacher.

William Wordsworth, *The Poetical Works of William Wordsworth*, edited by E. de Selincourt and Helen Darbishire, Oxford at the Clarendon Press, 1958, Volume IV, page 57, 'The Tables Turned,' st.iv, l.15

To me the meanest flower that blows can give
Thoughts that do often lie too deep for tears.

William Wordsworth, *The Poetical Works of William Wordsworth*, edited by E. de Selincourt and Helen Darbishire, Oxford at the Clarendon Press, 1958, Volume IV, page 285, 'Ode: Intimations of Immortality,' xi, l.203

O Nature all-sufficient! over all!
Enrich me with the knowledge of thy works.
Snatch me to heaven.

James Thomson, *The Seasons and The Castle of Indulgence*, edited by J. Logie Robertson, Oxford at the Clarendon Press, 1891, 'Autumn,' page 152, l.1352

The losing of Paradise is enacted over and over again by the children of Adam and Eve. We clothe our souls with messages and doctrines and lose the touch of the great life in the naked beast of Nature.

Rabindranath Tagore, *Letters to a Friend*, George Allen & Unwin Ltd., 1928, page 138

I do not count the hours I spend
In wandering by the sea;

The forest is my loyal friend,
Like God it useth me.

Ralph Waldo Emerson, *The Works of Ralph Waldo Emerson*, edited by George Sampson, George Bell & Sons Ltd., 1906, Volume V, *Poems*, 'Waldeinsamkeit,' page 180

There is undoubtedly a deep affinity, probably psychic and chemical, between every individual human being and some particular type of landscape. It is well to find out as soon as possible what kind this is; and then to get as much of it as you can.

John Cowper Powys, *The Meaning of Culture*, Jonathan Cape Ltd., 1932, page 177

His are the mountains, and the vallies his,
And the resplendent rivers. His t'enjoy
With a propriety that none can feel,
But who, with filial confidence inspir'd,
Can lift to heaven an unpresumptuous eye,
And smiling say—My Father made them all!

William Cowper, *The Poetical Works of Cowper*, edited by H.S. Milford, Oxford University Press, 1950, page 216, 'The Task,' Book V, l.742

The year's at the spring
And day's at the morn;
Morning's at seven;
The hill side's dew-pearled;
The lark's on the wing;
The snail's on the thorn;
God's in his heaven—
All's right with the world!

Robert Browning, *The Poetical Works of Robert Browning*, Smith, Elder & Co., 1899, Volume I, page 202, 'Pippa Passes,' Part I

In looking at objects of Nature while I am thinking, as at yonder moon dim-glimmering through the dewy window-pane, I seem rather to be seeking, as it were *asking* for, a symbolic language for something within me that already and for ever exists, than observing anything new. Even when that latter is the case, yet still I have always an obscure feeling as if that new phenomena were the dim awaking of a forgotten or hidden truth of my inner nature.

Samuel Taylor Coleridge, *Coleridge, Select Poetry & Prose*, edited by Stephen Potter, The Nonesuch Press, page 175, Notebooks: 14th April, 1805

The same stream of life that runs through my veins night and day runs through the world and dances in rhythmic measures.

It is the same life that shoots in joy through the dust of the earth in numberless blades of grass and breaks into tumultuous waves of leaves and flowers.

It is the same life that is rocked in the ocean-cradle of birth and of death, in ebb and in flow.

I feel my limbs are made glorious by the touch of this world of life. And my pride is from the life-throb of ages dancing in my blood at this moment.

Rabindranath Tagore, *Gitanjali*, Macmillan & Co. Ltd., 1971, page 64

There is a pleasure in the pathless woods,
There is a rapture on the lonely shore,
There is society, where none intrudes,
By the deep Sea, and music in its roar:
I love not Man the less, but Nature more,
From these our interviews, in which I steal
From all I may be, or have been before,
To mingle with the Universe, and feel
What I can ne'er express, yet can not all conceal.

Lord Byron, *The Complete Poetical Works*, edited by Jerome J. McCann, Oxford at the Clarendon Press, 1980, Volume II, page 184, 'Childe Harold's Pilgrimage,' Canto IV, st.clxxviii, l.1594

All are but parts of one stupendous whole,
Whose body Nature is, and God the soul;
That, changed through all, and yet in all the same;
Great in the earth, as in the ethereal frame;
Warms in the sun, refreshes in the breeze,
Glows in the stars, and blossoms in the trees, . . .
As full, as perfect, in vile man that mourns,
As the rapt seraph that adores and burns:
To him no high, no low, no great, no small:
He fills, he bounds, connects, and equals all.

Alexander Pope, *An Essay on Man*, Cassell and Company Ltd., 1905, Epistle 1, page 23

Man is free to indulge in riotous living and to live by overthrowing the order of things, but on his way he will surely meet the suffering that will prostrate him.

He is free to separate himself from God who is order, nature and life, but God then surrounds him with a hedge and fills his path with thorns so that he sees that it is better to stop and perhaps even turn round and go back again.

Nature is one of God's great signs and man will never manage to elude it.

Nor will he succeed in ridding himself of the fear, indeed the terror, that death lays upon him. In the last analysis, what matters is to stop in time.

I am reminded of the story of Pinnochio. He is made of wood so is insensitive to pain.

But when he let his leg loll in the fireplace near the fire his insensitivity to pain became a great danger and threatened his life.

It seems absurd to say it, but: what would happen if there were no pain to sensitize us in time, to warn us?

Carlo Carretto, *The Desert in the City*, translated by Barbara Wall, William Collins Sons & Co. Ltd., 1979, page 66

The beauty of nature is a distinct revelation made to the human mind, from that of its use . . . When the materialist has exhausted himself in efforts to explain utility in nature, it would appear to be the peculiar office of beauty to rise up suddenly as a confounding and baffling *extra*, which was not even formally provided for in his scheme . . . The glory of nature in reality resides in the mind of man; there is an inward intervening light through which the material objects pass, a transforming medium which converts the physical assemblage into a picture. It must be remarked that the whole of what any scene of earth or sky is materially, is stamped upon the retina of the brute, just as it is upon the man's; and that the brute sees all the same objects which are beautiful to man, only without their beauty: which aspect is inherent to man, and part of his reason. He possesses the key to the sight; and that which makes the appearance what it is, resides in him; and is an inner light or splendour reflected from his reason upon the surface of the universal frame of things.

J.B. Mozley, *University and Other Sermons*, Rivingtons, 1876, page 124

NEIGHBOUR

'Neighbour'—dweller in the same street or district, or one having claims on others' friendliness.

S omewhere I have come across a description of a neighbour as 'anyone close by in need'. Within half an hour of being ordained there was a knock on the clergy house door, and there was a young woman with a baby in her lap, 'close by in need'—of money and food.

This was the start of coming close to hundreds of people in need during the last thirty years of ministry. Some have been destitute men and women in need of food and sustenance. Others have been sick, physically, mentally and spiritually, in need of healing.

Another group have been the elderly and the infirm, in need of care. I also have taken on individuals with special needs. I remember trying to help a young 'drop-out' over a three-year period, and he was followed by another man, with serious psychological problems, whom I saw regularly for fifteen years.

When I worked in Nigeria I was caught up freeing a man who was being blackmailed and I can also recall taking in relief supplies to Biafra during the Nigerian Civil War in the late 1960s.

As a college chaplain I have been confronted by almost every student problem imaginable. Many of these spring from broken relationships, whether at home or at college. Loneliness is still a major problem in universities, and stress and strain have led to an increase in anxiety and worry. Depression afflicts a number of people and mental breakdowns are not uncommon. Being resident in college means being exposed and vulnerable throughout a term to neighbours—i.e. 'anyone close by in need'.

You shall love your neighbour as yourself: I am the Lord.
Leviticus 19.18

Do not plan evil against your neighbour who dwells trustingly beside you.
Proverbs 3.29

So whatever you wish that men would do to you, do so to them; for this is the law and the prophets.
Matthew 7.12

If you really fulfil the royal law, according to scripture, 'You shall love your neighbour as yourself,' you do well.
James 2.8

You cannot love a fellow-creature fully till you love God.
C.S. Lewis, *The Great Divorce*, William Collins Sons & Co. Ltd., 1982, page 84

All is well with him, who is beloved of his neighbours.
George Herbert, *The Works of George Herbert*, edited by F.E. Hutchinson, Oxford at the Clarendon Press, 1972, page 321, 'Outlandish Proverbs,' No.10

The love of our neighbour is the only door out of the dungeon of self.
George Macdonald, *Unspoken Sermons*, First Series, Alexander Strahan, Publisher, 1867, page 214

We are made *one for another*; and each is to be a Supply to his Neighbour.
Benjamin Whichcote, *Moral and Religious Aphorisms*, 1930, page 16, Century II, No.122

The good neighbour looks beyond the external accidents and discerns those inner qualities that make all men human, and therefore, brothers.
Martin Luther King, *Strength to Love*, William Collins Sons & Co. Ltd., 1980, page 29

We cannot be sure if we are loving God, although we may have good reasons for believing that we are, but we can know quite well if we are loving our neighbour.
St Teresa of Avila, *Complete Works of St. Teresa of Jesus*, translated by E. Allison Peers, Sheed & Ward Ltd., 1978, page 261, *Interior Castle*

A man must not choose his neighbour; he must take the neighbour that God sends him . . . The neighbour is just the man who is next to you at the moment, the man with whom any business has brought you into contact.
George Macdonald, *Unspoken Sermons*, First Series, Alexander Strahan, Publisher, 1867, page 210

True neighbourliness must begin within our own psychological attitudes. I must accept my neighbour for what he is, I must let him be himself, respect his 'isness' and self-understanding. I must not impose my pattern on him or exploit him for my own purposes. I must be interested in him as a person, so that our relationship will encourage mutual development in maturity. I must be ready to take initiatives, to engage in adventures of understanding and friendship.

George Appleton, *Journey for a Soul*, William Collins Sons & Co. Ltd., 1976, page 60

The second great commandment of the Law of the Lord was a miracle of inspiration, combining divine inspiration and human perception. To love my neighbour as myself, to give him equal value and equal rights, to do nothing to him which I would not want done to myself, and more positively to do to him only those deeds that I would like done to me, is a principle that makes for a humane and satisfying society, and it makes for a heart at peace and moving out in love.

George Appleton, *Journey for a Soul*, William Collins Sons & Co. Ltd., 1976, page 59

Today there is an inescapable duty to make ourselves the neighbour of every man, no matter who he is, and if we meet him, to come to his aid in a positive way, whether he is an aged person abandoned by all, a foreign worker despised without reason, a refugee, an illegitimate child wrongly suffering for a sin he did not commit, or a starving human being who awakens our conscience by calling to mind the words of Christ: 'As you did it to one of the least of these my brethren, you did it to me.' (Mt.25.40)

Vatican Council II, *The Conciliar and Post Conciliar Documents*, 1981 Edition, general editor, Austin Flannery, OP, Fowler Wright Books Ltd., page 928

People can sense when we are concerned and interested. Sometimes it may be that we are preoccupied with some problems or too much under pressure of time, or it may be that we cannot take the trouble. We need to give our whole attention to our neighbour, to identify ourselves with him, to have an open ear, an open mind and an open heart. This applies not only to individual relationships, but also to the relationship of our social, national and religious groupings as we meet similar neighbourhood groups.

George Appleton, *Journey for a Soul*, William Collins Sons & Co. Ltd., 1976, page 73

By love, I do not mean natural tenderness, which is more or less in people, according to their constitutions; but I mean a larger principle of the soul, founded in reason and piety, which makes us tender, kind, and benevolent to all our fellow creatures as creatures of God, and for His sake.

It is this love, that loves all things in God, as His creatures as the images of His power, as the creatures of His goodness, as parts of His family, as members of His society, that becomes a holy principle of all great and good actions.

The love, therefore, of our neighbour, is only a branch of our love to God. For when we love God with all our hearts, and with all our souls, and with all our strength, we shall necessarily love those beings that are so nearly related to God, that have everything from Him, and are created by Him to be objects of His own eternal love.

William Law, *A Serious Call to a Devout and Holy Life*, J.M. Dent & Co. Ltd., 1898, page 334

When we hear those great, solemn, beautiful words intoned—'Listen O Israel... You must love the Lord your God with all your heart and all your soul, with all your mind and all your strength'—we can feel deeply moved. They resound in our soul as the very meaning of life.

But what are we actually doing to live out this totality of love which constitutes the very existence of Jesus himself?

The love of God is almost impossible to evaluate. Love of neighbour is the only guide to existence let alone its depths.

It is only in loving our neighbour that we can be set on loving God all the time and everywhere. There is no meaning to our human existence but this.

The more earnestly we want to surrender to God, the more determinedly we must work to love our neighbour.

Ruth Burrows, *Living Love and Our Father*, Darton, Longman & Todd, 1990, page 48

'In the evening of life you will be examined on love.'

In the parable of the sheep and the goats Jesus makes it devastatingly clear that in the end it is only love of neighbour that counts—nothing else.

We shall not be examined on prayer, poverty, obedience, or any of the other virtues; not because they are inessential but because they are real only insofar as we are wholly concerned with our neighbour.

You can't pray, obey, or be truly poor, says our Lord, unless you are wholly taken up with your brother's needs . . .

No human heart is capable of such devotion, but Jesus asks it because what is impossible to man is possible to God. He has identified himself with us completely—'you did it, did not . . . to me'—so that he may be our life.

What he asks we can therefore fulfil if we really want to, if we pray from our hearts, if we really take the trouble to do all we can do.

Ruth Burrows, *Living Love and Our Father*, Darton, Longman & Todd, 1990, page 41

OBEDIENCE

'Obedience'—obeying the will of God; doing God's will rather than doing one's own.

When the faith I had been trained in at theological college broke down, one of the books which helped me was *From Darkness to Light*, by Victor Gollancz.

Victor Gollancz himself went through a long period of darkness in his life, and eventually came through to light by 'waiting on God'. This involved a certain obedience which is described in a quotation in this section taken from *From Darkness to Light*. The observations expressed in this short passage very much mirror my own experience.

For me (as for Victor Gollancz), obeying the will of God, or doing God's will rather than my own, came in learning to cooperate, quietly, and in complete freedom, with his blessed and blessing will, that will of his which I discover deep in my own heart as my will also—as the best, essential me—and which, discovering it also deep in the heart of everything else, I find to be not only vaster, but also saner and more fruitful of life and peace and joy. He went on to compare this with the self-regarding wilfulness that would deceive me with its appearance of leading me to my goal, but would in fact cut me off, if it had its way, from my birthright of unity with all things.

I have quoted this almost verbatim as it coincides with what I have experienced. I don't think God wants me to obey him as some Stalin or Hitler—but prefers quiet cooperation.

Link this up with reflection, using *Visions of Grace*, and we find a wonderful way of obedience to the will of God.

Now therefore, if you will obey my voice and keep my covenant, you shall be my own possession among all peoples; for all the earth is mine, and you shall be to me a kingdom of priests and a holy nation.

Exodus 19.5

Teach me thy way, O Lord; and lead me on a level path.

Psalm 27.11

We must obey God rather than men.

Acts 5.29

What you have learned and received and heard and seen in me, do.

Philippians 4.9

Obedience is the key to every door.

George Macdonald, *The Marquis of Lossie*, Everett & Co. Ltd., 1912, page 207

God does not desire that we should abound in spiritual lights, but that in all things we should submit to His will.

Henry Suso, in St Alphonsus de Liguori, *On Conformity with the Will of God*, translated by the Rev. James Jones, Catholic Truth Society, 1892, page 7

Had he done as the Master told him, he would soon have come to understand. Obedience is the opener of eyes.

George Macdonald, *Unspoken Sermons*, Second Series, Longmans, Green & Co. Ltd., 1885, page 22

If a man does not keep pace with his companions, perhaps it is because he hears a different drummer. Let him step to the music which he hears, however measured or far away.

Henry David Thoreau, *Walden*, The New American Library of World Literature, Inc., 1960, page 216

Henceforth I learn, that to obey is best,
And love with fear the only God, to walk
As in his presence, ever to observe
His providence, and on him sole depend.

John Milton, *The Poetical Works of John Milton*, edited by the Rev. H.C. Beeching, Oxford at the Clarendon Press, 1900, page 446, *Paradise Lost*, Book XII, l.561

Obedience is a complicated act of virtue, and many graces are exercised in one act of obedience. It is an act of humility, of mortification and self-denial, of charity to God, of care of the public, of order and charity to ourselves and all our society, and a great instance of a victory over the most refractory and unruly passions.

Jeremy Taylor, *Holy Living*, abridged by Anne Lamb, The Langford Press, 1970, page 85

We have no code of rules that can only be obeyed in the circumstances of their origin, no scheme of thought which can only be understood in the terms in which it was first conceived, but a Person to whom we can be loyal in all circumstances whatever, with that infinite flexibility and delicacy of adjustment which are compatible with a loyalty that remains absolute and unalterable.

William Temple, *Thoughts On Some Problems Of The Day*, Macmillan & Co. Ltd., 1931, page 28

True and perfect obedience is a virtue above all virtues. No great work can be accomplished without it; nor can there be any task, however small or insignificant, which will not be done to better purpose in obedience... Obedience brings out the best of everything; it never fails or errs in any matter; and no matter what you do, if you do it in true obedience, it will not miss being good.

Obedience has no cares; it lacks no blessing. Being obedient, if a man purifies himself, God will come into him in course; for when he has no will of his own, then God will command for him what God would command for himself.

Meister Eckhart, *Meister Eckhart*, translated by Raymond B. Blakney, Harper & Row, Publishers, Inc., 1941, page 3

I dislike talk about obeying God, as if he were some Stalin or Hitler: I cannot think that he wants me to obey him: what he wants, I think, is that I should learn to cooperate, quietly and in complete freedom, with his blessed and blessing will, that will of his which I discover deep in my own heart as my own will also—as the best, essential me—and which, discovering it also deep in the heart of everything else, I find to be not only vaster, but also saner and more fruitful of life and peace and joy, than the self-regarding wilfulness that would deceive me with its appearance of leading me to my goal, but would in fact cut me off, if it had its way, from my birthright of unity with all things.

Victor Gollancz, *From Darkness to Light*, Victor Gollancz Ltd., 1965, page 245

To commit ourselves to Jesus and the Father whom he reveals means a deliberate choosing to move off ourselves, to refuse to stand on ourselves, to be our own judges of reality.

We have to discover Jesus' vision and make it our own even against what our senses and reason tell us. It means trying to live our human lives as he lived his in obedience to the Father. Faith has no reality if it is not love. Love chooses. Love moves out of self to the other; it is a movement of surrender. Faith, hope and love: these are different aspects of the one human surrender to the God of love.

Biblical faith is not a mere intellectual assent to this or that piece of information; it is an act of the whole person surrendering to the God who calls in love, or rather, offers himself in love. It is the human 'yes' to the infinite mystery of love. It is obedience.

Ruth Burrows, in *The Watchful Heart*, edited by Eliabeth Ruth Obbard, Darton, Longman & Todd, 1988, page 12

We are servants, called upon to obey. Has not the idea of obedience as a Christian virtue rather slipped out of our contemporary religion? We think much about the response of faith, love, sonship, friendship in our relation to God or to our Lord. But obedience? We tend to think that it smacks of legalism, and not to dwell upon it. But it has an ineradicable place in the New Testament. Jesus was 'obedient unto death' (Phil 2.8), and 'he learned obedience through what he suffered' (Heb 5.8). The apostle is Christ's slave... Our obedience calls for 'loins girded and lamps burning'. 'Loins girded' suggests an alertness which is ready to meet emergencies and interruptions. Do not be encumbered. Be ready to move, rapidly and unexpectedly. Our faithfulness is again and again tested by our power to deal with interruptions. You plan your day according to some rule, with so many hours for this and so many for that. Then all seems thrown into disorder by interruptions... If the will of God is that you should accept this or that interruption, and you accept them with gladness, then a day which might seem tempestuous is really filled with plan and peace and order; for where the will of God is there is God's presence and God's peace, and where that will is obeyed there is pattern and harmony. In his will is your peace.

Michael Ramsey, *The Christian Priest Today*, SPCK, 1972, page 62

So many people need to learn that Obedience must often come before Faith; that it is by going on patiently obeying the commandments of God and the teaching of Christ that faith will come to them; that faith is neither something to which they are entitled nor something which is either given or withheld, but something which has to be earned by a life of discipline and obedience. It is really no good saying: 'I find it so difficult to believe' when we are doing little or nothing to build up faith by using the means of grace which God has provided for us and by bringing our lives under the control of his will. And if we are to practise obedience we can scarcely do better than begin with the three commands which Jesus gave to Peter in the boat. 'Thrust out a little from the land'; do not allow yourself to become earthbound, your life dominated by things of this world; withdraw a little from the pleasures and interests and anxieties of what happens in this life and devote a little more of your time to the things of eternity. And then 'launch out into the deep' and explore the depths of God's love; consider his nature, his goodness, his strength; let the thought of his majesty and of his tender mercy and compassion flow into your heart; learn to be alone with him in the deep. And then 'Let down your nets for a draught'; learn to accept what God gives of his grace, his peace, his strength; spread your nets wide for that miraculous draught of all that your soul can need.

J.R.H. Moorman, *The Path to Glory*, SPCK, 1960, page 54

But there are hours, and they come to us all at some period of life or other, when the hand of Mystery seems to lie heavy on the soul—when some life-shock scatters existence, leaves it a blank and dreary waste henceforth for ever, and there appears nothing of hope in all the expanse which stretches out, except that merciful gate of death which opens at the end—hours when the sense of misplaced or ill-requited affection, the feeling of personal worthlessness, the uncertainty and meanness of all human aims, and a doubt of all human goodness, unfix the soul from its old moorings—and leave it drifting—drifting over the vast Infinite, with an awful sense of solitariness. Then the man whose faith rested on outward Authority and not on inward life, will find it give away: the authority of the Priest: the authority of the Church: or merely the authority of a document proved by miracles and backed by prophecy: the soul—conscious life hereafter—God—will be an awful desolate Perhaps. Well! in such moments you doubt all—whether Christianity be true: whether Christ was man, or God, or a beautiful fable. You ask bitterly, like Pontius Pilate, What is Truth? In such an hour what remains? I reply, Obedience. Leave those thoughts for the present. Act—be merciful and gentle—honest: force yourself to abound in little services: try to do good to others: be true to the Duty that you know. *That* must be right whatever else is uncertain. And by the laws of the human heart, by the word of God, you shall not be left to doubt. Do that much of the will of God which is plain to you, and 'You shall know of the doctrine, whether it be of God.'

F.W. Robertson, *Sermons*, Kegan Paul, Trench, Trubner & Co. Ltd., 1897, Second Series, page 104

OPPORTUNITY

*'Opportunity'— favourable juncture, good chance,
opening (of doing, to do, for action)*

One of my guiding principles in life is—'Observe the opportunity'. A simple illustration of this is our expedition to Nepal of 1963. This began with a casual conversation in the Examination Schools. Two of us were chatting away, waiting for a lecture to begin. We were talking about what we had done before coming up to university. I happened to mention I had been in the Gurkhas for national service. My acquaintance asked me who the Gurkhas were and where they came from. I told him they were hillmen from the mountains of Nepal. 'Let's go there,' he said, and before the lecturer arrived the expedition was born.

We made careful plans during the next eighteen months. We began by inviting a third member, a medical student, and then another medical student, who agreed to come on the expedition provided he could lead it. As he was already a seasoned explorer we readily agreed.

From then onwards we had a meeting each week. Minutes were taken so we were accountable to each other. A good scientific project presented itself. The World Health Organization were doing a worldwide survey of blood groupings and had no data on Nepal. We volunteered to collect blood samples in three areas, and link up with a scheme setting up a blood transfusion service in Kathmandu, the capital of Nepal.

We completed both projects on time, and went on a three-week trek in the Annapurna region. This enjoyable expedition all came out of our openness to the principle 'observe the opportunity'.

… the place on which you are standing is holy ground.

Exodus 3.5

Observe the opportunity.

Ecclesiasticus 4.20 (AV)

Now the Lord is the Spirit, and where the Spirit of the Lord is, there is freedom.

2 Corinthians 3.17

For you were called to freedom, brethren; only do not use your freedom as an opportunity for the flesh, but through love be servants of one another.

Galatians 5.13

Dawn does not come twice to awake a man.

Arab proverb

A man must make his opportunity, as oft he find it.

Francis Bacon, *The Advancement of Learning and New Atlantis*, edited by Arthur Johnston, Oxford at the Clarendon Press, 1974, page 172

No great man ever complained of want of opportunity.

Ralph Waldo Emerson, *The Heart of Emerson's Journals*, edited by Bliss Perry, Constable & Co. Ltd., 1927, Volume V, page 534

A wise man will make more opportunities than he finds.

Francis Bacon, *The Moral and Historical Works of Francis Bacon*, Henry G. Bohn, 1852, page 140

God often gives in one brief moment what he has long been keeping from you.

Thomas à Kempis, *The Imitation of Christ*, translated by Betty I. Knott, William Collins Sons & Co. Ltd., 1979, page 244

Yet he who grasps the moment's gift,
He is the proper man.

Johann Wolfgang von Goethe, *Faust*, translated by Bayard Taylor, Sphere Books Ltd., 1974, page 78, Part I, Act I. sc.iv. l.2017

Who seeks and will not take, when once 'tis offer'd,
Shall never find it more.

William Shakespeare, *Anthony and Cleopatra*, Act II. sc.vii. l.83

Our hands are full of business, let's away,
Advantage feeds them fat while men delay.

William Shakespeare, *Henry IV*, Part I, Act III. sc.ii. l.180

To improve the golden moment of opportunity, and catch the good that is within our reach, is the great art of life.

Samuel Johnson, *The Works of Samuel Johnson*, Talboys and Wheeler, 1825, Volume VI, page 214, 'The Patriot'

For age is opportunity no less
Than youth itself, though in another dress,
And as the evening twilight fades away
The sky is filled with stars, invisible by day.

Henry Wadsworth Longfellow, *The Poetical Works of Longfellow*, Humphrey Milford, Oxford University Press, 1913, page 708, 'Morituri Salutamus,' final stanza

'Now, Mr. Tapley,' said Mark, giving himself a tremendous blow in the chest by way of reviver, 'just you attend to what I've got to say. Things is looking about as bad as they *can* look, young man. You'll not have such another opportunity for showing your jolly disposition, my fine fellow, as long as you live. And therefore, Tapley, Now's your time to come out strong; or Never!'

Charles Dickens, *Martin Chuzzlewit*, edited by Margaret Cardwell, Oxford University Press, 1982, page 383

There is a tide in the affairs of men,
Which, taken at the flood, leads on to fortune;
Omitted, all the voyage of their life
Is bound in shallows and in miseries.
On such a full sea are we now afloat,
And we must take the current when it serves,
Or lose our ventures.

William Shakespeare, *Julius Caesar*, Act IV. sc.iii. l.217

To every man there openeth
A Way, and Ways, and a Way,
And the High Soul climbs the High Way,
And the Low Soul gropes the Low,
And in between, on misty flats,
The rest drift to and fro.
But to every man there openeth
A High Way, and a Low.
And every man decideth
The Way his soul should go.

John Oxenham, *The King's High Way, Some More Helpful Verse*, Methuen & Co. Ltd., 1916, 'The Ways,' page 10

Jesus, holy and beloved
hold me always in your 'yes'.
Let nothing matter to me from this moment
but the Father's good pleasure,
the coming of his kingdom.

Let me not matter to myself.
I have only one short life in which to love
In difficulty and pain,
trusting in the dark and non-seeming.
Opportunities come and pass forever,
never to return.
Let me not miss one,
let my life be lived in total love:
There is no other way of living a truly human life.

Ruth Burrows, *Living Love and Our Father*, Darton, Longman & Todd, 1990, page 93

PACIFISM

'Pacifism'—the doctrine that the abolition of war is both desirable and possible.

P acifism implies *peace-making*. To get to the heart of what this means, we go back once more to the Genesis story of the creation of man. In that story God is depicted as fashioning and shaping man in his own image and likeness and he then breathes into his nostrils the breath of life, and man becomes a living being. At the very least this speaks of there being something of God in man. We notice also that which was fashioned in the image and likeness of God was taken from the dust of the earth, thus giving man an earthy and creaturely side to his nature.

If we wish to see this fully worked out in a life we go to the person of Jesus Christ. During his life he discovered something of the Father in the depths of himself, as well as divine attributes such as the Holy Spirit, Life, Light, Truth, Joy, Love, and so on. These were integrated with Christ's earthy and creaturely side of his nature so those who knew him described him as 'very God and very Man'. As such he epitomized peace and peace-making. This in turn is part of our inheritance.

To understand this further let us now look at the Hebrew word *shalom*—peace. This word is about man's well-being, wholeness, harmony, peace—an inner integration of the divine and human, held in a creative tension in a constant state of movement, horizontally and vertically (spiritually)—man most fully and truly alive—peace, *shalom*. When we live this out to the full and encourage *shalom* in the lives of others close to us we are engaged in 'pacifism'. The abolition of war then becomes both desirable and possible.

Wisdom is better than weapons of war.
Ecclesiastes 9.18

No weapon that is fashioned against you shall prosper.
Isaiah 54.17

Blessed are the peacemakers, for they shall be called sons of God.
Matthew 5.9

Salt is good; but if the salt has lost its saltness, how will you season it? Have salt in yourselves, and be at peace with one another.
Mark 9.50

We ought not to retaliate or render evil for evil to any one, whatever evil we may have suffered from him.
Socrates, *The Dialogues of Plato*, translated by B. Jowett, Oxford at the Clarendon Press, 1875, Volume I, page 390, 'Crito' 49

[Non-violence] is not a garment to be put on and off at will. Its seat is in the heart, and it must be an inseparable part of our very being.
Mohandas K. Gandhi, *Non-violence in Peace & War*, Navajivan Publishing House, 1948, Volume I, page 61

In a conversation with his friend, the Rev. J.J. Doke, a Baptist minister of Johannesburg, Gandhi said that he got the idea of passive resistance in the spirit of Ahimsa from the sayings of Jesus, 'But I say unto you, that ye resist not evil,' and 'Love your enemies... pray for them which despitefully use you and persecute you; that ye may be the children of your Father which is in heaven'. And then his idea developed under the influence of the Bhagavad-Gita and Tolstoi's *The Kingdom of God is Within You.*

Albert Schweitzer, *Indian Thought and Its Development*, translated by Mrs C.E.D. Russell, Hodder & Stoughton Ltd., 1936, page 234

A nation following the way of Christ, might feel called upon to adopt a policy of total disarmament. But it would do so, in the first instance, not with the deliberate purpose of courting martyrdom, but with the conviction that the best safety from the perils against which nations arm is to be found in a new national way of life, which would remove causes of provocation and lead progressively to reconciliation and peace. It, too, would risk everything on the conviction that God's way would work. But such a nation must also be willing, if necessary, to incur the risk of national martyrdom by refusing to equip itself against the possibility of aggression. And it may be that the world must wait for its redemption from warfare until one nation is ready to risk crucifixion at the hands of its possible enemies. It might lose its own national life; but it would set free such a flood of spiritual life as would save the world.

G.H.C. Macgregor, *The New Testament Basis of Pacifism*, James Clarke & Co., 1936, page 103

... there were men in China who travelled all over the empire as preachers of love and peace. It is there that we find the first pacificists, probably in the fifth century B.C. In a record which has come down to our time with the writings of the philosopher, Chwang-Tsz, this is said about them:—

'They sought to unite men through an ardent love in universal brotherhood. To fight against lusts and evil desires was their chief endeavour. When they were reviled, they did not consider it a shame; they were intent on nothing but the redemption of men from quarrelling. They forbade aggression, and preached disarmament in order to redeem mankind from war. This teaching they carried throughout the world. They admonished princes and instructed subjects. The world was not ready to accept their teachings, but they held to it all the more firmly. It was said that high and low tried to avoid meeting them, but that they forced themselves upon people.'

Albert Schweitzer, *Christianity and the Religions of the World*, translated by J. Powers, George Allen & Unwin Ltd., 1923, page 56

Through the centuries probably only a minority of considering Christians have held that Christ's teaching demands the totally pacifist position. I would hold myself that the injunction to turn the other cheek and to offer no resistance to evil, like many other of Christ's injunctions, concerns motive. Faced with a violent attack the follower of Christ must have total selflessness in motive; so far as his own pride or comfort or security is concerned he must be ready to accept death and have no self-concern. But given that selflessness in motive which Christ demands, he may strike, or risk killing, or even kill if his concern is to protect others, whether family, friends, neighbours, enemies, or the community itself. It has been found possible, however hazardous, to strike in defence of others without hatred, anger, or self-concern; and conversely it is possible to be physically passive while bearing anger and hatred. It is such considerations which cause many conscientious Christians not to endorse total pacifism.

Michael Ramsey, *Canterbury Pilgrim*, SPCK, 1974, page 129

... when a Christian meets with injustice, he no longer clings to his rights and defends them at all costs. He is absolutely free from possessions and bound to Christ alone...

The only way to overcome evil is to let it run its course, so that it does not find the resistance it is looking for. Resistance merely creates further evil and adds fuel to the flames. But when evil meets no opposition and encounters no obstacle but only patient endurance, its sting is drawn... By his willingly renouncing self-defence, the Christian affirms his absolute adherence to Jesus, and his freedom from the tyranny of his own ego...

He addresses His disciples as men who have left all to follow Him, and the precept of non-violence applies equally to private life and official duty...

It looked as though evil had triumphed on the cross, but the real victory belonged to Jesus ... Jesus calls those who follow Him to share His passion. How can we convince the world by our preaching of his passion when we shrink from that passion in our own lives? ... The cross is the only power in the world which proves that suffering love can avenge and vanquish evil.

Dietrich Bonhoeffer, The Cost of Discipleship, translated by R.H. Fuller, SCM Press Ltd., 1948, page 122

He (Gandhi) is confident that by the non-worldly he can completely spiritualise and ennoble what is worldly, and he really seriously believes that he can practise passive resistance entirely in the spirit of freedom from hatred and of love. Again and again he points to his followers that the justification, the reason and the success of what they join him in undertaking for the good of the people is dependent on whether their minds are completely purified. And again and again he emphasizes his conviction that passive resistance, exercised in the spirit of Ahimsa, must not only be concerned with the achievement of this purpose or that, but that its real aim must be to bring about a mutual understanding founded on love. The non-violent violence of passive resistance must merely form the river-bed for the flood-waters of the spirit of love.

Thus, then, does Gandhi try to solve the problem whether, along with action by ethical and spiritual means, action by worldly means can also be justified—he sets up the first as a principle and at the same time retains a minimum of worldly procedure, the exercise, namely, of non-violent force; and this he places at the service of the ethical and the spiritual.

It must remain a question whether the restriction to non-violent force and the combination of this (as being the procedure regarded as the least worldly) with the ethical and spiritual method is the right solution of the problem. All mixing up of what is different in essence is an unnatural and dangerous proceeding.

Albert Schweitzer, Indian Thought and Its Development, translated by Mrs C.E.B. Russell, Hodder & Stoughton Ltd, 1936,
page 232

PATIENCE

'Patience'—calm endurance of pain or any provocation;
perseverance.

I n 1968 I went to Nigeria for six months, looking after All Saints Church, Jericho, Ibadan, whilst the regular priest came back to England on long leave.

I soon discovered Nigerians have a different concept of time from ours. This really came home to me officiating at my first wedding. The service was scheduled to start at 11.00 a.m. At 10.55 a.m. hardly anyone had arrived, and there was certainly no sign of the bridal party. At 12.00 noon about half the guests had arrived, but there was still no sign of the bride, the bridegroom or the bridesmaids.

I was beginning to get uptight and impatient, but, looking round, everyone seemed to be relaxed; in fact, all the guests were boisterously happy and pleased to see each other. There was much loud laughter, and a general feeling all was well.

At 1.00 p.m. the bride and her father arrived, and much to my relief the bridegroom and best man suddenly appeared from nowhere. The bridesmaids, however, were still not to be seen.

I eventually started the wedding at 1.30 p.m. and the service ended an hour later. Whilst the happy couple were proceeding down the aisle after the final blessing, six beautifully dressed bridesmaids arrived—supposedly for the start of the service. Amidst much laughter and hilarity we set off for the reception.

I learnt a great deal about patience in my six months in Nigeria. As I have gone through life I value more and more my 'apprenticeship' in patience and am grateful for the six-month stay at All Saints Church, Jericho, Ibadan.

But they who wait for the Lord shall renew their strength, they shall mount up with wings like eagles, they shall run and not be weary, they shall walk and not faint.

Isaiah 40.31

A patient man will bear for a time, and afterward joy shall spring up unto him.

Ecclesiasticus 1.23 (AV)

And as for that in the good soil, they are those who, hearing the word, hold it fast in an honest and good heart, and bring forth fruit with patience.

Luke 8.15

As an example of suffering and patience, brethren, take the prophets who spoke in the name of the Lord.

James 5.10

Possess your soul with patience.

John Dryden, *The Poems of John Dryden*, edited by James Kinsley, Oxford at the Clarendon Press, 1958, Volume II, page 525, 'The Hind and the Panther,' The Third Part, l.839

Calumnies are answer'd best with silence.

Ben Jonson, *Ben Jonson*, edited by C.H. Herford and Percy Simpson, Oxford at the Clarendon Press, 1965, Volume V, page 50, *Volpone*, Act II. sc.ii

Endurance is nobler than strength, and patience than beauty.

John Ruskin, *The Two Paths*, George Allen, 1905, page 179

I worked with patience, which means almost power.

E.B. Browning, *Elizabeth Barrett Browning's Poetical Works*, Smith, Elder, & Co., 1873, Volume V, page 96, *Aurora Leigh*, Third Book

One of the principal parts of faith is patience.

George Macdonald, *Weighed and Wanting*, Sampson Low, Marston, Searle & Rivington, 1882, Volume III, page 191

Endurance is the crowning quality,
And patience all the passion of great hearts.

J.R. Lowell, *The Poetical Works of James Russell Lowell*, Ward, Lock & Co. Ltd., 1911, page 58, 'Columbus'

Patience is not passive; on the contrary, it is active; it is concentrated strength.

Anon.

To climb steep hills
Requires slow pace at first.

William Shakespeare, *King Henry VIII*, Act I. sc.i. l.131

One moment of patience may ward off great disaster, one moment of impatience may ruin a whole life.

Chinese wisdom

Sorrow and silence are strong, and patient endurance is godlike.

Henry Wadsworth Longfellow, *The Poetical Works of Longfellow*, Humphrey Milford, Oxford University Press, 1913, page 158, *Evangeline*, Part the Second, I, l.60

How poor are they that ha' not patience!
What wound did ever heal but by degrees?

William Shakespeare, *Othello*, Act II. sc.iii. l.360

Be you content to lend your patience to us,
And we shall jointly labour with your soul
To give it due content.

William Shakespeare, *Hamlet*, Act IV. sc.v. l.207

The time of life arming myself with patience
To stay the providence of some high powers
That govern us below.

William Shakespeare, Julius Caesar, Act V. sc.i. l.131

Let patience have her perfect work. Statue under the chisel of the sculptor, stand steady to the blows of his mallet. Clay on the wheel, let the fingers of the divine potter model you at their will. Obey the Father's lightest word; hear the Brother who knows you, and died for you.

George Macdonald, Unspoken Sermons, Third Series, Longmans, Green & Co. Ltd., 1889, page 227

But patience is more oft the exercise
Of Saints, the trial of their fortitude,
Making them each his own Deliver,
And Victor over all
That tyranny or fortune can inflict.

John Milton, Milton's Poetical Works, edited by Helen Darbishire, Oxford at the Clarendon Press, 1955, Volume II,
'Sampson Agonistes', l.1287

God is unwearied patience, a meekness that cannot be provoked; He is an ever-enduring mercifulness; He is unmixed goodness, impartial, universal love; His delight is in the communication of Himself, His own happiness to everything according to its capacity. He does everything that is good, righteous, and lovely for its own sake, because it is good, righteous and lovely. He is the good from which nothing but good comes, and resisteth all evil only with goodness. This ... is the nature and Spirit of God.

William Law, Selected Mystical Writings of William Law, edited by Stephen Hobhouse, Rockliff, 1948, page 113

The patient man is already experiencing a deep and healthful purging. When he receives an injury, he is more distressed for the other's unkind thought than for the hurt he has received; he gladly prays for those who put obstacles in his path, forgives others their faults from his heart, and is not slow in seeking their forgiveness. He is more ready to feel pity for others than anger, but his own feelings he often treats roughly, and he tries to keep his natural impulses obedient to his spirit.

Thomas à Kempis, The Imitation of Christ, translated by Betty I. Knott, William Collins Sons & Co. Ltd., 1979, page 75

PEACE

*'Peace'—freedom from, cessation of war, freedom from civil
disorder, quiet tranquillity; mental calm; bring person, oneself, back
into friendly relations.*

I n this definition of peace, the words I want to concentrate on are 'quiet tranquillity'. The quotation which best unfolds the meaning of these words in this section comes from John Tauler's book *The History and Life of the Reverend Doctor John Tauler*. John Tauler tells us peace is to be found in the spirit and the inner life. What he means by this is 'the Kingdom of God ... and His righteousness'—found, in the first instance, within us.

In quiet times of reflection, meditation and contemplation we can sometimes experience 'the peace of God which passes all understanding' at first hand. The peace of God may be experienced in many ways. For some this may be a certain oneness with the presence of the Father, the Son and the Holy Spirit. Others may experience this peace as a oneness with the presence of divine attributes such as light, life, joy, truth, love, grace, glory, power, goodness, and so on. Jesus described the kingdom of God in a number of important parables. He likened it to treasure hidden in a field, which a man found and covered up; then in his joy he goes and sells all that he has and buys that field. He further likened it to a merchant in search of fine pearls, who, on finding one pearl of great value, went and sold all that he had and bought it. Others might just experience the kingdom of God as a feeling of harmony, wholeness and well-being.

John Tauler felt this inner peace so valuable, nothing in life should ever be allowed to take its place.

Agree with God, and be at peace; thereby good will come to you.

Job 22.21

In peace I will both lie down and sleep; for thou alone, O Lord, makest me dwell in safety.

Psalm 4.8

And the peace of God, which passes all understanding, will keep your hearts and your minds in Christ Jesus.

Philippians 4.7

May the God of peace himself sanctify you wholly; and may your spirit and soul and body be kept sound and blameless at the coming of our Lord Jesus Christ.

1 Thessalonians 5.23

Peace is always beautiful.

Walt Whitman, *The Complete Poems*, edited by Francis Murphy, Penguin Books Ltd., 1982, page 447, 'The Sleepers,' l.147

Where there is peace, God is.

George Herbert, *The Works of George Herbert*, edited by F.E. Hutchinson, Oxford at the Clarendon Press, 1972, page 345, 'Outlandish Proverbs,' No.733

Live in peace yourself and then you can bring peace to others.

Thomas à Kempis, *The Imitation of Christ*, translated by Betty I. Knott, William Collins Sons & Co. Ltd., 1979, page 87

You touched me, and I am inflamed with love of your peace.

St Augustine, *Confessions*, translated by R.S. Pine-Coffin, Penguin Books Ltd., 1964, page 232

The more a man gives up his heart to God, to his vocation and to men, forgetful of himself and of that which belongs to him—the greater poise he will acquire, until he reaches peace, quiet, joy—the apanage of simple and humble souls.

Father Yelchaninov, in *A Treasury of Russian Spirituality*, edited by G.P. Fedotov, Sheed & Ward Ltd., 1977, page 445

To thee, O God, we turn for peace... but grant us too the blessed assurance that nothing shall deprive us of that peace, neither *ourselves*, nor our foolish, earthly desires, nor my wild longings, nor the anxious cravings of my heart.

Søren Kierkegaard, *The Journals of Søren Kierkegaard*, a selection edited and translated by Alexander Dru, Oxford University Press, 1938, page 85

A soul divided against itself can never find peace. Peace cannot exist where there are contrary loyalties. For true peace there has to be psychological and moral harmony. Conscience must be at rest.

Hubert van Zeller, *Considerations*, Sheed & Ward Ltd., 1974, page 43

People are always expecting to get peace in heaven; but you know whatever peace they get there will be ready made. Whatever making of peace *they* can be blest for, must be on earth here.

John Ruskin, *The Eagle's Nest*, George Allen & Sons, 1910, page 222

Children, that peace which is found in the spirit and the inner life is well worth our care, for in that peace lies the satisfaction of all our wants. In it the Kingdom of God is discovered and His righteousness is found. This peace a man should allow nothing to take from him, whatever betide, come weal or woe, honour or shame.

John Tauler, *The History and Life of the Reverend Doctor John Tauler*, translated by Susanna Winkworth, Smith, Elder & Co., 1857, page 381

My son, I will teach you the way of peace and true liberty... try to do another's will rather than your own. Always choose to have less than more. Always choose the lowest place and to be less than everyone else. Always long and pray that the will of God may be fully realized in your life. You will find the man who does all this walks in the land of peace and quietness.

Thomas à Kempis, *The Imitation of Christ*, translated by Betty I. Knott, William Collins Sons & Co. Ltd., 1979, page 147

Every good man, in whom religion rules, is at peace and unity with himself, is as a city compacted together. Grace doth more and more reduce all the faculties of the soul into a perfect subjection and subordination to itself. The union and conjunction of the soul with God, that primitive Unity, is that which is the alone original and fountain of all peace, and the centre of rest.

John Smith the Platonist, *Select Discourses*, Cambridge at the University Press, 1859, page 421

Peace can only be manifested in society when there is peace within the human heart. The cause of peace is sometimes pursued with aggressiveness. This is the case when peace is no more than a concept or an ideal.

Peace communicates itself wordlessly. In India the great example of the power of peace was seen in Mahatma Gandhi whose inner peace influenced the whole nation.

Work for peace must first of all be a work within ourselves.

Bede Griffiths OSB, in *The Universal Christ*, edited by Peter Spink, Darton, Longman & Todd, 1993, page 25

The dominant meaning of the word in common parlance is freedom from war, 'that condition of a nation or community in which it is not at war with another' (*Shorter Oxford English Dictionary*). When used of individuals it has the equivalent meaning of freedom from disturbance or dissension. And in spirituality it has tended similarly to denote cessation of divine wrath, freedom from the disturbing sense of guilt or from inner turmoil and conflict.

This somewhat negative idea of peace is part of our classical heritage. For particularly in Greek, peace means primarily the opposite of war, the state without which there can be no prosperity, classically expressed in the absence of internal strife within the Empire during the reign of Augustus, the golden age of the *pax Romana*.

In Hebrew thought, however, peace was a much more positive concept. It embraced the idea of absence of war (as in Deut.20.12; Judg.4.17; I Sam.7.14; I Kings 2.5; Isa.36.16), or indeed, victory in war (Judg.8.9; I Chron.22.18; Jer.43.12; Mic.5.5). But its basic meaning was something like 'well-being'. For the ancient Israelite, *salom* (peace) was all that makes for wholeness and prosperity (e.g. Deut.23.6; Ps.72.3,7; 147.14; Isa.48.18; 55.12; Zech.8.12).

Two aspects are worthy of particular note. 1. *Salom* did not refer simply to a 'spiritual' condition. 'Peace is growth and expansion, fertility in husbandry and family, health and strength throughout life.' (J. Pedersen). This did not make it any the less a gift of God (e.g. Num.6.26; Judg.6.24; Ps.29.11; Isa.66.12; Jer.29.11). On the contrary, it was precisely the correlation of 'spiritual' and 'material' which was in view in the wholeness of peace (Ps.85). Not just war, not just private sins, but injustice and oppression destroy peace (Isa.59.8; Jer.6.14; Zech.8.16).

2. In Hebrew thought peace was primarily a relational, a social concept. Thus it could be used of a relationship of friendly co-operation and mutual benefit (as in I Kings 5.12; Zech.6.13), whereas there is no obvious text where it denotes an individual's sense of inner peace (G. von Rad). Peace was something visible and usually included the idea of a productively harmonious relationship between people (family, covenant partners, nations).

This richer concept is carried over into the earliest Christian vocabulary—peace as spiritual and physical wholeness (Luke 7.50; 8.48), peace characterized by unselfish, active concern for one's neighbour, both within the community of faith (Rom.14.17,19; I Cor.14.33; Eph.4.3) and beyond (I Cor.7.15). To develop and maintain such positively beneficial relationships is a duty urged on the first Christians by several authors (Rom.12.18; II Tim.2.22; Heb.12.14; I Peter 3.11). The 'peacemaker' whom Jesus called 'blessed' (Matt.5.9), therefore, does not simply prevent or stop conflict; rather he seeks to promote those spiritual and social relationships which remove the causes of conflict (James 3.18).

For the first Christians it was particularly important that the good news they proclaimed was the gospel of peace (Luke 2,14· 10 5 6, Acts 10.36; Eph.6.15). Through their faith in Christ they had found a breaking down of barriers both between God and man (Rom.5.1; Col.1.20) and between man and man (Eph.2.14,17). Hence the characteristic greeting of the risen Christ was 'Peace to you' (Luke 24.36; John 20.19, 21, 26), and Paul especially used the same word again and again to sum up all his most heartfelt hopes for his readers, both in his opening salutation and in his parting blessing.

More distinctive among the first Christians was peace in the sense of inward spiritual calm, the serenity of a secure relationship with God which is sustained by grace through all kinds of tribulation and pressures (John 14.27; 16.33; Rom.15.13; Gal.5.22; Phil.4.7; Col.3.15). It was presumably this sense of being a recipient of God's peace which inspired and sustained the first Christians in their proclamation of the gospel of peace and in their peace-making between Jew and Gentile (cf. Rom.8.6).

In the history of the church, thought about peace has tended to fall into two strands—a political concern for matters of war and peace, focused classically in the doctrine of the just war, and a spiritual, often mystical or pietistic concern for the individual's peace of soul. If the biblical concept is to guide our thought, however, spiritual should never be divorced from social (including political), nor the individual's peace from the well-being of the wider community. Only so can the Christian truly 'live in peace' and the Christian blessing retain its richness: 'May the Lord of peace himself give you peace at all times in all ways' (II Thess.3.16).

James D.G. Dunn, in *A Dictionary of Christian Spirituality*, edited by Gordon S. Wakefield, SCM Press Ltd., 1983, page 290

PERFECTION

'Perfection'—completion; making perfect; full development;
faultlessness; comparative excellence; perfect person or thing;
highest pitch, perfect specimen or manifestation.

Whilst in the army doing National Service, I spent four months at Mons Officer Cadet School in Aldershot, training to be commissioned. I greatly enjoyed the wide variety of the training programme and the friendship of the other members of our platoon. We spent many hours perfecting our drill on the parade ground, under the eagle eye of Sergeant Fawcett of the Irish Guards. We attended a whole batch of lectures, and periodically sat examinations to check how much we had assimilated. Failure meant we would be 'back-squadded' and none of us liked the idea of being put back to a lower intake. There were military exercises in the field, culminating in a fortnight's battle camp in the Welsh mountains. An old soldier told us this would be the fittest time of our lives, and in retrospect he was right.

Everything pointed forward to the Passing-Out Parade and perfection in turn out. For instance, we had a special pair of boots we 'bulled' with spit and polish for four months, and these were to be used only on this one occasion. Countless hours were spent in blancoing our white belts and polishing brass parts. We knew a fault in turn out detected in the Passing-Out Parade meant instant back-squadding.

On the day it poured with rain as we were marching on to the parade ground. What a relief. We all knew at this point none of us could be 'back-squadded'. The weather had frustrated our attempts at perfection of turn out, and prevented any kind of inspection. We were safe, and through.

The law of the Lord is perfect, reviving the soul; the testimony of the Lord is sure, making wise the simple.
Psalm 19.7

The righteousness of the blameless keeps his way straight, but the wicked falls by his own wickedness.
Proverbs 11.5

You, therefore, must be perfect, as your heavenly Father is perfect.

Matthew 5.48

Let steadfastness have its full effect, that you may be perfect and complete, lacking in nothing.

James 1.4

The very best and utmost of attainment in this life is to remain still and let God act and speak in thee.

Meister Eckhart, *Meister Eckhart*, Franz Pfeiffer, translated by C. de B. Evans, John M. Watkins, 1956, Volume I, page 6

The great aim of culture [is] the aim of setting ourselves to ascertain what perfection is and to make it prevail.

Matthew Arnold, *The Complete Prose Works of Matthew Arnold*, Volume V, *Culture and Anarchy*, edited by R.H. Super, Ann Arbor, The University of Michigan Press, 1965, 'Sweetness and Light,' page 93

Perfection is finally attained not when there is no longer anything to add but when there is no longer anything to take away.

Antoine de Saint-Exupéry, *Wind, Sand and Stars*, translated by Lewis Galantière, William Heinemann Ltd., 1939, page 54

God's purpose is to lead man into perfection of growth, which is the attainment of a unity comprehending an immense manifoldness.

Rabindranath Tagore, *Letters to a Friend*, George Allen & Unwin Ltd., 1928, page 116

We always find a restless appetite within ourselves which craves for some supreme and chief good, and will not be satisfied with any thing less than infinity itself.

John Smith the Platonist, *Select Discourses*, Cambridge at the University Press, 1859, page 138

So slow
The growth of what is excellent; so hard
T'attain perfection in this nether world.

William Cowper, *The Poetical Works of Cowper*, edited by H.S. Milford, Oxford University Press, 1950, page 131, 'The Task,' i. l. 83

He has made the soul according to his own most perfect nature, pouring into her the whole of his own light in all its pristine purity, while he himself remains all undefiled.

Meister Eckhart, *Meister Eckhart*, Franz Pfeiffer, translated by C. de B. Evans, John M. Watkins, 1956, Volume I, page 222

In this broad earth of ours,
Amid the measureless grossness and the slag,
Enclosed and safe within its central heart,
Nestles the seed perfection.

Walt Whitman, *The Complete Poems*, edited by Francis Murphy, Penguin Books Ltd., 1982, page 255, 'Song of the Universe', i. l. 4

The Church recalls to mind that culture must be subordinated to the integral development of the human person, to the good of the community and of the whole of mankind. Therefore one must aim at encouraging the human spirit to develop its faculties of wonder, of understanding, of contemplation, of forming personal judgements and cultivating a religious, moral and social sense.

Vatican Council II, *The Conciliar and Post Conciliar Documents*, 1981 Edition, general editor, Austin Flannery, OP, Fowler Wright Books, page 963

All that can be expected from the most perfect institutions is that they should make it possible for individual excellence to develop itself, not that they should produce the excellent individual. Virtue and genius, grace and beauty, will always constitute a *noblesse* such as no form of government can manufacture. It is of no use, therefore, to excite oneself for or against revolutions which have only an importance of the second order—an importance which I do not wish either to diminish or to ignore, but an importance which, after all, is mostly negative.

Henri Frédéric Amiel, *Amiel's Journal*, translated by Mrs Humphry Ward, Macmillan & Co. Ltd., 1918, page 177

I suppose others feel the same intense delight, which one cannot describe any more than one can explain how it comes, when some verse in the Gospels which one has read for years and years without a second thought suddenly expands in some new direction of thought and goes on from point to point of one's whole idea of the beginning and method and ultimate object of the great fact of Life, from birth and beginning to death and completion. Everything in life which comes anywhere near this delight has the same foundation; it is just simply the realization of beauty, just a glimpse of something nearing perfection, just a momentary sense of the presence of something which will last, which cannot be done away with or lost, something, however little, of the perfect Love of God.

Edward Wilson, in The Faith of Edward Wilson, George Seaver, John Murray Ltd., 1949, page 16

We acknowledge that there are broken lives, pieces of lives which have begun in this world to be completed, as we believe, in another state of being. And some of them have been like fragments of ancient art, which we prize not for their completeness but for their quality, and because they seem to give us a type of something which we can hardly see anywhere upon earth. Of such lives we must judge, not by what the person said or wrote or did in the short span of human existence, but by what they were: if they exercised some peculiar influence on society and on friends, if they had some rare grace of humility, or simplicity, or resignation, or love of truth, or self-devotion, which was not to be met with in others. God does not measure men's lives only by the amount of work which is accomplished in them. He who gave the power to work may also withhold the power. And some of these broken lives may have a value in His sight which no bustle or activity of ordinary goodness could have attained. There have been persons confined to a bed of sickness, blind, palsied, tormented with pain and want, who yet may be said to have led an almost perfect life. Such persons afford examples to us, not indeed of a work carried out to the end (for their circumstances did not admit of this), but of a work, whether finished or unfinished, which at any moment is acceptable to God. And we desire to learn of them, and to have an end like theirs when the work of active life is over and we sit patiently waiting for the will of God.

Benjamin Jowett, Select Passages from the Theological Writings of Benjamin Jowett, edited by Lewis Campbell, John Murray Ltd., 1902, page 231

PERSONALITY

'Personality'—being a person, personal existence or identity; distinctive personal character.

There are two quotations in this section which I feel are extremely important. The first is by Rufus Jones from his book *Spiritual Reformers in the 16th and 17th Centuries.* I would like to pinpoint what he has written about the deepest note of present-day Christianity—'the appreciation of personality as the highest thing in earth or heaven'.

Rufus Jones goes on to mention the initiation of a movement to find the vital sources and resources of the inner kindling of the spirit, and for raising the whole personal life to higher functions and to higher powers.

If someone was to ask how can this be done, I would advise them to take a good hard look at my second recommended quotation. This is the long passage at the end of the section, by Carl Gustav Jung, taken from his book *The Development of Personality.* The good hard look would involve reflecting, meditating and contemplating on this passage with the aid of paper and pen, and to unfathom the meaning would probably take several hours. This would initiate a movement to find the vital sources and resources for the inner kindling of the spirit. For raising the whole personal life to higher functions and to higher powers, the combined contents of *Visions of Faith, Hope, Love, Glory* (and *Visions of Grace*) would need to be reflected on and the findings put into practice. What is in mind here is a lifelong practice involving what might be called 'the daily increase'. The outcome would be a joyful discovery of a distinctive personal character.

So God created man in his own image, in the image of God he created him; male and female he created them.

Genesis 1.27

A good name is to be chosen rather than great riches, and favour is better than silver or gold.

Proverbs 22.1

Do you not believe that I am in the Father and the Father in me?

John 14.11

I have been crucified with Christ; it is no longer I who live, but Christ who lives in me; and the life I now live in the flesh I live by faith in the Son of God, who loved me and gave himself for me.

Galatians 2.20

Nothing endures but personal qualities.

Walt Whitman, *The Complete Poems*, edited by Francis Murphy, Penguin Books Ltd., 1982, page 218, 'Song of the Broad-Axe', iv. 99

The secret of the universe, as by slow degrees it reveals itself to us, turns out to be personality.

John Cowper Powys, *The Complex Vision*, Dodd, Mead & Co., 1920, page 194

Man's main task in life is to give birth to himself, to become what he potentially is. The most important product of his effort is his own personality.

Erich Fromm, *Man For Himself*, Routledge & Kegan Paul Ltd., 1975, page 237

One whose greatest power lay in unfolding the love of God by speech and action, and in helping individual men and women to find the meaning and the glory, the purpose and the joy of life, in that surrender to the all-pervading presence of God which for him gave earth the character of heaven.

G.A. Studdert Kennedy, *By his Friends*, Hodder & Stoughton Ltd., 1929, page 63

The present state of the world calls for a moral and spiritual revolution, revolution in the name of personality, of man, of every single person. This revolution should restore the hierarchy of values, now quite shattered, and place the value of human personality above the idols of production, technics, the state, the race or nationality, the collective.

Nicolas Berdyaev, *The Fate of Man in the Modern World*, translated by Donald A. Lowrie, SCM Press Ltd., 1935, page 83

Here is the genuine beginning in modern times of what has come to be the deepest note of present-day Christianity, *the appreciation of personality as the highest thing in earth of heaven*, and the initiation of a movement to find the vital sources and resources for the inner kindling of the spirit, and for raising the whole personal life to higher functions and to higher powers.

Rufus M. Jones, *Spiritual Reformers in the 16th and 17th Centuries*, Macmillan & Co. Ltd., 1914, page xlix

To live is the rarest thing in the world. Most people exist... Have we ever seen the full expression of a personality?... A perfect man is one who develops under perfect conditions; one who is not wounded, or worried, or maimed, or in danger. Most personalities have been obliged to be rebels. Half their strength has been wasted in friction... and these battles do not always intensify strength, they often exaggerate weakness... The note of the perfect personality is not rebellion but peace.

Oscar Wilde, in *The Note Books of a Woman Alone*, edited by M.G. Ostle, J.M. Dent & Sons Ltd., 1935, page 160

It is by the body that we come into contact with Nature, with our fellow-men, with all their revelations of God to us. It is through the body that we receive all the lessons of passion, of suffering, of love, of beauty, of science. It is through the body that we are both trained outwards from ourselves, and driven inwards into our deepest selves to find God. There is glory and might in this vital evanescence, this slow glacier-like flow of clothing and revealing matter, this ever uptossed rainbow of tangible humanity. It is no less of God's making than the spirit that is clothed therein.

George Macdonald, *Unspoken Sermons*, First Series, Alexander Strahan, Publisher, 1867, page 238

It is as a body that I am most aware of myself, and my strongest and most elemental instincts are directed to satisfy the needs and desires of the body. The body is a wonderful organism —breathing, circulation of the blood, digestion and sewerage, sexual feeling and the capacity for union and the procreation of children. The body has a marked effect on the feeling tone of its owner. It is an integral part of our being; it is basically good because given us by God. It must be the servant of the total personality, through which the person expresses himself in demeanour and behaviour.

George Appleton, *Journey for a Soul*, William Collins Sons & Co. Ltd., 1976, page 15

A great many people think their body is themselves. Others think the personality is themselves. 'This personality is me, this is my self', and so they are satisfied.

Others reflect that this personality of mine— -my thoughts, feelings, desires is going to pass away when the body decays. This is not the self I am seeking, for it also belongs to the changing world.

The basic orientation of the Upanishads is found in the search for the inner self, the self beyond the body and the mind.

This is a hidden mystery. We look into the depths of our being and find this hidden mystery. In Christian terms you have discovered yourself in God. In the words of St Paul in Ephesians 3, 'The mystery long hidden is revealed, it is Christ in you, the hope of glory'.

Bede Griffiths OSB, in *The Universal Christ*, edited by Peter Spink, Darton, Longmans & Todd, 1993, page 43

The achievement of personality means nothing less than the optimum development of the whole individual human being. It is impossible to foresee the endless variety of conditions that have to be fulfilled. A whole lifetime, in all its biological, social, and spiritual aspects, is needed. Personality is the supreme realization of the innate idiosyncrasy of a living being. It is an act of high courage flung in the face of life, the absolute affirmation of all that constitutes the individual, the most successful adaptation to the universal conditions of existence coupled with the greatest possible freedom for self-determination. To educate a man to *this* seems to me no light matter. It is surely the hardest task the modern mind has set itself. And it is dangerous too... It is as dangerous as the bold and hazardous undertaking of nature to let women bear children...

Just as the child must develop in order to be educated, so the personality must begin to sprout before it can be trained. And this is where the danger begins. For we are handling something unpredictable, we do not know how and in what direction the budding personality will develop, and we have learned enough of nature and the world to be somewhat chary of both. On top of that, we were brought up in the Christian belief that human nature is intrinsically evil. But even those who no longer adhere to the Christian teaching are by nature mistrustful and not a little frightened of the possibilities lurking in the subterranean chambers of their being. Even enlightened psychologists like Freud give us an extremely unpleasant picture of what lies slumbering in the depths of the human psyche. So it is rather a bold venture to put in a good word for the development of personality... 'Anything might happen then,' people say. Or they dish up the old, feeble-minded objection to 'individualism.' But individualism is not and never has been a natural development; it is nothing but an unnatural usurpation, a freakish, impertinent pose that proves its hollowness by crumpling up before the least obstacle. What we have in mind is something very different... The development of personality means... fidelity to the law of one's own being... Fidelity to the law of one's own being is a trust in this law, a loyal perseverance and confident hope; in short, an attitude such as a religious man should have towards God. It can now be seen how portentous is the dilemma that emerges from behind our problem: personality can never develop unless the individual chooses his own way, consciously and with moral deliberation. Not only the causal motive—necessity—but conscious moral decision must lend its strength to the process of building the personality. If the first is lacking, then the alleged development is a mere acrobatics of the will; if the second, it will get stuck in unconscious automatism. But a man can make a moral decision to go his own way only if he holds that way to be the best. If any other way were held to be better, then he would live and develop that other personality instead of his own. The other ways are conventionalities of a moral, social, political, philosophical, or religious nature. The fact that the conventions always flourish in one form or another only proves that the vast majority of mankind do not choose their own way, but convention, and consequently develop not themselves but a method and a collective mode of life at the cost of their own wholeness...

To develop one's own personality is indeed an unpopular undertaking, a deviation that is highly uncongenial to the herd... Small wonder, then, that from earliest times only the chosen few have embarked upon this strange adventure. Had they all been fools, we could safely dismiss them as, *idiotai*, mentally 'private' persons who have no claim on our interest. But, unfortunately, these personalities are as a rule the legendary heroes of mankind, the very ones who are looked up to, loved, and worshipped, the true sons of God whose names perish not. They are the flower and the fruit, the ever fertile seeds of the tree of humanity... They towered up like mountain peaks above the mass that still clung to its collective fears, its beliefs, laws, and systems, and boldly chose their own way. To the man in the street it has always seemed miraculous that anyone should turn aside from the beaten track with its known destinations, and strike out on the steep and narrow path leading into the unknown. Hence it was always believed that such a man, if not actually crazy, was possessed by a daemon or a god...

What is it, in the end, that induces a man to go his own way and to rise out of unconscious identity with the mass as out of a swathing mist? Not necessity, for necessity comes to many, and they all take refuge in convention. Not moral decision, for nine times out of ten we decide for convention likewise. What is it, then, that inexorably tips the scales in favour of the *extra-ordinary*?

It is what is commonly called *vocation:* an irrational factor that destines a man to emancipate himself from the herd and from its well-worn paths. True personality is always a vocation and puts its trust in it as in God, despite its being, as the ordinary man would say, only a personal feeling. But vocation acts like a law of God from which there is no escape. The fact that many a man who goes his own way ends in ruin means nothing to one who has a vocation. He *must* obey his own law as if it were a daemon whispering to him of new and wonderful paths. Anyone with a vocation hears the voice of the inner man: he is *called.* That is why the legends say that he possesses a private daemon who counsels him and whose mandates he must obey. The best known example of this is Faust, and an historical instance is provided by the daemon of Socrates... The original meaning of 'to have a vocation' is 'to be addressed by a voice.' The clearest examples of this are to be found in the avowals of the Old Testament prophets...

Vocation, or the feeling of it, is not, however, the prerogative of great personalities; it is also appropriate to the small ones all the way down to the 'midget' personalities, but as the size decreases the voice becomes more and more muffled and unconscious... until finally it merges indistinguishably with the surrounding society, thus surrendering its own wholeness and dissolving into the wholeness of the group. In the place of the inner voice is the voice of the group with its conventions, and vocation is replaced by collective necessities...

(Likewise) to become a personality is not the absolute prerogative of the genius, for a man may be a genius without being a personality. In so far as every individual has the law of his life inborn in him, it is theoretically possible for any man to follow this law and so become a personality, that is, to achieve wholeness...

Only the man who can consciously assent to the power of the inner voice becomes a personality; but if he succumbs to it he will be swept away by the blind flux of psychic events and destroyed. That is the great and liberating thing about any genuine personality: he voluntarily sacrifices himself to his vocation, and consciously translates into his own individual reality what would only lead to ruin if it were lived unconsciously by the group.

One of the most shining examples of the meaning of personality that history has preserved for us is the life of Christ... Obeying the inner call of his vocation, Jesus voluntarily exposed himself (in the Temptations) to the assaults of the imperialistic madness that filled everyone, conqueror and conquered alike. In this way he recognized the nature of the objective psyche which had plunged the whole world into misery and had begotten a yearning for salvation that found expression even in the pagan poets. Far from suppressing or allowing himself to be suppressed by this psychic onslaught, he let it act on him consciously, and annimilated it. Thus was world-conquering Caesarism transformed into spiritual kingship, and the Roman Empire in the universal kingdom of God that was not of this world. While the whole Jewish nation was expecting an imperialistically minded and politically active hero as a Messiah, Jesus fulfilled the Messianic mission not so much for his own nation as for the whole Roman world, and pointed out to humanity the old truth that where force rules there is no love, and where love reigns force does not count. The religion of love was the exact psychological counterpart to the Roman devil-worship of power.

The example of Christianity is perhaps the best illustration of my previous abstract argument. This apparently unique life became a sacred symbol because it is the psychological prototype of the only meaningful life, that is, of a life that strives for the individual realization—absolute and unconditional—of its own particular law. Well may we exclaim with Tertullian: *anima naturaliter christiana!*

Just as the great personality acts upon society to liberate, to redeem, to transform, and to heal, so the birth of personality in oneself has a therapeutic effect. It is as if a river that had run to waste in sluggish side-streams and marshes suddenly found its way back to its proper bed, or as if a stone lying on a germinating seed were lifted away so that the shoot could begin its natural growth.

C.G. Jung, *The Collected Works of C.G. Jung*, Volume VXII, *The Development of Personality*, translated by R.F.C. Hull, Routledge & Kegan Paul Ltd., 1954, page 171

POETRY

'Poetry'—art, work, of the poet; elevated expression of elevated thought or feeling in metrical form; quality (in any thing) that calls for poetical expression.

One of our greatest poets was for a short time an undergraduate at University College, Oxford—Percy Bysshe Shelley. He was sent down in his first year for writing a treatise on 'The Necessity of Atheism'. Visitors still come to the college specifically to see the Shelley memorial.

In 1894 a domed chamber was built to receive the naked figure of the drowned poet, the work of the sculptor Edward Onslow Ford. This lies on a slab of Connemara marble supported by two winged lions in bronze; in front is seated a bronze figure of the Poetic Muse. The memorial, originally intended to be placed over Shelley's grave in the Protestant Cemetery at Rome, was presented to the college by Lady Shelley.

Some years ago a group of undergraduates (bent on mischief) filled the sunken space with water during the night. To add to their prank they managed to procure some sizeable fish. These happily splashed around entertaining a grim-faced Dean as he surveyed the scene the following morning.

Shelley as a poet qualifies better than most, to fit in with the definition of poetry above. His poems are indeed an elevated expression of elevated thought or feeling in metrical form. I sometimes wonder if he might have had a certain sympathy for the vision underlying *Visions of Grace*. In *A Defence of Poetry* he wrote, 'A poem is the image of life expressed in its eternal truth,' and later backed this up with 'Poetry is indeed some thing divine.' Hence his inclusion in these anthologies.

My heart overflows with a goodly theme; I address my verses to the king; my tongue is like the pen of a ready scribe.

Psalm 45.1

That they should seek God, in the hope that they might feel after him and find him. Yet he is not far from each one of us, for 'In him we live and move and have our being'; as even some of your poets have said, 'For we are indeed his offspring.'

Acts 17.27-28

A poem is the very image of life expressed in its eternal truth.

Percy Bysshe Shelley, *The Prose Works of Percy Bysshe Shelley*, edited by H. Buxton Forman, Reeves & Turner, 1880, Volume III, page 108, 'A Defence of Poetry'

God is the perfect poet,
Who in his person acts his own creations.

Robert Browning, *The Poetical Works of Robert Browning*, Smith, Elder & Co., 1899, Volume I, *Paracelsus*, II, page 36

Most people do not believe in anything very much and our greatest poetry is given us by those who do.

Cyril Connolly, in, *The Making of a Poem*, Stephen Spender, Hamish Hamilton, 1955, page 26, in a review of Keats' *Collected Letters*

Poetry is the record of the best and happiest moments of the happiest and best minds.

Percy Bysshe Shelley, *The Prose Works of Percy Bysshe Shelley*, edited by H. Buxton Forman, Reeves and Turner, 1880, Volume III, page 138, 'A Defence of Poetry'

[Poetry] was ever thought to have some participation of divineness, because it doth raise and erect the mind.

Francis Bacon, *The Advancement of Learning*, Cassell and Company Ltd., 1905, page 79

Poetry, therefore, we will call *musical Thought*. The Poet is he who *thinks* in that manner.

Thomas Carlyle, *Sartor Resartus*, Lectures on Heroes, Chapman & Hall Ltd., 1840, page 247

Poetry should be great and unobtrusive, a thing which enters into one's soul, and does not startle it or amaze it with itself, but with its subject.

John Keats, *The Works of John Keats*, edited by H. Buxton Forman, Reeves & Turner, 1883, Volume III, page 113, Letter to J.H. Reynolds

Poetry should be vital—either stirring our blood by its divine movement, or snatching our breath by its divine perfection. To do both is supreme glory; to do either is enduring fame.

Augustine Birrell, *Obiter Dicta*, Elliot Stock, 1884, 'Mr. Browning's Poetry,' page 92

The essence of all poetry is to be found, not in high-wrought subtlety of thought, nor in pointed cleverness of phrase, but in the depths of the heart and the most sacred feelings of the men who write.

John Keble, *Keble's Lectures on Poetry*, translated by E.K. Francis, Oxford at the Clarendon Press, 1912, Volume II, page 201

When a poet takes words as his instruments... the very sound of the words is now part of the meaning; that meaning can never be apprehended or recovered except by re-hearing physically or in imagination the actual sound of the words... Here we are near to a sacrament.

William Temple, *Nature, Man and God*, Macmillan & Co. Ltd., 1934, page 484

Poetry turns all thing to loveliness; it exalts the beauty of that which is most beautiful, and it adds beauty to that which is most deformed; it marries exultation and horror, grief and pleasure, eternity and change; it subdues to union, under its light yoke, all irreconcilable things. It transmutes all that it touches, and every form moving within the radiance of its presence is changed by wondrous sympathy to an incarnation of the spirit which it breathes: its secret alchemy turns to potable gold the poisonous waters which flow from death through life; it strips the veil of familiarity from the world, and lays bare the naked and sleeping beauty, which is the spirit of its forms...

It purges from our inward sight the film of familiarity which obscures from us the wonder of our being. It compels us to feel that which we perceive, and to imagine that which we know.

Percy Bysshe Shelley, *The Prose Works of Percy Bysshe Shelley*, edited by H. Buxton Forman, Reeves & Turner, 1880, Volume III, page 139, 'A Defence of Poetry'

What is a Poet? To whom does he address himself? And what language is to be expected from him? He is a man speaking to men: a man, it is true, endowed with more lively sensibility, more enthusiasm and tenderness, who has a greater knowledge of human nature, and a more comprehensive soul, than are supposed to be common among mankind; a man pleased with his own passions and volitions, and who rejoices more than other men in the spirit of life that is in him...

The Poet writes under one restriction only, namely, the necessity of giving immediate pleasure to a human Being possessed of that information which may be expected from him, not as a lawyer, a physician, a mariner, an astronomer, or a natural philosopher, but as a Man...

He is the rock of defence for human nature; an upholder and preserver, carrying everywhere with him relationship and love. In spite of difference of soil and climate, of language and manners, of laws and customs: in spite of things silently gone out of mind, and things violently destroyed; the Poet binds together by passion and knowledge the vast empire of human society, as it is spread over the whole earth, and over all time. The objects of the Poet's thoughts are everywhere though the eyes and senses of man are, it is true, his favourite guides, yet he will follow wheresoever he can find an atmosphere of sensation in which to move his wings. Poetry is the first and last of all knowledge—it is as immortal as the heart of man.

William Wordsworth, *The Poems of William Wordsworth*, edited by Nowell Charles Smith, Methuen & Co. Ltd., 1908, Volume III, Preface to the Second Edition of *Lyrical Ballads*, page 490

The most beautiful poem there is, is life—life which discerns its own story in the making, in which inspiration and self-consciousness go together and help each other, life which knows itself to be the world in little, a repetition in miniature of the divine universal poem. Yes, be man; that is to say, be nature, be spirit, be the image of God, be what is greatest, most beautiful, most lofty in all the spheres of being, be infinite will and idea, a reproduction of the great whole. And be everything while being nothing, effacing thyself, letting God enter into thee as the air enters an empty space, reducing the *ego* to the mere vessel which contains the divine essence. Be humble, devout, silent, that so thou mayest hear in the depths of thyself the subtle and profound voice; be spiritual and pure, that so thou mayest have communion with the pure spirit. Withdraw thyself often into the sanctuary of thy inmost consciousness; become once more point and atom, that so thou mayest free thyself from space, time, matter, temptation, dispersion,—that thou mayest escape thy very organs themselves and thine own life. That is to say, die often, and examine thyself in the presence of this death, as a preparation for the last death.

Henri Frédéric Amiel, *Amiel's Journal*, translated by Mrs Humphry Ward, Macmillan & Co. Ltd., 1918, page 28

Browning's poetry... deals with what is essentially the business of prayer, the responsive Yes that a man must endeavour to make in those moments when the engagement is offered to him, when to be truly himself he must speak the truth in love, when he is presented with the opportunity and the responsibility of framing his reply 'in spirit and in truth.' Browning knew that the eternal Word waited to be embodied in human speech. In such moments all the divine events from the Nativity to the Passion are in our human key re-enacted. The Word may be given no room, may be misunderstood, treated with contempt, entirely rejected, but it is certain that, because of His love, it will not cease to be uttered. It is in this sense that the language of poetry is the serious speech to which all prayer aspires. The poet knows only too well that he himself is failing again and again to speak as he should, now wrestling with unmanageable perceptions, now giving way to the deceptions of easy speech, now intruding a false self consciousness into the area where openness should prevail. The poet can just as easily get in the way of the movement of the Word as anyone else. He may be all that Shelley said so magnificently about the poet and still betray his calling. None the less, he shares in the forgiveness extended to us all. It is his job to enable words to become bearers of the Word, to permit the Word to take our flesh and dwell among us, to speak the words that hallow all that God has given and man has received, to translate them all into a Yes to God.

Alan Ecclestone, Yes To God, Darton, Longman & Todd, 1975, page 69

POVERTY

'Poverty'—indigence, want; scarcity, deficiency; inferiority;
poorness; meanness.

M other Teresa of Calcutta gave me a new insight into the nature of poverty. From her standpoint she wrote: 'You in the West have the spiritually poorest of the poor much more than you have physically poor people. Very often among the rich there are very, very spiritually poor people.'

This fits in with what I have observed and experienced in the West. A few weeks ago I received a letter from a wealthy acquaintance of mine. In this letter he mentioned four men in his circle of friends who had committed suicide in the last few years. This saddened me, but did not shock me. Years ago, as a part-time Hospital Chaplain, I had come across a number of patients who had tried to commit suicide. I was dismayed at the time. On the evidence before me I did some calculations—reaching the conclusion there were far more suicides than I was aware of—indicating the presence of spiritual poverty.

Mother Teresa added: 'I find it not difficult to give a plate of rice to a hungry person, to furnish a bed to a person who has no bed, but to console or to remove that bitterness, to remove that anger, to remove that loneliness takes a very long time.'

This also fits in with my experience. I frequently come across bitter, angry and lonely people, but to console them and remove these negative states of heart and mind takes a very long time. This is one reason why I encourage people to reflect, meditate and contemplate—to give the grace of God a chance. In this way, richness of life can eradicate spiritual poverty.

For the poor will never cease out of the land; therefore I command you, You shall open wide your hand to your brother, to the needy and to the poor, in the land.

Deuteronomy 15.11

But he saves the fatherless from their mouth, the needy from the hand of the mighty. So the poor have hope, and injustice shuts her mouth.

Job 5.15-16

And he sat down opposite the treasury, and watched the multitude putting money into the treasury. Many rich people put in large sums. And a poor widow came, and put in two copper coins, which make a penny. And he called his disciples to him, and said to them, 'Truly, I say to you, this poor widow has put in more than all those who are contributing to the treasury. For they all contributed out of their abundance; but she out of her poverty has put in everything she had, her whole living.'

Mark 12.41-44

Blessed are you poor, for yours is the kingdom of God.

Luke 6.20

The greatest man in history was the poorest.

Ralph Waldo Emerson, The Works of Ralph Waldo Emerson, edited by George Sampson, George Bell & Sons Ltd., 1906, Volume III, Society and Solitude: Letters and Social Aims: Addresses, page 62

There is nothing perfectly secure but poverty.

Henry Wadsworth Longfellow, *Final Memorials*, edited by Samuel Longfellow, Ticknor and Company, 1887, page 197

I want nothing whatever. I am quite happy.

William Blake, cited by Crabb Robinson's Diary for 10th December, 1825

The town's poor seem to me often to live the most independent lives of any.

Henry David Thoreau, *Walden*, The New American Library of World Literature, Inc., 1960, page 218

Oh Poverty, high wisdom! to be subject to nothing, and by despising all to possess all created things ...

God will not lodge in a narrow heart; and it is as great as thy love. Poverty has so ample a bosom that Deity Itself may lodge therein ...

Poverty is naught to have, and nothing to desire: but all things to possess in the spirit of liberty.

Jacopone da Todi, in Evelyn Underhill, *Mysticism*, Methuen & Co. Ltd., 1912, page 250, footnote, 'Lauda,' l. ix

'Blessed are the poor in spirit' means: Blessed is the man who has realised his own utter helplessness, and has put his whole trust in God.

If a man has realised his own utter helplessness, and has put his whole trust in God, there will enter into his life two things which are opposite sides of the same thing. He will become completely *detached from things*, for he will know that things have not got it in them to bring happiness or security; and he will become completely *attached to God*, for he will know that God alone can bring him help, and hope, and strength. The man who is poor in spirit is the man who has realised that things mean nothing, and that God means everything.

William Barclay, *The Gospel of Matthew*, The Saint Andrew Press, 1974, Volume I, page 86

Theologians and philosophers have no special expertise at all, except in the asking of awkward questions, and a certain acquaintance with the answers that men in past generations have offered themselves. But this is precisely why they are needed now, to ask us what our objects are, what we are aiming at, what sort of society we really want to create, what sort of people we really want to be ...

The point I am trying to make is excellently illustrated by the moon landings. Nothing could demonstrate better the capacity of human hearts to accomplish what they set their hearts on, and their equal capacity to set their hearts on the wrong things. The moon landings are, of course, magnificent. But to the underprivileged, undernourished two-thirds of the world they are a magnificent irrelevance. We are clever enough to reach the moon, but not sensible enough to share out the world's resources with anything approaching equity.

Henry McKeating, *Living with Guilt*, SCM Press Ltd., 1970, page 65

Death was for Jesus the supreme moment of his supreme poverty. God had chosen the path of poverty to save man, and no moment of his journey was so steeped in poverty as the moment of his death. A dead God was absolute poverty: it was impossible to go further than that.

By reaching the depths of this dark abyss, Christ had reached all the people whom the Father had chosen to be his sons but who had forfeited this sonship through disobedience.

By entering into the chaos produced by the perversity of a confused and deluded mankind, Jesus had identified himself with what was lost through showing that there was salvation even for sin.

By taking hardness-of-heart into its embrace, the power of love had been able to melt it. The prodigal son's flight had become a positive act because it brought to light the depths of the father's mercy.

Love had won, man was saved.

Freedom had inherited the earth.

Carlo Carretto, *Blessed Are You Who Believed*, translated by Barbara Wall, Burns & Oates Ltd., 1982, page 51

The poor man is really poor, but the poor of Yahweh has God at his disposal.

The realization is enough to make one's head spin. God at the disposal of my faith! What an awesome thought!

Jesus has left us an echo of that sense of vertigo. We are told in the Gospel of his being tempted by the possibility of changing stones into bread, or of casting himself from the pinnacle of the temple without doing himself any harm.

He says himself that he recovered his equilibrium by crying out in the midst of temptation: 'You must not put the Lord your God to the test' (Mt 4.7).

Yes, it is a terrible thing to feel that God is at the disposal of our poverty.

All things are possible for him who believes. That is the secret of the poor of Yahweh.

I am nothing, but God is my all. *I have nothing, but God is the fulness of being and I will lose myself in him.* I believe this is the most radical experience man can have here on earth, the most dramatic struggle man can have with God, the face-to-face encounter of Israel with Yahweh in the night of the Passover under the moon of bare faith.

Carlo Carretto, In Search of the Beyond, translated by Sarah Fawcett, Darton, Longman & Todd, 1975, page 35

The state of indigence or want.

When unqualified, the reference is usually to material poverty, the lack of sufficient resources to sustain an adequate standard of life. By extension, however, the word is also used to refer to spiritual poverty, usually understood as a lack of a sense of purpose, or of adequate stimulation to the capacity for imagination or for the formation of relationships.

In the more common, material, sense the specific definition of what constitutes poverty is a matter of intense debate, not least because upon the type of definition chosen depend both the diagnosis of the causes of poverty and the type of pastoral care and remedial action thought to be appropriate. Definitions generally fall into one of two types, *absolute* and *relative.*

Defined in an *absolute* sense, poverty is the lack of sufficient resources to maintain life, measured in terms of such items as food, clothing or housing. On the basis of such absolute definitions poverty is a finite problem, and caring for the poor consists in lifting the standard of those who are poor to the point where they are no longer poor. Statements such as, 'There is not the kind of poverty around that you used to see in the 1930's,' are based on such absolute definitions.

Relative definitions of poverty take account of the fact that the perceptions of poverty, and the experience of the poor, changes according to social context. If the standard of living generally is rising, so is likely to be the level below which people are perceived to be in poverty. Further, the experience of being poor is changed if the situation of a person ceases to be in the midst of a community in which poverty is general to one in which people are generally better off and expectations are rising. It is because of this relative element in the definition of poverty that the list of those necessities without which a person is poor is constantly revised to take account of general changes in the general standard of life, and therefore of expectations.

Parallel to the debate of definition in relation to poverty is the debate about causes, and these are directly related to suggested means of caring for the poor. Such definitions may broadly be categorized as *natural, individual* and *structural.*

The *natural* causes of poverty are differences in the resources of the land or of the country, harvest failures and natural disasters. It may also be claimed that there are natural differences in individual endowment and inheritance which make it inevitable that there will be differences in attainment and therefore in the rewards gained. Those who see such natural, or inevitable, differences as the chief cause of poverty would see care for the poor first in terms of alleviation—by means of charity or social provision—of a problem which, like the poor, will always be with us. They would secondly seek to bring the poor to an understanding and acceptance of the inevitable.

Those who see the causes of poverty lying primarily in the individuals who are poor focus on the higher incidence of crime, idleness and bad financial management among the poor, and see care for the poor principally as an educational task concerned with the reform of the individual. On that understanding, welfare provision can be seen as often counter-productive, since it lowers the sense of personal responsibility among the poor and therefore their motivation to improve their own lot.

Those who see poverty as structual, originating in the way society is ordered, focus on the injustices of which the poor are the victims, and regard the crime and the apathy found among the poor as the results rather than the causes of poverty. The right means of pastoral care for the poor is, therefore, political action with or on behalf of them, so that those with power, those who are not poor, may take responsibility for their part in bringing poverty into being. Such pastoral care finds theological support in liberation or political theology.

Peter Selby, in *A Dictionary of Pastoral Care*, edited by Alastair Campbell, SPCK, 1987, page 211

PRAISE

'Praise'—glorify, extol the attributes of God.

P raise comes to me most naturally when singing, or when viewing a marvellous spectacle of nature. At the age of ten I joined Huddersfield Parish Church Choir and greatly enjoyed singing in the services—the Versicles and Responses, the Magnificat, Nunc Dimittis, and Anthems. Many years later when I was serving my title at Bradford Cathedral I was privileged to lead Choral Evensong at 4.00 p.m. on Sundays for a whole year. This was a sheer delight, and an excellent opportunity for praise.

In this section we find three quotations coming from the pen of Thomas Traherne. Traherne was the last of the mystical poets following in the steps of George Herbert and Henry Vaughan. Through these quotes he has taught me something of 'the unsearchable extent and illimited greatness of 'my' own soul; the length and breadth and depth, and height of 'my' own understanding.' He adds: 'Because it is the House of God, a Living Temple, and a Glorious Throne of the Blessed Trinity... to see Eternity, to fill His Omnipresence, to possess His greatness, to admire His love; to receive His gifts, to enjoy His world, and to live in His image.' He concludes: 'Let all your actions proceed from a sense of this greatness, let all your affections extend to this wideness, let all your prayers be animated by this spirit and [this is the best one] let all your praises arise and ascend from this fountain.'

This is a purple passage for me and describes the very essence of what I believe, as well as getting to the heart of praise. In addition to singing and to viewing a marvellous spectacle of nature, reflecting has become for me a valuable medium of praise.

I call upon the Lord, who is worthy to be praised.

Psalm 18.3

Those who seek him shall praise the Lord! May your hearts live for ever!

Psalm 22.26

I will sing with the spirit and I will sing with the mind also.

1 Corinthians 14.15

But you are a chosen race, a royal priesthood, a holy nation, God's own people, that you may declare the wonderful deeds of him who called you out of darkness into his marvellous light.

1 Peter 2.9

Thou awakest us to delight in Thy praise.

St Augustine, *The Confessions of St Augustine* revised from a former translation by the Rev. E.B. Pusey, Library of the Fathers, Volume I, J.G. and F. Rivington, 1838, page 1

The whole wood-world is one full peal of praise.

Alfred, Lord Tennyson, *The Poems of Tennyson*, edited by Christopher Ricks, Longmans, Green & Co. Ltd., 1969, page 1588, No.468, Balin and Balan, l.444

Praised be to God who has given us a mind that cannot be satisfied with the temporal.

Nicolas Cusanus, *Of Learned Ignorance*, translated by Fr. Germain Heron, Routledge & Kegan Paul Ltd., 1954, page 168

Our meditation in this present life should be in the praise of God; for the eternal exultation of our life hereafter will be the praise of God; and none can become fit for the future life, who hath not practiced himself for it now.

St Augustine, *An Augustine Synthesis*, arranged by Erich Przywara, SJ, Sheed & Ward Ltd., 1945, page 397

What else can a lame old man as I am do but chant the praise of God? If, indeed, I were a nightingale I should sing as a nightingale, if a swan, as a swan; but as I am a rational creature I must praise God. This is my task, and I do it: and I will not abandon this duty, so long as it is given me; and I invite you all to join in this same song.

Epictetus, *The Stoic and Epicurean Philosophers*, edited by Witney J. Oates, Random House Inc., 1940, page 253

By an act of the understanding therefore be present now with all the creatures among which you live: and hear them in their beings and operations praising God in an heavenly manner. Some of them vocally, others in their ministry, all of them naturally and continually. We infinitely wrong ourselves by laziness and confinement. All creatures in all nations and tongues and peoples praise God infinitely; and the more, for being your sole and perfect treasures. You are never what you ought till you go out of yourself and walk among them.

Thomas Traherne, *Centuries, Poems, and Thanksgivings*, edited by H.M. Margoliouth, Oxford at the Clarendon Press, 1958, ii. 76

Man's chief work is but to praise God. To Him it belongs to satisfy thee by His beauty, to thee to praise Him in acts of thanksgiving. If thy works be not the praise of God, thou art beginning to love thyself ... Be dissatisfied with thyself; find satisfaction in Him Who made thee, in that thou art dissatisfied with that in thee which thou thyself hast made. Let therefore thy work be the praise of God. For it is not He that increaseth by our praise, but we. God is neither the better if thou praise Him, nor worse if thou disparage Him; but thou, by praising Him that is good, art the better; by disparaging thou art the worse, for He remaineth good, as He is.

St. Augustine, *An Augustine Synthesis*, arranged by Erich Przywara, SJ, Sheed & Ward Ltd., 1945, page 398

Let all thy creatures bless thee O Lord, and my soul praise and bless thee for them all. I give thee thanks for the being thou givest unto the heavens, sun, moon, stars, and elements; to beasts, plants, and all other bodies of the earth; to the fowls of the air, and fishes of the sea. I give thee thanks for the beauty of colours, for the harmony of sounds, for the pleasantness of odours, for the sweetness of meats, for the warmth and softness of our raiment, and for all my five senses, and all the pores of my body, so curiously made, as before recited, and for the preservation as well as use of all my limbs and senses, in keeping me from precipes, fractures, and dislocations in my body, from a distracted, discomposed, confused, discontented spirit. Above all, I praise thee for manifesting thyself unto me, whereby I am made capable to praise and magnify thy name for evermore.

Thomas Traherne, *Centuries, Poems, and Thanksgivings*, edited by H.M. Margoliouth, Oxford at the Clarendon Press, 1958, Volume II, *Poems and Thanksgivings*, page 228

We should praise God by means of everything that we can offer to Him. To praise God means that all his life long a man glorifies, reverences and venerates the Divine Omnipotence. The praise of God is the meet and proper work of the angels and the saints in heaven, and of loving men on earth. God should be praised by desire, by the lifting up of all our powers, by words, by works, with body and with soul, and with whatsoever one possesses; in humble service, from without and from within. He who does not praise God while here on earth shall in eternity be dumb. To praise God is the dearest and most joyous work of every loving heart; and the heart which is full of praise desires that every creature should praise God. The praise of God has no end, for it is our bliss; and most justly shall we praise Him in eternity.

John of Ruysbroeck, *The Adornment of the Spiritual Marriage*, translated by C.A. Wynshenk Dom, edited by Evelyn Underhill, John M. Watkins, 1951, page 65

We are on retreat. Very cold morning... I left for the woods before dawn, after a conference on sin. Pure dark sky, with only the crescent moon and planets shining; the moon and Venus over the barns, and Mars over in the west over the hills and the fire tower.

Sunrise is an event that calls forth solemn music in the very depths of man's nature, as if one's whole being had to attune itself to the cosmos and praise God for the new day, praise Him in the name of all the creatures that ever were or ever will be. I look at the rising sun and feel that now upon me falls the responsibility of seeing what all my ancestors have seen, in the Stone Age and even before it, praising God before me. Whether or not they praised Him then, for themselves, they must praise Him now in me. When the sun rises each one of us is summoned by the living and the dead to praise God.

Thomas Merton, *Conjectures of a Guilty Bystander*, Burns & Oates Ltd., 1968, page 256

As it becometh you to retain a glorious sense of the world, because the Earth and the Heavens and the Heaven of Heavens are the magnificent and glorious territories of God's Kingdom, so are you to remember always the unsearchable extent and illimited greatness of your own soul; the length and breadth and depth, and height of your own understanding. Because it is the House of God, a Living Temple, and a Glorious Throne of the Blessed Trinity: far more magnificent and great than the Heavens; yea, a person that in Union and Communion with God, is to see Eternity, to fill His Omnipresence, to possess His greatness, to admire His love; to receive His gifts, to enjoy the world, and to live in His Image. Let all your actions proceed from a sense of this greatness, let all your affections extend to this wideness, let all your prayers be animated by this spirit and let all your praises arise and ascend from this fountain. For you are never your true self, till you live by your soul more than by your body, and you never live by your soul till you feel its incomparable excellency, and rest satisfied and delighted in the unsearchable greatness of its comprehension.

Thomas Traherne, *Centuries*, The Faith Press Ltd., 1969, page 100

PRESENCE

'Presence'—being present; real presence, place where person is.

Once more the Genesis story of the creation of man enables us to understand the meaning of presence. In this story God is depicted as fashioning and shaping man in His own image and likeness and the last thing he does is breathe into man and man becomes a living being. This points to the possibility of experiencing the presence of God in the life of man.

If we want to see this fully worked out in a life we go to the person of Jesus Christ. As he went through life he discovered something of the presence of the Father in the depths of himself, something of the Holy Spirit, and divine attributes such as life, light, truth, joy and love. Following his resurrection and the coming of the Holy Spirit, his last words to the disciples in St Matthew's Gospel were a promise his presence would be with them always, to the close of the age. I rely heavily on Christ's experience of the presence and the final words of his promise.

I am also indebted to William Law. In the eighteenth century he wrote in *The Spirit of Prayer* —'Though God be everywhere present, yet He is only present to Thee in the deepest, and most central Part of thy Soul.' I have found in the spirit of prayer, particularly reflection, a way of experiencing the presence.

A well-known exponent of *The Practice of the Presence of God*, is Brother Lawrence, a Carmelite lay brother of the seventeenth century. In this simple mode of prayer use is made of the imagination and the intellect. For many years he ran the monastery kitchen. Amid the noise and clatter of the kitchen he was able to possess God in as great a tranquillity as if he was upon his knees at the Blessed Sacrament.

Even though I walk through the valley of the shadow of death, I fear no evil; for thou art with me; thy rod and thy staff, they comfort me.

Psalm 23.4

Fear not, for I am with you, be not dismayed, for I am your God; I will strengthen you, I will help you, I will uphold you with my victorious right hand.

Isaiah 41.10

And lo, I am with you always, to the close of the age.

Matthew 28.20

All who keep his commandments abide in him, and he in them. And by this we know that he abides in us, by the Spirit which he has given us.

1 John 3.24

Though God be everywhere present, yet He is only present to Thee in the deepest, and most central Part of thy Soul.

William Law, *The Spirit of Prayer*, full text, edited by Sidney Spencer, James Clarke & Co. Ltd., 1969, page 44

Speak to Him thou for He hears, and Spirit with Spirit can meet—
Closer is He than breathing, and nearer than hands and feet.

Alfred, Lord Tennyson, *The Poems of Tennyson*, edited by Christopher Ricks, Longmans, Green & Co. Ltd., 1969, page 1205, No. 353, 'The Higher Pantheism,' l.11

The doctrine of the presence of God, to be realized here and now, should give to the habitually unhappy both the light to see what Christian hope is all about and the grace to act upon this light.

Hubert van Zeller, *Considerations*, Sheed & Ward Ltd., 1974, page 100

The time of business does not with me differ from the time of prayer; and in the noise and clutter of my kitchen, while several persons are at the same time calling for different things, I possess God in as great a tranquillity as if I were upon my knees at the Blessed Sacrament.

Brother Lawrence, *The Practice of the Presence of God*, A.R. Mowbray & Co. Ltd., 1977, page 23

The practice of the presence of God may involve very many hours of hard work; but the reward is great; for this is the joy that no man can take from us; this is the faith which is the human side of divine grace, an experiment which is becoming an experience, a foretaste and assurance of the rest remaineth for the people of God.

W.R. Inge, *Personal Religion and the Life of Devotion*, Longmans, Green & Co. Ltd., 1924, page 32

What if it be true that the key to the correct understanding of the Second Coming is indeed to be found in John's Gospel in the words which tell how Father and Son will come and make their dwelling in the loving and obedient heart? (John 14.23). The cosmic upheaval may well stand for the destruction of the old life and the creation of the new when Christ enters into life. The judgement may well stand for the confrontation of the soul with Christ. The blessedness may well stand for the new life which is the life lived in Christ. For us it may well be that the Second Coming is not meant to be a dream of the future but a challenge to each individual Christian to make that sort of submission which will bring the coming again of the Spirit and the presence of Jesus Christ into his own soul.

William Barclay, *The Plain Man Looks at the Apostles' Creed*, William Collins Sons & Co. Ltd., 1967, page 197

You ought to know yourself as you really are … so that you may understand of what nature you are and whence you have come into this world, and for what purpose you were created, and in what your happiness and your misery consist, for within you are combined the qualities of the animals and the wild beasts and the angels, but the spirit is your real essence and all beside it is, in fact, foreign to you. So strive for the knowledge of your origin, so that you may know how to attain to the Divine Presence and the contemplation of the Divine Majesty and Beauty, and deliver yourself from the fetters of lust and passion … for God did not create you to be their captive, but that they should be your thralls, under your control, for the journey which is before you, to be your steed and your weapon, so that you may therewith pursue your happiness and then cast them under your feet.

Al-Ghazali, in *Al-Ghazali, The Mystic*, Margaret Smith, Luzac & Co., 1944, page 151

In those rare glimpses of Christ's own life and prayer which the Gospels vouchsafe to us, we always notice the perpetual reference to the unseen Father; so much more vividly present to Him than anything that is seen. Behind that daily life into which He entered so generously, filled as it was with constant appeals to His practical pity and help, there is ever the sense of that strong and tranquil Presence, ordering all things and bringing them to their appointed end; not with a rigid and mechanical precision, but with the freedom of a living, creative, cherishing thought and love. Throughout His life, the secret, utterly obedient conversation of Jesus with His Father goes on. He always snatches opportunities for it, and at every crisis He returns to it as the unique source of confidence and strength; the right and reasonable relation between the soul and its source.

Evelyn Underhill, *Abba*, Longmans, Green & Co. Ltd., 1940, page 12

It is easier to attain knowledge of this presence by personal experience than by reading books, for it is life and love, strength and light, joy and peace to a chosen soul. A soul that has once experienced it cannot therefore lose it without pain; it cannot cease to desire it, because it is so good in itself, and brings such comfort …

The awareness of special grace that accompanies the invisible presence of God and makes the soul perfect in love, does not always continue at its highest intensity, but comes and goes unpredictably … Sometimes He comes secretly when you are least aware of Him, but you will recognize Him unmistakably before He goes, for He stirs your heart in a wonderful way, and moves it strongly to contemplate His goodness. Then your heart melts with delight at the tenderness of His love like wax before the fire, and this is the sound of His voice.

Walter Hilton, *The Ladder of Perfection*, translated by Leo Sherley-Price, Penguin Books Ltd., 1957, page 233

… how wrong it is to use God as a stop-gap for the incompleteness of our knowledge. For the frontiers of knowledge are inevitably being pushed back further and further, which means that you only think of God as a stop-gap. He also is being pushed back further and further, and is in more or less continuous retreat. We should find God in what we do know, not in what we don't; not in outstanding problems, but in those we have already solved …

It just isn't true to say that Christianity alone has the answers. In fact the Christian answers are no more conclusive or compelling than any of the others. Once more, God cannot be used as a stop-gap. We must not wait until we are at the end of our tether: he must be found at the centre of life; in life, and not only in death; in health and vigour, and not only in suffering; in activity, and not only in sin. The ground for this lies in the revelation of God in Christ. Christ is the centre of life, and in no sense did he come to answer our unsolved problems.

Dietrich Bonhoeffer, *Letters and Papers from Prison*, edited by Eberhard Bethge, translated by R.H. Fuller, SCM Press Ltd., 1953, page 142

One of the hardest battles in the spiritual life, perhaps I should say the hardest, is the struggle to see God in our trivial human happenings. How often we have to renew our act of faith! At first we are tempted to see only ourselves, to believe only in ourselves, to value only ourselves. Then gradually we perceive that the thread of life has a rationale, a mysterious unity, and we are led to think that we meet God in its basic stages. Then again, as our religious experience grows, we begin to realize that we meet God not only in the big events of our lives but in all the events, however small and apparently insignificant. God is never absent from our lives, He cannot be, because 'in Him we live, and move, and exist' (Acts 17.28). But it requires so much effort to turn this truth into a habit!

We need repeated acts of faith before we learn to sail with confidence on the 'immense and endless sea' which is God (St Gregory of Nazienzen), knowing that if we founder we do so in Him, the divine, eternal, ever-present God. How fortunate we are if we can learn to navigate our frail craft on this sea and remain serene even when the storm is raging!

Carlo Carretto, *Love is for Living,* translated by Jeremy Moiser, Darton, Longman & Todd, 1976, page 109

I went out one afternoon for a walk alone. I was in the empty unthinking state in which one saunters along country lanes, simply yielding oneself to the casual sights around which give a town-bred lad with country yearnings such intense delight. Suddenly I became conscious of the presence of some one else. I cannot describe it, but I felt that I had as direct a perception of the being of God all about me as I have of you when we are together. It was no longer a matter of inference, it was an immediate act of spiritual (or whatever adjective you like to employ) apprehension. It came unsought, absolutely. I remember the wonderful transfiguration of the far-off woods and hills as they seemed to blend in the infinite being with which I was thus brought into relation. This experience did not last long. But it sufficed to change all my feeling. I had not found God because I had never looked for him. But He had found me; he had, I could not but believe, made himself personally known to me. I had not gone in search of a satisfying emotion. I did not work myself up into this state by any artificial means. But I felt that God had come to me, I could now not only believe in him with my mind, but love him with my heart. I cannot tell you how often this has come back to me both with thankfulness and with humiliation... I am often perplexed to know why such revealings do not come to other souls. But I cannot regard this as a mere piece of romanticism, though I shall not be surprised or offended if you do. This event has never happened to me again... It was not necessary. The sense of a direct relation to God then generated in my soul has become a part of my habitual thought and feeling.

Joseph Carpenter, *Joseph Estlin Carpenter,* edited by C.H. Herford, Oxford at the Clarendon Press, 1929, page 9

PROGRESS

'Progress'—forward or onward movement in space, advance, development.

M artin Luther King put his finger on a crucial point when he wrote we must work passionately and indefatigably to bridge the gulf between our scientific progress and our moral progress. He went on to add one of the great problems of mankind is that we suffer from a poverty of spirit which stands in glaring contrast to our scientific and technological abundance.

The scientific and technological revolution has been truly impressive in the last hundred years, and we have witnessed awe-inspiring progress in both these spheres in the twentieth century. Just think for a moment of the recent progress made in the computer industry and the vast possibilities being opened up for the future. This form of progress can be seen in every technical area of life, but for some reason similar progress has not been forthcoming in the spiritual and moral spheres of life.

In some ways I blame the Church for this. What I think is now needed is a spiritual and moral revolution, similar to the one we have experienced in science and technology. *Visions of Grace,* along with *Visions of Faith, Hope, Love* and *Glory,* is a small attempt to gather together the core of our spiritual and moral heritage, and to make this readily available for future generations in the twenty-first century.

The practice of reflection, meditation and contemplation, is a practical way of bringing this spiritual and moral heritage to bear on everyday life and transforming it. In this way we hope to bridge the gulf between scientific progress and moral progress and approach the twenty-first century in a spirit of optimism.

Blessed are the men whose strength is in thee... They go from strength to strength.

Psalm 84.5,7

But the path of the righteous is like the light of dawn, which shines brighter and brighter until full day.

Proverbs 4.18

But when the perfect comes, the imperfect will pass away. When I was a child, I spoke like a child, I thought like a child, I reasoned like a child; when I became a man, I gave up childish ways.

1 Corinthians 13.10-11

Rather, speaking the truth in love, we are to grow up in every way into him who is the head, into Christ, from whom the whole body, joined and knit together by every joint with which it is supplied, when each part is working properly, makes bodily growth and upbuilds itself in love.

Ephesians 4.15-16

I consider that the way of life in urbanised, rich countries, as it exists today, and as it is likely to go on developing, is probably the most degraded and unillumined ever to come to pass on earth.

Malcolm Muggeridge, *Jesus Rediscovered*, William Collins Sons & Co. Ltd., 1982, page 52

So long as all the increased wealth which modern progress brings goes but to build up great fortunes, to increase luxury and make sharper the contrast between the House of Have and the House of Want, progress is not real and cannot be permanent.

Henry George, *Progress and Poverty*, Kegan Paul & Co., 1881, page 9

It is therefore the opinion of the present writer that even in this age there are no supersonic flights to the Celestial City or even to the Palace Beautiful. Increased awareness can be obtained only by a journey on foot by way of the Slough of Despond, the Hill of Difficulty, Doubting Castle, and the rest.

H A Williams, in *Soundings*, edited by A.R. Vidler, Cambridge at the University Press, 1962, page 72

A man's ability to be a pioneer of progress, that is, to understand what civilization is and to work for it, depends, therefore, on his being a thinker and on his being free. He must be the former if he is to be capable of comprehending his ideals and putting them into shape. He must be free in order to be in a position to launch his ideals out into the general life. The more completely his activities are taken up in any way by the struggle for existence, the more strongly will the impulse to improve his own condition find expression in the ideals of his thought. Ideals of self-interest then get mixed up with and spoil his ideals of civilization. Material and spiritual freedom are closely bound up with one another. Civilization presupposes free men, for only by free men can it be thought out and brought to realization.

Albert Schweitzer, *The Philosophy of Civilization*, Part I, *The Decay and Restoration of Civilization*, translated by C.T. Campion, A & C Black Ltd., 1932, page 16

When a Christian hath begun to think of spiritual progress, he beginneth to suffer from the tongues of adversaries. Whoever hath not yet suffered from these, hath not yet made progress and whoever suffereth them not, doth not even endeavour to progress. Doth he wish to know what we mean? Let him experience at the same time what we have to listen to. Let him begin to progress, let him begin to wish to ascend, to wish to despise earthly, perishable, temporal things, to hold the happiness of this world as nothing, to think of God alone, not to rejoice in gain, not to pine at losses, to wish to sell all his goods and give them to the poor, and to follow Christ; let us see how he suffereth the tongues of detractors and many things from opponents, and—a still graver thing—the efforts of pretended counsellors who lead him away from salvation.

St. Augustine, *An Augustine Synthesis*, arranged by Erich Przywara, SJ, Sheed & Ward Ltd., 1945, page 430

When people ask how they can tell if they are making progress since they are not supposed to analyse or assess their actual periods of meditation, the answer is usually self-evident.

A greater rootedness in self, a deeper emotional stability, a greater capacity to centre in others and away from self are the signs of spiritual growth.

If you want to ask the question, 'Am I making progress?' do not look at your meditation. There is only one way we can judge our progress and that is by the quality of our love.

As the mantra leads us ever further from self-centredness we turn more generously to others and receive their support in return. Indeed, our love for others is the only truly Christian way of measuring our progress on the pilgrimage of prayer.

If we try to force the pace or to keep a constant self-conscious eye on our progress we are, if there is such a word, non-meditating because we are concentrating on ourselves, putting ourselves first, thinking about ourselves.

John Main OSB, in *The Joy of Being*, selected by Clare Hallward, Darton, Longman & Todd, 1989, page 37

The world is a-building. This is the basic truth which must first be understood so thoroughly that it becomes an habitual and as it were natural springboard for our thinking. At first sight, beings and their destinies might seem to us to be scattered haphazard or at least in an arbitrary fashion over the face of the earth; we could very easily suppose that each of us might *equally well* have been born earlier or later, at this place or that, happier or more ill-starred, as though the universe from the beginning to end of it's history formed in space-time a sort of vast flower-bed in which the flowers could be changed about at the whim of the gardener. But this idea is surely untenable. The more one reflects, with the help of all that science, philosophy and religion can teach us, each in its own field, the more one comes to realize that the world should be likened not to a bundle of elements artificially held together but rather to some organic system animated by a broad movement of development which is proper to itself. As the centuries go by it seems that a comprehensive plan is indeed being slowly carried out around us. A process is at work in the universe, an issue is at stake, which can best be compared to the processes of gestation and birth; the birth of that spiritual reality which is formed by souls and by such material reality as their existence involves. Laboriously, through and thanks to the activities of mankind, the new earth is being formed and purified and is taking on definition and clarity. No, we are not like the cut flowers that make us a bouquet: we are like the leaves and buds of a great tree on which everything appears at its proper time and place as required and determined by the good of the whole.

Pierre Teilhard de Chardin, *Hymn of the Universe*, William Collins Sons & Co. Ltd., 1961, page 92

In the great mystics we see the highest and widest development of that consciousness to which the human race has yet attained. We see its growth exhibited to us on a grand scale, perceptible to all men... The germ of that same transcendent life, the spring of the amazing energy which enables the great mystic to rise to freedom and dominate his world, is latent in all of us; an integral part of our humanity. Where the mystic has a genius for the Absolute, we have each a little buried talent, some greater, some less; and the growth of this talent, this spark of the soul, once we permit its emergence, will conform in little, and according to its measure, to those laws of organic growth, those inexorable conditions of transcendence which we found to govern the Mystic Way.

Every person, then, who awakens to consciousness of a Reality which transcends the normal world of sense... is put of necessity upon a road which follows at low levels the path which the mystic treads at high levels...

I do not care whether the consciousness be that of artist or musician, striving to catch and fix some aspect of the heavenly light or music, and denying all other aspects of the world in order to devote themselves to this: or of the humble servant of Science, purging his intellect that he may look upon her secrets with innocence of eye: whether the higher reality be perceived in the terms of religion, beauty, suffering; of human love, of goodness, or of truth. However widely these forms of transcendence may seem to differ, the mystic experience is the key to them all...

Each brings the self who receives its revelation in good faith, does not check it by self-regarding limitations, to a humble acceptance of the universal law of knowledge: the law that 'we behold that which we are' and hence that 'only the Real can know Reality.' Awakening, Discipline, Enlightenment, Self surrender, and Union, are the essential processes of life's response to this fundamental fact: the conditions of our attainment of Being...

Evelyn Underhill, *Mysticism*, Methuen & Co. Ltd., 1912, page 532

PSYCHOLOGY

'Psychology'—science of nature; functions, and phenomena, of human soul or mind.

M orris West wrote in his book *The Shoes of the Fisherman*, 'The human psyche is the meeting ground between God and man.' On reading these words, I was tempted to have another look at the Genesis story of the creation of man. In the Authorized Version of the Bible the wording of Genesis chapter 2, verse 7, is: 'And the Lord God formed man of the dust of the ground, and breathed into his nostrils the breath of life; and man became a living soul.' I was delighted to see these words point to the life of God in man.

As I have already written, if we want to see this fully worked out in a life, we go to the person of Jesus Christ. In the Gospels we notice he discovered something of the Father in his soul, along with other divine attributes—Holy Spirit, life, light, truth, joy and love. Herein lay the secret of his life. Those close to him concluded—here was 'very God and very Man'.

Paul made the crucial discovery that what Christ had experienced we can all in some measure also experience. In Colossians chapter 2, verses 9–10, he wrote: 'For in him [in Christ] the whole fulness of deity dwells bodily, and you have come to fulness of life in him.'

I was struck by these words. They prompted me to ask a crucial question: Does the priest have a vital psychological role in society which has been allowed to slip away unperceived?

Over the last few years I have undergone a re-discovery of 'the cure of souls'. In reflection we can experience 'the cure of souls' through a release of the divine in man, leading on to new life—and finally to wholeness of mind, body and soul.

You will be secure, and will not fear.

Job 11.15

Keep your tongue from evil, and your lips from speaking deceit.

Psalm 34.13

I wish above all things that thou mayest prosper and be in health, even as thy soul prospereth.

3 John 2 (AV)

... I am he who searches mind and heart.

Revelation 2.23

The human psyche is the meeting ground between God and man. It is possible, I think, that some of the meaning of the mystery of Divine Grace may be revealed when we understand better the working of the subconscious mind, where buried memories and buried guilts and buried impulses germinate for years and then break out into a strange flowering... I must encourage competent men inside the Church to pursue this study, and to co-operate with those outside it, to make the best use possible of their discoveries...

The sick mind is a defective instrument in the great instrument which is God's dialogue with man. Here perhaps we may see a fuller revelation of the meaning of human responsibility and God's compassion for His creatures. Here we may be able to illuminate the difference between formal guilt and the true status of the soul in the sight of God.

Morris West, *The Shoes of the Fisherman*, William Heinemann Ltd., 1963, page 79

It is one of the great discoveries of modern psychology that our attitudes towards ourselves are just as complicated as our attitudes toward others—sometimes more so. The great commandment of religion, 'Thou shalt love thy neighbour as thyself,' might now be better interpreted to mean. 'Thou shalt love thyself properly, and *then* thou wilt love thy neighbour'...

This condemnation of selfishness and exaltation of altruism is the traditional attitude of religion. It holds up a worthy goal to be sure, but there are many errors in its estimate of human nature. Is it *true* that we are spontaneously good to ourselves? The evidence points in quite the opposite direction. Men may *wish* to be good to themselves, but how misguided and unwise they are in their attempts to reach that goal! The fact is that we often treat ourselves more rigidly, more fanatically, more vengefully, than we do others. Suicide, self-mutilation, and more subtle forms of self-degradation such alcoholism, drug addiction, and promiscuity are pitiful proofs of this. Such self-hate is not restricted to the weak and the insane... Violent forms of aggression against the self occur daily and less dramatically in the lives of ordinary men and women...

He who hates himself, who does not have proper regard for his own capacities, powers, compassions, actually can have no respect for others. Deep within himself he will hate his brothers when he sees in them his own marred image. Love for oneself is the foundation of a brotherly society and personal peace of mind. By loving oneself I do not mean coddling oneself, indulging in vanity, conceit, self-glorification. I do, however, insist on the necessity of a proper self-regard as a prerequisite of the good and the moral life...

Psychology reveals the underlying causes of false self-love and destructive self-hatred. Religion, allied with psychology, can demonstrate just what true self-regard means.

Theoretically, religion has always been concerned with the achievement of true self-love. It eternally proclaims the value of every human personality, the sanctity of every man. But it has been strangely impotent to implement that sanctity... All the streets of the world are teeming with men and women who mutilate themselves spiritually and mentally in the invisible ways of self-criticism and self-degradation... It is important that all of us become wise enough to recognize where we go astray in our attitudes toward ourselves and how we become enslaved to false notions of what we are and what we ought to be. Some of us think we are loving ourselves when we are really strangling or suffocating ourselves with morbid self-concern. We maintain a cruel contempt for our own capabilities and virtues or become unconscious victims of a paralyzing egocentricity. When we free ourselves from that false self-love which is narcissism, that destructive self-hatred which is masochism, we become for the first time integrated enough to become friendly with ourselves and with others. We are on the road to proper self-love. Such self-love implies many things, but above everything else it is rooted in self-respect. And no man or woman can have self-respect unless he has learned the art of renunciation and the equally vital art of self-acceptance.

Joshua Loth Liebman, *Peace of Mind*, William Heinemann Ltd., 1946, page 38

It is in this aiding of people to find meaning for their lives that religion and depth-psychology are in partnership. The field of meaning in life is essentially the religious area, but the technique of discovering why persons fail to find meaning—why they suffer hindrances, complexes, irrational fears—is the modern contribution of depth-psychology.

But many modern persons have been unable to quench their thirst for meaning in the stream of organized religion. Numerous reasons could be given for this—the stagnation that results from any large organization, the preaching of dry forms in which the vitality has run dry, and the great upheavals in our Western culture of the last century, and so forth. Whatever the reason, multitudes of modern intelligent people have been unable to find the guidance they wished in conventional religion. They have been told so oppressively often to believe in life and love their neighbours, that the words ring with the cant of mere verbal repetition.

And so at the threshold of the present century, a new endeavour to understand the human personality sprang up as an answer to a great need. Beginning with the sage of Vienna, Sigmund Freud, this 'psychoanalysis' was an attempt to be scientific about the human soul. We cannot achieve health or happiness, Freud pointed out, by the dishonest means of repressing all tendencies that our Victorian moralism finds unpalatable, and we are deceiving ourselves if we think that our arrogant 'egos' standing at the thresholds of our minds can arbitrarily decide the great issues of life as the whim strikes them... The new understanding of human motives worked out in Vienna constitutes probably the outstanding discovery of the twentieth century...

(The practical application of the knowledge which depth-psychology has discovered was developed through various contributions,) by Dr. C.G. Jung, who terms his subject 'analytical psychology,' Alfred Adler, who calls his work, 'individual psychology,' Fritz Kunkel, Otto Rank, and others. The fact that so many of Freud's disciples have dissented from the master, rather than a mutiny of the ranks, was like the independent searching for gold of a number of prospectors—since there was so much gold to be found...

In the past twenty years it has become recognized that most psychological problems are intertwined with religious, and that religious problems have in most cases a very clear psychological aspect... Dr. Jung expresses in vivid and perhaps extreme fashion what psychologists of all sorts were beginning to observe: 'Among all my patients in the second half of life—that is to say over thirty-five—there has not been one whose problem in the last resort was not that of finding a religious outlook on life. It is safe to say that every one of them fell ill because he had lost that which the living religions of every age have given to their followers, and none of them has been really healed who did not regain his religious outlook.' Dr. Jung goes on to caution us that this has nothing to do with the dogmas of a particular church; it is rather... the reaching out of the human soul for basic meaning by which it can live...

The psychoanalyst, or consulting psychologist, or whatever he may call himself, is concerned with helping the individual overcome fears and rationalizations and inhibitions so that he can move ahead with success... This neurotic man who refuses to meet people and who holds that all women are demons must first understand the detours in his background that have led him to the impasse—here the sheer technique of analysis comes into its own. But then, having been helped back on the road, he must believe in the worth of love and friendship in order that he may move down the road with courage... So psychotherapy, the technique, points inevitably toward religion, the goal and meaning...

Dr. Adler holds in his last book that we should view life *sub specie aeternitatis* and at the time of his death he was engaged in collaborating with clergymen in work on pastoral psychology. 'The best conception hitherto gained,' he writes, 'for the elevation of humanity is the idea of God.'

'It is doubtless true,' writes Dr. Menninger, 'that religion has been the world's psychiatrist throughout the centuries.'... One can be coldly scientific in segments of the technique of analysis; but the closer the treatment comes to completion, the more the therapist must take into consideration aspects of life which are by no means coldly scientific, such as faith, hope, and love. 'The patient needs a world view,' Dr. Otto Rank aptly puts it, 'and will always need it, because man always needs belief, and this so much more, the more increasing self-consciousness brings him to doubt.'

Rollo May, *The Springs of Creative Living*, Abingdon Press, 1940

PURITY

'Purity'—pureness, cleanness, freedom from physical or moral pollution.

I n his book *What is the Kingdom of Heaven*, A. Clutton-Brock asks the question, 'What... does Christ mean by the pure in heart?' He goes on to answer his own rhetorical question. 'He means more than sexually or even morally pure. He means rather what we call single-minded.'

If we examine the Gospels carefully and the details of Christ's ministry we notice a certain pureness, cleanness, and freedom from physical or moral pollution, as in the definition above. We also become aware of that other quality mentioned by A. Clutton-Brock: single-mindedness. We see this worked out in the temptations in the wilderness. Here in this arid environment, Jesus worked out his strategy, and the result is a ruthless single-mindedness. We see this in action in his preaching and teaching of the kingdom of God, and healing all manner of sickness and disease. Apart from nights spent on mountains in prayer or being up a great while before day, he goes about his ministry, single-mindedly, to the very end—and beyond.

We know single-mindedness is a vital quality in the lives of experts, whether these be professional golfers, musicians, snooker players, or people in other areas of expertise— management consultants, politicians and the like. This is true also of the followers of Christ. What is enjoined is a certain pureness, cleanness, and freedom from physical or moral pollution, but more importantly a single-minded following of Christ—right to the end—and beyond. This is what we understand by the phrase: 'Blessed are the pure in heart, for they shall see God.'

The precepts of the Lord are right, rejoicing the heart; the commandment of the Lord is pure, enlightening the eyes.

Psalm 19.8

Create in me a clean heart, O God, and put a new and right spirit within me. Cast me not away from thy presence, and take not thy holy Spirit from me. Restore to me the joy of thy salvation, and uphold me with a willing spirit.

Psalm 51.10-12

The body is not meant for immorality, but for the Lord, and the Lord for the body.

1 Corinthians 6.13

To the pure all things are pure.

Titus 1.15

Chastity is a wealth that comes from abundance of love.

Rabindranath Tagore, *Stray Birds*, Macmillan & Co. Ltd., Indian Edition, 1941, page 19

Chastity—spiritually it is the devotion of all powers of body and soul to the service of God.

E.R. Hardy, in *A Dictionary of Christian Ethics*, edited by John Macquarrie, SCM Press Ltd., 1967, page 53, 'Chastity'

Even from the body's purity the mind
Receives a secret sympathetic aid.

James Thomson, *The Seasons and The Castle of Indulgence*, edited by J. Logie Robertson, Oxford at the Clarendon Press, 1891, page 99, 'Summer,' l.1267

My strength is as the strength of ten,
Because my heart is pure.

Alfred, Lord Tennyson, *The Poems of Tennyson*, edited by Christopher Ricks, Longmans, Green & Co. Ltd., 1969, page 610, No.234, 'Sir Galahad,' l.3

Man flows at once to God as soon as the channel of purity, physical, intellectual, and moral, is open.

Henry David Thoreau, *The Journal of Henry D. Thoreau*, edited by Bradford Torrey and Francis H. Allen, Houghton Mifflin Company, Boston, The Riverside Press, 1949, Volume II, page 4

The essence of chastity is not the suppression of lust, but the total orientation of one's life towards a goal. Without such a goal, chastity is bound to become ridiculous. Chastity is the *sine qua non* of lucidity and concentration.

Dietrich Bonhoeffer, *Letters and Papers from Prison*, William Collins Sons & Co. Ltd., 1963, page 163

It is not necessary to search for God in heaven and earth and to send out our mind to seek Him in different places. Purify thy soul, o man, and strip thyself from the thought of recollections which are unnatural and hang before thy impulses the curtain of chastity and humility. Thereby thou wilt find Him that is within thee. For to the humble the mysteries are revealed.

Isaac of Nineveh, *Mystical Treatises of Isaac of Nineveh*, translated by E.J. Wensinck, 1923, page 36

Bless'd are the pure in heart,
For they shall see our God,
The secret of the Lord is theirs,
Their soul is Christ's abode.
Still to the lowly soul
He doth Himself impart,
And for His cradle and His throne
Chooseth the pure in heart.

John Keble, *The Christian Year*, edited by Ernest Rhys, J.M. Dent & Sons Ltd., 1914, page 185

The supreme reality is incomprehensible in the sense that it cannot be expressed in logical propositions but it is increasingly apprehensible by the purified mind. This apprehension is reached not so much by the exercise of reason as by the purification of the heart, by the process of turning the attention of the soul to its own central necessities. The conception of the ground of all existence in God and of the kinship of the human spirit to the divine is at the basis of the idea that the human spirit is an exile always longing for home.

It is the source of the urge in the heart towards union with the beloved.

Sir Sarvepalli Radhakrishnan, *Eastern Religions and Western Thought*, Oxford University Press, 1940, page 128

Unchangeableness and complete detachment from creatures, that sets me nearest to God and to the summit of perfection. Purity makes me all unmindful of things, and by purity God is always kept in me. Purity makes me uniform with God, purity forces me into the inner being of creatures, purity means farewell to all creatures. None but the pure in heart can see God. In purity only is God to be found. Intellect teaches me about things, purity makes me see God. By purity God is made captive in me, purity makes me God-conscious and conscious of naught beside God, purity begets detachment. The pure soul has a light-birth as it were, purity is satisfied with God alone.

Meister Eckhart, *Meister Eckhart*, Franz Pfeiffer, translated by C. de B. Evans, John M. Watkins, 1952, Volume II, page 143

He will shake heaven and earth, that only the unshakeable may remain: he is a consuming fire, that only that which cannot be consumed may stand forth eternal. It is the nature of God, so terribly pure that it destroys all that is not pure as fire, which demands like purity in our worship. He will have purity. It is not that the fire will burn us if we do not worship thus but that the fire will burn us until we worship thus; yea, will go on burning within us after all that is foreign to it has yielded to its force, no longer with pain and consuming, but as the highest consciousness of life, the presence of God.

George Macdonald, *Unspoken Sermons*, First Series, Alexander Strahan, Publisher, 1867, page 31

Learning to pray is learning to live as fully as possible in the present moment.

We may indeed begin meditating with a superficial concern for results, trying to estimate if our investment of time and energy is justified by returns in knowledge or 'extraordinary' experience. Perhaps anyone formed by our society is conditioned to begin in this way. But the ordinary practice of meditation purifies us of this spiritual materialism.

The hinge upon which we swing into the really transcendent experience is the fidelity and regularity of commitment that does not concern itself with 'good' meditations or 'bad' meditations.

The essential simplicity of simply saying the mantra; in this is the purification of our whole being.

John Main OSB, in *The Joy of Being*, selected by Clare Hallward, Darton, Longman & Todd, 1989, page 45

Love is the forgetfulness of self in the thought of the interests of another... What do 'my' wishes, 'my' feelings, 'my' wants matter? Why on earth should I bother about *them*?... Why 'me'— when there are so many others?

Pierce beneath the outer coverings of human sinfulness and see the real, though ruined, beauty of human souls.

Pure strong love let me have for what is still natural in my fellow creatures. Corrupt and artificial we have made ourselves, but the sweeter and more lovely is the glimpse of what we were as children in God's hands.

Pure and lovely were we when we left God's hands; let me hunt in everyone for traces of this beauty and purity; and for myself let me try and get back to it, back to my childhood with God...

Edward Wilson, in *The Faith of Edward Wilson*, George Seaver, John Murray Ltd., 1949, page 23

'Blessed are the pure in heart: for they shall see God.' Who is pure in heart? Only those who have surrendered their hearts completely to Jesus that He may reign in them alone. Only those whose hearts are undefiled by their own vices—and by their own virtues too. The pure in heart have a child-like simplicity like Adam before the fall, innocent alike of vice and virtue: their hearts are not ruled by their conscience but by the will of Jesus. If men renounce their own vice and virtue, if in penitence they have renounced their own hearts, if they rely solely upon Jesus, then His word purifies their hearts. Purity of heart is here contrasted with all outward purity, even purity of an honest mind. The pure heart is pure alike of good and evil, it belongs exclusively to Christ and looks only to Him who goes on before. Only they will see God, who in this life have looked solely unto Jesus Christ, the Son of God. For then their hearts are free from all defiling phantasies and are not distracted by conflicting desires and intentions.

Dietrich Bonhoeffer, *The Cost of Discipleship*, translated by R.H. Fuller, SCM Press Ltd., 1948, page 101

Meditation... is a purifying process. In Blake's phrase: 'If the doors of perception were cleansed, everything will appear to man as it is, infinite' (*A Memorable Fancy: The Ancient Tradition*). By means of the mantra we leave behind all passing images and learn to rest in the infinity of God Himself. St Paul urges us to do just this when he implores us in Romans 12:

'... by God's mercy to offer your very selves to Him: a living sacrifice, dedicated and fit for His acceptance, the worship offered by mind and heart. Adapt yourselves no longer to the pattern of this present world, but let your minds be remade and your whole nature thus transformed' (Rom.12.1-2).

This transformation of our nature is put before us as a real and an immediate possibility. It is the essential Christian experience, the experience of being born again in the Holy Spirit, born again when we realize the power of the living Spirit of God within us.

John Main OSB, *Word into Silence*, Darton, Longman and Todd, 1980, page 16

QUIETNESS

*'Quietness'—silence, stillness; being free from disturbance or
agitation or urgent tasks; rest, repose; peace of mind.*

One of my favourite places for quietness is the village of Mürren, high up in the
Bernese Oberland, Switzerland. I go there once a year to look after the English
Church over the Christmas and New Year period. I always get excited when the train pulls
in to Lauterbrunnen station. As Mürren is not accessible by road, the journey onwards is
either by funicular railway or cable car. In a few minutes I know I will be virtually cut off
from the rest of the world.

Mürren is a quiet village. There are no cars, only a few vehicles needed for catering.
Set at an altitude of 5,361 feet on a cliff top, Mürren faces south and is a natural suntrap.
Looking eastwards across the Lauterbrunnen valley are spectacular views of the Eiger,
Monch and the Jungfrau. Behind Mürren, at a height of nearly 10,000 feet, is the
Schilthorn, with its revolving cafe, (the Piz Gloria), made famous by the James Bond film,
On Her Majesty's Secret Service. Mürren is renowned for skiing, and this is where
downhill racing skiing first began.

I love to go out late at night and experience the silence and the stillness of the
mountains. Sometimes the moon is shining brightly, and the night sky is alive with the
beauty of the stars. If the snow is not too deep I go for long walks on rough tracks in pine
forests. Here is a place of rest and repose, and a rare opportunity to enjoy peace of mind.

As well as looking after the church, I go skiing during the day and experience different
forms of quietness. When it is snowing heavily I stay indoors—for quiet reflection.

Be quiet, for this day is holy.
Nehemiah 8.11

In returning and rest you shall be saved; in quietness and in trust shall be your strength.
Isaiah 30.15

Study to be quiet.
1 Thessalonians 4.11 (AV)

Let it be the hidden person of the heart with the imperishable jewel of a gentle and quiet
spirit, which in God's sight is very precious.
1 Peter 3.4

In silence alone does a man's truth bind itself together and strike root.
Antoine de Saint-Exupéry, *The Wisdom of the Sands*, translated by Stuart Gilbert, Hollis & Carter, 1952, page 45

Tranquillity! thou better name
Than all the family of Fame!
Samuel Taylor Coleridge, *Coleridge's Poetical Works*, edited by Ernest Hartley Coleridge, Oxford University Press, 1978,
page 360, 'Ode to Tranquillity,' l.1

I have discovered that all the unhappiness of men arises from one single fact, that they
cannot stay quietly in their own chamber.
Blaise Pascal, *Pensées*, translated by W.F. Trotter, Random House Inc., 1941, page 48

To go up alone into the mountain and come back as an ambassador to the world, has ever been the method of humanity's best friends.

Evelyn Underhill, *Mysticism*, Methuen & Co. Ltd., 1912, page 210

Silence is the element in which great things fashion themselves together, that at length they may emerge, full-formed and majestic, into the daylight of Life, which they are henceforth to rule.

Maurice Maeterlinck, *The Treasure of the Humble*, translated by Alfred Sutro, George Allen, 1897, page 3

All I can prescribe out of my own experience is to abide patiently till the soul relaxes—it is sprung up. It needs to be let free from all thought and strain, and simply to bathe itself in the ocean of God's love. Do nothing itself—but let God do it all. Utter surrender. Then it becomes still, tranquil, and goes out to God and rests.

William of Glasshampton, *William of Glasshampton, Friar: Monk: Solitary*, Geoffrey Curtis, CR, SPCK, 1947, page 148

The more we receive in silent prayer, the more we can give in our active life. We need silence in order to be able to touch souls. The essential thing is not what we say, but what God says to us and through us. All our words will be useless unless they come from within—words which do not give the light of Christ increase the darkness.

Mother Teresa of Calcutta, in *Something Beautiful for God*, Malcolm Muggeridge, William Collins Sons & Co. Ltd., 1983, page 66

Christ's existence was ruled by a great silence. His soul was 'listening'. It was given over to the needs of others. In his innermost being he was silent, not asserting himself, detached. He did not grasp at anything in the world. Thus he overcame in his life the power of habit and daily routine, of dullness and fatigue, and created within himself a carefree tranquillity, a place for every encounter.

Ladislaus Boros, *In Time of Temptation*, translated by Simon and Erika Young, Burns & Oates Ltd., 1968, page 18

Come now, little man,
turn aside for a while from your daily employment,
escape for a moment from the tumult of your thoughts.
Put aside your weighty cares,
let your burdensome distractions wait,
free yourself awhile for God
and rest awhile in him.
Enter the inner chamber of your soul,
shut out everything except God
and that which can help you in seeking him,
and when you have shut the door, seek him.

St Anselm, *The Prayers and Meditations of Saint Anselm*, Penguin Books Ltd., 1973, page 239

Inner stillness is necessary if we are to be in perfect control of our faculties and if we are to hear the voice of the Spirit speaking to us.

There can be no stillness without discipline, and the discipline of external silence can help us towards that inner tranquillity which is at the heart of authentic religious experience.

In meditation we take steps to achieve this stillness. We quieten our bodies and our emotions, then gradually allow the mind to become single-pointed.

Stillness within one individual can affect society beyond measure.

Bede Griffiths OSB, in *The Universal Christ*, edited by Peter Spink, Darton, Longman & Todd, 1993, page 31

Every great spiritual tradition has known that the human spirit begins to be aware of its own Source only in profound stillness.

In the Hindu traditions the Upanishads speak of the spirit of One who created the universe as dwelling in our heart. The same spirit is described as the One who in silence is loving to all.

In our own Christian tradition Jesus tells us that the Spirit who dwells in our heart is the Spirit of love.

The meeting of East and West in the Spirit is one of the great features of our time, but it can only be fruitful if it is realized on the level of deep prayer. This, surely, is also true of the union of the different Christian denominations.

John Main OSB, in *The Joy of Being*, selected by Clare Hallward, Darton, Longman & Todd, 1989, page 21

One may not be so given to contemplation as to forget the good of one's neighbour, nor so given over to action as to forget divine speculation.

Our saviour Jesus lived a life in public, sociable, humane, charitable, free and common. And yet, for opportunity of special devotion, retired to prayer and contemplation.

It was in solitude that he kept his fasts. Rocks and mountains heard his prayers. Among beasts was he born, and in the wilderness he fed his thousands. Upon a mountain he prayed, upon a mountain he was transfigured, upon a mountain he died, to a mountain in Galilee he invited his disciples, and from a mountain he ascended.

In which retirements his devotions received a great advantage of freedom from distractions. So that solitude is a good school to learn piety and virtue in, and the world the best theatre to practise it.

Thomas Traherne, in *Landscapes of Glory*, edited by A.M. Allchin, Darton, Longman & Todd, 1989, page 39

Let your mind be quiet, realising the beauty of the world, and the immense the boundless treasures that it holds in store. All that you have within you, all that your heart desires, all that your Nature so specially fits you for—that or the counterpart of it waits embedded in the great Whole, for you. It will surely come to you.

Yet equally surely not one moment before its appointed time will it come. All your crying and fever and reaching out of hands will make no difference.

Therefore do not begin that game at all.

Do not recklessly spill the waters of your mind in this direction and in that, lest you become like a spring lost and dissipated in the desert.

But draw them together into a little compass, and hold them still, so still;

And let them become clear, so clear,—so limpid, so mirror-like; At last the mountains and sky shall glass themselves in peaceful beauty,

And the antelope shall descend to drink, and to gaze at his reflected image, and the lion to quench his thirst,

And Love himself shall come and bend over, and catch his own likeness in you.

Edward Carpenter, *Towards Democracy*, George Allen & Unwin Ltd., 1931, page 372

RELATIONSHIPS

'Relationships'—what one person or thing has to do with another,
way in which one stands or is related to another.

T he Swiss psychologist C. G. Jung once wrote the love problem is part of mankind's heavy toll of suffering, and nobody should be ashamed that he must pay his tribute.

I am one of those who is unashamedly paying his tribute. Over the years I have found Jung's words helpful, especially in the wake of a number of broken relationships.

As a college chaplain I have also been involved in working through a large number of hurt feelings, resulting from broken relationships. I remember being in London, in charge of a chaplaincy house, where ten students lived for a year. One summer evening I stood outside the house, and looked back, and thought about each occupant in turn. All ten were involved in relationships and all were experiencing difficulties. Bearing this in mind imagine a mixed community of 450 undergraduates and postgraduates living in an Oxford college, and we soon realize how important and how complex relationships are in this milieu.

I have also been helped in my understanding of the nature of relationships by some words of R.E.C. Browne. In *The Ministry of the Word* he wrote in the sphere of human relationships there are no rules to be found for knowing the appropriate behaviour in a particular situation. Perhaps this helps us to understand why relationships are so difficult. No fixed guidance to follow.

One thing I am learning from my experience of relationships is to be honest, in our thoughts and in our feelings. This is difficult, and sometimes painful.

Three things are too wonderful for me; four I do not understand: the way of an eagle in the sky, the way of a serpent on a rock, the way of a ship on the high seas, and the way of a man with a maiden.
Proverbs 30.18-19

Set me as a seal upon your heart, as a seal upon your arm; for love is strong as death . . . Many waters cannot quench love, neither can floods drown it. If a man offered for love all the wealth of his house, it would be utterly scorned.
Song of Solomon 8.6-7

Love is patient and kind; love is not jealous or boastful, it is not arrogant or rude. Love does not insist on its own way; it is not irritable or resentful; it does not rejoice at wrong, but rejoices in the right. Love bears all things, believes all things, hopes all things, endures all things. Love never ends.
1 Corinthians 13.4-8

And above all these put on love, which binds everything together in perfect harmony.
Colossians 3.14

Talk not of wasted affection, affection never was wasted;
If it enrich not the heart of another, its waters, returning
Back to their springs, like the rain, shall fill them full of refreshment.
Henry Wadsworth Longfellow, *The Poetical Works of Longfellow*, Humphrey Milford, Oxford University Press, 1913, page 158, *Evangeline*, Part the Second, I, l.55

I have often wondered why it is that men should be so fearful of new ventures in social relationships... Most of us fear, actually fear, people who differ from ourselves, either up or down the scale.

David Grayson, *The Friendly Road*, Andrew Melrose Ltd., 1946, page 117

Forgiving love is a possibility only for those who know that they are not good, who feel themselves in need of divine mercy, who live in a dimension deeper and higher than that of moral idealism.

Reinhold Niebuhr, *An Interpretation of Christian Ethics*, SCM Press Ltd., 1936, page 236

There is hardly anything that can make one happier than to feel that one counts for something with other people. What matters here is not numbers, but intensity. In the long run, human relationships are the most important thing in life.

Dietrich Bonhoeffer, *Letters and Papers from Prison*, edited by Eberhard Bethge, translated by R.H. Fuller, SCM Press Ltd., 1967, Second Revised Edition, page 212

The life and destiny of the least of human beings has an absolute meaning in respect of eternity: his life and his destiny are everlasting. For that reason one may not do away with a single human creature and escape punishment; we must consider the divine image and likeness in every one, from the most noble to the most despicable.

Nicolas Berdyaev, *Dostoievsky*, translated by Donald Attwater, Sheed & Ward Ltd., 1934, page 106

The woman is increasingly aware that love alone can give her her full stature, just as the man begins to discern that spirit alone can endow his life with its highest meaning. Fundamentally, therefore, both seek a psychic relation one to the other; because love needs the spirit, and the spirit, love, for their fulfilment.

C.G. Jung, *Contributions to Analytical Psychology*, translated by H.G. and Cary F. Baynes, Kegan Paul, Trench, Trubner & Co. Ltd., 1928, page 185

No matter how genuine a relationship may be, there will always be stresses and storms, to bring unexpected words, to make one impotent and afraid, to make one feel the terribleness of not being able to count on the other person, to create the despairing feeling that breaks in love can never be repaired. But one lives and loves, and suffers and forgets, and begins again—perhaps even thinking that this time, this new time, is to be permanent. But man is not permanent and man is not predictable.

Clark Moustakas, *Creativity and Conformity*, D. Van Nostrand Company Inc., 1967, page 21

The first [danger] is that a man lives for himself alone, deciding everything in the light of his own advantage, disregarding the rights and needs of his fellow-men. The second [danger] is that we should think of people impersonally, in the mass, with numbers rather than names, thinking of them as cast in the same mould, with no individuality of their own. Each man wants value in himself, wants to be himself, thinking of others in the same way. Neither individualism or collectivism is the right way of human relationship.

George Appleton, *Journey for a Soul*, William Collins Sons & Co. Ltd., 1976, page 27

In order to attain the being-with in love, our own existence must, so to speak, be given up; it must give up making use of the other person and treating him as a possession. Quite simply, man is meant to come to a personal fulfilment. His existence has not yet really come 'to be'; it has first to be created in a community of persons, in the last analysis that means— in love; but love means powerlessness.

To love means, of course, to renounce any exercise of power and desire to interfere with, to 'manage', to gain for oneself or to 'possess' any other person. Love leaves the other person free; indeed love creates freedom in the other person; and in this case, creating freedom means self-effacement and renunciation. Love is realised in a great movement of self-emptying and, when once realized, is no more 'our own' love, but comes to us from the other person; it is pure gift. In this gift and as gift we become what we 'are'; that is, it is as gift that we begin 'to be'. The soul's trusting readiness to surrender itself and be at another's disposal... creates the possibility of love and, therefore, of being. In order to be, one must surrender oneself.

Ladislaus Boros, The Moment of Truth, Burns & Oates Ltd., 1962, page 43

The deepest need of man... is the need to overcome his separateness, to leave the prison of his aloneness...

The full answer lies in the achievement of interpersonal union, of fusion with another person, in *love*.

This desire for interpersonal fusion is the most powerful striving in man. It is the most fundamental passion, it is the force which keeps the human race together, the clan, the family, society...

Mature *love is union under the condition of preserving one's integrity*, one's individuality.

Love is an active power in man; a power which breaks through the walls which separate man from his fellow men, which unites him with others; love makes him overcome the sense of isolation and separateness, yet it permits him to be himself, to retain his integrity. In love the paradox occurs that two beings become one yet remain two... Envy, jealousy, ambition, any kind of greed are passions; love is an action, the practice of a human power, which can be practised only in freedom and never as the result of a compulsion.

Love is an activity, not a passive affect... The active character of love can be described by stating that love is primarily *giving*, not receiving...

Giving is more joyous than receiving, not because it is a deprivation, but because in the act of giving lies the expression of my aliveness...

Whoever is capable of giving himself is rich...

Beyond the element of giving, the active character of love becomes evident in the fact that it always implies certain basic elements, common to all forms of love. These are *care, responsibility, respect* and *knowledge*.

Erich Fromm, The Art of Loving, George Allen & Unwin Ltd., 1974, pages 14–25

RENEWAL

'Renewal'—restoration to original state; making (as good as) new; resuscitating, revivifying, regenerating; getting, beginning, making, saying, or giving, anew; become new again.

I n one of the quotations of this topic, Thomas Merton writes, 'By the reading of Scripture I am so renewed that all nature seems renewed around me and with me.'

I have also found this sort of renewal taking place when reflecting on the material in *Visions of Grace*, and the other anthologies which make up this series—*Visions of Faith, Hope, Love* and *Glory*. Positively speaking, renewal takes place not only when reading Scripture, but also when reflecting on this other material, taken from a wide variety of sources.

In reflection, great use is made of the mind and the heart, intuition and imagination, and our experience of life so far. When we reflect, we also open ourselves to receive something of 'the God within'—found in the depths of our being. As we mull over the contents we become aware, from time to time, of 'something' which renews us, 'something' of the Father, the Son, the Holy Spirit, and divine attributes such as life, light, truth, joy, grace, love and so on. This is what Christ meant when he said the kingdom of God is within you (or among you).

I can remember this happening in one of our reflection groups. We had been silently reflecting for about ten minutes on 'Maturity' when one of our women undergraduates suddenly broke the silence, exclaiming, 'Gosh, yes, that's it.' The penny had dropped in a big way and she experienced some sort of renewal. My experience has been less dramatic, but reflecting regularly does lead to a constant renewal of one's life.

He restores my soul. He leads me in paths of righteousness for his name's sake.

Psalm 23.3

Bless the Lord, O my soul; and all that is within me, bless his holy name! Bless the Lord, O my soul, and forget not all his benefits, who forgives all your iniquity, who heals all your diseases, who redeems your life from the Pit, who crowns you with steadfast love and mercy, who satisfies you with good as long as you live so that your youth is renewed like the eagle's.

Psalm 103.1-5

So we do not lose heart. Though our outer nature is wasting away, our inner nature is being renewed every day.

2 Corinthians 4.16

Do not lie to one another, seeing that you have put off the old nature with its practices and have put on the new nature, which is being renewed in knowledge after the image of its creator.

Colossians 3.9-10

By the reading of Scripture I am so renewed that all nature seems renewed around me and with me. The sky seems to be a pure, a cooler blue, the trees a deeper green, light is sharper on the outlines of the forest and the hills and the whole world is charged with the glory of God and I feel fire and music in the earth under my feet.

Thomas Merton, *The Sign of Jonas*, Sheldon Press, 1976, page 215

If men can be found who revolt against the spirit of thoughtlessness, and who are personalities sound enough and profound enough to let the ideals of ethical progress radiate from them as a force, there will start an activity of the spirit which will be strong enough to evoke a new mental and spiritual disposition in mankind.

Albert Schweitzer, *My Life and Thought*, translated by C.T. Campion, George Allen & Unwin Ltd., 1924, page 281

It behoves the doctor, if he will be called a doctor, to study the whole process, how God has restored the *universal* in man; which is fully clear and manifest in the person of Christ, from his entrance into the humanity, even to his ascension, and the sending of the Holy Ghost. Let him follow this entire process, and then he may find the universal, provided he be born again of God.

Jacob Boehme, *The Signature of All Things and Other Discourses*, Everyman's Library 1912–1934, (from William Law's English Edition—4 volumes), page 110

Regeneration or the renewal of our first birth and state is something entirely distinct from this first sudden conversion or call to repentance... it is not a thing that is done in an instant, but is a certain process, a gradual release from our captivity and disorder, consisting of several stages and degrees, both of death and life, which the soul must go through before it can have thoroughly put off the old man.

William Law, *Selected Mystical Writings of William Law*, edited by Stephen Hobhouse, Rockliff, 1948, page 25

Remember, the supreme wonder of the history of the Christian Church is that always in the moments when it has seemed most dead, out of its own body there has sprung up new life; so that in age after age it has renewed itself, and age after age by its renewal has carried the world forward into new stages of progress, as it will do for us in our day, if only we give ourselves in devotion to its Lord and take our place in its service.

William Temple, *Christian Faith and Life*, SCM Press Ltd., 1963, page 133

The depth and nature of a radical renewal of spirit is not within our active power to bring about. What we have to do is to prepare ourselves for the power that will effect it.

Our preparation is our openness, our vulnerability to the power of God dwelling in us. This is prayer.

This means transferring our conscious hopes for a renewal of the Church's relevance and effectiveness in the world from politics to prayer, from mind to heart, from committees to communities, from preaching to silence.

Religious renewal is a renewal in prayer.

John Main OSB, in *The Joy of Being*, selected by Clare Hallward, Darton, Longman & Todd, 1989, page 6

To have learned through enthusiasms and sorrows what things there are within and without the self that make for more life or less, for fruitfulness or sterility; to hold to the one and eschew the other; to seek to persuade and reveal and convince; to be ready to readjust one's values at the summons of a new truth that is known and felt; to be unweary in learning how to discriminate more sharply between the false and the true, the trivial and the significant, in life and in men and in works; to be prepared to take a risk for what seems the finer and better thing—that is, perhaps all we can do. Yet somehow, as I write the words, that 'perhaps all we can do' seems a very meagre phrase. The endeavour to be true to experience strikes me at this moment as the most precious privilege of all. To have found a loyalty from which one cannot escape, which one must for ever acknowledge—no, one cannot ask for more.

John Middleton Murry, *To An Unknown God*, Jonathan Cape Ltd., 1924, page 22

Here it is necessary to distinguish two paths through the crisis to a new start. We call the first one the human or earthly path. It ends in a certain sense of fellowship in a We that consists of humans—an earthly or human We. The second one may be characterized as the religious path. Its outlet is—at least in our time—Christianity with its sense of the manifestation of God in the We.

In the first case, the person has renounced all the former aims and values of his Ego. In anticipation this process seemed to be death itself, yet now, having passed through it, he realizes that he is alive in spite of the terrible breakdown. Now he sees that the world is quite different from what he formerly believed it to be. He seems to look upon life with new eyes, seeing connections, facts, values, goals, ways, possibilities he never saw before. A serious offence, which yesterday seemed to be unbearable, is now a mere trifle. Like old clothes, worn out and worthless, his egocentric prejudices, notions, and ideas have been discarded for something better. Formerly it was supposed that without these egocentric values life would be empty, meaningless, nothing at all—that when these old egocentric ideas had been dropped nothing would be left, that the rest of life would be emptiness. But now the person discovers how mistaken he was. For a new world opens up before him with a whole new life, richer and more colourful and more differentiated than anything he knew before.

This appearance in his life of the new values, new feelings and new aims, which completes the new insight into the actual realities of life, is the very essence of the crisis, and perhaps the essence of human life itself. As has been said before, it is inexplicable, and we must limit ourselves to describing it as carefully as possible. In the case of the human or earthly path through crisis, we come to feel that this 'miracle of rebirth' seems to be a natural element in human life. In the case of the religious path, we feel behind the sunrise of the new life a higher Living Power who brings it about.

Fritz Kunkel and Roy E. Dickerson, in *The Choice is Always Ours*, edited by Dorothy Berkley Phillips, Harper & Row, Publishers, Inc., 1960, page 95

New, Old, Renew, Refresh. These words are, of course, frequently used in the Bible in their ordinary everyday sense. But the word 'new' acquires its distinctively biblical meaning whenever it takes on an eschatological significance and implies the passing away of the old order—this present world-age—and the breaking in of the new, 'the world to come'. Thus the Old Testament looks forward to the making of a 'new covenant' (Jer.31.31; cf. Ezek.34.25, 37.26), the imparting of a 'new spirit' (Ezek.11.19, 18.31, 36.26), the making of new heavens and a new earth (Isa 65.17, 66.22), and so on. The New Testament claims that the 'new age' has already broken in and has manifested itself in Jesus and his Church (cf. Heb.6.5); the new covenant has been made and sealed in the death of Jesus as Messiah (Mark 14.24, Heb.9.15); the 'new Spirit' has been given and brings 'seasons of refreshing from the presence of the Lord' (Acts 3.19); the new creation has been achieved (II Cor.5.17, Gal.6.15, Eph.2.15, 4.24, Col.3.10). There is thus a very distinctive Christian meaning in the word 'new' in the 'New' Testament: Christians have a new song (Rev.5.9, 14.3) and a new commandment (John 13.34, 1 John 2.8); in their baptism, being new persons, they receive a new name (cf. Rev.2.17). The very proclamation (*kerugma*)—the message heralded—is *news*, good news (*euangelion*). Religious truth always strikes one afresh and is always news, however often we have previously experienced or heard it (cf. Lam.3.23: 'Thy mercies are new every morning') and this is supremely true of the news of Jesus' Resurrection. But over and beyond this in-breaking of the new age, which was manifest in Christ and the Kingdom of God which he proclaimed, the New Testament looks forward to a full and utter realization of the eschatologically new—at the end of this age, the Parousia or Second Coming of Christ. The word 'new' can be used in an absolute sense only in respect of the Parousia. The new heavens and new earth will then be revealed (II Pet.3.12f., Rev.21.1,5), and the New Jerusalem will be established (Rev.3.12, 21.2); until this time comes, the heavens must receive Jesus—'until the times of the restoration of all things' (Acts 3.21).

Alan Richardson, in *A Theological Word Book of the Bible*, edited by Alan Richardson, SCM Press Ltd., 1975, page 159

SACRAMENTS

'Sacraments'—religious ceremonies or acts regarded as an outward and visible sign of an inward and spiritual grace.

T he sacrament of baptism is a good illustration of an outward and visible sign of an inward and spiritual grace. The outward and visible sign is water, and the inward and spiritual grace is a rebirth (following the divine inbreathing of the Genesis story of the creation of man) 'in the name of (nature of) the Father, in the name of (nature of) the Son, and in the name of (nature of) the Holy Spirit'. In some modern baptism services there is a further sacramental element. A lighted candle (an outward and visible sign) is given to the godparents (suitably named) and the inward and spiritual grace is Christ the light of the world, now coming into the baptized person's life.

In the sacrament of Holy Communion, the outward and visible sign is bread and wine, and the inward and spiritual grace is the body and blood of Christ, now taken afresh into the life of the communicant. We are just beginning to appreciate once again the immense value of this inward and spiritual grace. At one level we receive the body and blood of Christ. At another level we are at one and the same time receiving the Father, the Holy Spirit, and divine attributes of life, light, truth, joy, love and so on.

In reflection groups I have also noticed something akin to the sacramental at work. The outward and visible sign is the words of the chosen topic, and the inward and spiritual grace is the effect these words have on us. I have often seen people deeply moved by a new truth they have spotted for the first time in a reflection group. To an outward observer it looks as though the inward and spiritual grace has just taken root.

Unless you eat the flesh of the Son of man and drink his blood, you have no life in you; he who eats my flesh and drinks my blood has eternal life, and I will raise him up at the last day. For my flesh is food indeed, and my blood is drink indeed. He who eats my flesh and drinks my blood abides in me, and I in him.
John 6.53-56

And Peter said to them, 'Repent, and be baptized every one of you in the name of Jesus Christ for the forgiveness of your sins; and you shall receive the gift of the Holy Spirit.'
Acts 2.38

For I received from the Lord what I also delivered to you, that the Lord Jesus on the night when he was betrayed took bread, and when he had given thanks, he broke it, and said, 'This is my body which is for you. Do this in remembrance of me.' In the same way also the cup, after supper, saying, 'This cup is the new covenant in my blood. Do this, as often as you drink it, in remembrance of me.'
1 Corinthians 11.23-25

And let him who is thirsty come, let him who desires take the water of life without price.
Revelation 22.17

An outward and visible sign of an inward and spiritual grace.
Book of Common Prayer, Catechism

Embodied acts, such as the Sacramental act, are beneath acts purely *mental* and spiritual; such as Prayer is.
Benjamin Whichcote, *Moral and Religious Aphorisms*, 1930, page 124, Century XI, No.1082

Whatever we see, wherever we look, whether we recognize it as true or not, we cannot touch or handle the things of earth and not, in that very moment, be confronted with the sacraments of heaven.

C.A. Coulson, *Science and Christian Belief*, Oxford University Press, 1955, page 102

A sacrament is something more than a divine poem, because it conveys (as is believed by those who make use of it) not only God's meaning to the mind, but God Himself to the whole person of the worshipper.

William Temple, *Nature, Man and God*, Macmillan & Co. Ltd., 1934, page 484

When faith exists as a struggle to believe in spite of empirical and temperamental pressure to unbelief, when the whole life of feeling is dead, when nothing is left but stark loyalty to God as He is dimly and waveringly apprehended to be—then the sheer objectivity, even the express materialism, of a sacrament gives it a value that nothing else can have.

William Temple, *Nature, Man and God*, Macmillan & Co. Ltd., 1934, page 491

The particular sacraments are meant to teach us that all life is sacramental. Every deliberate act should be, in a sense, the outward sign of inward grace. A sacrament is more than a symbol. A symbol leads us from the lower to the higher; a sacrament brings us back again to earth, but infuses a heavenly meaning and divine potency into common things and actions.

W.R. Inge, *Personal Religion and the Life of Devotion*, Longmans, Green & Co. Ltd., 1924, page 47

Let me ask you a question: are we still able to understand what a sacrament means? The more we are estranged from nature, the less we can answer affirmatively. That is why, in our time, the sacraments have lost so much of their significance for individuals and Churches. For in the sacraments nature participates in the process of salvation. Bread and wine, water and light, and all the great elements of nature become the bearers of spiritual meaning and saving power. Natural and spiritual powers are united—reunited—in the sacrament. The word appeals to our intellect and may move our will. The sacrament, if its meaning is still alive, grasps our unconscious as well as our conscious being. It grasps the creative ground of our being. It is the symbol of nature and spirit, united in salvation.

Paul Tillich, *The Shaking of the Foundations*, SCM Press Ltd., 1949, page 86

The great central act of our religion is not of our devising, it is given to us. We do not have to make our worship; we enter into, claim as our own, a worship God himself has given to us. God has done and does everything for us; all is pure grace. The sacraments affirm this.

Never are we more truly Christian than when we approach the sacraments with the Christian community. This is where God 'touches' us. Here, at this moment, is our guarantee.

What need have we of a word spoken inwardly when we hear the word spoken outwardly: 'My Body for you', 'Your sins are forgiven'.

Our religion is historical; earthly because divine. God affirms the whole of our human being, wants it all, sanctifies it all, comes to us through its reality. In our sacred liturgy we have the concrete certainty of divine encounter and action. We are grounded on objectivity rather than on the quicksands of our poor subjectivity which can, in certain states, seem so sure, so divine.

Ruth Burrows, in *The Watchful Heart*, edited by Elizabeth Ruth Obbard, Darton, Longman & Todd, 1988, page 25

When psalmist or prophet calls Israel to lift their eyes to the hills, or to behold how the heavens declare the glory of God, or to listen to that unbroken tradition, which day passes to day and night to night, of the knowledge of the Creator, it is not proofs to doubting minds which he offers: it is spiritual nourishment to hungry souls. These are not arguments—they are sacraments.

When we Christians go to the Lord's Supper, we go not to have the Lord proved to us, but to feed upon a life and a love of whose existence we are past all doubt. Our sacrament fills all the mouths by which needy faith is fed—such as outward sight, and imagination, and memory, and wonder, and love. Now very much what the Lord's Supper is to us for fellowship with God and feeding upon Him, that were the glory of the heavens, and the everlasting hills, and the depths of the sea, and the vision of the stars to the Hebrews. They were the sacraments of God. By them faith was fed, and the spirit of man entered into the enjoyment of God, whose existence indeed he had never doubted, but whom he had lost, forgotten, or misunderstood.

George Adam Smith, *The Book of Isaiah*, Hodder & Stoughton Ltd., 1927, Volume II, page 91

The sacraments are a perpetual witness that man thus needs something done to him, here and now. They declare that an access of Supernature is needed, which he cannot get alone: and that this access of Supernature will reach him most easily along natural paths. Their whole emphasis is on this given-ness. They remind us that our innate thirst for the Infinite is not the governing fact of our religious life, and cannot be satisfied by any effort we are able to make. That Infinite must come to us before we can go to it and it is within the sensory and historical frame of human experience that such supernatural gifts are best and most surely received by our successive and sense-conditioned souls. Thus the sacramental principle continues to press upon us that profound truth which the Incarnation so vividly exhibits: that the whole of man's spiritual history, both corporate and solitary, involves and entirely rests in the free self-giving of God—is conditioned from first to last by the action of His all-penetrating, prevenient and eternal love . . . Through the Christian sacraments that self-giving, of which the Incarnation is the supreme example, finds another and a continuous expression: sense here becoming the vehicle through which the very Spirit of Life enters into the little lives of men.

Evelyn Underhill, *Man and the Supernatural*, Methuen & Co. Ltd., 1927, page 180

SACRIFICE

'Sacrifice'—giving up of thing for the sake of another that is higher or more urgent.

I was born a few months before the outbreak of the Second World War, so my early years were dominated by an atmosphere of war. One of the verses from the Bible I soon came to know was about *sacrifice*: 'Greater love has no man than this, that a man lay down his life for his friends.' I sometimes wonder if this verse has been influential in the development of my life, for an element of sacrifice seems to have been built into my psyche.

The importance of sacrifice can easily be detected in our college chapel. If one can avert one's eyes from the beautifully painted van Linge windows, and focus on the centre of the East Window, there is a figure of Christ on the cross. I remember coming into the chapel early one summer's morning and the rising sun was shining brilliantly around the cross. We are not meant to like this East Window (it is inferior to the van Linge windows) but on that particular morning it was glorious.

Immediately beneath the centre of the East Window, behind the altar, is an intricate and delicate ancient woodcarving. Here we find the legendary pelican feeding her fledgelings on her own blood, considered as an emblem of Jesus Christ, who fed or redeemed his flock with his own blood.

In this section Carlo Carretto asks the question: Do you want to know the secret of true happiness? of deep and genuine peace? Do you want to solve at a blow all your difficulties in relations to your neighbour, bring all polemic to an end, avoid all dissension? Well, decide here and now to love things and men as Jesus loved them, that is to the point of self-sacrifice.

The sacrifice of the wicked is an abomination to the Lord, but the prayer of the upright is his delight.

Proverbs 15.8

For I desire steadfast love and not sacrifice, the knowledge of God, rather than burnt offerings.

Hosea 6.6

Present your bodies as a living sacrifice, holy and acceptable to God, which is your spiritual worship.
Romans 12.1

Do not neglect to do good and to share what you have, for such sacrifices are pleasing to God.
Hebrews 13.16

Was anything real ever gained without sacrifice of some kind?
Arthur Helps, *Friends in Council*, George Routledge & Sons Ltd., 1907, page 165

In common things the law of sacrifice takes the form of positive duty.
J.A. Froude, *Short Studies on Great Subjects*, Longmans, Green & Co. Ltd., 1907, Volume IV, page 165

Inwardness, mildness, and self-renouncement do make for man's happiness.
Matthew Arnold, *The Complete Prose Works of Matthew Arnold*, Volume VI, *Dissent and Dogma*, edited by R.H. Super, Ann Arbor, The University of Michigan Press, 1968, 'Literature and Dogma,' Ch.3, page 229

Too long a sacrifice,
Can make a stone of the heart.
W.B. Yeats, *The Collected Poems of W.B. Yeats*, Macmillan & Co. Ltd., 1973, page 204, 'Easter 1916'

Sacrifice is the first element of religion, and resolves itself in theological language into the love of God.
J.A. Froude, *Short Studies on Great Subjects*, Longmans, Green & Co. Ltd., 1907, Volume IV, page 176

Standing before God the only thing we have to offer him is ourselves. And the extraordinary part is that this is exactly what he wants.
Hubert van Zeller, *Considerations*, Sheed & Ward Ltd., 1974, page 123

The church's glory is not its power and numerical superiority, nor its system or its discipline or its theology. Its glory lies in its willingness to sacrifice.
Hubert van Zeller, *Considerations*, Sheed & Ward Ltd., 1974, page 79

Without sacrifice there is no resurrection. Nothing grows and blooms save by giving. All you try to save in yourself wastes and perishes.
André Gide, *Fruits of the Earth*, Penguin Books Ltd, in association with Secker & Warburg, 1976, page 156

Measure thy life by loss instead of gain;
Not by the wine drunk, but the wine poured forth;
For love's strength standeth in love's sacrifice;
And whoso suffers most hath most to give.
Harriet Eleanor Hamilton King, *The Disciples*, Kegan Paul & Co., 1880, page 100

The vine lives to give its life blood. Its flower is small, its fruit abundant; and when that fruit is mature and the vine has for a moment become glorious, the treasure of the grapes is torn down and the vine is cut back to the stem and next year blooms again,
Not bitter for the torment undergone. Not barren for the fulness yielded up.
William Temple, *Readings in St. John's Gospel*, First and Second Series, Macmillan & Co. Ltd., 1947, page 252

If sacrifice, total self-giving to God's mysterious purpose, is what is asked of us, His answer to that sacrifice is the gift of power. Easter and Whitsuntide complete the Christian Mystery by showing us first Our Lord Himself and then His chosen apostles possessed of a new power—the power of the Spirit—which changed every situation in which they were placed. That supernatural power is still the inheritance of every Christian, and our idea of Christianity is distorted and incomplete unless we rely on it. It is this power and only this which can bring in the new Christian society of which we hear so much. We ought to pray for it; expect it and trust it; and as we do this, we shall gradually become more and more sure of it.
Evelyn Underhill, *The Fruits of the Spirit*, Longmans, Green & Co. Ltd., 1949, page 71

Do you want to know the secret of true happiness? of deep and genuine peace?

Do you want to solve at a blow all your difficulties in relations with your neighbour, bring all polemic to an end, avoid all dissension?

Well, decide here and now to love things and men as Jesus loved them, that is, to the point of self-sacrifice.

Don't bother with the book-keeping of love; love without keeping accounts.

If you know someone who is decent and likeable, love him, but if someone else is very *un*likeable, love him just the same.

If someone greets you and smiles, greet him and smile back, but if someone else treads on your feet, smile just the same. If someone does you a good turn, thank the Lord for it, but if someone else slanders you, persecutes you, curses you, strikes you, thank him and carry on.

Do not say: 'I'm right, he's wrong.' Say: 'I must love him as myself.' This is the kind of love Jesus taught: a love which transforms, vivifies, enriches, brings peace.

Carlo Carretto, *Love is for Living*, translated by Jeremy Moiser, Darton, Longman & Todd, 1976, page 144

The act of making a sacrifice consists in the first place in giving something which belongs to me. Everything which belongs to me bears the stamp of 'mineness,' that is, it has a subtle identity with my ego . . .

In other words, out of the natural state of identity with what is 'mine' there grows the ethical task of sacrificing oneself . . . One ought to realize that when one gives or surrenders oneself there are corresponding claims attached, the more so the less one knows of them. The conscious realization of this alone guarantees that the giving is a real sacrifice. For if I know and admit that I am giving myself, foregoing myself, and do not want to be repaid for it, then I have sacrificed my claim, and thus a part of myself. Consequently, all absolute giving, a giving which is a total from the start, is a self-sacrifice. Ordinary giving for which no return is received is felt as a loss; but a sacrifice is meant to be like a loss, so that one may be sure that the egoistic claim no longer exists . . . Yet, looked at in another way, this intentional loss is also a gain, for if you can give yourself it proves that you possess yourself. Nobody can give what he has not got. So anyone who can sacrifice himself and forgo his claim must have had it; in other words, he must have been conscious of the claim. This presupposes an act of considerable self-knowledge, lacking which one remains permanently unconscious of such claims . . .

The sacrifice proves that you possess yourself, for it does not mean just letting yourself be passively taken: it is a conscious and deliberate self-surrender, which proves that you have full control of yourself, that is, of your ego. The ego thus becomes the object of a moral act, for 'I' am making a decision on behalf of an authority which is supraordinate to my ego nature. I am, as it were, deciding against my ego and renouncing my claim . . .

. . . in giving up my egoistic claim I shall challenge my ego personality to revolt. I can also be sure that the power which suppresses this claim, and thus suppresses me, must be the self. Hence it is the self that causes me to make the sacrifice; nay, more, it compels me to make it . . .

. . . We have seen that a sacrifice only takes place when we feel the self actually carrying it out on ourselves. We may also venture to surmise that in so far as the self stands to us in the relation of father to son, the self in some sort feels our sacrifice as a sacrifice of itself. From that sacrifice we gain ourselves—our 'self'—for we have only what we give. But what does the self gain? We see it entering into manifestation, freeing itself from unconscious projection, and, as it grips us, entering into our lives and so passing from unconsciousness into consciousness, from potentiality into actuality. What it is in the diffuse unconscious state we do not know; we only know that in becoming ourself it has become man.

C.G. Jung, *Psychology of Religion: East and West*, Volume II of *The Collected Works of C.G. Jung*, Second Edition, translated by R.F.C. Hull, Routledge & Kegan Paul Ltd., 1969, page 255

SEEKING

'Seeking'—making search or inquiry for; trying to be anxious to find or get, asking (thing or person) for advice.

Several years ago I was on a chalet reading party in the French Alps with a dozen undergraduates. One of our Junior Research Fellows dropped in for a couple of days. He wanted to see as much of Mont Blanc as possible in the limited time available; so the two of us went for a walk by the Bionnassay glacier, up to a place called *Le Nid d'Aigle*, and back.

We had not gone very far before he made a direct request. 'Bill, tell me what do you believe in.' 'Oh, gosh,' I thought to myself, 'he's so bright, he is never going to believe this.'

Anyway a direct request warrants a direct answer so I gave him an outline of my vision of faith; of the divine inbreathing of the Genesis story of the creation of man; of this being fully worked out in the life of Jesus Christ; of St Paul realizing what Christ had experienced we can all in some measure also experience—something of the presence of the Father in ourselves, the Son, the Holy Spirit, and divine attributes such as life, light, joy, truth and love. This seemed to strike a chord in him.

We both paused for a breather and gazed up the Bionnassay glacier. Suddenly, in this magnificent scenery, we were both gripped by an amazing sight—the actual start of an avalanche. For a split second we saw a great mass of ice suspended in mid-air, before it slowly crashed down on the ice below.

Something clicked into place in my companion. To my great surprise he found what he had been seeking. As a result of this experience I now encourage those who are 'seeking' to have a good look at the *Visions* series—in the best possible scenery.

> You who seek God, let your hearts revive.
> Psalm 69.32

> You will seek me and find me; when you seek me with all your heart, I will be found by you.
> Jeremiah 29.13-14

> Seek, and you will find.
> Matthew 7.7

> For whoever would draw near to God must believe that he exists and that he rewards those who seek him.
> Hebrews 11.6

> A man travels the world over in search of what he needs and returns home to find it.
> George Moore, *The Brook Kerith*, William Heinemann Ltd., 1927, page 121

> Even in the midst of the lowest pleasures, the most abandoned voluptuary is still seeking God; nay more, as far as regards what is positive in his acts, that is to say in all that makes them an analogue of the true Love, it is God Himself Who, in him and for him, seeks Himself.
> Etienne Gilson, *The Spirit of Mediaeval Philosophy*, translated by A.H.C. Downes, Sheed & Ward Ltd., 1950, page 274

> Know that, by nature, every creature seeks to become like God... Nature's intent is neither food nor drink, nor clothing, nor comfort, nor anything else in which God is left out. Covertly, nature seeks, hunts, tries to ferret out the track on which God may be found.
> Meister Eckhart, *Meister Eckhart*, translated by Raymond B. Blakney, Harper & Row, Publishers, Inc., 1941, page 167

> Hold fast to God and he will add every good thing. Seek God and you shall find him and all good with him... To the man who cleaves to God, God cleaves and adds virtue. Thus, what you have sought before, now seeks you; what once you pursued, now pursues you; what once you fled, now flees you. Everything comes to him who truly comes to God, bringing all divinity with it, while all that is strange and alien flies away.
> Meister Eckhart, *Meister Eckhart*, translated by Raymond B. Blakney, Harper & Row, Publishers, Inc., 1941, page 7

The God of faith is not a God who is silent, a God who is inactive, a God who is not present to us.

To you who are a person, He is a person; to you who have life, He is life; to you who have love, He is love. He is the 'Other' who is searching for you.

He has always been searching for you.

And you, too, are looking for the 'Other', even when—and it often happens—you feel you are doing something quite different.

In the end everything we do on this earth is pushed on solely by this search for the 'Other'. We search for Him first in things. Then in creatures, with ever more intimate relationships. Finally, in the maturity of faith, the 'Other' shows Himself to us as a transcendent and autonomous presence, detached from things and creatures, beyond creation: the Absolute.

I can never insist enough that this beginning of the life of faith is governed by God himself. It is His gift, and we cannot anticipate it by a single instant, however many mountains of virtue we may heap up.

Carlo Carretto, *The God Who Comes*, translated by Rose Mary Hancock, Darton, Longman & Todd, 1974, page 27

Your servant Isaiah loved to describe you as a '*hidden God*' (Isaiah 45.15).

You hide in the creation.

You hide in history.

You hide in the Incarnation.

You hide in the Eucharist.

You hide within us.

You hide all the time.

And you want us to discover you … like this … on our own … in our own time … when we need you.

Generally, need is what impels us to seek you.

The need for the absolute, for eternity, light, freedom, love. Above all, we seek you in our difficulties, when we no longer know which way to turn, when we are disillusioned by our pleasures.

But even then you hide what you are doing and give us the impression that we ourselves are conducting the search.

I believe that your motive is always the same: you do not want to force us.

You do not want a marriage of convenience, you do not want to damage our freedom.

And when we get up and come to you, taking the road prepared by you from the outset, we feel perfectly free.

Carlo Carretto, *Summoned by Love*, translated by Alan Neame, Darton, Longman & Todd, 1977, page 48

Seek and ye shall find. But what is one to seek? A conscious and living communion with the Lord. This is given by the grace of God, but it is also essential that we ourselves should work, that we ourselves should come to meet Him. How? By always remembering God, who is near the heart and even present within it. To succeed in this rememberance it is advisable to accustom oneself to the continual repetition of the Jesus Prayer, 'Lord Jesus Christ, Son of God, have mercy upon me,' holding in mind the thought of God's nearness, His presence in the heart. But it must also be understood that in itself the Jesus Prayer is only an outer oral prayer; inner prayer is to stand before the Lord, continually crying out to Him without words.

By this means remembrance of God will be established in the mind, and the countenance of God will be in your soul like the sun. If you put something cold in the sun it begins to grow warm, and in the same way your soul will be warmed by the remembrance of God, who is the spiritual sun. What follows on from this will presently appear.

Your first task is to acquire the habit of repeating the Jesus Prayer unceasingly. So begin: and continually repeat and repeat, but all the time keep before you the thought of our Lord. And herein lies everything.

Theophan the Recluse, *The Art of Prayer, An Orthodox Anthology*, compiled by Igumen Chariton of Valamo, translated by E. Kadloubovsky and E.M. Palmer, edited by Timothy Ware, Faber & Faber Ltd., 1973, page 121

I remember one day in the early spring-time I was listening to the sounds of a wood, and thinking only of one thing, the same of which I had constantly thought for two years—I was again seeking for a God.

I said to myself, 'It is well, there is no God, there is none that has a reality apart from my own imaginings, none as real as my own life—there is none such. Nothing, no miracle can prove there is, for miracles only exist in my own unreasonable imagination.'

And then I asked myself, 'But my conception of the God whom I seek, whence comes it?' And again life flashed joyously through my veins. All around me seemed to revive, to have a new meaning. My joy, though, did not last long, for reason continued its work: 'The conception of God is not God. Conception is what goes on within myself; the conception of God is an idea which I am able to rouse in my mind or not, as I choose; it is not what I seek, something without which life could not be.' Then again all seemed to die around and within me, and again I wished to kill myself.

After this I began to retrace the process which had gone on within myself, the hundred-times-repeated discouragement and revival. I remembered that I had lived only when I believed in a God. As it was before so it was now; I had only to know God, and I lived; I had only to forget Him, not to believe in Him, and I died. What was this discouragement and revival? I do not live when I lose faith in the existence of God; I should long ago have killed myself if I had not had a dim hope of finding Him. I only really live when I feel and seek Him. 'What more, then, do I seek?' A voice seemed to cry within me, 'This is He, He without whom there is no life! To know God and to live are one. God is life! Live to seek God, and life will not be without Him.' And stronger than ever rose up life within and around me, and the light that then shone never left me again.

Leo Tolstoy, *How I Came to Believe*, C.W. Daniel Ltd., 1922, page 50

SELF

'Self'—person's or thing's own individuality or essence, person or thing as object of introspection or reflexive action.

S ome writers in previous generations have made a distinction between the False Self and the Real Self.

The False Self is usually made up of a number of elements. Firstly, self-centredness or selfishness, often cunningly disguised. Secondly, a single-minded pursuit of wealth and what money can buy. Thirdly, a striving for status and success; i.e. an ego trip. Fourthly, a quest for happiness and pleasure, often with sexual connotations. In brief, the False Self is completely taken up with the 'earthy and creaturely'.

A person with a False Self seems to be wearing a mask and appears unreal. I remember attending a conference in which the organizers had set up a whiteboard so participants could record thoughts and feelings about the Conference. Someone had written (somewhat unkindly) the following comment about one of the speakers: 'Could the real Dr ... please stand up.'

The Real Self is rather different. In this section W.R. Inge enables us to understand the nature of the Real Self: '*We* are potentially all things; our personality is what we are able to realise of the infinite wealth which our divine-human nature contains hidden in its depths.'

The Real Self discovers the 'infinite wealth' of our 'divine-human nature' (the God within) and in this finds fulfilment, contentment and peace. This is integrated with the 'earthy-creaturely', producing a whole well-balanced person, at ease with oneself, and with other people. There is now no longer any need for pretence and cut-throat competition.

Keep your heart with all vigilance; for from it flow the springs of life.

Proverbs 4.23

A man without self-control is like a city broken into and left without walls.
Proverbs 25.28

Do not labour for the food which perishes, but for the food which endures to eternal life, which the Son of man will give to you; for on him has God the Father set his seal.
John 6.27

We know that our old self was crucified with him so that the sinful body might be destroyed, and we might no longer be enslaved to sin. For he who has died is freed from sin. But if we have died with Christ, we believe that we shall also live with him.
Romans 6.6-8

The true value of a human being is determined primarily by the measure and the sense in which he has attained liberation from the self.
Albert Einstein, *Ideas and Opinions*, Souvenir Press (Educational & Academic) Ltd., 1973, page 12

We are potentially all things; our personality is what we are able to realise of the infinite wealth which our divine-human nature contains hidden in its depths.
W.R. Inge, *The Philosophy of Plotinus*, Longmans, Green & Co. Ltd., 1918, Volume I, page 248

Not in the clamour of the crowded street,
Not in the shouts and plaudits of the throng,
But in ourselves, are triumph and defeat.
Henry Wadsworth Longfellow, *The Poetical Works of Longfellow*, Humphrey Milford, Oxford University Press, 1913, page 717, 'The Poems,' l.12

Begin to search and dig in thine own Field for this *Pearl of Eternity*, that lies hidden in it; it cannot cost Thee too much, nor canst thou buy it too dear, for it is *All*, and when thou hast found it, thou wilt know, that all which thou hast sold or given away for it, is as mere a Nothing, as a Bubble upon the Water.
William Law, *The Spirit of Prayer*, full text, edited by Sidney Spencer, James Clarke & Co. Ltd., 1969, page 44

But can one actually find oneself in someone else? In someone else's love? Or even in the mirror someone else holds up for one? I believe that true identity is found, as Eckhart once said, by 'going into one's own ground and knowing oneself.' It is found in creative activity springing from within. It is found, paradoxically, when one loses oneself. One must lose one's life to find it.
Anne Morrow Lindbergh, *Gift from the Sea*, Chatto & Windus Ltd., 1974, page 68

Sincerity is the act whereby each of us at once knows and makes himself...
It is the quality of sincerity to oblige me to be myself, that is to become, by my own agency, what I am. It is a search for my own essence, which begins to be adulterated as soon as I borrow from outside the motives of my actions. For this essence is never an object that I contemplate, but a work that I carry out, the bringing into play of certain powers that are within me, and which atrophy if I cease to exercise them. Sincerity consists in a certain tranquil courage by which we dare to enter existence, as we are.
Louis Lavelle, in *Existentialism*, Paul Foulquié, translated by Kathleen Raine, Dennis Dobson Ltd., 1947, page 119

Fully realized human beings are more than body and soul (psyche). They are body, soul and spirit. This spirit is there within every human being.
To relate consciously to the 'spirit' is, in the words of Jesus, to find the true self.
Without this 'self-realization' we live as isolated human beings. We are unfulfilled and falling short of our destiny as human beings.
United to our true or transcendental selves we find our union with Christ.
Beyond this we find a true unity or communion with others. All barriers of separation are transcended. Further still, we find a unity with all creation. The unity of mankind can

never be attained on the level of body and soul alone. Only when we awaken to the true self can we find that true harmony with others and with the created order.

Bede Griffiths OSB, in *The Universal Christ*, edited by Peter Spink, Darton, Longman & Todd, 1990, page 38

The all-one idea can definitely be realized or embodied only in the fulness of completed individualities, this means that the final aim of the whole matter is the higher development of each individuality in the perfected unity of all, but this latter necessarily comprises in itself also our own life-aim, which for us therefore no consideration or possibility separates or isolates from the aim common to all. We are just as necessary to the world, as the world is to us. The universe from time immemorial is interested in the preservation, development and perpetuation of all that is really necessary and desirable for us, all that is absolute and of worth in our individuality. And it remains to us only to accept, if possible more consciously and actively, our share in the general historical process—for our own selves and for all others *inseparably.*

Vladimir Solovyev, *The Meaning of Love*, translated by Jane Marshall, Geoffrey Bles Ltd., The Centenary Press, 1945, page 72

The question is always: *Who am I?* and until that is discovered I don't see how one can really direct anything in one's self. *Is there a me?* One must be certain of that before one has a real unshakeable leg to stand on. And I don't believe for one moment these questions can be settled by the head alone. It is this life of the head, this intellectual life at the expense of all the rest which has got us into this state. How can it get us out of it? I see no hope of escape except by learning to love in our emotional and instinctive being as well, and to balance all three.

You see, if I were allowed one single cry to God, that cry would be: *I want to be REAL.* Until I am that I don't see why I shouldn't be at the mercy of old Eve in her various manifestations for ever... At this present moment all I know really, really, is that though one thing after another has been taken from me, I am not annihilated, and that I hope—more than hope—believe. It is hard to explain.

Katherine Mansfield, *The Letters of Katherine Mansfield*, edited by J. Middleton Murry, Constable & Co. Ltd., 1928, Volume II, page 266

If we are to love sincerely and with simplicity, we must first of all overcome the fear of not being loved. And this cannot be done by forcing ourselves to believe in some illusion, saying that we are loved when we are not. We must somehow strip ourselves of our greatest illusions about ourselves, frankly recognize in how many ways we are unlovable, descend into the depths of our being until we come to the basic reality that is in us, and learn to see that we are lovable after all, in spite of everything!

This is a difficult job. It can only really be done by a lifetime of genuine humility. But sooner or later we must distinguish between what we are not and what we are. We must accept the fact that we are not what we would like to be. We must cast off our false, exterior self like the cheap and showy garment that it is. We must find our real self, in all its elemental poverty but also in its very great and very simple dignity: created to be a child of God, and capable of loving with something of God's own sincerity and His unselfishness.

Thomas Merton, *No Man is an Island*, Hollis & Carter, 1955, page 178

Man is not himself. He has lost himself in the falsities and illusions of a massive organization. How can he recover his authenticity and his true identity? What is meant by identity?... Many facets of the concept could be considered.

For practical purposes here we are talking about one's own authentic and personal beliefs and convictions, based on experience of oneself as a person, experience of one's ability to choose and reject even good things which are not relevant to one's own life.

One does not receive 'identity' in this sense along with life and vegetative existence. To have identity is not merely to have a face and a name, a recognizable physical presence,

Identity in this deep sense is something that one must create for oneself by choices that are significant and that require a courageous commitment in the face of anguish and risk. This means much more than just having an address and a name in the telephone book. It means having a belief one stands by; it means having certain definite ways of responding to life, of meeting its demands, of loving other people, and in the last analysis, of serving God. In this sense, identity is one's witness to truth in one's life.

Thomas Merton, *Contemplation in a World of Action*, George Allen & Unwin Ltd., 1971, page 58

Every moment and every event of every man's life on earth plant something in his soul. For just as the wind carries thousands of winged seeds, so each moment brings with it germs of spiritual vitality that come to rest imperceptibly in the minds and wills of men...

We must learn to realize that the love of God seeks us in every situation, and seeks our good. His inscrutable love seeks our awakening. True, since this awakening implies a kind of death to our exterior self, we will dread His coming in proportion as we are identified with this exterior self and attached to it...

There is an irreducible opposition between the deep, transcendent self that awakens only in contemplation, and the superficial, external self which we commonly identify with the first person singular. We must remember that this superficial 'I' is not our real self. It is our 'individuality' and our 'empirical self' but it is not truly the hidden and mysterious person in whom we subsist before the eyes of God. The 'I' that works in the world, thinks about itself, observes its own reactions and talks about itself is not the true 'I' that has been united to God in Christ... Contemplation is precisely the awareness that this 'I' is really 'not I' and the awakening of the unknown 'I' that is beyond observation and reflection and is incapable of commenting upon itself.

Thomas Merton, *New Seeds of Contemplation*, Burns & Oates Ltd., 1962, pages 12 and 5

SERENITY

'Serenity'—calmness, placidity, tranquillity, being unperturbed.

C.S. Duthie, in his book *God in His World*, wrote: 'The serenity relevant for our time is a serenity that does not bypass the turmoil and torment of the atomic age but sends its roots down through the agonies to the life and power of God.'

I find this sentence helpful because it fits in with the vision of faith which has evolved for me during the last twenty years. Most of us experience turmoil, torment and agonies in everyday life. If we balance this by developing an inner life, we become rooted in the life and power of God, and at times experience serenity. As I have indicated elsewhere there is an enormous resource of divine life in the depths of our being— Father, Son, Holy Spirit, and divine attributes such as life, light, truth, love, joy, grace and power and so on. When we tap into this resource we experience precious moments of serenity.

I am very fond of my set of rooms in University College. Sometimes during a hectic term, especially towards the end of a term, I feel surrounded by turmoil, torment and agonies. In spite of this there is an atmosphere of peace in my sitting-room. Perhaps this is because the outer walls are a metre thick, or it may have something to do with the artistic design of the room. In these surroundings I can cope with stress and strain provided I keep up a regular pattern of reflection. In reflection I become rooted in the life and power of God. In this way I can recharge my batteries and get things into perspective. St Augustine wrote: 'You made us for yourself and our hearts find no peace until they rest in you.' This is what serenity means to me.

He made the storm be still, and the waves of the sea were hushed. Then they were glad because they had quiet, and he brought them to their desired haven.

Psalm 107.29-30

I have calmed and quieted my soul, like a child quieted at its mother's breast; like a child that is quieted is my soul.

Psalm 131.2

Be patient, therefore, brethren, until the coming of the Lord. Behold, the farmer waits for the precious fruit of the earth, being patient over it until it receives the early and late rain. You also be patient. Establish your hearts.

James 5.7 8

We call those happy who were steadfast.

James 5.11

You made us for yourself and our hearts find no peace until they rest in you.

St Augustine, *Confessions*, translated with an introduction by R.S. Pine-Coffin, Penguin Books Ltd., 1964, page 21

All men who live with any degree of serenity live by some assurance of grace.

Reinhold Niebuhr, *Reflections on the End of an Era*, Charles Scribner's Sons, 1936, page 284

He who would be serene and pure needs but one thing, detachment.

Meister Eckhart, *Meister Eckhart*, Franz Pfeiffer, translated by C. de B. Evans, John M. Watkins, 1956, Volume I, page 341

Serenity of Mind, and Calmness of Thought are a better Enjoyment; than any thing *without* us.

Benjamin Whichcote, *Moral and Religious Aphorisms*, 1930, Century III, No.280

Serene yet strong, majestic yet sedate,
Swift without violence, without terror great.

Matthew Prior, *The Poetical Works of Matthew Prior*, edited by Charles Cowden Clarke, William P. Nimmo, 1868, page 116, 'Carmen Seculare for the Year MDCC,' 1.282

He who is of a calm and happy nature will hardly feel the pressure of age, but he who is of an opposite disposition will find youth and age equally a burden.

Plato, *The Republic of Plato*, translated by B. Jowett, Oxford at the Clarendon Press, 1881, page 3, Book I, 329

Calm's not life's crown, though calm is well.
'Tis all perhaps which man acquires,
But 'tis not what our youth desires.

Matthew Arnold, *The Poems of Matthew Arnold*, edited by Kenneth Allott, Longmans, Green & Co. Ltd., 1965, page 225, 'Youth and Calm,' 1.23.

Serene will be our days and bright,
And happy will our nature be,
When love is an unerring light,
And joy its own security.

William Wordsworth, *The Poetical Works of William Wordsworth*, edited by E. de Selincourt and Helen Darbishire, Oxford at the Clarendon Press, 1958, Volume IV, page 84, 'Ode to Duty,' 1.17

A sense of rest, of deep quiet even. Silence within and without. A quietly burning fire. A sense of comfort… I am not dazed or stupid, but only happy in this peaceful morning. Whatever may be the charm of emotion, I do not know whether it equals the sweetness of those hours of silent meditation, in which we have a glimpse and foretaste of the contemplative joys of Paradise. Desire and fear, sadness and care, are done away. Existence is reduced to the simplest form, the most ethereal mode of being, that is, to pure self-consciousness. It is a state of harmony, without tension and without disturbance, the dominical state of the soul, perhaps the state which awaits it beyond the grave. It is happiness as the Orientals understand it, the happiness of the anchorite, who neither struggles nor wishes any more, but simply adores and enjoys. It is difficult to find words in which to express this moral situation, for our languages can only render the particular and localised vibrations of life; they are incapable of expressing this motionless concentration, this divine quietude, this state of the resting ocean, which reflects the sky, and is master of its own profundities. Things are then reabsorbed into their principles; memories are swallowed up in memory; the soul is only soul, and is no longer conscious of itself in its individuality and separateness. It is something which feels the universal life, a sensible atom of the Divine, of God. It no longer appropriates anything to itself, it is conscious of no void. Only the Yoghis and Soufis perhaps have known in its profundity this humble and yet voluptuous state, which combines the joys of being and of non-being, which is neither reflection nor will, which is above both the moral existence and the intellectual existence, which is the return to unity, to the pleroma, the vision of Plotinus and of Proclus,—Nirvana in its most attractive form.

It is clear that the western nations . . . know very little of this state of feeling. For them life is devouring and incessant activity. They are eager for gold, for power, for dominion; their aim is to crush men and to enslave nature. They show an obstinate interest in means, and have not a thought for the end. They confound being with individual being, and the expansion of the self with happiness,—that is to say, they do not live by the soul; they ignore the unchangeable and the eternal; they live at the periphery of their being, because they are unable to penetrate to its axis. They are excited, ardent, positive, because they are superficial. Why so much effort, noise, struggle, and greed?—it is all a mere stunning and deafening of the self. When death comes they recognise that it is so,—why not then admit it sooner? Activity is only beautiful when it is holy—that is to say, when it is spent in the service of that which passeth not away.

Henri Frédéric Amiel, *Amiel's Journal*, translated by Mrs Humphry Ward, Macmillan & Co. Ltd., 1918, page 263

SEX

'Sex'—act of intercourse, for procreation or pleasure.

I n trying to get sex in line with the vision in *Visions of Grace*, I thought a combination of a New Testament verse with some words of William Temple would be appropriate and seemly.

The New Testament verse goes as follows: 'Do you not know that your body is a temple of the Holy Spirit within you which you have from God.' This sets the scene for William Temple: 'The first necessity for a truly Christian philosophy of sex is to pass from the phase where sex is a matter of shame to that where it becomes an object of reverence. Through it God allows to men (and women) the incomparable privilege of co-operating with Him in the creation of His own sons and daughters, called to eternal fellowship with Him. How sacred a thing is this!'

I wonder if we have debased and devalued sex and the time has now come to pass from the phase where sex is a matter of shame to that where it becomes an object of reverence. If the body is indeed made in the image and likeness of God and is a temple of the Holy Spirit then we ought to treat our bodies as such. This attitude can be found in the marriage service of the *Alternative Service Book*, with the reciprocal vow of the bride and bridegroom: 'With my body I honour you.' The physical union then becomes an expression, in the fullest possible way (body, mind and spirit) of the feelings of the one for the other and vice versa, and is best experienced, we believe, in the context of a lasting relationship. Add to this the possibility of bringing children into the world, also made in the image and likeness of God, called to an eternal fellowship with him, then what a sacred thing sex is—an incomparable privilege.

Be fruitful and multiply.
Genesis 1.28

For I am sick with love. O that his left hand were under my head, and that his right hand embraced me!

Song of Solomon 2.5-6

Do you not know that your body is a temple of the Holy Spirit within you, which you have from God?

1 Corinthians 6.19

For this is the will of God, your sanctification; that you abstain from unchastity.

1 Thessalonians 4 3-4

The first necessity for a truly Christian philosophy of sex is to pass from the phase where sex is a matter of shame to that where it becomes an object of reverence. Through it God allows to men the incomparable privilege of co-operating with Him in the creation of His own sons and daughters, called to eternal fellowship with Him. How sacred a thing is this!

William Temple, *Thoughts On Some Problems Of The Day*, Macmillan & Co. Ltd., 1931, page 42

Chastity is the most unpopular of the Christian virtues. There is no getting away from it: the Chrisian rule is, 'Either marriage, with complete faithfulness to your partner, or else total abstinence.' Now this is so difficult and so contrary to our instincts, that obviously either Christianity is wrong or our sexual instinct, as it now is, has gone wrong. One or the other. Of course, being a Christian, I think it is the instinct which has gone wrong.

C.S. Lewis, *Mere Christianity*, William Collins Sons & Co. Ltd., 1961, page 85

The monstrosity of sexual intercourse outside marriage is that those who indulge in it are trying to isolate one kind of union (the sexual) from all the other kinds of union which were intended to go along with it and make up the total union. The Christian attitude does not mean that there is anything wrong with sexual pleasure, any more than about the pleasure of eating. It means that you must not isolate that pleasure and try to get it by itself, any more than you ought to try to get the pleasures of taste without swallowing and digesting, by chewing things and spitting them out again.

C.S. Lewis, *Mere Christianity*, William Collins Sons & Co. Ltd., 1961, page 92

Sex, being a strong natural appetite in animals, and being enormously strengthened in man by the use of imagination, is very liable in human nature to grow in a degree entirely disproportionate. So there is a peculiar difficulty in maintaining, in this respect, that true economy of nature in which to every impulse there is given its own proper, but no more than its own proper, exercise. If our ancestors were wrong in their suggestions that there was about sex something wrong, they were quite right in thinking there was about it something which gave the greatest ground for the most anxious caution.

William Temple, *Christian Faith and Life*, SCM Press Ltd., 1963, page 55

One thing, however, marriage has done for me. I can never again believe that religion is manufactured out of our unconscious, starved desires and is a substitute for sex. For those few years H. and I feasted on love; every mode of it—solemn and merry, romantic and realistic, sometimes as dramatic as a thunderstorm, sometimes as comfortable and unemphatic as putting on your soft slippers. No cranny of heart or body remained unsatisfied. If God were a substitute for love we ought to have lost all interest in Him. Who'd bother about substitutes when he has the thing itself? But that isn't what happens. We both knew we wanted something besides one another—quite a different kind of something, a quite different kind of want.

C.S. Lewis, *A Grief Observed*, Faber & Faber Ltd., 1961, page 10

Sex-love, if it is love at all, is a personal communion in which a man and a woman meet in the full integrity of their personal reality. And the law of reality in the relationship of persons is this. 'The integrity of persons in inviolable. You shall not use a person for your own ends, or indeed for any ends, individual or social. To use another person is to violate his personality by making an object of him and in violating the integrity of another you violate your own.' In all enjoyment there is a choice between enjoying the other and enjoying yourself through the instrumentality of the other. The first is the enjoyment of love, the second is the enjoyment of lust. When people enjoy themselves through each other, that is merely mutual lust. They do not meet as persons at all; their reality is lost. They meet as ghosts of themselves and their pleasure is a ghostly pleasure that cannot begin to satisfy a human soul, and which only vitiates its capacity for reality.

John Macmurray, *Reason and Emotion*, Faber & Faber Ltd., 1972, page 141

The practice of Christian sex ethics is not to be recovered by preaching the ethics... A renewed, creative and fully personal fulfilment of sexuality will only come from people who are aware of the pressure of a debilitated civilisation, and without contracting out of it, can put down their roots in an alternative culture. Christianity is such a culture. Its moral demands are not its main contribution. Underneath those demands is a whole way of life, of deep emotional power bringing its believers in touch with the ultimate mystery of existence, more permanent than the ups and downs of histories and culture. Religion and sex have been closely linked in the history of the human race. That is the ground upon which I assert that religion provides the kind of security and resources which men and women are now vainly seeking by an exaltation of sex in order to counterbalance the impoverishing influence of an over-sophisticated culture. You can only really live in the world fruitfully, happily and co-operatively if you have resources not given by the world. You can only appreciate fruitfully the good things of the world—and sexual love is one of the greatest—if you don't trust them overmuch or seek salvation in them.

V.A. Demant, *Christian Sex Ethics*, Hodder & Stoughton Ltd., 1963, page 121

SORROW

'Sorrow'—grief, sadness, caused by loss of good or occurrence of evil.

O ne of the greatest areas of sorrow in my work is the loss of a young person. I was very upset when one of our women students was killed in a horse riding accident, shortly after leaving college. Nobody knows for certain what happened. She had gone out early one afternoon for a ride. Horse and rider were last seen cantering along a country lane by a housewife, glancing out of her kitchen window. A few minutes later the housewife noticed the horse trotting back without its rider. She decided to investigate and found our former student lying by the roadside, unconscious. She raised the alarm, an ambulance arrived, but sadly our former student died in hospital, without ever regaining consciousness.

We were all very upset. I had known her well as she had lived in our chaplaincy house for a short time during a summer vacation. A group of us went to her funeral which took place in her home church. At the end of the funeral I suddenly broke down and burst into tears. This happened on recalling a very happy memory of her from the previous summer. A group of us were on a pilgrimage, walking round the Cornish coastal path, before striking inland to our destination—Truro Cathedral. We stopped for a picnic lunch on the beach of a secluded bay, and changed in to our swimming gear. She re-appeared, in her bikini and a very dainty sun hat. We were extremely happy. The academic year was over, the weather set fair, and the long vacation lay ahead.

Recalling this occasion threw me. Anger at the accident and sorrow she was no longer with us, issued forth in tears. Sometimes there is a place for expressing deeply felt sorrow.

If you set your heart aright, you will stretch out your hands toward him . . . You will forget your misery; you will remember it as waters that have passed away.

Job 11.13,16

Turn thou to me, and be gracious to me, for I am lonely and afflicted. Relieve the troubles of my heart, and bring me out of my distresses.

Psalm 25.16-17

Rejoice with those who rejoice, weep with those who weep.

Romans 12.15

Behold, the dwelling of God is with men. He will dwell with them, and they shall be his people, and God himself will be with them; he will wipe away every tear from their eyes, and death shall be no more, neither shall there be mourning nor crying nor pain any more, for the former things have passed away.

Revelation 21.3-4

A deep distress hath humanised my Soul.

William Wordsworth, *The Poetical Works of William Wordsworth*, edited by E. de Selincourt and Helen Darbishire, Oxford at the Clarendon Press, 1958, Volume IV, page 259, 'Elegaic Stanzas,' l.36

The busy bee has no time for sorrow.

William Blake, *The Complete Writings of William Blake*, edited by Geoffrey Keynes, Oxford University Press, 1974, page 151, *The Marriage of Heaven and Hell*, Plate 7, 'Proverbs of Hell,' l.11

Where there is sorrow there is holy ground.

Oscar Wilde, *The Works of Oscar Wilde*, edited by G.F. Maine, William Collins Sons & Co. Ltd., 1948, *De Profundis*, page 854

True sorrow makes a silence in the heart.

Robert Natham, *A Cedar Box*, The Bobbs-Merrill Company, Publishers, 1929, page 35

Sorrow makes us all children again,—destroys all differences of intellect. The wisest knows nothing.

Ralph Waldo Emerson, *The Heart of Emerson's Journals*, edited by Bliss Perry, Constable & Co. Ltd., 1927, page 173

Sorrow is a kind of rust of the soul, which every new idea contributes in its passage to scour away.

Samuel Johnson, *The Yale Edition of the Works of Samuel Johnson*, edited by W.J. Bate and Albrecht B. Strauss, Yale University Press, 1969, Volume III, page 258, 'The Rambler,' No.47

Take this sorrow to thy heart, and make it a part of thee, and it shall nourish thee till thou art strong again.

Henry Wadsworth Longfellow, *Hyperion*, George Routledge & Sons Ltd., 1887, page 245

The groundwork of life is sorrow. But that once established, one can start to build. And until that is established one can build nothing: no life of any sort.

D.H. Lawrence, *The Selected Letters of D.H.Lawrence*, edited by Diana Trilling, Farrar, Straus & Cudahy, 1958, page 188

Sorrow is the most tremendous of all realities in the sensible world, but the transfiguration of sorrow after the manner of Christ is a more beautiful solution of the problem than the extirpation of sorrow.

Henri Frédéric Amiel, *Amiel's Journal*, translated by Mrs Humphry Ward, Macmillan & Co. Ltd., 1918, page 285

We wasters of sorrows! How we stare away into sad endurance beyond them, trying to foresee their end! Whereas they are nothing else than our winter foliage, our sombre evergreen, *one* of the seasons of our interior year,—not only season—they're also place, settlement, camp, soil, dwelling.

Rainer Maria Rilke, *Duino Elegies*, translated by J.B. Leishman and Stephen Spender, Chatto & Windus Ltd., 1975, page 91

If it were possible for us to see further than our knowledge extends and out a little over the outworks of our surmising, perhaps we should then bear our sorrows with greater confidence than our joys. For they are the moments when something new, something unknown, has entered into us; our feelings grow dumb with shy confusion, everything in us retires, a stillness supervenes, and the new thing that no one knows stands silent there in the midst.

Rainer Maria Rilke, *Letters to a Young Poet*, translated by Reginald Snell, Sidgwick & Jackson, 1945, page 35

Sorrow is one of the things that are lent, not given. A thing that is lent may be taken away; a thing that is given is not taken away. Joy is given; sorrow is lent. We are not our own, we are bought with a price, 'and our sorrow is not our own' (Samuel Rutherford said this a long time ago), it is lent to us for just a little while that we may use it for eternal purposes. Then it will be taken away and everlasting joy will be our Father's gift to us, and the Lord God will wipe away all tears from off all faces. So let us use this 'lent' thing to draw us nearer to the heart of Him Who was once a Man of Sorrows (He is not that now, but He does not forget the feeling of sorrow). Let us use it to make us more tender with others, as He was when on earth and is still, for He is touched with the feeling of our infirmities.

Amy Carmichael, *Edges Of His Ways*, SPCK, 1955, page 193

Unrest, disappointment and pain are our lot in this short span of time which lies between our entrance on life and our departure from it. What is spiritual is in a dreadful state of dependence on our bodily nature. Our existence, is at the mercy of meaningless happenings and can be brought to an end by them at any moment. The will-to-live gives me an impulse to action, but the action is just as if I wanted to plough the sea, and sow in furrows. What did those who worked before me effect? What significance in the endless chain of world-happenings had their efforts had? With all its illusive promises, the will-to-live only means to mislead me into prolonging my existence, and allowing to enter on existence other beings to whom the same miserable lot has been assigned as to myself, so that the game may go on without end.

The discoveries in this field of knowledge which the will-to-live encounters when it begins to think, are therefore altogether pessimistic. It is not by accident that all religious world-views, except the Chinese, have a more or less pessimistic tone and bid man expect nothing from his existence here.

Who will prevent us from making use of the freedom we are allowed, and casting existence from us? Every thinking human being makes acquaintance with this thought...

What determines us, so long as we are comparatively in our right mind, to reject the thought of putting an end to our existence. An instinctive feeling of repulsion from such a deed. The will-to-live is stronger than the pessimistic facts of knowledge. An instinctive reverence for life is within us, for we are will-to-live.

Albert Schweitzer, *The Philosophy of Civilization*, Part II, *Civilization and Ethics*, translated by C.T. Campion, Third English Edition, revised by Mrs Charles E.B. Russell, A. & C. Black Ltd., 1946, page 210

THINKING

*'Thinking'—considering; being of opinion; forming conception of; exercising
the mind otherwise than by passive reception of another's idea; imagining.*

A lbert Schweitzer in his book *My Life and Thought*, recommends 'the rekindling of the
fire of thought' as a recipe for the future. A common reaction of those involved in
reflection groups is: 'They really make me think.'

D.H. Lawrence opens up thinking in his poem on *Thought*.

> Thought is the welling up of unknown life into consciousness,
> Thought is the testing of statements on the touchstone of the conscience,
> Thought is gazing onto the face of life, and reading what can be read,
> Thought is pondering over experience, and coming to a conclusion.
> Thought is not a trick, or an exercise, or a set of dodges,
> Thought is a man in his wholeness wholly attending.

All this sounds rather like reflection. In reflection full use is made of our minds, as in
the poem above. Full use is also made of our hearts, meaning our feelings and emotions,
our instinct and intuition. Full use is made too of our imagination, and our experience of
life so far. More importantly we open ourselves to what D.H. Lawrence described as 'the
welling up of unknown life into consciousness'. In doing this we are only remembering
an important part of New Testament teaching: 'Let this mind be in you, which was also in
Christ Jesus.'

Seen in this way, thinking can be a great adventure. Let D.H. Lawrence have the final
word: 'Thought is a man in his wholeness wholly attending.'

Let the words of my mouth and the meditation of my heart be acceptable in thy sight, O
Lord, my rock and my redeemer.

Psalm 19.14

We have thought on thy steadfast love, O God, in the midst of thy temple.

Psalm 48.9

What do you think of the Christ?

Matthew 22.42

Take thought for what is noble in the sight of all.

Romans 12.17

One thought fills immensity.

William Blake, *The Complete Writings of William Blake*, edited by Geoffrey Keynes, Oxford University Press, 1974,
page 151, *The Marriage of Heaven and Hell*, Plate 8, 'Proverbs of Hell,' l.15

What is the hardest task in the world? To think.

Ralph Waldo Emerson, *Essays*, Bernhard Tauchnitz Edition, 1915, page 191, 'Intellect'

Reading is sometimes an ingenious device for avoiding thought.

Arthur Helps, *Friends in Council*, George Routledge & Sons Ltd., 1907, page 169

My own thoughts
Are my companions.

Henry Wadsworth Longfellow, *The Poetical Works of Longfellow*, Humphrey Milford, Oxford University Press, 1913, page 688, *The Masque of Pandora*, Part III

It is thy very energy of thought
Which keeps thee from thy God.

John Henry Newman, *The Dream of Gerontius*, Burns & Oates Ltd., 1886, page 25

It is thoughts of God's thinking which we need to set us right, and, remember, they are not as our thoughts.

W.M. Macgregor, *Jesus Christ the Son of God*, T. & T. Clark, 1907, page 99

Christianity has need of thought that it may come to the consciousness of its real self.

Albert Schweitzer, *Out of My Life and Thought*, Henry Holt and Company, Inc., 1949, page 236

Thought that can emerge wholly into feeling, feeling that can merge wholly into thought—these are the artist's highest joy.

Thomas Mann, *Death in Venice*, translated by H.T. Lowe-Porter, Penguin Books Ltd., 1978, page 52

When we ask the ultimate questions, whether about the direction of our own lives or about the meaning of existence, the outcome of thinking is not an answer but a transformed way of thinking, not propositions to assent to but heightened power of apprehension.

Helen Merrell Lynd, *On Shame and the Search for Identity*, Routledge & Kegan Paul Ltd., 1958, page 251

Elemental thinking is that which starts from the fundamental questions about the relations of man in the universe, about the meaning of life, and about the nature of goodness. It stands in the most immediate connexion with the thinking which impulse stirs in everyone. It enters into that thinking, widening and deepening it.

Albert Schweitzer, *My Life and Thought*, translated by C.T. Campion, George Allen & Unwin Ltd., 1933, page 260

Today we overrate the rational values and behave as if thinking were a substitute for living. We have forgotten that thought and the intuition that feeds it only become whole if the deed grows out of it as fruit grows from the pollen on a tree. So everywhere in our civilized world there tends to be a terrible cleavage between thinking and doing.

Laurens van der Post, *The Lost World of the Kalahari*, Penguin Books Ltd., 1983, page 61

Full well aware that all has failed, yet, side by side with the sadness of that knowledge, there lives on in me an unquenchable belief, thought burning like the sun, that there is yet something to be found, something real, something to give each separate personality sunshine and flowers in its own existence now. Something to shape this million-handed labour to an end and outcome, leaving accumulated sunshine and flowers to those who shall succeed. It must be dragged forth by might of thought from the immense forces of the universe.

Richard Jefferies, *The Story of My Heart*, Duckworth & Co., 1923, page 73

None the less strong than the will to truth must be the will to sincerity. Only an age which can show the courage of sincerity can possess truth which works as a spiritual force within it.

Sincerity is the foundation of the spiritual life.

With its depreciation of thinking our generation has lost its feeling for sincerity and with it that for truth as well. It can therefore be helped only by its being brought once more on to the road of thinking.

Because I have this certainty I oppose the spirit of the age, and take upon myself with confidence the responsibility of taking my part in the rekindling of the fire of thought.

Albert Schweitzer, *My Life and Thought*, translated by C.T. Campion, George Allen & Unwin Ltd., 1933, page 259

On many occasions we can do a lot of thinking; there are plenty of situations in our daily life in which we have nothing to do except wait, and if we are disciplined—and this is part of our spiritual training—we will be able to concentrate quickly and fix our attention at once on the subject of our thoughts, of our meditation. We must learn to do it by compelling our thoughts to attach themselves to one focus and to drop everything else. In the beginning, extraneous thoughts will intrude, but if we push them away constantly, time after time, in the end they will leave us in peace. It is only when by training, by exercise, by habit, we have become able to concentrate profoundly and quickly, that we can continue through life in a state of collectedness, in spite of what we are doing.

Anthony Bloom, *Living Prayer*, Darton, Longman & Todd, 1966, page 55

The rational mind always thinks in terms of duality; subject and object, mind and matter, body and soul, time and space. These are all categories of the rational mind.

These categories are of course valuable and necessary, for they enable us to operate within the world of time and space, the world of sense perception. We cannot discard them, but as we begin to contemplate so we go beyond these dualities. We transcend reason and logical thought, and open ourselves to the direct experience of the spirit. This is the unifying experience.

Thoughts may take us to the furthest outreach of space, but they neither find nor relate to God. God cannot be realized or known by the processes of the mind. Thought can give birth to further thoughts about God.

The hope of humanity today is to get beyond the experience of duality. A spiritual awakening in this direction is taking place all over the world. Beyond thought is where, in the words of St Paul, we find God to be 'all in all' (I Corinthians 15.28).

Bede Griffiths OSB, in *The Universal Christ*, edited by Peter Spink, Darton, Longman & Todd, 1993, page 57

It seems, indeed, little better than mockery that we should urge men to anything so remote as a return to reflection about the meaning of life at a time when the passions and the follies of the nations have become so intense and so extended, when unemployment and poverty and starvation are rife, when power is being used on the powerless in the most shameless and senseless way, and when organized human life is dislocated in every direction. But only when the general population begins to reflect in this way will forces come into being which will be able to effect something to counterbalance all this chaos and misery. Whatever other measures it is attempted to carry out will have doubtful and altogether inadequate results.

When in the spring the withered grey of the pastures gives place to green, this is due to the millions of young shoots which sprout up freshly from the old roots. In like manner the revival of thought which is essential for our time can only come through a transformation of the opinions and ideals of the many brought about by individual and universal reflection about the meaning of life and of the world.

Albert Schweitzer, *The Philosophy of Civilization*, Part I, *The Decay and the Restoration of Civilization*, translated by C.T. Campion, A. & C. Black Ltd., 1932, page 100

UNDERSTANDING

'Understanding'—comprehending, perceiving the meaning of,
grasping mentally, perceiving the significance or explanation or
cause or nature of, knowing how to deal with, having insight.

When I was chaplain *to* University College, London, my old faith broke down and I was struggling to find a new faith. A law student I knew well introduced me to the writings of Herman Hesse, and insisted I read *The Glass Bead Game*. His advice was excellent, and helped me back on the road of faith. In this book I came across an outstanding passage on understanding, and I am going to quote it in full because it is so good.

'Oh, if only it were possible to find understanding,' Joseph exclaimed. 'If only there were a dogma to believe in. Everything is contradictory, everything tangential; there are no certainties anywhere. Everything can be interpreted one way and then again interpreted in the opposite sense. The whole of world history can be explained as development and progress and can also be seen as nothing but decadence and meaninglessness. Isn't there any truth? Is there no real and valid doctrine?'

The Master had never heard him speak so fervently. He walked on in silence for a little, then said: 'There is truth, my boy. But the doctrine you desire, absolute, perfect dogma that alone provides wisdom, does not exist. Nor should you long for a perfect doctrine, my friend. Rather, you should long for the perfection of yourself. The deity is within *you*, not in ideas and books. Truth is lived, not taught. Be prepared for conflicts, Joseph Knecht—I can see they have already begun.'

This passage greatly helped me. It can be found in *Visions of Grace* under 'God Within'. I know it has helped others as well.

Wisdom is the principal thing; therefore get wisdom: and with all thy getting get understanding.

Proverbs 4.7 (AV)

I shall light a candle of understanding in thine heart, which shall not be put out.

2 Esdras 14.25 (AV)

As for what was sown on good soil, this is he who hears the word and understands it; and he indeed bears fruit, and yields, in one case a hundredfold, in another sixty, and in another thirty.

Matthew 13.23

That their hearts may be encouraged as they are knit together in love, to have all the riches of assured understanding and the knowledge of God's mystery, of Christ, in whom are hid all the treasures of wisdom and knowledge.

Colossians 2.2-3

All the glory of greatness has no lustre for people who are in search of understanding.

Blaise Pascal, *Pensées*, translated by W.F. Trotter, Random House Inc., 1941, page 277

That which enables us to know and understand aright in the things of God, must be a living principle of holiness within us.
John Smith the Platonist, *Select Discourses*, Cambridge at the University Press, 1859, page 3

If one is master of one thing and understands one thing well, one has at the same time insight into and understanding of many things.
Vincent van Gogh, *Dear Theo: An Autobiography of Vincent van Gogh*, edited by Irving Stone, Constable & Co. Ltd., 1937, page 28

Of course, *understanding* of our fellow-beings is important.
But this understanding becomes fruitful only when it is sustained by sympathetic feeling in joy and in sorrow.
Albert Einstein, *Ideas and Opinions*, Souvenir Press (Educational & Academic) Ltd, 1973, page 53

I want, by understanding myself, to understand others. I want to be all that I am capable of becoming... This all sounds very strenuous and serious. But now that I have wrestled with it, it's no longer so. I feel happy—deep down. *All is well.*
Katherine Mansfield, *Journal of Katherine Mansfield*, edited by John Middleton Murry, Constable & Co. Ltd., 1927, page 251

The Hebrew word (*bin*) means discern, consider; and the cognate nouns (*binah, tebunah*) can mean both the act and the faculty of understanding and also the object understand. The relevant Greek verbs are similar in meaning, (*noeo*), as Mark 13.14; *suniemi*, as Mark 4.12). 'They that seek the Lord understand all things', says Prov.28.5. Contact with God, faith, is the spring of understanding as of wisdom. Alternatively, God is the most important object of understanding: Isa.43.10, Jer.9.24; though in the more intellectual sense God is beyond man's understanding: Isa.40.28, Rom.11.33ff.
The verbs 'understand' and 'know' are in frequent juxtaposition, especially in the Old Testament, and their meaning often is synonymous.
E.C. Blackman, in *A Theological Word Book of the Bible*, edited by Alan Richardson, SCM Press Ltd., 1975, page 273

Know, knowledge—Old Testament: The Heb. *yada'*, means know (whether person or thing), perceive, learn, understand, have skill; and also, with a wider sweep of meaning than our 'know', experience good or bad (including the sexual sense: Gen.4.1, etc.). Knowledge for the Hebrews was not knowledge of abstract principles, or of a reality conceived of as beyond phenomena. Reality was what happens, and knowledge meant apprehension of that. Knowledge of God meant, not thought about an eternal Being or Principle transcending man and the world, but recognition of, and obedience to, one who acted purposefully in the world (Deut.11.2ff., Isa.41.20). This sometimes meant emphasis on the fact that God is one, and the later Hellenistic Judaism had to develop this in its Gentile propaganda (cf. Wisd.12.27), adding a more intellectual element to the Old Testament conception. For continuance of this emphasis in the New Testament, cf. John 17.3, Rom.1.18ff., I Cor.8.4-6, Gal.4.8f.
To know God is the chief duty of man: Deut.4.39, 29.2-6, Isa.43.10, Hos.6.6, Ps.46.10. In the case of God, knowledge means his providence and prosecution of his good purposes; and particularly his choice of a man or nation to play a part in those purposes: Amos 3.2, Jer.1.5. For this thought carried on in the New Testament, cf. I Cor.8.2f, Gal.4.9. For the Rabbis of later Judaism, knowledge was primarily knowledge of the Law; cf. Rom.2.20.
New Testament: In the New Testament generally the words used for 'know' and 'knowledge' have the various nuances of meaning which are familiar in English, and also contain the significance of the Old Testament *yada'* which was mediated by the Septuagint; e.g. for 'know' in the sense of 'have experience of', cf. the phrase 'know sin', Rom.7.7, II Cor.5.21. The phrase 'know the truth' is almost a synonym for 'become a Christian' or 'be converted'; it signifies not intellectual enlightenment, but enlightenment which is a stimulus to a new way of life, viz. love: Phil.1.9, Col.1.9f., 3.10ff. This conserves the Hebraic use of know, which has in view conduct rather than theory; cf. Jer.22.16; 'He judged the cause of the poor and needy... Was not this to know me? saith the Lord.'

For the noun (*gnosis*) in an absolute sense, meaning religious knowledge, cf. I Cor.8.7, 13.8. Some scholars regard this as due to Gnostic influence, together with Matt.13.11 and Col.2.2f., where we have also the word 'mystery', and Matt.11.27, the most Johannine of the sayings recorded in the Synoptic Gospels. The use of words which had a vogue in non-Christian religious circles need not be denied, but it must be insisted that in the passages above cited such non-Christian terminology is used in the service of distinctively Christian ideas, not for the importation of alien ones. In the light of Phil.3.8-15, it should be clear that the New Testament is trying to express the unique character of the believer's relation to Christ. This involves an element of knowledge. St. Paul's usuage as a rule makes faith include this, but sometimes he allows himself the more intellectualist word. Johannine usage, which is worthy of more detailed examination than can be given here, distinguishes 'know' and 'believe' roughly as fruit and seed, and then connects 'know' with 'love' in a distinctive fashion.

E.C. Blackman, in *A Theological Word Book of the Bible*, edited by Alan Richardson, SCM Press Ltd., 1975, page 121

UNION

*'Union'—uniting, being united, a whole resulting from a
combination of parts of members.*

I n *Visions of Faith, Hope, Love, Grace* and *Glory*, I have tried to include excerpts from writers with whom I have had some form of contact. C.S. Lewis, for instance, was an undergraduate at University College, Oxford, as was the poet, Percy Bysshe Shelley—before he was 'sent down' for writing a treatise *In Defence of Atheism*. When I was an undergraduate at Balliol the set of rooms allocated to me had been at one time occupied by William Temple, a former Archbishop of Canterbury. Another prominent writer from Balliol was Aldous Huxley. In one of his books, *The Devils of Loudun*, he comes out with a purple passage on union: 'In terms employed by Christian theology we may define realization as the soul's union with God as a Trinity, a three in one. It is simultaneously union with the Father, the Son, and the Holy Ghost—union with the source and Ground of all being, consciousness and union with the spirit which links the Unknowable to the known.'

This passage is sympathetic to the 'vision' underlying these anthologies. Union is a gift of God, and cannot be achieved by our own efforts. All we can do is be passive and open ourselves to receive this divine gift. The best approach lies in a passive form of reflection, meditation and contemplation. When we silence our thoughts and feelings and become receptive, it is then that the Spirit of God can move in and for a few precious seconds we might experience the bliss of union.

Let us join ourselves to the Lord in an everlasting covenant which will never be forgotten.
Jeremiah 50.5

And I will betroth you to me for ever. I will betroth you to me in righteousness and in justice, in steadfast love, and in mercy.
.   Hosea 2.19

I will not leave you desolate; I will come to you. Yet a little while, and the world will see me no more, but you will see me; because I live, you will live also. In that day you will know that I am in my Father, and you in me, and I in you.
John 14.18-20

Abide in me, and I in you. As the branch cannot bear fruit by itself, unless it abides in the vine, neither can you, unless you abide in me. I am the vine, you are the branches. He who abides in me, and I in him, he it is that bears much fruit, for apart from me you can do nothing.

John 15.4-5

Every rational soul should desire with all its strength to draw close to God, and to be united to Him by its awareness of His unseen presence.

Walter Hilton, *The Ladder of Perfection*, translated by Leo Sherley-Price, Penguin Books Ltd., 1957, page 233

We come closest to Him [God] not when, with our mind, we obtain a wide conspectus of truth, but when in our purposes we are united with His righteous purpose.

William Temple, *The Preacher's Theme To-day*, SPCK, 1936, page 8

As long as the soul has not thrown off all her veils, however thin, she is unable to see God. Any medium, but a hair's-breath, in betwixt the body and the soul stops actual union.

Meister Eckhart, *Meister Eckhart*, Franz Pfeiffer, translated by C. de B. Evans, John M. Watkins, 1956, Volume I, page 114

In the terms employed by Christian theology we may define realization as the soul's union with God as a Trinity, a three in one. It is simultaneously union with the Father, the Son, and the Holy Ghost—union with the source and Ground of all being, union with the manifestation of that Ground in a human consciousness and union with the spirit which links the Unknowable to the known.

Aldous Huxley, *The Devils of Loudon*, Penguin Books Ltd., 1973, page 74

If we look at what John of the Cross has to say about the transformed soul, one on the summit of the mountain, this is what we get. The Bride has no desires of the will, no acts of understanding, neither object nor occupation of any kind which she does not refer wholly to God, together with all her desires.

She is absorbed in God, all love. All her actions are love, all her energies and strength are intent on love. She has given up everything for the pearl of great price, total union with God.

She is never seeking her own gratification, her will is wanting his will alone. 'My sole occupation is love', 'I do always such things that please him'.

When we think of such selflessness, such love for God, we must, naturally speaking, feel only despair. It is impossible to achieve. But God wants it in us and everything is possible to God.

Here we touch the heart of Christianity and mysticism. It is all God's work. He wills it absolutely and we must choose to let him do it.

Ruth Burrows, in *The Watchful Heart*, edited by Elizabeth Ruth Obbard, Darton, Longman & Todd, 1988, page 14

... how can I say that I have found Him and found myself in Him if I never know Him or think of Him, never take any interest in Him or seek Him or desire His presence in my soul?

What good does it do to say a few formal prayers to Him and then turn away and give all my mind and all my will to created things, desiring only ends that fall far short of Him? Even though my soul may be justified, yet if my mind does not belong to Him then I do not belong to Him either. If my love does not reach out towards Him but scatters itself in His creation, it is because I have reduced His life in me to the level of a formality, forbidding it to move me with a truly vital influence ...

Set me free from the laziness that goes about disguised as activity when activity is not required of me, and from the cowardice that does what is not demanded, in order to escape sacrifice.

But give me the strength that waits upon You in silence and peace. Give me humility in which alone is rest, and deliver me from pride which is the heaviest of burdens.

Thomas Merton, *New Seeds of Contemplation*, Burns & Oates Ltd., 1962, page 34

No unity with God is possible except by an exceedingly great love. This we can see from the story of the woman in the Gospel, who was a sinner: God in His great mercy granted her the forgiveness of her sins and a firm union with Him, 'for she loved much' (Luke 7.47). He loves those who love Him, He cleaves to those who cleave to Him, gives Himself to those who seek Him, and abundantly grants fullness of joy to those who desire to enjoy His love.

To kindle in his heart such a divine love, to unite with God in an inseparable union of love, it is necessary for a man to pray often, raising the mind to Him. For as a flame increases when it is constantly fed, so prayer, made often, with the mind dwelling ever more deeply in God, arouses divine love in the heart. And the heart, set on fire, will warm all the inner man, will enlighten and teach him, revealing to him all its unknown and hidden wisdom, and making him like a flaming seraph, always standing before God within his spirit, always looking at Him within his mind, and drawing from this vision the sweetness of spiritual joy...

The principal thing is to stand with the mind in the heart before God, and to go on standing before Him unceasingly day and night, until the end of life.

St Dimitri of Rostov and Theophan the Recluse, in *The Art of Prayer, An Orthodox Anthology*, compiled by Igumen Chariton of Valamo, translated by E. Kadloubovsky and E.M. Palmer, edited by Timothy Ware, Faber & Faber Ltd., 1973, pages 47, 63

Who can tell of the intimacy of this union with God, for it is beyond compare!... God, when He is united with the soul, penetrates it wholly and enters all its secret chambers, till He is made one with its inmost being; and herein, when He has become soul of its soul and is straitly entwined with it, He enfolds it in the most intimate union...

And not merely in great part is God united with the soul, but He is united wholly; and not gradually, one part succeeding another, but all together and at once, with no waiting of one part for the other which is the reverse of that which takes place with the body, the good things of which (or that which it holds to be good things) come to it slowly and gradually, one after the other, now this, now that, so that before it can enjoy the second it has already lost the first...

From all this it may be concluded that not only is there delight in this betrothal and union of the soul with God, but that it is a delight which, from whatsoever aspect it be regarded, is greater than any other. For neither is it mingled with necessity, nor diluted with sorrow, nor is it given partially, nor corrupted in any degree soever. Neither is it born of lesser favours, nor of indifferent or weak embraces; neither is it a base delight nor lightly apprehended, as are the delights of our base and superficial senses. But it is wealth divine, and intimate fruition, abundance of delight, unsullied happiness, which bathes the whole soul, and inebriates it, and overwhelms it in such wise that its state can be described by none.

Luis de Leon, in *Studies of the Spanish Mystics*, E. Allison Peers, Sheldon Press, 1927, Volume I, page 336

That life is difficult, I have often bitterly realised. I now had further cause for serious reflection. Right up to the present I have never lost the feeling of contradiction that lies behind all knowledge. My life has been miserable and difficult, and yet to others and sometimes to myself, it has seemed rich and wonderful. Man's life seems to me like a long, weary night that would be intolerable if there were not occasionally flashes of light, the sudden brightness of which is so comforting and wonderful, that the moments of their appearance cancel out and justify the years of darkness. The gloom, the comfortless darkness, lies in the inevitable course of our daily lives. Why does one repeatedly rise in the morning, eat, drink, and go to bed again? The child, the savage, the healthy young person does not suffer as a result of this cycle of repeated activities. If a man does not think too much, he rejoices at rising in the morning, and at eating and drinking. He finds satisfaction in them and does not want them to be otherwise. But if he ceases to take things for granted, he seeks eagerly and hopefully during the course of the day for moments of real life, the radiance of which makes him rejoice and obliterates the awareness of time and all thoughts on the meaning and purpose of everything. One can call these moments creative, because they seem to give a feeling of union with the creator, and while they last, one is sensible of everything being necessary, even what is seemingly fortuitous. It is what the mystics call union with God. Perhaps it is the excessive radiance of these moments that makes everything else appear so dark, perhaps it is the feeling of liberation, the enchanting lightness and the suspended bliss that make the rest of life seem so difficult, demanding and oppressive, I do not know. I have not travelled very far in thought and philosophy. However I do know that if there is a state of bliss and a paradise, it must be an uninterrupted sequence of such moments, and if this state can be attained by suffering and dwelling in pain, then no sorrow or pain can be so great that one should attempt to escape from it.

Herman Hesse, *Gertrude*, Peter Owen Ltd., and Vision Press Ltd., 1955, page 134

VISION

'Vision'—act of faculty of seeing, things seen in dream or trance;
thing seen in the imagination, imaginative insight; statesmanlike
foresight.

I have never seen a vision in a dream or in a trance. My visions have been more down-to-earth, involving the imagination and imaginative insight. Thomas Traherne once wrote: 'And thus you have a Gate, in the prospect even of this world, whereby you may see into God's Kingdom.' In one sense these words could have been written of *Visions of Grace*. This book, along with *Visions of Faith*, Hope, Love and Glory, act as a gate in which one can 'see' a prospect (or a vision) of this world, and of God's kingdom. In reflecting on the contents of these anthologies the imagination is stimulated, and through imaginative insight we 'see' things not previously 'seen'.

As I mentioned in *Visions of Hope*, this vision came to me whilst reading a book entitled *The Choice is Always Ours*, by Dorothy Berkley Phillips. At the time I was travelling on a Greyhound bus in America, thoroughly absorbed reading the contents of this book.

The vision begins with man made in the image and likeness of God. We see this fully worked out in the life of Jesus Christ—'the image of the invisible God'. We move on to find the substance of the vision in the lives and writings of poets, novelists, playwrights, philosophers, theologians, artists, musicians, historians, scientists, psychologists, and so on, up to the present day. These findings have been arranged in topics.

We then bring reflection into play and open up a 'prospect even of this world,' whereby we 'may see into God's Kingdom'.

For God speaks in one way, and in two, though man does not perceive it. In a dream, in a vision of the night, when deep sleep falls upon men, while they slumber on their beds, then he opens the ears of men, and terrifies them with warnings.

Job 33.14-16

And it shall come to pass afterward, that I will pour out my spirit on all flesh; your sons and your daughters shall prophesy, your old men shall dream dreams, and your young men shall see visions.

Joel 2.28

And a vision appeared to Paul in the night: a man of Macedonia was standing beseeching him and saying, 'Come over to Macedonia and help us.' And when he had seen the vision, immediately we sought to go on into Macedonia.

Acts 16.9-10

I was not disobedient to the heavenly vision.

Acts 26.19

And thus you have a Gate, in the prospect even of this world, whereby you may see into God's Kingdom.

Thomas Traherne, *Centuries*, The Faith Press Ltd., 1969, page 71

Golden hours of vision come to us in this present life, when we are at our best, and our faculties work together in harmony.

Charles Fletcher Dole, *The Hope of Immortality*, Houghton Mifflin Company, The Riverside Press, 1906, page 59

The simple vision of pure love, which is marvellously penetrating, does not stop at the outer husk of creation; it penetrates to the divinity which is hidden within.

Malaval, in *Mysticism*, Evelyn Underhill, Methuen & Co. Ltd., 1912, page 305

Hundreds of people can talk for one who can think, but thousands can think for one who can see. To see clearly is poetry, prophecy, and religion,—all in one.

John Ruskin, *Modern Painters*, George Allen & Sons, 1910, Volume III, page 278, Part IV, Ch.16, section 28

An eternal trait of men is the need for vision and the readiness to follow it; and if men are not given the right vision, they will follow wandering fires.

Sir Richard Livingstone, *On Education*, Cambridge at the University Press, 1954, page 151

I but open my eyes,—and perfection, no more and no less,
In the kind I imagined, full-fronts me, and God is seen God
In the star, in the stone, in the flesh, in the soul and the clod.

Robert Browning, *The Poetical Works of Robert Browning*, Volume I, Smith, Elder & Co., 1899, page 278, 'Soul,' st.xvii, l.21

This made it more likely that he had seen a true vision; for instead of making common things look commonplace, as a false vision would have done, it had made common things disclose the wonderful that was in them.

George Macdonald, *Cross Purposes and The Shadows*, Blackie & Son, Ltd., 1891, page 62

Now, this state of 'spiritual unrest' can never bring you to a state of vision, of which the essential is peace. And struggling to see does not help one to see. The light comes, when it does come, rather suddenly and strangely I think. It is just like falling in love; a thing that never happens to those who are always trying to do it.

Evelyn Underhill, *The Letters of Evelyn Underhill*, edited by Charles Williams, Longmans, Green & Co. Ltd., 1947, page 51

All that is sweet, delightful, and amiable in this world, in the serenity of the air, the fineness of seasons, the joy of light, the melody of sounds, the beauty of colours, the fragrancy of smells, the splendour of precious stones, is nothing else but Heaven breaking through the veil of this world, manifesting itself in such a degree and darting forth in such variety so much of its own nature.

William Law, *Selected Mystical Writings of William Law*, edited by Stephen Hobhouse, Rockliff, 1948, page 44

There are two different ways of looking at God. You can think of him as above and you can pray to him and ask his grace to descend. You can kneel in penitence and ask for mercy.

Equally you can think of God as immanent, present in the earth, in the water, in the air.

These two different ways are complementary. Just as a Christian starting from above discovers the Holy Spirit as immanent and realizes the presence of God in the whole creation around him, so the Hindu starting with the immanence of God in creation, in the human heart, rises to the idea of God beyond the creation and beyond humanity.

These are two complementary visions and we have to bring them together in our lives so that each enriches the other.

Bede Griffiths OSB, in *The Universal Christ*, edited by Peter Spink, Darton, Longman & Todd, 1993, page 17

To share in the vision of God means that we have to pass beyond all concepts of the rational mind and all images derived from the senses. We must pass into the world of non-duality, in which our present mode of consciousness is transcended.

We so pass into that 'divine darkness' of which Dionysius speaks, which appears dark only because it is pure light. We must ascend to that state of 'unknowing' in which all human knowledge fades away, and we shall know truly 'even as we are known'.

In this view of the ultimate mystery of being, which is the beginning and the end of all our human aspirations, Hindu, Buddhist and Christian unite and in God all differences which appear in nature, and all distinctions known to the human mind, are transcended.

Bede Griffiths OSB, in *The Universal Christ*, edited by Peter Spink, Darton, Longman & Todd, 1993, page 48

It is only in exceptional moods that we realise how wonderful are the commonest experiences of life. It seems to me sometimes that these experiences have an 'inner' side, as well as the outer side we normally perceive. At such moments one suddenly sees everything with new eyes; one feels on the brink of some great revelation. It is as if we caught a glimpse of some incredibly beautiful world that lies silently about us all the time. I remember vividly my first experience of the kind when, as a boy, I came suddenly upon the quiet miracle of an ivy-clad wall glistening under a London street-lamp. I wanted to weep and I wanted to pray; to weep for the Paradise from which I had been exiled, and to pray that I might yet be made worthy of it. Such moments are rare, in my experience. But their influence is permanent. They import a tinge of unreality into our normal acceptances; we suspect them for the dull and purblind things that they are. There are analagous moments when one suddenly sees the glory of people. On some unforgettable evening one's friend is suddenly seen as the unique, irreplaceable, and utterly delightful being that he is. It is as if he had been freshly created. One is no longer concerned with his relations to oneself, with his *pragmatic* value. He exists wholly in his own right; his significance is eternal, and the essential mystery of his being is as fathomless as that of God Himself.

J.W.N. Sullivan, *But For the Grace of God*, Jonathan Cape Ltd., 1932, page 133

Religion is the vision of something which stands beyond, behind, and within, the passing flux of immediate things; something which is real, and yet waiting to be realised; something which is a remote possibility, and yet the greatest of present facts; something that gives meaning to all that passes, and yet eludes apprehension; something whose possession is the final good, and yet is beyond all reach; something which is the ultimate ideal, and the hopeless quest. The immediate reaction of human nature to the religious vision is worship. Religion has emerged into human experience mixed with the crudest fancies of barbaric imagination. Gradually, slowly, steadily the vision recurs in history under nobler form and with clearer expression. It is the one element in human experience which persistently shows an upward trend. It fades and then recurs. But when it renews its force, it recurs with an added richness and purity of content. The fact of the religious vision, and its history of persistent expansion, is our one ground for optimism. Apart from it, human life is a flash of occasional enjoyments lighting up a mass of pain and misery, a bagatelle of transient experience.

The vision claims nothing but worship; and worship is a surrender to the claim for assimilation, urged with the motive force of mutual love. The vision never overrules. It is always there, and it has the power of love presenting the one purpose whose fulfilment is eternal harmony. Such order as we find in nature is never force—it presents itself as the one harmonious adjustment of complex detail. Evil is the brute motive force of fragmentary purpose, disregarding the eternal vision. Evil is overruling, retarding, hurting. The power of God is the worship He inspires. That religion is strong which in its ritual and its modes of thought evokes an apprehension of the commanding vision. The worship of God is not a rule of safety, it is an adventure of the spirit, a flight after the unattainable. The death of religion comes with the repression of the high hope of adventure.

Alfred North Whitehead, *Science and the Modern World*, Cambridge at the University Press, 1932, page 238

WAR

*'War' quarrel usually between nations, conducted by force,
hostility or contention between persons.*

A lbert Camus wrote in his *Carnets*: 'We used to wonder where war lived, and what made it so vile. And now we realize that we know where it lives, that it is inside ourselves.'

This insight should come as no surprise to us. In the Genesis story of the creation of man, we have seen the divine inbreathing, and recognized the enormous potential resource of divine life in the depths of our being. In that story we have also seen that which was fashioned and shaped in the image and likeness of God was taken from the dust of the earth, so we also have an earthy and creaturely side to our nature. If we choose to ignore the enormous resource of divine life, there is a danger we centre ourselves on the earthy and creaturely side of our nature, and on a large scale, this can lead to war.

Conversely, if we accept the enormous resource of divine life in the depths of our being, and integrate this with the earthy and creaturely side of our nature we are able to transform a potentially destructive side of our nature into something creative and dynamic—which can ultimately lead to peace.

I wonder if Charles Kingsley thoroughly understood all this over a hundred years ago? To the question, 'What can a man do more than *die* for his countrymen?', he replied: 'Live for them. It is a longer work, and therefore a more difficult and a nobler one.'

Visions of Grace and the practice of reflection offers a way in which this can be done, a way that leads to peace, not war.

Scatter the peoples who delight in war.
Psalm 68.30

He shall judge between many peoples, and shall decide for strong nations afar off; and they shall beat their swords into plowshares, and their spears into pruning hooks; nation shall not lift up sword against nation, neither shall they learn war any more.
Micah 4.3

For all who take the sword will perish by the sword.
Matthew 26.52

For we are not contending against flesh and blood, but against the principalities, against the powers, against the world rulers of this present darkness, against the spiritual hosts of wickedness in the heavenly places. Therefore take the whole armour of God, that you may be able to withstand in the evil day, and having done all, to stand. Stand therefore, having girded your loins with truth; and having put on the breastplate of righteousness, and having shod your feet with the equipment of the gospel of peace; besides all these taking the shield of faith, with which you can quench all the flaming darts of the evil one. And take the helmet of salvation, and the sword of the Spirit, which is the word of God.
Ephesians 6.12-17

There is nothing that war has ever achieved we could not achieve without it.

Havelock Ellis, *Selected Essays*, J.M. Dent & Sons Ltd., 1936, page 221 (footnote)

We used to wonder where war lived, what it was that made it so vile. And now we realize that we know where it lives, that it is inside ourselves.

Albert Camus, *Carnets 1935–42*, translated by Philip Thody, Hamish Hamilton, 1962, page 79

The Church knows nothing of a sacredness of war. The struggle for existence is carried on here with inhuman means. The church which prays the 'Our Father' asks God only for peace.

Dietrich Bonhoeffer, *No Rusty Swords, Lectures, Lectures and Notes 1929–1936*, from *The Collected Works*, Volume I, edited by Edwin H. Robertson, translated by Edwin H. Robertson and John Bowden, William Collins Sons & Co. Ltd., 1965, page 145

We (Christians in war) are called to the hardest of all tasks: to fight without hatred, to resist without bitterness, and in the end, if God grant it so, to triumph without vindictiveness.

William Temple, *The Hope of a New World*, SCM Press Ltd., 1940, page 81

What we now need to discover in the social realm is the moral equivalent of war: something heroic that will speak to men as universally as war does, and yet will be as compatible with their spiritual selves as war has proved itself to be incompatible.

William James, *The Varieties of Religious Experience*, William Collins Sons & Co. Ltd., 1974, page 356

It is not merely cruelty that leads men to love war, it is excitement. It is not merely excitement, it is the excitement that discloses to them depths of power and averages of manhood far more in certain cases than belong to ordinary avocations in peace.

Henry Ward Beecher, *Proverbs From Plymouth Pulpit*, Charles Burnet & Co., 1887, page 51

I believe that Christianity does not necessarily demand pacifism. I believe that Christians can encourage and participate in a just war—that is, a war conducted by a state or states against oppression, for the protection of the weak, and for the restoration of justice. But in order to have a just war it is necessary that there should be some prospect of the outcome being just. That's why, on a world scale, it is very hard to see how today there *could* be a just war, because the result would be indiscriminate destruction.

As for a rebellion or revolution, there can, I believe, be a just revolution or rebellion which Christian people should support. But the condition of its justice must include the prospect that from it there is going to emerge not only the destruction of a bad order, but also the substitution for it of an order that is good and just.

Such conditions are very difficult indeed to foresee, but this is an area in which Christian thought must work out more precisely what *are* the conditions of a just rebellion, bearing in mind that all the conclusions of a just war are not necessarily admirable.

Michael Ramsey, *Through the Year with Michael Ramsey*, edited by Margaret Duggan, Hodder & Stoughton Ltd., 1975, page 133

It is our clear duty to spare no effort in order to work for the moment when all war will be completely outlawed by international agreement. This goal, of course, requires the establishment of a universally acknowledged public authority vested with the effective power to ensure security for all, regard for justice, and respect for law. But before this desirable authority can be constituted, it is necessary for existing international bodies to devote themselves resolutely to the exploration of better means for obtaining common security, But since peace must be born of mutual trust between peoples instead of being forced on nations through dread of arms, all must work to put an end to the arms race and make a real beginning of disarmament, not unilaterally indeed but at an equal rate on all sides, on the basis of agreements and backed up by genuine and effective guarantees.

Vatican Council II, *The Conciliar and Post Conciliar Documents*, 1981 Edition, general editor, Austin Flannery, OP, Fowler Wright Books Ltd., page 991

The more I have reflected on the experience of history the more I have come to see the instability of solutions achieved by force and to suspect even those instances where force has had the appearance of resolving difficulties. But the question remains whether we can afford to eliminate force in the world as it is without risking the loss of such ground as reason has gained...

There is at least one solution that has yet to be tried—that the masters of force should be those who have mastered all desire to employ it...

If armed forces were controlled by men who have become convinced of the wrongness of using force there would be the nearest approach to a safe assurance against its abuse. Such men might also come closest to efficiency in its use, should the enemies of civilization compel this. For the more complex that war becomes the more its efficient direction depends on understanding its properties and effects; and the deeper the study of modern war is carried the stronger grows the conviction of its futility.

Sir Basil Liddell Hart, *Why Don't We Learn from History?*, George Allen & Unwin Ltd., 1971, page 72

Undoubtedly, armaments are not amassed merely for use in wartime. Since the defensive strength of any nation is thought to depend on its capacity for immediate retaliation, the stockpiling of arms which grows from year to year serves, in a way hitherto unthought of, as a deterrent to potential attackers. Many people look upon this as the most effective way known at the present time for maintaining some sort of peace among nations.

Whatever one may think of this form of deterrent, people are convinced that the arms race, which quite a few countries have entered, is no infallible way of maintaining real peace and that the resulting so-called balance of power is no sure and genuine path to achieving it. Rather than eliminate the causes of war, the arms race serves only to aggravate the position. As long as extravagant sums of money are poured into the development of new weapons, it is impossible to devote adequate aid in tackling the misery which prevails at the present day in the world. Instead of eradicating international conflict once and for all, the contagion is spreading to other parts of the world. New approaches, based on reformed attitudes, will have to be chosen in order to remove this stumbling block, to free the earth from its pressing anxieties, and give back to the world a genuine peace.

Vatican Council II, *The Conciliar and Post Conciliar Documents*, 1981 Edition, general editor, Austin Flannery, OP, Fowler Wright Books Ltd., page 990

WISDOM

'Wisdom'—being wise, (possession of) experience and knowledge together with the power of applying them critically or practically, sagacity, prudence, common sense.

'For wisdom will come into your heart...' So wrote the author of the book of Proverbs on the source of wisdom. If we want to see this fully worked out in a life we go to the New Testament. In the Gospels some of those who heard our Lord's teaching were astonished, saying, 'Where did this man get all this? What is the wisdom given to him?' The Apostle Paul went one stage further and enthusiastically wrote 'of Christ, in whom are hid all the treasures of wisdom and knowledge'.

In the sacrament of baptism a seed or spark of wisdom is brought to life, through the cleansing of water and spiritual rebirth. The teaching of the Church is that we daily increase in wisdom—through Bible reading, prayer and sacrament. In confirmation we 'confirm' the promises made on our behalf by godparents, and receive the gifts of the Holy Spirit one of which is wisdom.

At this stage we might be helped forward by taking to heart some words of Christopher Bryant. In his book *The Heart in Pilgrimage* he wrote: 'It is part of the Christian spiritual tradition that God dwells in the centre of every man, an unseen, largely unknown Strength and Wisdom, moving him to be human, to grow and to expand his humanity to the utmost of its capacity.'

I wonder if this is best done by reflection. *Visions of Grace* is a repository of wisdom and provides a way and a means 'moving him [or her] to be human, to grow and to expand his [or her] humanity to the utmost of its capacity'.

For wisdom will come into your heart, and knowledge will be pleasant to your soul; discretion will watch over you; understanding will guard you.

Proverbs 2.10-11

Wisdom exalteth her children, and layeth hold of them that seek her. He that loveth her loveth life... If a man commit himself unto her, he shall inherit her; and his generations shall hold her in possession. For at the first she will walk with him by crooked ways, and bring fear and dread upon him, and torment him with her discipline, until she may trust his soul, and try him by her laws. Then will she return the straight way unto him, and comfort him, and shew him her secrets. But if he go wrong she will forsake him, and give him over to his own ruin.

Ecclesiasticus 4.11-19 (AV)

Every one then who hears these words of mine and does them will be like a wise man who built his house upon the rock.

Matthew 7.24

He is the source of your life in Christ Jesus, whom God made our wisdom, our righteousness and sanctification and redemption.

1 Corinthians 1.30

Wisdom cometh by suffering.

Aeschylus, *Agamemnon*, translated by Herbert Weir Smyth, William Heinemann Ltd., 1952, page 19

The wisdom of the wise is an uncommon degree of common sense.

W.R. Inge, in *Wit and Wisdom of Dean Inge*, selected and arranged by Sir James Marchant, Longmans, Green and Co. Ltd., 1927, page 112

Wisdom is oftimes nearer when we stoop
Than when we soar.

William Wordsworth, *The Poetical Works of William Wordsworth*, edited by E. de Selincourt and Helen Darbishire, Oxford at the Clarendon Press, 1959, Volume V, page 82, 'The Excursion,' Book III, l.231

More wisdom is latent in things-as-they-are than in all the words men use.

Antoine de Saint-Exupéry, *The Wisdom of the Sands*, translated by Stuart Gilbert, Hollis & Carter, 1952, page 89

Tracing our Wisdom, Power, and Love,
In earth or sky, in stream or grove.

John Keble, *The Christian Year*, edited by Ernest Rhys, J.M. Dent & Sons Ltd., 1914, page 6

Some hold... that there is a wisdom of the Head, and that there is a wisdom of the Heart.

Charles Dickens, *Hard Times*, The Gresham Publishing Company, 1904, page 155

The true sage is not he who sees, but he who, seeing the furthest, has the deepest love for mankind.

Maurice Maeterlinck, *Wisdom and Destiny*, translated by Alfred Sutro, George Allen, 1898, page 38

To know
That which before us lies in daily life,
Is the prime wisdom.

John Milton, *The Poetical Works of John Milton*, edited by the Rev. H.C. Beeching, Oxford at the Clarendon Press, 1900, page 339, *Paradise Lost*, Book VIII, l.192

We do well to believe less than we are told, and to keep a wary eye on our own impulses; whatever it is, we should think the matter over slowly and carefully, referring it to God.

Thomas à Kempis, *The Imitation of Christ*, translated by Betty I. Knott, William Collins Sons & Co. Ltd., 1979, page 43

Knowledge dwells
In heads replete with thoughts of other men;
Wisdom in minds attentive to their own.

William Cowper, *The Poetical Works of Cowper*, edited by H.S. Milford, Oxford University Press, 1950, page 221, 'The Task,' Book VI, l.89

And we shall be truly wise if we be made content; content, too, not only with what we can understand, but, content with what we do not understand — the habit of mind which theologians call—and rightly—faith in God.

Charles Kingsley, *Health and Education*, W. Isbister & Co., 1874, page 194

Wisdom alone is true Ambition's aim,
Wisdom the Source of Virtue, and of Fame,
Obtain'd with Labour, for Mankind employ'd,
And then, when most you share it, best enjoy'd.

William Whitehead, *Miscellaneous Poems*, 1744, 'On Nobility,' page 12

Here is the test of wisdom,
Wisdom is not finally tested in schools,
Wisdom cannot be pass'd from one having it to another not having it,
Wisdom is of the soul, is not susceptible of proof, is its own proof.

Walt Whitman, *The Complete Poems*, edited by Francis Murphy, Penguin Books Ltd., 1982, page 182, 'Song of the Open Road,' section 6, l.77

The spirit of Savouring Wisdom ... is a ghostly touch or stirring within the unity of our spirit, and it is an inpouring and a source of all grace, all gifts and all virtues ... And we feel this touch in the unity of our highest powers, above reason, but not without reason.

John of Ruysbroeck, *The Adornment of the Spiritual Marriage*, translated by C.A. Wynschenk Dom, edited by Evelyn Underhill, John M. Watkins, 1951, page 146

By 'a new nativity,'—initiated by obedient response to the inward Light... of God the indwelling Spirit—he may put on the new man, created after the likeness of God, and become the recipient of heavenly Wisdom springing up within him from the Life of the Spirit.

Rufus M. Jones, *Spiritual Reformers in the 16th and 17th Centuries*, Macmillan & Co. Ltd., 1914, page 150

So, from this glittering world with all its fashion,
Its fire, and play of men, its stir, its march,
Let me have wisdom, Beauty, wisdom and passion,
Bread to the soul, rain where the summers parch.
Give me but these, and, though the darkness close
Even the night will blossom as the rose.

John Masefield, *Collected Poems*, William Heinemann Ltd., 1926, page 671, 'On Growing Old', l.23

What is the price of Experience? do men buy it for a song?
Or wisdom for a dance in the street? No, it is bought, with the price
Of all that a man hath, his house, his wife, his children.

Wisdom is sold in the desolate market where none come to buy,
And in the wither'd field where the farmer plows for bread in vain.

William Blake, *The Complete Writings of William Blake*, edited by Geoffrey Keynes, Oxford University Press, 1974, page 290, 'Vale or the Four Zoas,' l.397

This love of wisdom (or philosophy) is the illumination of the intelligent mind by that pure wisdom (defined as the self-sufficient living mind and sole primaeval reason of all things), and is a kind of return and recall to it, so that it seems at once the pursuit of wisdom, the pursuit of divinity and the friendship of that pure mind. So that this wisdom gives to the whole class of minds the reward of its own divinity and returns it to its proper constitution and purity of nature.

Migne, in *The Consolation of Philosophy*, Boethius, translated by V.E. Watts, Penguin Books Ltd., 1969, page 21

The whole secret of remaining young in spite of years, and even of gray hairs, is to cherish enthusiasm in oneself, by poetry, by contemplation, by charity,—that is, in fewer words, by the maintenance of harmony in the soul. When everything is in its right place within us, we ourselves are in equilibrium with the whole work of God. Deep and grave enthusiasm for the eternal beauty and the eternal order, reason touched with emotion and a serene tenderness of heart—these surely are the foundations of wisdom.

Henri Frédéric Amiel, *Amiel's Journal*, translated by Mrs Humphry Ward, Macmillan & Co. Ltd., 1918, page 95

The Wisdom of God is working through all created life, and far and wide is the sustainer and the inspirer of the thought and the endeavour of men. The Church will therefore reverence every honest activity of the minds of men; it will perceive that therein the Spirit of God is moving, and it will tremble lest by denying this, in word or in action, it blaspheme the Spirit of God. But Wisdom cannot be thus learnt in all its fulness. The mind and the eye of man are distorted by sin and self-worship; and the Wisdom which the Spirit of God unfolds throughout the world can lead to blindness and to deceit unless men face the fact of sin and the need for redemption.

Michael Ramsey, *The Gospel and the Catholic Church*, Longman, Green & Co. Ltd., 1936, page 125

Western science is slowly beginning to rediscover the ancient tradition of wisdom, according to which mind and matter are interdependent and complementary aspects of one reality. This same process can also be observed in Western medicine where there is a gradual recognition that all disease is psychosomatic and that the human body cannot be properly treated apart from the soul.
A knowledge is slowly being recovered which was universal in the ancient world that there is no such thing as matter apart from mind or consciousness.
Consciousness is latent in every particle of matter and the mathematical order which science discovers in the universe is due to the working of this universal consciousness within it. In human nature latent consciousness begins to come into actual consciousness, and as human consciousness evolves it grows more and more conscious of the universal consciousness in which it is grounded—God the very ground of our being.

Bede Griffiths OSB, in *The Universal Christ*, edited by Peter Spink, Darton, Longman & Todd, 1993, page 13

Intuition is knowledge which derives not from observation and experience or from concepts and reason, but from the mind's reflection on itself.
What distinguishes the human mind above all else is not its powers of observation and experiment which animals also possess in some degree, not its powers of logical deduction, but its power of self-reflection. For the human mind is so structured that it is always present to itself.
Intuition may be described as the passive intellect. It may be likened to a still, clear pool of reflection. It cannot be produced but the condition which permits the intuition to function is that of the mind 'stayed upon God'.
Wordsworth describes the process in 'Lines composed a few miles above Tintern Abbey':

Felt in the blood, and felt along the heart,
And passing even into the purer mind with tranquil restoration.

Only when we offer our minds to God do we receive the illumination of his wisdom.

Bede Griffiths OSB in *The Universal Christ*, edited by Peter Spink, Darton, Longman & Todd, 1990, page 7

Then said a teacher, Speak to us of Teaching. And he said: No man can reveal to you aught but that which already lies half asleep in the dawning of your knowledge.

The teacher who walks in the shadow of the temple, among his followers, gives not of his wisdom but rather of his faith and lovingness.

If he is indeed wise he does not bid you enter the house of his wisdom but rather leads you to the threshold of your own mind.

The astronomer may speak to you of his understanding of space, but he cannot give you his understanding.

The musician may sing to you of the rhythm which is in all space, but he cannot give you the ear which arrests the rhythm, nor the voice that echoes it.

And he who is versed in the science of numbers can tell of the regions of weight and measure, but he cannot conduct you thither.

For the vision of one man lends not its wings to another man.

And even as each one of you stands alone in God's knowledge, so must each one of you be alone in his knowledge of God and in his understanding of the earth.

Kahlil Gibran, *The Prophet*, William Heinemann Ltd., 1970, page 67

WONDER

'Wonder'—emotion excited by what surpasses expectation or experience or seems inexplicable, surprise mingled with admiration or curiosity or bewilderment.

I was very excited on discovering an insight on wonder by Rabindranath Tagore. In his book *Sadhana* he wrote this very simple, yet profound sentence: 'The idea of God that man has in his being is the wonder of all wonders.' I think this sentence sums up the vision in *Visions of Grace* in a most succinct way.

Throughout this book I have tried to point out the spiritual or divine element 'that man has in his being'. In strict theological terms this can be Father, Son, and Holy Spirit. Not quite so theological, but certainly biblical, the spiritual or divine element might be experienced as life, light, truth, joy, grace, glory, love and so on. When we experience the spiritual or divine element in our being it is not long before we become conscious of a sense of awe and wonder.

Rollo May encourages us also to look outside ourselves. In *Man's Search For Himself* he had this to say of wonder:

'Wonder ... is essentially an "opening" attitude— an awareness that there is more to life than one has yet fathomed, an experience of new vistas in life to be explored as well as new profundities to be plumbed.'

Once we have got used to Tagore's words (above) and look outside ourselves on the lines suggested by Rollo May, all sorts of people we come across become a source of wonder. This is true also of nature and the world we live in. Evelyn Underhill reminds us 'Wonder and love are caught, not taught; and to catch them we must be in an atmosphere where we are sure to find the germs.'

Remember the wonderful works that he has done.

Psalm 105.5

Let them thank the Lord for his steadfast love, for his wonderful works to the sons of men!
Psalm 107.15

And all spoke well of him, and wondered at the gracious words which proceeded out of his mouth.
Luke 4.22

And all the people saw him walking and praising God, and recognized him as the one who sat for alms at the Beautiful Gate of the temple; and they were filled with wonder and amazement at what had happened to him.
Acts 3.9-10

Wonder is involuntary praise.
Edward Young, *Cumberland's British Theatre*, Volume XV, John Cumberland, 1827, 'The Revenge,' page 35

Wonder (which is the seed of knowledge).
Francis Bacon, *The Advancement of Learning*, Cassell and Company Ltd., 1905, page 16

To be surprised, to wonder, is to begin to understand.
José Ortega Y Gasset, *The Revolt of the Masses*, George Allen & Unwin Ltd., 1932, page 12

Wonder . . . is essentially an 'opening' attitude—an awareness that there is more to life than one has yet fathomed, an experience of new vistas in life to be explored as well as new profundities to be plumbed.
Rollo May, *Man's Search For Himself*, George Allen & Unwin Ltd., 1953, page 212

The most beautiful experience we can have is the mysterious. It is the fundamental emotion which stands at the cradle of true art and science. Whoever does not know it and can no longer wonder, no longer marvel, is as good as dead, and his eyes are dimmed. It was the experience of mystery—even if mixed with fear—that engendered religion. A knowledge of the existence of something we cannot penetrate, our perceptions of the profoundest reason and the most radiant beauty, which only in their most primitive forms are accessible to our minds—it is this knowledge and this emotion that constitutes true religiosity.
Albert Einstein, *Ideas and Opinions*, Souvenir Press (Educational & Academic) Ltd., 1973, page 11

No man or woman begins to live a full life until they realise they live in the presence of something greater, outside and beyond themselves. Self-consciousness truly means that you are standing over against that other than yourself and you cannot be living in truth. Wonder is at the base of true living, and wonder leads to worship and after that the great other than self; it is yet kin to you, you are one with it. Then you begin to live more completely and realise the kinship between you and nature, that out of nature you came and are part and parcel with it, this brings nearer faith which is self-conscious life (opposed to birds, trees, etc.), reaching out to perfection.
G.A. Studdert Kennedy, *The New Man in Christ*, edited by the Dean of Worcester, Hodder & Stoughton Ltd., 1932, page 132

And when the wonder has gone out of a man he is dead . . . When all comes to all, the most precious element in life is wonder. Love is a great emotion, and power is power. But both love and power are based on wonder. Love without wonder is a sensational affair, and power without wonder is mere force and compulsion. The one universal element in consciousness which is fundamental to life is the element of wonder . . .

Plant consciousness, insect consciousness, fish consciousness, all are related by one permanent element, which we may call the religious element inherent in all life, even in a flea: the sense of wonder. That is our sixth sense. And it is the *natural* religious sense.
D.H. Lawrence, *Phoenix II*, William Heinemann Ltd., 1968, page 598

When I was younger and more impatient I used to get bored when the junior scouts opened their tents and gazed curiously and affectionately at the woods and at the tiny animals under the yellowing leaves. It seemed a waste of time. I would have preferred to have them taught catechism in some church.

I was immature and did not understand that the best catechism is to fix our eyes on created things, because through things God begins to speak to us.

It may be, through teaching catechism to bored students sitting on benches, teaching abbreviated formulas and intellectual summaries, that we have destroyed everything, leaving them sad and absent before the mystery of God.

Today, so many years later, how I should like to replace a catechism lesson with a walk in the fields, offering to a boy who lives buried in the inhuman cemetery of the city, the wonderful discovery of a sparrow's nest!

For is not wonder the first, unconscious meeting with mystery? Does not wonder give birth to the first prayer? Does not the power to contemplate involve first the power to be awed?

Carlo Carretto, *The God Who Comes*, translated by Rose Mary Hancock, Darton, Longman & Todd, 1974, page 5

The spirit has its own senses by which to see, feel and be guided; these grow out of our ordinary ones and are related to them, as inward eyes, ears and feelings, which as yet are only partly formed and rudimentary, but which develop as we dare to trust them. Mystical experience and knowledge of guidance are becoming commoner in these times and perhaps this is because the great Unseen is building up power to help us in these dark days. At last we are ready on a great scale to begin to understand what is happening in the polarization of old and new. I believe it will not be too many years ahead before we begin to educate children in a fuller use of their mind's and spirit's potential ...

This way is open to every one; the seed of divine consciousness of which Christ's incarnation is the herald is not out in space but here, right under our hands to be experienced in fullness of life as we learn to look for it: as we dig in the garden, sit by the bedside of the dying, hold a young baby in our arms, study the patterns of nature through microscope and telescope, puzzle over philosophical problems and above all as we sit in the silence both alone and together in the meeting for worship.

Damaris Parker-Rhodes, *Truth: A Path and not a Possession*, Swarthmore Lecture, Friends Home Service Committee, 1977, page 51

Now if it is these moments of recognition and awareness that change our minds and change our lives, if these can be the true turning points of human history, then something of enormous power must be at work in such commonplace experiences. One might say that a flash of recognition has a higher voltage than a flash of lightning, that the power that makes us suddenly aware is the secret of all evolution and the spark that sets off most revolutions.

But what is this force which causes me to see in a way in which I have not seen? What makes a landscape or a person or an idea come to life for me and become a presence towards which I surrender myself? I recognize, I respond, I fall in love, I worship—yet it was not I who took the first step. In every such encounter there has been an anonymous third party who makes the introduction, acts as a go-between, makes two beings aware of each other, sets up a current of communication between them. What is more, this invisible go-between does not simply stand between us but is activating each of us from inside. Moses approaching the burning bush is no scientific observer; the same fiery essence burns in his own heart also. He and the thorn-bush are caught and held, as it were, in the same magnetic field.

John V. Taylor, *The Go-Between God*, SCM Press Ltd., 1972, page 16

WORD OF GOD

'Word of God'—Christ as mediator or manifestation of God to men and women.

I n the early years of faith, I was attracted by the great prophets of the Old Testament— Elijah, Elisha, Isaiah, Jeremiah and Ezekiel. These were men who seemed to be particularly tuned in to hearing the Word of God.

Later on I was influenced by the writings of one of my great mentors—William Temple. His writings encouraged me to focus on the Gospels and to look at Christ as the mediator or the manifestation of God to men. In his *Readings in St. John's Gospel*, he wrote: 'Our reading of the Gospel story can be and should be an act of personal communion with the living Lord.' I spent several years putting this into practice, and sometimes wonder if I overdid it, becoming rather narrow and blinkered.

Rufus Jones has some useful words in this section. He tells us he prefers the holy scriptures before all human treasure. I wonder how many of us can echo that sentiment. He obviously values the Bible, as the Word of God, very highly. He then goes on to add— 'yet I do not so much esteem them as I do the Word of God which is living, potent, and eternal, and which is free from all the elements of this world: For that is God Himself, Spirit, and no letter, written without pen or ink, so that it can never be obliterated.'

I found these words very liberating, and have been encouraged to look for the living, potent, and eternal Word of God not just in the scriptures but in the writings of the last two thousand years. By reflecting on these in silence something of the Word of God has come to me—relevant to our day and age.

By the word of the Lord the heavens were made, and all their host by the breath of his mouth.

Psalm 33.6

If I say, 'I will not mention him, or speak any more in his name,' there is in my heart as it were a burning fire shut up in my bones, and I am weary with holding it in, and I cannot.

Jeremiah 20.9-10

As for what was sown among thorns, this is he who hears the word, but the cares of the world and the delight in riches choke the word, and it proves unfruitful.

Matthew 13.22

Lord, to whom shall we go? You have the words of eternal life.

John 6.68

In the midst of the silence there was spoken in me a secret Word.

Meister Eckhart, Meister Eckhart, Franz Pfeiffer, translated by C. de B. Evans, John M. Watkins, 1956, Volume I, page 4

Our reading of the Gospel story can be and should be an act of personal communion with the living Lord.

William Temple, Readings in St. John's Gospel, First and Second Series, Macmillan & Co. Ltd., 1947, page 15

And so the Word had breath, and wrought
With human hands the creed of creeds
In loveliness of perfect deeds,
More strong than all poetic thought.

Alfred, Lord Tennyson, The Poems of Tennyson, edited by Christopher Ricks, Longmans, Green & Co. Ltd., 1969, page 894, No. 296, 'In Memoriam A.H.H.,' st.xxxvi, 1.9

'A still small voice' comes through the wild,
(Like a Father consoling his fretful child),
Which banishes bitterness, wrath, and fear,—
Saying—MAN IS DISTANT, BUT GOD IS NEAR!

Thomas Pringle, *Afar in the Desert: and Other South African Poems*, edited by John Noble, Longmans, Green & Co. Ltd., 1881, page 53

For it is impossible for language, miracles, or apparitions to teach us the infallibility of God's word, or to shew us the certainty of true religion, without a clear sight into truth itself, that is into the truth of things. Which will themselves when truly seen, by the very beauty and glory of them, best discover, and prove religion.

Thomas Traherne, *Centuries*, The Faith Press Ltd., 1969, page 134

Infallible direction for practical action is not to be had either from Bible or Church or Pope or individual communing with God; and this is not through any failure of a wise and loving God to supply it, but because in whatever degree reliance upon such infallible direction comes in, spirituality goes out. Intelligent and responsible judgement is the privilege and burden of spirit or personality.

William Temple, *Nature, Man and God*, Macmillan & Co. Ltd., 1934, page 353

I prefer the Holy Scriptures before all Human Treasure; yet I do not so much esteem them as I do the Word of God which is living, potent, and eternal, and which is free from all elements of this world: For that is God Himself, Spirit, and no letter, written without pen or ink, so that it can never be obliterated. True Salvation is in the Word of God; it is not tied up to the Scriptures. They alone cannot make a bad heart good, though they may supply it with information. But a heart illumined with the Light of God is made better by everything.

Rufus M. Jones, *Spiritual Reformers in the 16th and 17th Centuries*, Macmillan & Co. Ltd., 1914, page 242

We sometimes think that God spoke to men in the past in a more objective, external way than he speaks to us today. He speaks as he has always done, within the heart of man, in direct intuitive communication or through making relevant to us today, words that he spoke to prophets, saints, and thinkers, recorded in Scripture. Above all he speaks through his eternal word, who became man in Jesus our Christ, whose words and teaching as they were remembered and handed down are recorded in the gospels, and who is ever present with men

George Appleton, *Journey for a Soul*, William Collins Sons & Co. Ltd., 1976, page 199

There is no man in the world in whom this *logos*, this Word of God, this rational principle of all things, does not speak. The veriest atheist of them all thinks by the power of that which is perfectly revealed in Jesus Christ. It is the light that lighteth every man. You never get away from it, and there is nobody who is without it. That light which lighteth every man, and which shone by fits and starts elsewhere, that Word which was spoken in divers portions and divers manners in the prophets, shone out supremely and found perfect utterance in the Son.

William Temple, *Christian Faith and Life*, SCM Press Ltd., 1963, page 35

The Word whom we preach is the Word who created the world, who sustains its order and beauty, who is ever at work in the ups and downs of history, whose coming in Jesus is the key to the whole.

To the preacher the realisation of this is at once shattering and consoling: shattering because the preacher's theme is so vast, its scope is reminiscent of the title of a medieval treatise, *De Omnibus Rebus et Quibusdam Aliis* (Concerning All Things and Certain Other Things as Well); consoling because behind the preacher is the almighty action of God in all things, and he is called not to be wise or powerful himself, but to bid his hearers listen to what God is saying in his ceaseless action in the world.

The Word is not imprisoned in a sermon; for it is present in its sovereign power before the preacher's mouth is opened, and after the preacher's lips are closed.

Michael Ramsey, in *Through the Year with Michael Ramsey*, edited by Margaret Duggan, Hodder & Stoughton Ltd., 1975, page 234

There is one particular image which I ask you to look at closely. It is the image used by St. John which, more than any other, sums the matter up.

St. John writes, 'The Word became flesh and dwelt among us, and we beheld his glory'. *Word*: it is a biblical term, denoting one who is living, creative, imperishable, divine. *Flesh*: it is a biblical term denoting what is creaturely, frail, mortal, human. Here then is the paradox. The divine Creator has humbled himself to take on himself the entire experience of existence as man, in all conditions of humanity.

Is it credible? It is only just credible. It is credible because there already exists the affinity between God and man, through man being made in God's likeness. This affinity anticipates the closest final fellowship conceivable between God and man.

Again, it is credible because of the infinity of God's love, with love's power of entering into the experience of another beyond all the analogies of love's power which we know.

Michael Ramsey, in *Through the Year with Michael Ramsey*, edited by Margaret Duggan, Hodder & Stoughton Ltd., 1975, page 235

YOUTH

*'Youth'—being young; adolescence (the vigour or enthusiasm or
weakness or inexperience or other characteristic of the period
between childhood and full manhood or womanhood).*

I am greatly indebted to my housemaster at school. On the first evening of joining the
house he gave us some sound advice: 'Work hard, play hard, pray hard, and then you
will be happy.'

At first I was not too keen on the 'work hard' directive but at the age of fifteen I went
on a schools hockey festival to Oxford and this had a decisive influence on the future
course of my life. This short visit made me realize I wanted to come to the university as an
undergraduate—so work began in earnest. I now had a goal in life, and something to aim
for.

I greatly enjoyed the injunction to 'play hard' and entered fully into the sports life of
the school, gaining a great deal of fulfilment in the process.

Rather surprisingly I also responded to the injunction to 'pray hard.' I was confirmed
at the age of sixteen and followed closely the school chaplain's instructions on how to
pray. This was a simple, down-to-earth, daily form of prayer, consisting of thanksgiving,
confession, the Lord's Prayer, intercession and petition—praying for one's own needs.

'Work hard, play hard and pray hard' proved to be a good working pattern and
formed a firm foundation on which to build a future. This pattern has stayed with me and
has proved to be effective. The biggest change which has taken place over the years is in
prayer. The verbal form of prayer has given way to reflection, meditation and contemplation. This form of receptive prayer has turned out to be a valuable asset.

For thou, O Lord, art my hope, my trust, O Lord, from my youth. Upon thee I have leaned
from my birth; thou art he who took me from my mother's womb. My praise is continually
of thee.

Psalm 71.5-6

Rejoice, O young man, in your youth, and let your heart cheer you in the days of your youth;
walk in the ways of your heart and the sight of your eyes.

Ecclesiastes 11.9

Let no one despise your youth, but set the believers an example in speech and conduct, in
love, in faith, in purity.

1 Timothy 4.12

So shun youthful passions and aim at righteousness, faith, love, and peace, along with those
who call upon the Lord from a pure heart.

2 Timothy 2.22

Our most important are our earliest years

William Cowper, *The Poetical Works of Cowper*, edited by H.S. Milford, Oxford University Press, 1950, page 25, 'The
Progress of Error,' l.354

The thoughts of youth are long, long thoughts.

Henry Wadsworth Longfellow, *The Poetical Works of Longfellow*, Humphrey Milford, Oxford University Press, 1913, page
308, 'My Lost Youth,' st.i, l.10

Bliss was it in that dawn to be alive,
But to be young was very Heaven.

William Wordsworth, *The Prelude*, edited by E. de Selincourt, Second Edition revised by Helen Darbishire, Oxford at the
Clarendon Press, 1959, page 407, Book XI, l.108

Heaven lies about us in our infancy!
Shades of the prison-house begin to close
Upon the growing Boy.

William Wordsworth, *The Poetical Works of William Wordsworth*, edited by E. de Selincourt and Helen Darbishire,
Oxford at the Clarendon Press, 1958, Volume IV, page 281, 'Intimations of Immortality,' V, l.66

The imagination of a boy is healthy, and the mature imagination of a man is healthy; but
there is a space of life between, in which the soul is in a ferment, the character undecided,
the way of life uncertain, the ambition thick-sighted.

John Keats, *The Poems of John Keats*, edited by E. de Selincourt, Methuen & Co. Ltd., 1907, page 52, 'Preface to
Endymion'

Science, philosophy, theology, literature, art, education: all are in the quest for truth. In the
last analysis it is not a matter of culture but of religion. It is a matter of rightly ordered
spirituality. Why is this not more frankly put to the young?

Hubert van Zeller, *Considerations*, Sheed & Ward Ltd., 1974, page 64

'Youth is full of sunshine and love. Youth is happy, because it has the ability to see beauty.
When this ability is lost, wretched old age begins, decay, unhappiness.'
    'So age excludes the possibility of happiness?'
    'No, happiness excludes age.' Smiling, he bent his head forward, as if to hide it between
his hunched shoulders. 'Anyone who keeps the ability to see beauty never grows old.'

Gustav Janouch, *Conversations with Kafka*, translated by Goronwy Rees, S. Fischer Verlag GmbH, 1968, page 30

Youth is not a time of life... it is a state of mind.
Nobody grows old by merely living a number of years;
people grow old only by deserting their ideals.
Years wrinkle the skin, but to give up enthusiasm wrinkles
the soul. Worry, doubt, self-distrust, fear and despair ...
these turn the long, long years that bow the head and turn
the growing spirit back to dust.
Whether seventy or sixteen, there is in every being's
heart the love of wonder, the sweet amazement at the stars
and the starlike things and thoughts, the undaunted
challenge of events, and unfailing childlike appetite for what
next, and the joy of the game of life.
You are as young as your faith, as old as your doubt;
as young as your self-confidence, as old as your fear;
as young as your hope, as old as your despair.

Anon.

The future belongs to the young. It is a young and new world which is now under the
process of development and it is the young who must create it.
    But it is also a world of truth, courage, justice, lofty aspirations and straight-forward
fulfillment which we seek to create.
    Our ideal is a new birth of humanity into the spirit; our life must be a spiritually inspired
effort to create a body of action for the great new birth and creation.

Our ideal is not the spirituality that withdraws from life but the conquest of life by the power of the spirit.

It is to accept the world as an effort of manifestation of the Divine, but also to transform humanity by greater effort of manifestation than has yet been accomplished, one in which the veil between man and God shall be removed, the divine manhood of which we are capable shall come to birth and our life shall be remolded in the truth and light and power of the spirit.

It is the young who are free in mind and heart to accept a completer truth and labour for a greater ideal.

There must be men who will dedicate themselves not to the past or the present but to the future.

They will need to consecrate their lives to an exceeding of their lower self, to the realisation of God in themselves and in all human beings and to a whole-hearted and indefatigable labour for the nation and for humanity.

The ideal can be as yet only a little seed and the life that embodies it a small nucleus, but it is our fixed hope that the seed will grow into a tree and the nucleus be the heart of an ever-extending formation.

It is with a confident trust in the spirit that inspires us that we take our place among the standard-bearers of the new humanity that is struggling to be born.

Sri Aurobindo, published in the Auroville magazine, *One*, in *A Vision of the Aquarian Age*, George Trevelyan, Coventure Ltd., 1977, page 75

Index

A

Adams, Henry 140
Addison, Joseph 22, 45, 62, 116, 138, 194
Aelred of Rievaulx 90
Aeschylus 284
Al-Ansari 26, 106, 127
Al-Ghazali 84, 86, 233
Amiel, Henri Frédéric 18, 21, 23, 39, 42, 62, 66, 69, 71, 109, 110, 116, 119, 126, 151, 152, 179, 218, 225, 263, 267, 286
Anselm, St 244
Appleton, George 19, 42, 81, 84, 86, 148, 188, 201, 202, 221, 247, 291
Armstrong, John 125
Arnold, Matthew 26, 65, 68, 94, 110, 218, 255, 263
Auden, W.H. 95
Augustine, St 80, 145, 215, 229, 230, 235, 263
Aurelius, Marcus 115
Aurobindo, Sri 294

B

Bacon, Francis 207, 224, 288
Bailey, P.J. 91, 157
Barclay, William 47, 227, 232
Barkway, Bishop Lumsden 175
Barnes, Kenneth C. 50
Bassett, Elizabeth 163, 172
Beecher, Henry Ward 41, 45, 47, 134, 282
Berdyaev, Nicolas 34, 53, 86, 220, 247
Bettelheim, Bruno 191
Birrell, Augustine 224
Black, Hugh 89
Blackman, E.C. 273
Blake, William 18, 21, 121, 127, 184, 185, 227, 267, 269, 285
Blanton, Smiley 177
Bloom, Anthony 16, 50, 74, 101, 122, 123, 127, 271
Boehme, Jacob 48, 249
Boethius 68
Bondfield, Margaret 29, 82
Bonhoeffer, Dietrich 33, 47, 104, 119, 149, 211, 233, 241, 242, 247, 282
Boros, Ladislaus 244, 247
Borrow, George 66
Bourne, Randolph 119
Bradley, A.C. 144
Bridges, Robert 34, 124
Brockington, L.H. 98
Brooks, Phillips 110

Brown, John 23
Browne, R.E.C. 62
Browne, Sir Thomas 61, 67, 195, 198
Browning, E.B. 110, 174, 213
Browning, Robert 18, 65, 86, 112, 148, 152, 155, 194, 199, 224, 279
Bunyan, John 126
Burke, Edmund 65, 109
Burrows, Ruth 39, 48, 56, 66, 75, 76, 148, 161, 185, 202, 203, 205, 208, 253, 275
Butterfield, Herbert 104
Byron, Lord 53, 199

C

Campbell, Thomas 138, 198
Camus, Albert 282
Carlyle, Thomas 23, 37, 61, 62, 67, 95, 109, 110, 130, 158, 166, 194, 195, 224
Carmichael, Amy 268
Carpenter, Edward 29, 86, 120, 245
Carpenter, Joseph 234
Carretto, Carlo 19, 57, 125, 163, 164, 176, 200, 227, 228, 233, 256, 258, 289
Cassian, John 56
Casteel, John L. 172
Channing, William E. 60, 110, 167, 188
Chardin, Pierre Teilhard de 16, 19, 68, 77, 92, 113, 236
Church, R.W. 43
Churchill, Winston S. 59
Cloud of Unknowing 174
Coleridge, Hartley 86
Coleridge, Samuel Taylor 41, 46, 47, 68, 134, 140, 147, 199, 243
Connolly, Cyril 91, 224
Conrad, Joseph 21, 24, 134, 187
Cook, Joseph 53
Cooke, Grace 145, 176
Cotton, Charles 59
Coulson, C.A. 253
Cowper, William 52, 198, 199, 218, 285, 293
Cusanus, Nicolas 230
Cushing, Harvey 109

D

Demant, V.A. 266
Dickens, Charles 125, 208, 284
Dickerson, Roy E. 250
Dimitri of Rostov, St 276

Dimnct, Ernest 16, 55
Disraeli, Benjamin 174
Dole, Charles Fletcher 279
Donne, John 67
Dostoyevsky, Fyodor 50, 137, 175, 183
Dryden, John 59, 95, 103, 116, 166, 213
Dunn, James D.G. 216
Dyke, Henry Van 174, 179

E

Ecclestone, Alan 225
Eckhart, Meister 55, 68, 71, 97, 100, 127, 140, 160, 205, 218, 241, 257, 263, 275, 290
Edwards, Jonathan 121, 122
Einstein, Albert 131, 155, 198, 260, 273, 288
Eliot, George 26, 140
Ellis, Havelock 94, 282
Emerson, Ralph Waldo 34, 42, 45, 55, 68, 89, 95, 107, 119, 134, 137, 155, 158, 198, 207, 226, 267, 269
Epictetus 169, 230
Erskine, John 155

F

Faber, F.W. 151, 152
Falconer, L. 131
Fénelon, F. de la M. 185
Field, Joanna 195
Fiske, John 137
Forster, E.M. 167
Fosdick, Harry Emerson 34
Fox, George 161
Francis de Sales, St 89, 142
Francis of Assisi, St. 43
Frank, Anne 50
Fromm, Erich 53, 92, 163, 169, 183, 220, 248
Frost, Bede 141
Froude, J.A. 255
Fuller, Thomas 109, 121, 190

G

Gandhi, Mohandas K. 74, 182, 210
Gasset, José Ortega Y 288
George, Henry 235
Gibran, Kahlil 90, 174, 181, 287
Gide, André 255
Gilson, Etienne 257
Gissing, George 55
Glasson, Francis 74

Glubb, Sir John 146, 155, 191
Goethe, Johann Wolfgang von 25, 35, 86, 116, 120, 180, 208
Gogh, Vincent van 53, 89, 175, 273
Goldsmith, Oliver 125, 179, 190
Gollancz, Victor 205
Goodier, Alban 59
Gorman, George H. 158
Grayson, David 104, 247
Green, Thomas F. 16
Grensted, L.W. 174
Griffiths, Bede, OSB 56, 78, 81, 92, 93, 113, 188, 216, 221, 244, 260, 271, 279, 286

H

Habgood, John 78
Haecker, Theodor 109
Hammarskjöld, Dag 50, 157
Hardy, E.R. 240
Harries, Richard 195
Hart, Sir Basil Liddell 283
Haskins, Louise M. 160
Hawthorne, Nathaniel 137
Hazlitt, William 95
Heine, Heinrich 195
Helps, Arthur 255, 269
Henri, Robert 24
Herbert, George 201, 215
Herman, E. 188
Hesse, Herman 100, 166, 276
Hewlett, Maurice 180
Higgins, Ronald 175
Hilton, Walter 106, 160, 233, 275
Hindemith, Paul 195
Holmes, Edward 196
Houlden, J.L. 186
Houselander, Caryll 101
Hügel, Friedrich von 158
Hughes, Gerard J. 54
Huneker, James 23
Huxley, Aldous 56, 77, 107, 112, 143, 275

I

Ibsen, Henrik 61, 116, 178
Inge, W.R. 36, 43, 49, 50, 74, 75, 82, 116, 120, 122, 141, 149, 183, 232, 253, 260, 284
Irenacus, St 97
Isaac of Nineveh 241
Israel, Martin 112

J

James, William 71, 100, 103, 116, 131, 282
Janouch, Gustav 294
Jeanne D'Arc, Sister, OP 164
Jefferies, Richard 92, 270
Jefferson, Thomas 42
Johnson, Raynor C. 27
Johnson, Samuel 89, 92, 95, 124, 137, 157, 208, 267
Jones, E. Stanley 113
Jones, Rufus M. 31, 32, 47, 81, 84, 87, 97, 104, 157, 160, 174, 175, 220, 285, 291
Jonson, Ben 21, 213
Joubert, Joseph 18, 133
Jowett, Benjamin 32, 219
Julian of Norwich, Lady 107, 174, 185
Jung, C.G. 19, 24, 32, 100, 140, 145, 157, 179, 221, 247, 256

K

Kagawa, Toyohiko 131
Keats, John 35, 116, 124, 134, 145, 224, 294
Keble, John 163, 224, 241, 284
Keller, Helen 42
Kelly, Thomas 127
Kempis, Thomas à 26, 53, 106, 126, 174, 207, 214, 215, 216, 285
Kennedy, G.A. Studdert 220, 288
Ker, John 167
Kierkegaard, Søren 61, 140, 215
King, Harriet Eleanor Hamilton 255
King, Martin Luther 50, 53, 201
Kingsley, Charles 27, 285
Küng, Hans 72
Kunkel, Fritz 250

L

Lavelle, Louis 86, 260
Law, William 128, 142, 143, 161, 191, 194, 202, 214, 232, 249, 260, 279
Lawrence, Brother 232
Lawrence, D.H. 18, 61, 120, 158, 267, 288
Leeuw, J.J. van der 157
Leon, Luis de 276
Lewis, C.S. 22, 32, 59, 62, 89, 106, 111, 169, 180, 201, 265
Lewisohn, Ludwig 24
Liebman, Joshua Loth 238
Lindbergh, Anne Morrow 19, 158, 260

Livingstone, Sir Richard 47, 72, 279
Longfellow, Henry Wadsworth 23, 25, 35, 65, 110, 119, 121, 195, 208, 213, 227, 246, 260, 270, 294
Lowell, Amy 23
Lowell, J.R. 95, 110, 171, 213
Lynd, Helen Merrell 270

M

Macdonald, George 34, 65, 104, 112, 119, 138, 145, 159, 182, 201, 204, 213, 214, 220, 241, 279
Macgregor, G.H.C. 211
Macgregor, W.M. 270
Macmurray, John 86, 265
Maeterlinck, Maurice 244, 284
Main, John, OSB 81, 87, 113, 120, 148, 164, 176, 180, 242, 244, 250
Malaval 279
Mann, Horace 71
Mann, Thomas 270
Mansfield, Katherine 35, 71, 134, 261, 273
Masefield, John 285
Massinger, Philip 155
Maugham, W. Somerset 18, 35, 103, 133
May, Rollo 61, 62, 238, 288
McIntyre, J. 135
McKeating, Henry 227
Meredith, Owen 140
Merton, Thomas 20, 28, 36, 43, 97, 116, 117, 177, 231, 249, 261, 262, 275
Migne 286
Miller, Henry 91, 154-155
Milton, John 21, 26, 45, 62, 70, 103, 111, 205, 214, 285
Moore, George 257
Moorman, J.R.H. 206
Moustakas, Clark 247
Mozley, J.B. 200
Muggeridge, Malcolm 117, 235
Munby, D.L. 191
Murdoch, Iris 55
Murry, John Middleton 189, 250

N

Natham, Robert 267
Neill, Stephen 169
Newman, John Henry 270
Nicoll, Maurice 92
Niebuhr, Reinhold 247, 263

Nietzsche, Friedrich 179
Nouwen, Henri J.M. 27, 29, 51, 84, 125, 134, 149, 155, 170
Noüy, Lecomte du 26, 77

O

Overstreet, H.A. 103
Oxenham, John 208

P

Palmer, Samuel 95
Parker-Rhodes, Damaris 289
Parkhurst, Charles H. 198
Pascal, Blaise 115, 119, 120, 127, 145, 198, 243, 272
Pater, Walter 96
Patmore, Coventry 178, 179
Péguy, Charles 132, 146, 174
Penn, William 47, 89
Phillips, J.B. 146
Philo 34, 143
Plato 70, 138, 195, 263
Plotinus 143
Poe, Edgar Allan 194
Pope, Alexander 41, 124, 185, 200
Post, Laurens van der 157, 270
Powell, Cyril H. 163
Powys, John Cowper 199, 220
Powys, Llewelyn 157
Pringle, Thomas 291
Prior, Matthew 34, 263

Q

Quick, Oliver 74
Quoist, Michel 163

R

Radhakrishnan, Sir Sarvepalli 241
Ramsey, Michael 28, 45, 48, 56, 75, 97, 122, 149, 156, 181, 206, 211, 282, 286, 291, 292
Reymond, Lizelle 81
Richard of Saint-Victor 106
Richardson, Alan 192, 250
Rilke, Rainer Maria 62, 112, 119, 143, 267, 268
Robertson, F.W. 20, 206
Robinson, John A T 47
Rousseau, Jean Jacques 52, 151
Ruskin, John 23, 24, 71, 134, 213, 215, 279

Russell, Bertrand 110, 116, 117, 182
Ruysbroeck, John of 51, 122, 230, 285

S

Saint-Exupery, Antoine de 169, 179, 218, 243, 284
Santayana, George 18, 179
Sayers, Dorothy L. 191
Schiller, Friedrich 34
Schopenhauer, Arthur 191
Schreiner, Olive 152
Schweitzer, Albert 65, 81, 103, 131, 141, 152, 153, 161, 210, 211, 212, 235, 249, 268, 270, 271
Scott, Sir Walter 175
Scudder, Vida D. 16
Seeger, Alan 34
Selby, Peter 228
Seneca 109
Sertillanges, A.D. 61
Shaw, George Bernard 158, 169
Shelley, Percy Bysshe 124, 133, 224
Sidney, Sir Philip 26
Silesius, Angelus 119, 146
Smiles, Samuel 43
Smith, George Adam 253
Smith, John, the Platonist 42, 68, 98, 116, 138, 145, 216, 218, 273
Smith, Lillian 127
Smith, R.L. 93, 158
Socrates 138, 210
Solovyev, Vladimir 261
Solzhenitsyn, Alexander 167
Spencer, Herbert 70, 86, 145
Spenser, Edmund 58, 59, 97, 106, 184
Steiner, Rudolf 77
Stevenson, Robert Louis 71, 90, 115
Sullivan, J.W.N. 194, 280
Suso, Henry 204

T

Tagore, Rabindranath 65, 86, 87, 92, 110, 148, 198, 199, 218, 240
Tauler, John 215
Taylor, Jeremy 60, 205
Taylor, John V. 28, 289
Temple, William 16, 42, 48, 50, 53, 71, 74, 75, 77, 80, 83, 84, 97, 106, 122, 124, 128, 145, 152, 158, 160, 166, 174, 183, 187, 191, 205, 224, 249, 253, 255, 265, 275, 282, 290, 291
Tennyson, Alfred, Lord 26, 65, 126, 155, 168, 230, 232, 240, 290

Teresa of Avila, St 100, 201
Teresa of Calcutta, Mother 122, 147, 152, 244
Tertullian 47
Theophan the Recluse 120, 258, 276
Thomson, James 143, 198, 240
Thoreau, Henry David 37, 65, 96, 126, 131, 133, 166, 198, 205, 227, 241
Tillich, Paul 100, 125, 169, 253
Todi, Jacopone da 227
Tolstoy, Leo 259
Traherne, Thomas 36, 38, 39, 68, 104, 107, 148, 175, 176, 230, 231, 245, 278, 291

U

Underhill, Evelyn 16, 17, 35, 84, 157, 233, 236, 244, 254, 255, 279

V

Vann, Gerald 45
Vatican Council II 32, 53, 202, 218, 282, 283

W

Wagner, Richard 194
Waller, Edmund 19
Walton, Izaak 38, 127
Washington, George 52
Weil, Simone 124, 133, 163, 185
Wells, H.G. 190
West, Morris 238

Whichcote, Benjamin 201, 252, 263
Whipple, Edwin P. 95
Whitehead, Alfred North 187, 280
Whitehead, William 285
Whitman, Walt 18, 45, 89, 103, 160, 215, 218, 220, 285
Widor, C.M. 194
Wieman, Henry Nelson 132
Wilde, Oscar 112, 134, 220, 267
William of Glasshampton 244
Williams, Daniel D. 106, 107
Williams, H.A. 235
Wilson, Edward 117, 162, 171, 175, 219, 242
Wolfe, Thomas 148
Wolff, Toni 188
Woolf, Virginia 134
Wordsworth, William 15, 38, 71, 140, 152, 198, 225, 263, 267, 284, 294
Wyon, Olive 35

Y

Yeats, J.B. 95
Yeats, W.B. 95, 255
Yelchaninov, Father 180, 215
Young, Edward 37, 47, 143, 198, 288

Z

Zeller, Hubert van 26, 42, 65, 124, 157, 161, 163, 169, 179, 188, 215, 232, 255, 294

ACKNOWLEDGMENTS

Credit to authors and publishers of works quoted is given below each quotation. In addition, the publishers wish to acknowledge the following:

Quotation from J.W.N. Sullivan, *But For the Grace of God* reproduced by permission of Peters Fraser & Dunlop Group Ltd.

Henry Miller, *The Wisdom of the Heart*, copyright © 1941 by Henry Miller. Reproduced by permission of New Directions Pub. Corp.

D.H. Lawrence, *Phoenix II*, by permission of Laurence Pollinger Ltd and the Estate of Frieda Lawrence Ravagli.